BEST
SELLERS

Peter Sellers
A Life In Comedy

ROBERT ROSS

GREAT (N)ORTHERN

Great Northern Books
PO Box 1380, Bradford,
West Yorkshire, BD5 5FB

www.greatnorthernbooks.co.uk

ISBN: 978-1-914227-72-1

Design by David Burrill

CIP Data
A catalogue for this book is available from the British Library

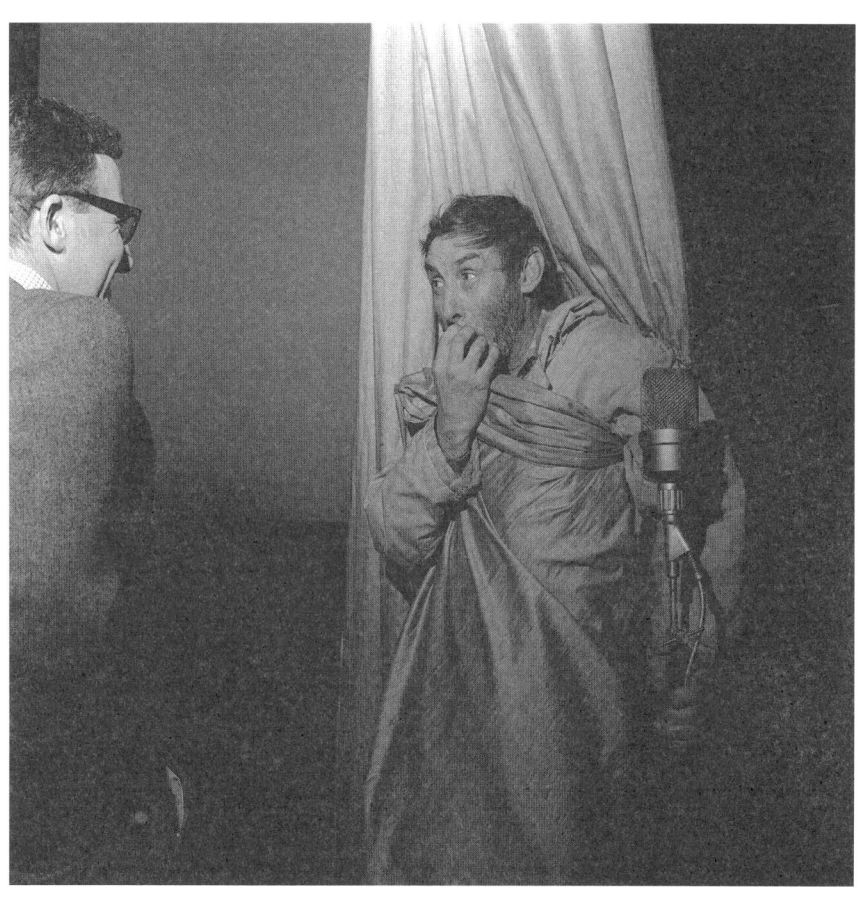

Dedicated to

SPIKE MILLIGAN

Peter's Life Partner in Laughter

CONTENTS

A Quick Foreword March

Conversation with Simon Williams

Simon Williams became immensely popular on television, as dashing James Bellamy in *Upstairs, Downstairs*, before playing the debonair and engaging and ever-so-slightly silly juveniles in the last two spirited Peter Sellers spoof films: Fritz in *The Prisoner of Zenda*, and Robert Townsend in *The Fiendish Plot of Dr. Fu Manchu*.

"I first met Peter Sellers, very briefly, backstage after a performance of Oscar Wilde's *An Ideal Husband*, in 1977. I was playing Lord Goring, a renowned dandy, and my father, Lord Caversham, was played by Peter's good friend and colleague Wilfred Hyde-White. They got on tremendously well, precisely because they were very similar. Both were maverick actors, brilliant but unpredictable. Very special talents. Both too were very superstitious, each with a grave abhorrence to wearing the colour green. As a result I have never worn green either!"

It wasn't long after this meeting that Simon was cast opposite Peter in *The Prisoner of Zenda*, and that eccentric and erratic personality was even more apparent. "I think the very nature of a genius – and Peter was undoubtedly a genius – is that you can't be a genius all the time. With Peter there were flashes of genius. On a good day he could be the funniest person you ever saw. He was spontaneously funny. He never seemed to work anything out in advance. All his comedy was based on the character, which is a sign of the very good actor he was. There was a truth to what he was doing. Conversely, on a bad day, he could be impossible. He simply would not work. You could tell, instantly. Just the look on Peter's face as he walked onto set in the morning would tell you he was in a bad mood. He just wouldn't or couldn't find the magic to be funny."

It was down to Peter's fellow performers to join in with the merriment that he wanted, and needed, to create the fun atmosphere on set in which he could work. As Simon remembers: "There would be endless pranks, and his insatiable desire for giggling. This could go on for days and days. We joined in with this, or else the mood on set would have been untenable." It worked: "Peter's head would lift; the scowl would vanish; the magic could begin. We would go straight onto the film set and shoot a scene". The fun and the funny within Peter was back.

"It certainly helped that he had old friends on the films I made with him. Lionel Jeffries was an utter delight, and he could rally Peter in a moment. David Tomlinson was another trusted friend. Peter's closest friend was Graham Stark, who was the greatly loved butt of all Peter's jokes". Graham took all the ribbing in good grace, happily joining in, and "essential for that mood to be lifted.

"Acting is a funny old game, you know, and that reassurance on having reliable stalwarts by Peter's side was crucial. I feel rather honoured that I was so quickly welcomed back to Peter's playground, which is exactly how he saw making comedy films. I certainly wasn't a threat to him, either in terms of his star clout or his love life, but it's nice to know I became one of his trusted allies."

Despite the fun on set, these final films were fraught with debate and delay. *The Fiendish Plot of Dr. Fu Manchu* was, if anything, even more difficult. As Simon recalls: "Peter's mood could dip without any warning. He hadn't got on with Richard Quine, who had directed *The Prisoner of Zenda*. Unlike Blake Edwards, Richard didn't know that Peter wouldn't want to do covering-shots and lots of takes. Blake would set up multi-cameras to get everything in one. Richard wasn't like that. Peter would get frustrated, rip off his wig and moustache, mutter 'See you around', and vanish . . . back to Switzerland! By the time we started on *Fu Manchu* Peter had sacked three directors and, during the making of it, he sacked director Piers Haggard".

Peter's health had visually deteriorated in the short time between *Zenda* and *Fu Manchu*. "He also seemed to be living in the past. He would often say that he had never been happier than when he was recording *The Goon Show* and, sure enough, if you prompted him to lapse into some of his favourite Goon characters not only would he do so, with great alacrity, but the process of doing it would put him in a very good mood for the rest of the day. Peter got through that film by doing silly voices. To amuse us, for sure, but also to amuse himself.

"Believe me, it was needed. Peter would call me up while he was making *Being There*". Both were going through a few problems at the time, and "he was very excited about making *Fu Manchu*. He would say how much he was looking forward to having a jolly time with me in Paris. Well . . ."

Philosophical in the fact that: "my association with Peter was in two absolute turkeys, either side of his masterpiece *Being There*"; for Simon, "the great sadness of *Being There* is that, in Chance, is a performance that proved he could have gone on to do much more, Oscar-worthy work. Peter displayed such depth, and such understanding".

The legacy of Peter Sellers is assured though. "Peter was a complex genius", without doubt, but a man who could, and still does, make us laugh, hard and long. Even in the two flaky and frantic comic epics that Sellers and Simon made together: "if you can chuckle once or twice at the silly films I was in with Peter, then that makes me happy". That's why they were made.

Peter's relevance is still powerful too. The satire he created with Stanley Kubrick in *Dr. Strangelove* is about to be resurrected, on the West End stage, at the Noel Coward Theatre, via a couple of colossal talents, actor Steve Coogan and writer Armando Iannucci. That the film remains disquieting and prescient "some sixty years on is quite remarkable.

"It also shows, in the publication of this brilliant book, a sense of comedy timing that Peter would be proud of! Robert Ross has dug with affection and understanding into Peter's life's work. His comedy". Peter Sellers could be irrational; indulgent; infuriating . . . but, above all, he was very, very funny. *Best Sellers* is, as Simon concludes, "a celebration of Peter's towering talent to amuse; his ability to cheer an audience up; and his skill at allowing us to get the joke, and laugh".

September 2024

Introduction

This is by no means the first book dedicated to Peter Sellers. It is unlikely to be the last. For we are endlessly fascinated by the man behind that gallery of beloved screen characters and wireless eccentrics. Fittingly for such a comic chameleon, Sellers is many different people. In the scant thirty years he was in the public eye he was the chubby, tousle-haired impersonator; he was the international jet-set playboy; he was the relentlessly physical slapstick Hollywood clown. Also he was undoubtedly the finest comedy actor this country has ever produced. And all of those different shades of Sellers are characters in this story. The plot, however, is single-minded and focused: the life Peter Sellers lived through his comedy.

Certainly Sellers was a complex personality. In those thirty years in the spotlight he married four times and fuelled his creative juices with intoxicating substances both illegal and alcoholic. These trials and tribulations, the wives and wealth and weirdness, are only referred to if and when they collided and conflicted with the comedy, as they frequently did. For this is by no means a hagiology. Nor is it a hatchet-job. It is an abstract ramble through a body of work which gives me incalculably huge waves of pleasure.

I encountered him first as a disembodied voice in my subconscious. Well, a wailing, whining cornucopia of deliciously silly voices emanating from an ancient reel-to-reel tape player of my dad's. My dad, you see, had been a fan of *The Goon Show* since the beginning; and frequently and vehemently blessed the thirty minutes of barely-controlled hysteria that had lifted his week of National Service with the Royal Air Force. The show took him out of his daily humdrum into a delirium of daydreams. It was profitable too. A gang of them would huddle round the NAAFI radio set, with a wager on the table.

Each serviceman would contribute a coin of the realm. The pooled kitty of cash was not to be sneezed at. Then, the test of will-power was to suppress any laughs out loud during the broadcast, and thus, being responsible for obliterating a treasured gag. Those listeners who lacked self-control of their chuckle muscle would forfeit their stake. My dad won a lot of money by biting his cheeks, and, as a result, made a mental note of every manic mutter and bilious burp.

No such restriction was put upon me, however. As a mere babe-in-arms I was free to gurgle like the proverbial drain as much as I wanted to. I was also a captive audience. Those merrie misadventures from radio days long gone were as much a part of my teething regime as soggy nappies and Farley's Rusks.

Perhaps my earliest memory is of seeing my dad, convulsed with laughter, tears rolling down his cheeks, enraptured by those voices; those wonderful voices, from nearly twenty years earlier. An aural portal to a time before fatherhood, before marriage, from a more carefree life when he wore a younger man's clothes, a younger man's uniform, and longed to return home to Blighty. The Goons were a part of him, a part of his nation, and, by the early 1970s, a part of the fibre of his heritage. They soon became a part of mine. They still are.

And, reassuringly, at that same time in the early 1970s, they were still a part of the very fibre of Peter Sellers. Despite all his many, international achievements, Sellers was happiest as a man of silly voices; an impersonator of the famous, and the infamous.[1]

It was my dad's pristine copy of *The Best of Sellers* – the 1958 long-playing, 33 revolutions per minute, in the shape of a diminutive 78 rpm record – that was probably the first time I saw what Sellers actually looked like. That image: a bowler-hatted businessman. More accountant than anarchist. Funny? Not really. Odd and intriguing? Yes. The cover image, that is. And the elements that stuck: the classic car; the sensible spectacles. Eternal shorthand for Sellers:

---

1 In the opening line of Gary Arnold's *Washington Post* obituary of 25th July 1980, Sellers is described as: "the gifted British mimic and comic actor . . ." Film-maker and friend Sidney Gilliat, who directed Sellers in *Only Two Can Play*, always maintained that: "mimic is too minor a word for the talent that Sellers possessed. He was an actor of rare distinction." Interview with the author, August 1991.

both comedic, and personal.

In interviews Sellers would hide his natural shyness at being himself by inevitably lapsing into impersonation and insanity – channelling, perfectly, everybody from Michael Caine to (more than anyone else) Adolf Hitler. Still, behind that ever-changing array of stylish and hugely expensive pairs of glasses, flashed the eyes of a very deep-thinking man. A man who relished the convoluted giggles that his merest quip or playful facial expression could instantly engender from his audience.

John Mortimer, who was part of the production team for the film of his play *The Dock Brief*, in which Sellers starred, wrote that he was: "a man who stood empty, waiting to be inhabited by other people",[1] while Sellers himself would relentlessly endorse that view in interviews.

The recurring cliche of this journalistic shortcut is the oft-quoted Sellers claim that there wasn't a real him: "I had it surgically removed!" Still, that was a scripted quip. For *The Muppet Show*. The real Peter Sellers is in actual fact a fascinating man, and throughout this book he will be glimpsed time and time again, forever preserved behind and within the comic characters he has left behind.

Basking in the success of *The Pink Panther* and its swift sequel, he insisted that: "I have no idea who Peter Sellers is. I have no concrete personality of my own, you see. I hop into a new personality as often as I can. I'm a character actor. I couldn't play Peter Sellers the way Cary Grant plays Cary Grant – though I could *play* Cary Grant!"[2]

Perhaps this is why Sellers was and remains such a towering, relatable actor. He is not just the nondescript self but all of us. The glamorous Cary Grant image; and the shy Bristolian Archie Leach that Grant had been. The everyman. The pretender at the workplace. When Sellers put on a costume to become Fred Kite or Inspector Clouseau or Queen Victoria, it was the exact same act of everyday subterfuge deployed by a nervous worker in order that he may become authoritative. The strength of leadership lies within the military

---

1 *Clinging to the Wreckage: A Part of Life*, by John Mortimer (Weidenfeld & Nicolson, 1982).
2 *ABC Film Review*, June 1965.

uniform or the matronly garb or the university professor's gown. The art of Peter Sellers as an actor is that his mastery of disguise touches and reassures an inner fear within all humanity. You have to hide the real you or else you may well be found out; and, horror of horrors, get sent back to the beginning. That power and respect and position can be swiftly taken away.

That fear; that anxiety; that vulnerability made Sellers the greatest of actors. His mental place of performance was a brilliant blank canvas, ever poised to embrace and absorb an entire character for a complete, totally convincing transformation. The ultimate vessel for comedy.

So that is the agenda, if I have an agenda at all. Simply to celebrate the imperishable verve of a master comic performer. As Sellers's old comrade of craziness Michael Bentine wrote in 1984: "the films of Peter Sellers repay further viewing with their wide range of good-humoured caricatures."[1]

And as long-serving member of the Pink Panther repertory company Herbert Lom remembered: "The only thing Peter Sellers could do was make the entire world laugh, but he was very, very good at that."[2] While Peter's sheer professionalism at his craft can never be questioned, Joe McGrath, who went through both heaven and hell directing Peter Sellers over a twenty-year period, maintained that: "once you got Peter on set he was a gift from the comedy Gods. He would always come in, word perfect. He was very much like an American movie star in that respect. He didn't want to flesh it out on the floor, in-front of the camera. He knew the dialogue, he knew the business he was going to do, and he just wanted to get on with it. He expected everybody else to know what they were doing too. Not unreasonably. And if he loved a script, he really loved it. He once said to me, 'I need to know the character, and I mean really

---

1 *The Shy Person's Guide to Life*, by Michael Bentine (Granada Publishing Limited). And let me say from the outset, that that will be the last time I type Sellers's. For fear of sounding like Hissing Sid – from the fevered nightmares of the good animal folk of the Captain Beaky band – there are far too many Ss in that word. So, without trying to sound matey or over-familiar – although I do feel I now know his comedic soul, if not his inner demons – I shall, when he is in possession, call him Peter throughout.
2 Interview with the author, July 2000.

know him. If I don't know the character, it can't be funny. It has to be real.""[1]

It is the architect of his comic psyche, Spike Milligan, that summed Sellers up with most assurance and conviction: "Peter is one of the true comedy greats of the 20th century. He can hold his head up with the very best."[2]

This then is the life story of a man through the only prism that matters: the laughter he still generates.

Robert Ross
Buckinghamshire
January 2024

---

1 Interview with the author, July 2003.
2 Interview with the author, July 2000.

Chapter 1

"Enters Stage Left. Adopts Heroic Stance in Cardboard Nightgown.
Instant Applause."

Bluebottle

"I've arrived – and to prove it, I'm here! Oh, sorry, folks! That's Max Bygraves. I must really try being myself for a change! I am so used to impersonating people on the radio that it's getting a habit!" So said Sellers as a comic prelude to a brief potted history of his career so far – and it had only just taken flight – for a column in popular children's comic paper *Radio Fun*, in January 1951.[1] He would spend the rest of his life at his happiest being other people.

Richard Peter Sellers wasn't so much born in a trunk as a sea-chest. In Southsea, a picturesque seaside resort in Portsmouth, Hampshire. The date was 8th September 1925. It was a Tuesday, so the infant was full of grace. He was also full of energy. Young Sellers couldn't help but entertain, for his heritage was steeped in it.

Peter was fiercely proud of his great-grandfather, the celebrated bareknuckle prize fighter Daniel Mendoza. In July 1787 nationwide interest for Mendoza's book, *The Art of Boxing*, knocked news of the storming of the Bastille in Paris off the front pages! Sellers shared his enthused thoughts with fellow music-hall and radio funny voices man Jon Pertwee: "It was almost childish. He would tell you about his great-grandfather's exploits often. It was that thing of if my dad couldn't have beaten up your dad then my great-grandfather could have beaten

---

1 6th January 1951, to be precise. This was abridged from a snatched stage-door interview from the end of 1950 and written up, on behalf of Sellers, by Stanley Gooch, Managing Editor of publisher Amalgamated Press. The column bills Sellers as the "Character-Comedian from *Ray's a Laugh* programme", which was indeed his biggest credit at the time.

up your great-grandfather! Like the boasting banter of schoolboys in the playground, you know. Apparently his great-grandfather had taught George IV how to box. It was all this *Boy's Own* yarns that Peter had read and re-read and absorbed as gospel truth."[1]

Peter's maternal grandmother, Ma Ray, toured Britain, with her ten – count 'em – ten children in tow. Ma's most notable achievement was a variety show entitled *Splash Me!* The world's first travelling, underwater revue, the show featured a bevy of bathing beauties performing such hitherto unseen spectacles as consuming a banana whilst submerged! Be honest. The end of this venture was wet and final: the tank in which these wonders were performed sprang a leak during a performance in Huddersfield. The bottom literally fell out of the market after that.

Still, the troupe soldiered on, delivering rumbustious song and dance fare. Albeit in a rather more standard manner. Peter's mother, Peg, was one of the ten siblings in the show. She had taken rather a fancy to a dashing young Yorkshireman pianist who had joined the company. The name was Bill Sellars and, at the time, he was a confident and easy-going sort of chap. He also held the gene for Peter's swanky fantasist storyteller, for Bill would eagerly tell anybody who listened that it had been he who had taught George Formby to play the banjolele. Bill and Peg were married, at the Bloomsbury Registrar's Office, in 1923; their only surviving son would inherit a passion for the uke, and impersonations of the Lancastrian Toreador were a staple part of his act for the rest of his days.[2]

It had indeed turned out nice again that faithful autumn day in 1925. As Peter recalled: "My parents were on the stage so I suppose it was quite natural for me to follow suit – although at one time I wanted to be a doctor."[3] Goodness, gracious me. The sheer thrill of getting a laugh swiftly put paid to that ambition though. Besides, he was a theatre veteran from the age of just a few weeks. That canny

---

1 Interview with the author, July 1995.
2 From those wartime years when Formby was the highest paid and most popular of Churchill's comedians, to Peter's final album, *Sellers Market*, when Formby was long dead and an anachronistic staple on early evening television.
3 *Radio Fun*, January 1951.

old pro Ma Ray knew very well that a baby on stage would always get a gleeful audience reaction. The baby would make something of a fuss too! Thus it was that Peter, unwittingly but willingly, joined the gang show, proudly shown off by his mother, and getting the expected cheers and huge bursts of applause.

Then came speech, and soon after mimicry! As Peter remembered: "I have been doing impersonations ever since I was a schoolboy at St. Aloysius College, Highgate, London." This was swiftly curtailed by the early stages of the Second World War, when the family moved out to the relative safety of Ilfracombe, in Devonshire.

Peg had roots in the county, and a favourite uncle, or, at least, the uncle of family friend Derek Altman, rather fortuitously, ran a theatre there. It was Peter's paradise: "Here I was general odd-job boy. I took the tickets at the door, helped with the stage-lighting and scene-shifting and did the sweeping-up afterwards."[1] Eventually Peter worked his way up to the position of Assistant Stage Manager, but never lost that essential knowledge that every cog in a production was vital – regardless of how lowly they may be. Super-Stardom would certainly suggest that this all-embracing attitude did not last but, according to Joe McGrath: "Sellers was very good to all the crew, but only if he thought they were good at what they were doing. It's fair enough, really, by the time I was directing his films the production would sink or swim on his name. It was Peter Sellers the people were paying to see. He felt a very tangible responsibility. That could be seen as arrogance, even aggression, but it was nothing personal. Actually, it *was* very personal. Maybe it was insecurity, maybe it was egomania, but the source for all the angst was Sellers himself. You had to learn not to let him reflect that on to you. But, fundamentally, he was a team player. In the heart of the game."[2]

By the spring of 1941, with London facing the height of the Blitz, fifteen-year-old Peter formed a comedy double act with Derek Altman. Father Bill may or may not have taught all the chords to George Formby, but he certainly taught his own son how to pluck

1 *Radio Fun*, January 1951.
2 Interview with the author, July 2003.

out a few tunes on a ukulele, and with a couple of half-remembered amusing tall tales, the act was ready to conquer the world. Or not. It lasted no more than a rehearsal or two, but still the intention and ambition was piqued.

However, it was the tap rather than the pluck, the skin rather than the string, that really fired-up Peter's passion as a wannabe musician. Peter's great hero was Gene Krupa, and this fascination with drums provided the beat to each of his performances.[1] The drumbeat and the heartbeat aligned. It would be at the very core of Peter's work. With a £200 drum kit and experience with jazz combo Joe Daniels and His Hot Shots, Peter's career path was encouraged by his father, Bill, who printed out his son's business cards: 'The Young Ultra-Modern Swing Drummer and Uke Entertainer'.

At the time Bill was entertaining the troops in ENSA,[2] in a company featuring none other than George's wife, manager, and champion clog dancer, Beryl Formby.

In the meantime, Peter, Bill's young, ultra-modern offspring, was in Blackpool, earning the princely sum of eight pounds a week: "I obtained a job with Syd Seymour's band". Then, on 8th September 1943, Peter's eighteenth birthday, fascism inconveniently got in the way: "I was getting along fine", he jokingly lamented, "when the war came along and spoiled everything. Instead of fitting myself into a career I found myself fitting guns into aircraft – as an armourer in the R.A.F.! It was not long before Ralph Reader enlisted me in his famous Gang Show, and I toured the theatres of war instead of the music halls."[3]

Service with the Royal Air Force was duty rather than adventure, although Sellers did live vicariously through the cinematic antics of

---

1 New Yorker Krupa had revolutionised the instrument during his tenure with the Benny Goodman Orchestra, and in particular on the 1937 recording of 'Sing, Sing, Sing'. By the time the war in Europe began, Krupa was heading up his own jazz outfit.
2 The Entertainments National Service Association or, as beleaguered servicemen far from home unkindly dubbed it, Every Night Something Awful.
3 *Radio Fun*, January 1951.

one of his big idols, Errol Flynn, in *The Dawn Patrol*.[1] Still, Peter's life in uniform was less derring-do than play-acting, and his cinephile delight continued through his early fame and into superfame.[2] And some of those far-off postings to faraway places certainly indulged his wanderlust and desire for the high life – in every way: "I went to India, Burma, France and Germany entertaining the troops."[3]

It was during these world war zone skirmishes that Airman 2nd Class No. 2223033, Sellers, RP met his lifelong friend and colleague David Lodge. By 1945 the two chums were going through the motions for the Gang Show, at the Théatré Marigny, Paris. Sellers had come to detest live theatre. David Lodge agreed with Peter.[4]

Although he never gave up on the drumming – for sheer joy of musical expression – and, by the time he had joined the Jive Bombers he was: "a pretty good drummer", even if he did say so himself.[5] However, what Sellers enjoyed, nay adored, was the thrill he got when a moment of comedy landed. Boom! The feeling swiftly became an addiction.

Frank Thornton, later the officious Captain Peacock in *Are You Being Served?*, was his R.A.F. Entertainment Unit Commanding Officer and noted that not only did Sellers live out a fantasy of pretending to know every leading light in show business, but he was extraordinarily good at pretending to be other people. Indeed, the source of any joy was Peter's instinctive, near supernatural ability to capture the peaks, troughs and vocal mannerisms of a myriad of personalities, record them onto the tape within his head, and

---

1 The remake of the 1930 adventure film, directed by Edmund Goulding, and recruiting David Niven as a fellow Great War aviator, was released for Christmas 1938. With its dramatic tension of ill-fated, inexperienced airmen, and its gung-ho comic-strip dog-fights with the Red Baron, it became a much-celebrated cultural reference point during World War II.

2 In the Milligan script for *The Goon Show*'s 'The Phantom Head-Shaver' of 15th October 1955, he embellished Bluebottle's spoken stage direction about striking a defiant Alan Ladd pose – but trousers fall down and ruin effect – with a reference to the Ladd historical adventure *The Black Knight*, which Peter had recently seen.

3 *Radio Fun*, January 1951.

4 Asked about his ambitions for the *Radio Fun* piece, Peter replied: "Firstly, I should like to be an actor on the legitimate stage", which certainly sounded in earnest, not to mention impressive. Mind you, so did: "I'd like to be a professional cricketer", but neither came to fruition. Not really.

5 *Parkinson Meets the Goons*, BBC Television, 28th October 1972.

duplicate the voice for the merriment of his mates. From Stan Laurel to Winston Churchill and through nondescript but equally hilarious character voices of his own crazed inventiveness, this was Peter's talent to amuse. Incarnate. He would deploy the skill well. For the rest of his days. Even when he had become one of the biggest radio stars in the country, he would eagerly slip into obscurity and exercise his dexterous vocal chords for a tiny scraping off the top of the budget. Indeed for the 1956 war film *The Man Who Never Was*, Sellers provided the narration as spoken by Winston Churchill.[1]

Peter never really left childhood. He certainly never left the ethos of *The Goon Show*. Peter's entire working life, and much of his downtime, was a maelstrom of silly voices. The pretty much continued reliance on these silly voices to defuse an awkward situation; impress a pretty girl; win friends and influence people. That is Peter Sellers.

As Sellers eagerly related, the knack could not only get him out of a tricky situation but just as easily into one:

"Sometimes, for a joke, I ring up my friends on the telephone, imitating someone else's voice. You'd be surprised what I hear about myself!

"You've got to be careful, though. Once I was doing an impression of a politician and someone mistook me for the real person. I nearly had to run for my life. Oh, yes, this voice-imitating can get you into trouble.

"On my way to the studio to-day a man came up to me.

"'Would you mind accompanying me to the police-station?' he asked.

"'What for?' I asked, wondering what I had done wrong.

"'Because I'm scared of crossing the road alone,' was the reply.

1 Directed by Ronald Neame and starring Clifton Webb as Royal Naval Lieutenant Commander Ewen Montagu, *The Goon Show* parodied the BAFTA-winning screenplay, although Sellers was not afforded the opportunity to reprise his Churchillian tones. However, Peter's Churchill impression did invade the show, on Valentine's Day 1956, when 'The Choking Horror' was sprouting hair on all of London's beloved monuments. It even made a knitted cover over the controversial Churchill portrait recently unveiled by artist Graham Sutherland. Sellers, as the dour Prime Minister, mutters: "Thank heavens for that!", much to the audience's glee. Wondrous contemporary political and cultural satire. Glorious finger on the pulse stuff.

"Ha, ha! That relieved me no end."[1]

Never really a joke-teller, as proved there, Peter's limitless talent for sounding exactly like somebody else did change his life. Completely. And forever.

Upon demobilisation Peter secured gainful employment at the legendary and notorious Windmill Theatre – well the clientele needed something to laugh at as a distraction between the naked lovelies performing historical tableaux. Peter's impressions and funny stories were as welcome as any other comedian – in other words, not much – but he impressed entrepreneur Vivian Van Damm and the powers that be, and, starting from Monday, 17th March 1948, secured a six-week assignment in Revudeville, for £25 a week. It was enough to have his name emblazoned in bronze on the venue's proud roll-call of 'Stars of Today Who Started Their Careers in This Theatre'. Peter's name immediately followed that of one Harry Secombe.[2]

And Peter never lost the glee in using his impressions to play a practical joke; or, indeed, a practical career move. As he remembered at the dawn of his fame: "it was the joke I played on a BBC producer which really set me on the road to success." The producer in question was Roy Speer, who, at the time, was working on the ventriloquist comedy show *Educating Archie*, as well as the variety package *Starlight Hour*. In 1957 Speer would take over the reins of *The Goon Show*. That was nearly a decade away though. Sellers remembered that fateful call from 1948. How could he forget it? It was a pivotal moment in his life: "I phoned him one day and pretended I was Henry Hall." Hall, the genteel host of *Henry Hall's Guest Night*, would have had his call accepted by anyone at the BBC, even Director General William Haley.

Sellers, shy but desperate, summoned up every ounce of courage: "'This is Henry Hall speaking,' I said, imitating the well-known voice

---

1 *Radio Fun*, January 1951.

2 Less than ten years later, and on the verge of fame and fortune in British Film, Peter was interviewed for the BBC Television documentary *The Windmill Theatre: Twenty-Five Years*. Produced by Alan Chivers and Ernest Maxin, the great and the good were rounded up, including Jimmy Edwards, Benny Hill, Bob Monkhouse and, yes, Harry Secombe! The thirty-minute retrospective was hosted by Richard Murdoch, and transmitted on 4th February 1957.

of the band-leader. 'I've got Dicky Murdoch with me and we have both seen a very promising young fellow you might be interested in. His name is Peter Sellers. Here's Dicky to have a word with you!' Thereupon I changed my voice and imitated Richard Murdoch![1] The conversation went on for quite a while and when I revealed my identity I got invited up to the producer's office in reward for my cool cheek!"

In actual fact it was Peter's nerve that finally gave out and, with the fruity calmness of Murdoch gone, the young performer gulped, broke cover, and muttered: "Actually, Mr. Speer. This isn't Richard Murdoch speaking, and that wasn't Henry Hall. My name is Peter Sellers . . ." The bluster and bewilderment and belligerence were almost immediately blown away by an offer: "Why, you cheeky young . . . Are you available on Wednesday evening . . .?" Speer was impressed, and Sellers was in.

As Sellers recalled: "I was given a broadcast in *Show Time*, and I also appeared in *Music Hall*."[2]

Clearly Speer had shared Peter's name about the Corporation, for *Show Time* was produced by Bill Ward. It was a cavalcade of variety turns compered by the Australian comic and *Take It From Here* star Dick Bentley. Sellers was gifted a five-minute spot. His turn that evening was 'My Nightmare', a tried and tested playground for his celebrity impersonations. And in light of that phone call, Peter was on television, with these accurate celebrity voices clearly coming out of the one, unknown cherubic face. Although he would be other people on radio hundreds of times, this was a canny move. No trickery here. Fittingly, the boy did good; the audience approval was high; and

---

1 The frightfully nice Murdoch was a star of radio comedy *Much-Binding-in-the-Marsh* and he too would have been fast-tracked through to any high-up at the Corporation. By January 1948 the series was so popular that Murdoch was writing *The Chronicles of Much-Binding-in-the-Marsh*, a monthly column in *The Strand Magazine*; while the last recording of 1948 was by Royal Command, with Queen Mary, Elizabeth and Philip, and other members of the household in attendance. In apocryphal re-telling of this tale some historians have insisted on repeating the embellished version Sellers related to Michael Parkinson in November 1974, with an impersonation of Murdoch's radio co-star Kenneth Horne rather than Henry Hall, but let's assume that Peter himself, less than three years after the event, had crystal clarity of this moment in time.

2 *Radio Fun*, January 1951.

the ruse had worked. Sellers was in the inner sanctum. In fact, he had made his broadcasting debut from 3 p.m. on Monday, 3rd May 1948, in a variety show suitably entitled *New to You*. Billed simply as 'Comedian' in the *Radio Times*, in the surviving script extracts, there's a tentative confidence in his cheery closing ditty: "I'm glad you've heard my name – it's Peter Sellers! Peter Sellers can be gay as well as zealous! And now it's my due, from the programme *New to You*, as one of Britain's up and coming fellas – perhaps."

And those formative weeks and months would see Sellers be new to lots of people, both on radio (*Workers' Playtime*, *Variety Bandbox*) and on the stages of Britain's variety theatre circuit. Even so, some powerful movers and shakers remained unmoved and unshakable. Some felt there was a calculated, almost clinical, feel to his act: Peter Sellers – Speaking for the Stars. That Playbill matter was quite a claim, but Sellers could deliver. However, whether it was born of the man himself, or the chilling accuracy of his talent, this view of cold calculation was also held, rather unfortunately, by Peter's own agent Joe Collins[1] who feared he would keep on struggling to win favour with live theatre crowds. Unlike his fledgling Crazy Person and cuddlesome chum Harry Secombe, Collins noted that: "when facing an audience . . . Sellers lacked personal warmth and communication."[2]

That critique notwithstanding, Sellers was getting bookings. Besides, if Secombe was any judge – and of course he was – Sellers was head and shoulders above the competition: "I couldn't fail to be impressed by Peter", he recalled in 1972, "because I've never known anyone who is as good at impressions as he is."[3]

Peter's early stage act was a gimmick, for sure, a human voice-box of the great and the good of screen and radio; from recreating entire scenes from *The Maltese Falcon*, with Humphrey Bogart, Peter Lorre, and Sydney Greenstreet, to the best-loved radio comedian of

---

1 Yes, the father of future film megastar Joan Collins, and bedroom-romping novelist Jackie Collins.

2 *A Touch of Collins* by Joe Collins (Headline, 1987).

3 *Radio Times*, interview by Ray Connolly, 28th September 1972.

the day, Tommy Handley. Sellers was a one-man, cheaper tribute act to the famous folk that the audiences would tune in to or queue up for at their local Odeons and Regals. For Sellers the warmth was irrelevant. It was his technical skill at doing the voices that mattered. Although Eddie Braben, later the pivotal scribe for Eric Morecambe and Ernie Wise, recalled one radio routine he wrote for Sellers which played out to absolutely no audience laughter whatsoever. However, undeterred by this, Sellers soldiered on. For the price of admission you got variety, folks, complemented by Peter's speciality: the quick-fire brilliance of his flexible larynx. If they wanted warmth, they could bring a blanket. Or wait for Harry Secombe to come on. The warmth could come later. Not on the stage; but in the studio. There was something about a microphone, the isolation, the womb of a recording booth, with nobody but the necessary technicians and turns about him that would inspire that same larynx, and make it more relaxed, more at ease. Then he would give them warmth.

The key architect for this, of course, was Spike Milligan: "it was actually in 1948 that I first met Sellers. It was at a bar. I was spending a lot of time at bars in those days. This fateful bar was the one at the Hackney Empire. Michael Bentine introduced him to me. Sellers was quite posh, you know. He was well-dressed, or more to the point, over-dressed. He looked like a funeral director . . . who could do funny voices."[1]

The first tentative steps away from the impressive but uninspiring "and this is Wilfred Pickles" stage banter, was *Third Division*, a madcap and ragbag collection of comic sketches and hootenanny off-kilter characters described as 'Some Vulgar Fractions' in the *Radio Times*, and pulled together by Frank Muir and Denis Norden. As the scriptwriters of the series *Take It From Here*, Muir and Norden were the leaders in the field of radio comedy. Six episodes of *Third Division* were recorded between the 6th and 29th December 1948. *Third Division* was broadcast on the Third Programme, from 26th January 1949, on a Wednesday evening, usually from 8 p.m. Sellers

---

1 Interview with the author, July 2000.

was joined by other up and coming performers, including two he would get to know extremely well – Harry Secombe and Michael Bentine – alongside *Educating Archie*'s first tutor, the frightfully funny Robert Moreton, Patricia Hayes, taking time off from being a small boy in the *Children's Hour* favourite *Norman and Henry Bones, the Boy Detectives*, and a puppy-fat Benny Hill, cutting his teeth and biding his time. In September 1954, half a decade or so after the episodes were broadcast and then lost forever, Jimmy Grafton, the man who pulled the Goons together and mixed them up in a blender, observed in a *Radio Times* column that *Third Division* was not only a "super-intellectual advanced comedy show", but pretty much the birth of the Goons. Sellers wasn't so sure when he read that. Milligan was horrified. For it had been Milligan, undoubtedly, that had fired up this obsession for lunatic jokes and scattergun comic situations that would inspire and fuel Sellers. Full stop. As we will see, once Milligan found his muse in Sellers, Sellers would always, but always, inject some Milligan breath of insanity into a script. Whether Milligan was there or not; or even aware of it or not.

Certainly for Denis Norden: "it was pretty mad but nothing ground-breaking. I just remember how excited and excitable Sellers was. He caressed that BBC microphone as if it was one of the girls from his Windmill Theatre days. He was brilliant too. Pitch-perfect. A frantic Italian one sketch; a dour Russian the next."[1] Norden wasn't alone in finding Sellers the standout of the extremely outstanding ensemble. So much so that Jimmy Grafton concocted a radio show tailormade as Peter's own starring vehicle, *Sellers' Castle*. This was to co-star Spike, alongside husband-and-wife team Peter Butterworth and Janet Brown.

By that blistering summer of 1949 – the hottest in thirty years – Peter had dropped Joe Collins and Collins had dropped Peter Sellers. The feeling was mutual. As a result, Peter found even more solace in the domestic comfort of his parents, or at the very least, his barley-fed, mollycoddling Jewish Earth Mother. Having survived the war

---

1 Interview with the author, July 2000.

entertaining the troops with Mrs. George Formby, father Bill was something of a worn-out variety pianist who, as Spike Milligan observed at the time, "looked like he had died some years before and no one had bothered to tell him".[1] This stifling quagmire, both professional and personal, was brightened by the arrival in our story of a confident and skilful theatrical agent from Brighton: Dennis Selinger. This twenty-eight-year-old took on the twenty-three-year-old Sellers. He was sure, not to say cocksure, that he could mine the moonshine and gemstones within Peter's cluttered creativity. As far as Selinger was concerned too, Peter's stage personality and comic presence was not just impressive but bankable. As for his fledgling grip on the cosy confines of BBC Radio: Gold dust. Today the Third Programme; Tomorrow the World. Well, in ten years at any rate. The timing was perfect.

Off the ramshackle but interesting back of *Third Division*, it was opportune that the biggest radio comedian of the day, Ted Ray, was not only an admirer but also in the market. He was recruiting supporting talent for his own starring vehicle. The dexterous vocal prowess of Peter Sellers was just what *Ray's a Laugh* needed. First broadcast on 4th April 1949, the show was scripted by Ronnie Hanbury and George Wadmore, and in the safe producing hands of George Inns it proved an instant hit. Tommy Handley, the star of flag-waving World War II and beyond sketch smash hit *It's That Man Again* – or *ITMA* for short – had died suddenly in the January of 1949. A gaping hole was left, and *Ray's a Laugh* would fill it, even to the extent of securing the vocal talents of Tommy's old team member Fred Yule to growl and howl at odd intervals.

Sellers was the new kid on the block. The young pretender. Still, he loved and respected Ted Ray. This was an old-school showbiz charmer. And the feeling was mutual. Ted saw in Sellers a brilliant comedy voice man. The characters would be rather one-dimensional and gloriously silly, like weekly comic creations from the *Beano* or the *Dandy*, but in the hands of Sellers the star of the show felt

1 *Sellers' Best?* Lucida Productions, Channel 4, 1992.

comforted. Ray was safe in the knowledge that his supporting team were the cream of the crop.

It certainly didn't hurt Peter's variety theatre assignments either, securing a two-week engagement, from 3rd October 1949, at the London Palladium. Performing his 'Speaking for the Stars' routine, his position on the bill came immediately after Jose Moreno: Juggler on the Slack Wire and, rather more impressively, immediately before that Top of the Bill Lancashire Lassie 'Our Gracie' Fields.

The old showbiz adage used to be that a performer would ask the vital question: "How do I get to the London Palladium?", and the seasoned veteran would mutter: "Practice!", rather than: "Turn right outside the Oxford Circus tube station!" For Sellers to have made it to the world's most famous variety theatre was an achievement. A picture of Peter, from this appearance, hangs in the London Palladium stalls Variety Bar to this day. Immortality. It provided a tasty financial incentive too, in the fee of £100 per performance. As such it was one in the eye for his old agent Joe Collins.

It was the dawn of a bright new decade. A decade that would see and, most importantly, hear Peter's comedy revelation. Moreover his vibrant new agent had already introduced Sellers to the woman who would become his first wife.

Chapter 2

"More voices are always possible because there are people who exist!"

Peter Sellers, 1955

The 1950s certainly was a roller-coaster for Sellers. A decade that saw Peter remorselessly climbing the fame ladder, and outgrowing his fine line in unfussy impersonations. Most fundamentally of all, it would be the decade of *The Goon Show*. And from cheerful radio comic to BAFTA-winning film actor, Dennis Selinger steered Peter Sellers to the top. He was such a seamless fit, and was tirelessly sculpting and shaping Sellers into a star.

He liked to think of himself as something of a matchmaker too. Selinger had befriended Australian Anne Howe while they were both studying at the Royal Academy of Dramatic Art. From the dying days of the summer of 1949, and appearing under her stage name of Anne Hayes, she was in rehearsals for Alan Melville's diplomatic farce *Top Secret*. When it transferred from the Theatre Royal, Newcastle, to the West End's Winter Garden Theatre that October it quickly became apparent it would be a rare flop for the playwright. In the event, it ran in London for just twenty-one performances.

From that very first meeting, however, it was clear that the West End's loss would be Peter's gain. Remembering that first encounter, some forty years on, Anne thought Sellers a rather nondescript sort of chap. That was before Anne saw him on stage and was taken by that sparkle in his eyes that shone so brightly when Peter was making people laugh: "It wasn't instant attraction", she remembered. "That came when I saw him on stage for the first time, doing his act at the Regal, Edmonton. He was doing impressions, and he was absolutely wonderful. I think I fell in love with him on the stage."[1]

With the laughter came the love, and with the love came a sense of security within his own comedic skin.

By the time Peter and Anne were engaged in April 1950, that first series of *Ray's a Laugh* was still enjoying its unbroken run, only coming to an end that summer, after a staggering sixty-five weeks. Everything was coming up roses, both professionally and emotionally. Speaking in January 1951, the pivotal year of this oh-so-pivotal decade, Sellers explained that it was Ted Ray, personally, who invited him: "to play in his show, *Ray's a Laugh*, and I have enjoyed every minute of this series. They are the happiest crowd I have ever worked with."

That happy crowd, aside from Ray himself, included such seasoned radio talents as Kitty Bluett, whose domestic sketches within the show were blueprints for pretty much every domestic situation comedy that would follow, and Bob & Alf Pearson, the popular double act of brothers who performed close harmony renditions of the popular songs of the day. Bob also helped out with character acting, usually as high-pitched young ladies! Leslie Perrins was also in the company. A distinguished RADA-trained stage and screen actor since 1922, Sellers was rather in awe of his reputation and talent. Then there was the ubiquitous Patricia Hayes, not only a fabulous actress but a close and trusted ally, and good chum. No wonder he was enjoying himself so much.

Peter's gallery of gigglesome grotesques included Serge Suit, the bewildered Russian, Al K. Traz, a fast-talking American gangster, and Soppy, the high-pitched schoolboy who cheekily shouted out "Just like your big red conk!" As the character developed a nasal fascination for girls, the wisps of a fledgling Bluebottle can be heard. The bumfluff of a comic child that would reach heights of hilarity. There is even an embryonic Willium Mate in the armoury. He's less stylised, and less wheezing, and less bats, frankly, but maybe it's because he's a Londoner and that he calls Ted Ray "mate" a lot. He's

---

1 *Private Lives: You*, interview by Sue Summers, 5th February 1995.

also one of life's chancers and one of life's losers. However, most imperishable of all Peter's *Ray's a Laugh* creations is the outrageous, chuckling, and flirtatious old lady who would forever introduce herself thus: "My name's Crystal Jollibottom, you saucebox!" Listening to those earliest surviving broadcasts, from 1949, you can hear young genius at work. This really is Peter Sellers juvenilia. The audience's reaction was warm and tickled too. A lot of this was, undoubtedly, due to the fact that he was a fresh-faced, rather handsome, very personable young man . . . from whose youthful mouth emitted this barking mad female with slightly salacious sayings. Sellers had the ability to make the most innocent, though loaded, observations sound like pure filth. An excited exclamation of: "You've pushed me down on my hearth rug!" could glean gales of laughter. Ted Ray too, despite writing the jokes, alongside Eddie Maguire, would often crack up with laughter when cheek-by-jowl with Sellers at the mic. Invariably Crystal Jollibottom would pop up in the long-running sketch focused on Ted as George, a sheepish newspaper reporter with a conscience. In the episode broadcast on 22nd November 1949 Jollibottom is with the "last of the GIs down on the docks." The inference that she is now a lady of the night is clear, but it's the transatlantic jokes that tickle Ted. At one point Peter screams: "You're dribbling down my Gettysburg Address!" It's almost too much for the star of the show. He gulps back a laugh, and carries on. This was the very magic Peter lived for. And the character made him a national sensation. And a lasting one too.

Yes, Sellers would resurrect these caricatures for a good few years yet, particularly Jollibottom, who was a signifier for instant audience laughter. Something of a Godsend, in fact. Peter's jukebox of funny voices and zestful eagerness to accept work saw him join the cast of *Horace Washes It Out!*, a Boxing Day 1950 afternoon comedy variety package for the Light Programme, alongside Harry Hemsley, Jean Carson and Bob Monkhouse.

The radio marquee value certainly heightened his appeal on the variety circuit, and heightened his bank balance. Certainly by the start of 1951 he was suitably able to indulge: "My hobbies . . ." which he listed as: "golf, motor-cars, and collecting unusual gramophone records." The motor-cars would remain a lifetime passion, and would soon become an oft-repeated joke in his radio broadcasts. The unusual gramophone records also remained something of a constant, informing his own recording career and leading him down exciting rabbit warrens in experiments with sound comedy. It was an obsession that also influenced Peter's comic acolytes such as Peter Butterworth, Dick Emery and Graham Stark.[1]

This thrilling financial buoyancy notwithstanding, it was *Those Crazy People* that put Peter's mind at ease. Sellers was a very happy wage slave, earning enough money to get married, buy a house, and start a family. This domestic idyll was thanks completely to the focus of Dennis Selinger and the friendly influence of Jimmy Grafton. And, most importantly, the alcohol-flowing conviviality of Jimmy's pub, the Grafton Arms, in Victoria, south-west London.[2] It was the fertile breeding ground for a revolution in comedy which would shape Peter's entire life and career; and those other fledgling comic greats who drank alongside him. These included the aforementioned Peter Butterworth and his wife Janet Brown; Graham Stark; Dick Emery; Larry Stephens; not to mention Michael Bentine, Spike Milligan, and Harry Secombe. I told you not to mention them!

Those Crazy People was first broadcast on Monday 28th May 1951. On 15th September, just five days before the last of that inaugural series was transmitted and seven days after he had turned twenty-six years old, Sellers was a married man. Security and stability, for the intrigue and all-consuming appeal of the Goonish quartet was pretty much immediate. The 1951 documentary team at E.J. Fancey Productions, working on their eclectic round-up review *London Entertains* were impressed and piqued enough with the buzz

---

1 That same *Radio Fun* column, from January 1951, gave an early, jovial nod to Peter's superstitions. He revealed that: "My lucky number is 7 – because it was while playing a race-game at a fun-fair in Portsmouth with a horse numbered 7 that I won every time and cleared all the prizes off the stall!"

2 Any self-respecting comedy connoisseur needs to have a pint here: 2 Strutton Ground, SW1P 2HP. The pub grub is pretty good too. Tell them I sent you!

surrounding the group that they filmed the four-man team in action, supported by Ray Ellington too. Although the film was conceived and written by Edwin John F.J. Fancey, the Goons sequence was conceived and written by Jimmy Grafton. In all fairness it had been Grafton who had suggested the showcasing of his boys. Moreover, Grafton's free and for nothing access all areas for the crew's filming of the Goons sequence was a blessing to the tiny budget.

Shot in the summer of 1951 and released that December, it stars presenter Eamonn Andrews escorting a group of young ladies round the cultural sites of the capital. Apart from Jimmy's comedy-centric boozer these included the Festival of Britain and the Windmill Theatre. But this is where you came in, folks . . .

Other radio personalities appearing as themselves included Canadian singer Bobby Breen, and straight man and host Tony Fayne. However, *London Entertains* remains historically crucial for that brief, vibrant glimpse of pure, infant Goonery. On the air the four were still very much individual performers, indulging their own individual talents, as honed on the variety stages across Britain. For Sellers, of course, this talent was for famous and silly voices.

Fancey had actually already utilised the Sellers voice to spruce up a vintage classic from the most famous comedian in cinema history. May 1951 saw New Realm Entertainment distribute Fancey's twist on Charlie Chaplin's *A Burlesque of Carmen*. Sellers was recruited to narrate the silent gem; while the unauthorised deployment of jangly comedy music and outlandish sound effects led to Chaplin skipping over from Hollywood to sue. Sellers was in the clear. He had taken the money and scarpered back to the BBC.[1]

Over at the Corporation it was Peter's skill for silly voices that were to the fore. All of which helped fuel the marketing of the team as the Junior Crazy Gang. During those earliest days of the Goons, the Crazy Gang proper were holding court at the Victoria Palace, in riotous comedy revues *Knights of Madness* and *Ring Out the Bells*.

---

1 Chaplin's original comedy had sat happily in the middle of two big budget serious productions released in 1915. His leading lady was Edna Purviance, with eye-crossing comic support from Ben Turpin.

The junior moniker was skilful shorthand in order to label these young comic bucks as anarchic and wacky. Still, Bud Flanagan, undisputed leader of the Gang, was a high profile and vocal admirer. It was a fact that amazed and elated Sellers. Here was true variety comedy royalty endorsing the Goons. Waxing lyrical, in print, in 1958 Bud revealed: "I've followed the Goons ever since they started on the air – in fact I've watched their careers very carefully, and I'm one of their biggest champions. They're brilliant – especially Sellers. We're 'crazy', but their humour is far more advanced than ours."[1]

Not only was he brilliant, but Sellers was a busy man. Spike was handcuffed into writing duties; while Sellers was free to accept a myriad of other, lucrative radio assignments. Most notably he duputised for an indisposed Valentine Dyall at the eleventh hour for *Bumblethorpe*. The notorious Man in Black would become a valued part of the Goon repertory company, but on this day, 19th November 1951, Sellers stepped into the breach when the bizarre ramblings of Spike Milligan and Larry Stephens were both recorded and transmitted. The supporting cast was awash with freewheelin' chums, including Avril Angers,[2] the fretfully earnest and diligent comedian Robert Moreton,[3] and reliable and esteemed members of the gang: Kenneth Connor, Alfred Marks and Graham Stark. These chaps were Peter's friends and allies. The nuts and bolts who kept him together. For decades, in some cases.

Stark certainly would step in, almost immediately, to essay the tongue-in-cheek romantic lead of Prince Charming in the Goon Christmas Special, 'Cinderella', recorded on 16th December 1951, ten days ahead of its broadcast as a Boxing Day treat. Cinders was played by soprano Lizbeth Webb. Sellers relished a Jollibottom-like Ugly Sister along the way, but a radio pantomime was as nothing to a feature film though. Oh yes it was; oh no it wasn't!

Peter would have loads of radio chums surrounding his first foray

---

1 'The Goons – as others see them', by Gale Pedrick, *Radio Times*, 31st October 1958.
2 Liverpudlian comedienne who was something of a fusion of Lucille Ball and Gracie Fields.
3 An urbane personality who delighted in telling bad jokes and who was the first tutor on *Educating Archie*.

into cinema; not to mention that determination and grit which indulged him in multi characterisation. In his heart Sellers was Alec Guinness at Ealing Studios; in reality he was nurtured and championed by a smaller, though no less pioneering, outfit: Adelphi Films. The home of great swathes of quota quickies, and instrumental in making and shaping the screen personas of Diana Dors and Sidney James, Adelphi produced *Let's Go Crazy*, with director Alan Cullimore, for Advance Productions.

Let's Go Crazy was Peter's first film proper. A short subject, and something of a cobbled-together rag-bag of silly skits and frantic farce, it was a big break nonetheless. Peter didn't have to do much save leap into the action and give one of five – count 'em – five comic turns. Fundamentally, it's a half-hour variety theatre package, presented as a cabaret in a select restaurant. The fun and frolics are overseen by Giuseppe, an irate Italian with an outrageously big handle-bar moustache. This is Sellers at his least subtle. A caricature of continental consternation, who is disgusted by the Brits' obsession with boiled beef and carrots, and desperately tries to push instead his gaff's speciality – what else but spaghetti.

In between the singers and contortionist dancers and mayhem music of the house band, Sellers is given hilarious vignettes that showcase his contemporaneous radio characters (Crystal Jollibottom, strangled tones set to stun, is whisked off in an energetic dance by a sheepish, sticky-fingered Wallace Eaton) and Peter's music-hall repertoire of impressions (notably an obvious, girl-chasing, cigar-chomping Groucho Marx). Peter's enthusiasm adds glee to this stable of stock performances. One-dimensional certainly, hilarious most assuredly, again like characters from a weekly comic. There's nothing particularly clever going on here, but Sellers is clearly having a great time flexing his comic muscles. In a film.

It may be as cheap as chips; and as mad as a box of frogs, but it is cinema; and the first rung on the ladder of a thirty-year star career in front of the cameras.

There's also slow-witted and pretentiously confident Cedric who mangles his way through the French menu and, somehow, continually impresses his easily pleased date. Last to appear is Izzy Gozunk. He is a soppy and pushy variation on the Flash Harry creation of variety character comedian Sid Field, who had died tragically young the previous February. Field was a firm favourite with Sellers and, here, in affectionate homage, he is as crooked and cocky as a spiv should be. His stooge in the scene is Spike Milligan – who also pops up as an Eccles-like waiter. In the encounter with the spiv, however, Spike plays it straight. Posh, in fact. Hoodwinked and bamboozled by Peter's fast-talking nonsense. And while Milligan is uncredited, Sellers enjoys top billing: five times. Clearly his name attached was deemed powerful enough to sell a short film as part of an evening's entertainment. None of the roles is a stretch; all of them are delightful. Even more so thanks to the primitive, almost embryonic nature of the performance. *Let's Go Crazy* has certainly earned its place in cinema's most treasured vault and, fittingly enough, was lovingly restored by the British Film Institute simply because of its historical importance.[1]

The final moment of *Let's Go Crazy*, as Sellers, in Groucho mode, ignites a TNT bomb with his cigar in order to speed up the orchestra, literally closes the film with a bang. Crucially, for all its ramshackle corner-cutting and corny comic quips, *Let's Go Crazy* straddles Peter's career as a mere impersonator of the famous, and a more interesting creator of unique comic characters.

Perhaps not surprisingly *Let's Go Crazy* had been something of an afterthought. An opportunistic, swiftly-assembled project off the back of another. It was shot at Brighton Film Studios, St. Nicholas Road, within a spare week in the schedule of an Adelphi Films feature film, *Penny Points to Paradise*. Sellers and Spike were in this as well, as was Harry Secombe. Thus, in hindsight, this is a Goon film that isn't. Not really. True to the show, Harry is, in fact, the lead in *Penny Points to Paradise*, although he's playing a slightly less manic version of himself: the likeable fool Harry Flakers, who,

---

1 It eventually found a Blu-ray home as a bonus feature on the 2016 BFI release of *Mr. Topaze*.

supposedly, wins £100,000 on the football pools – the winning penny points that will make his life a paradise, you see – and attracts the attention of a gang of crooked counterfeiters. Sellers plays just three roles – just three! – this time round, although two of these are much more rounded; and much more grounded than anything he conjured up for *Let's Go Crazy*. There's the Major, a kindly curmudgeon of a cove; and Arnold P. Fringe, a fast-talking irritant.

There's also a blink and you'll miss him role of a spectator during Secombe's sporting dream, in which he is a champion shot-putter. It's the sort of thing that, at the time, Sellers would always step up to the plate for. Someone, anyone, was needed to fill out a crowd scene. The budget was miniscule. He was on the budget, and he was game. Eager, even. A little more screen time experience was what he craved.

First and foremost Sellers was simply happy to be filming. Anything. The director was a breeze too. Tony Young would later produce *The Telegoons*, and shot *Penny Points to Paradise* in just three weeks. Those with a cynical streak may wonder what took him so long, but it's a jolly jamboree down in Brighton, largely in salute to slapstick silent comedy. Great swathes of the fun is under-cranked and accompanied by jubilant, jaunty music, while a chase sequence is a direct tip of the hat to the Keystone Kops, who had been making merry some thirty years earlier. Paddie O'Neill (Mrs. Alfred Marks) even mimes exaggeratingly in her imitation of Gloria Swanson.[1] Some of the gags aren't that much fresher. If he had been alive W.C. Fields would undoubtedly have demanded a percentage.

It's certainly fitting that at this same time Peter was lined up by Adelphi Films to record an English language narration over *Ca C'est du Cinema*, a cheap French compilation film the company had bought and plonked upon the desk of producer R.A. Bradford. This comprised hacked-up silent comedy classics, with Laurel and Hardy, 'Buster' Keaton, and Harry Langdon. In Britain these were newly

---

1 The silent screen goddess was in London at the time. Indeed footage of her visiting the building site of the Royal Festival Hall is featured in the Goons-celebrating documentary *London Entertains*.

edited by Hilary Long, who also wrote the linking commentary. Cleverly, all this meant it was now deemed a new British film, thus serving to fulfil the 'quota quickie' requirement for home-made material in British cinemas. As such the film emerged in 1953 as the gloriously entitled *The Slappiest Days of Our Lives*. The poster tagline promised that: "You'll laugh! You'll roar! You'll scream!" Well, quite.

That quote could certainly – on occasions – be used for *Penny Points to Paradise*. For because, and not despite, the catalogue of old jokes, there is also something unquestionably historic about Harry, Spike and Peter larking about together – be it in cross-talking, surrealist banter or the elongated play-acting with the dressing-up basket during the finale set in Louis Tussaud's waxworks.

Peter's highlight is undoubtedly the one-scene cameo as the fast-talking American salesman Arnold P. Fringe. He's got an answer and a product for everything. Sellers and Secombe clearly enjoy the scene immensely. However, the major Sellers contribution is, suitably enough, the Major: a lapel-tucking, Gilbert Harding-like bore who mutters on with endless nuggets of dull trivia. He's also not above the odd con trick himself, happily swindling the swindlers with worthless shares in a North Pole coconut mine; and pulling out the oldest pub trick in the book to wheedle out a couple of large gins from permanently sozzled variety theatre drunk Freddie Frinton. Sellers effortlessly milks the running bathroom gag too, and wholeheartedly throws himself into the slapstick homage. His stiff-legged galloping and wayward bicycle-riding antics are straight from the messy prattfalling playbook of Richard Hearne's Mr. Pastry.

Everybody is allowed to indulge their act: Spike stripped to the waist and looking goofy; Alfred Marks turning on the supercilious intellect and crooked eye-rolling contempt; Bill Kerr referencing and almost shoe-horning in his "I'm only here for four minutes" radio catchphrase; while Harry even verges into his old shaving routine. So, in this almost-Goon feature, Harry is Harry (in a near continual state of bemusement throughout) and Spike is Spike (mournful mumbler of often incoherent nonsense), but Sellers is certainly not Sellers – he's the chameleon. The complete character comedian.

For Sellers *Penny Points to Paradise* was an opportunity to display his skills at character comedy rather than the heightened reality of performance of *London Entertains*; or, more crucially, the manic impersonation of *Let's Go Crazy*. Thus, within his Adelphi Films experience, he became the film star he would remain for thirty years. A gloriously corny film which only granted him third billing, *Penny Points to Paradise* is arguably the one that made Peter Sellers Peter Sellers.

1952 saw the Goons officially billed as *The Goon Show* from Tuesday, 22nd January. Listings explained that the programme still featured those crazy people but now the expected madness was a little less variety and a little more structured. However, the programme for 12th February was pulled from the schedule, following the announcement of the death of King George VI. The Sellers and Bentine takeover of BBC Television was also scuppered in the wake of the monarch's demise. *Trial Gallop* was to have been a live sketch show, and was set for transmission from 8.55 p.m. the following day, Wednesday, 13th February. Testament to the clout and interest in the fledging Goons, this experimental television show was to have been linked, in vision, by newsreel commentator and announcer Leslie Mitchell. Thus containing the madness within BBC stability. With half the Goons present and correct, the supporting cast was to have comprised of Mrs. Sellers, Anne Hayes, Graham Stark, and Peter Butterworth. In the event, the broadcast could never be remounted.

Still, it was at around this time, early in 1952, that Stark and Sellers were gainfully employed on a jolly jape, when they took on Laurel and Hardy: "in a basement room in Wardour Street . . . redubbing film reels. A bright gentleman had bought some cheap footage of Stan and Ollie, obviously intending to put out a little film of them. I imagine it was cheap as it was soon discovered there was no sound track . . . Peter was booked as Hardy, he suggested me as Laurel. All day long we sat watching loops of film being projected on the screen . . . I know Peter always adored them and I think he was very influenced by their subtlety."[1] Sellers often recalled those sessions as some of the happiest of his professional life. Although, ironically, the real Stan and Ollie had docked in England, on the *Queen Mary*, on Monday, 28th January 1952, for a ten-week variety theatre tour. The originals being too busy and, more than likely, too expensive, Stark and Sellers became Laurel and Hardy. The films remain perhaps the most obscure in the entire Sellers canon. And there are a fair few in competition.

Indeed, it was a feverishly busy time for Sellers as a vocal nonentity, racking up those obscure credits at a rate of knots. He would be rushing from one BBC studio to another, as often as not to add a voice in *Meet the Huggetts* here, or a sound effect in *Life with the Lyons* there. He would also eagerly take on any voiceover assignment that happened to come along. Perhaps the most intriguing and important to the plot was for *Our Girl Friday*, a love triangle desert island comedy film, written and directed by Noel Langley, and starring Joan Collins, Kenneth More, and George Cole. Peter was cast as the voice of a decidedly cheeky cockatoo who shrieked with delight when the daughter of his ex-agent removed her clothes!; and was heard in cinemas across Britain when the film went on general release for the Christmas of 1953. Sellers had been lending his catalogue of voices to all sorts of weird and wonderful ventures at the time. He dubbed actor Alfonso Bedoya, as Lu Chung, the villainous leader of a merchant's caravan across 12th-century China, in Henry Hathaway's *The Black Rose* (1950); and, even more intriguing, provided additional snatches of dialogue as Humphrey Bogart, as Billy Dannreuther, in *Beat the Devil* (1953), John Huston's homage to his own past.

Sellers was very much Sellers, albeit in multiple characters, for his first ever record recording assignment. The producer was George Martin, who would helm Peter's funniest discs. This wasn't one of them. *Jakka and the Flying Saucers (An Interplanetary Fairy Tale)*

---

1 *Remembering Peter Sellers*, by Graham Stark (Robson Books, 1990)

is more charming whimsy, although our narrator is a space-travelling spin on *The Goon Show*'s Henry Crun. Here he is an even more aged Professor Crun, who relates the science-fiction nonsense across a double-sided 78 rpm Parlophone release.

The jokes are a little bit Goonish for the kiddies but far more Christmas Cracker japery: witness our space cadet's dog being called Dunker simply because he has a circular body and looks like a doughnut. These sweet trivialities were written by lyricist Ken Hare and composer Ron Goodwin. Goodwin had only just joined the label, as arranger and conductor, and both he and Hare would assist George Martin on *The Best of Sellers* album.

Thus, despite being a childlike trinket that failed to wobble the charts in terms of sales or air-play during the Coronation year of its release, it was extremely helpful in terms of experience for Sellers in the recording studio. *Jakka* also proved useful as a showcase for his winning ways as a comedy voice man. Giving it a spin you can certainly hear him having a whale of a time. There's delicious glee when Crun rambles on about the 'Space Horn'; while Winston Churchill makes an uncredited appearance as an elderly star in the stratosphere. There's a distinct exotic edge of Zsa-Zsa Gabor about the characterisation of Mother; while the comet is a variation on the Sidney Mincing character that chum Kenneth Connor had just introduced to *Ray's a Laugh*.

The hit and miss tomfoolery of *Jakka* was not Peter's bread and butter, for the dawning of the second Elizabethan Age saw the Goons return to the studio and cement their reputation for anarchic, authority-baiting comedy. The first episode of the second series was recorded on Sunday, 20th January 1952 for a broadcast the following Tuesday; while screens weren't safe from the team's antics either. *Goonreel*, a television newsreel, was transmitted from 8.45 p.m. on Wednesday, 2nd July. Goon announcer Andrew Timothy provided the commentary, with Sellers and Spike in the studio. Secombe made his contribution through a pre-recorded filmed insert, while the programme featured credited written contributions from Bentine.

Just four days later Bentine would record his last show as part of the team. The 25th and final episode in that second series, on Tuesday, 15th July, would be his last regular involvement with the programme. A moment in comedy history, and the end of an era, for sure, but a series of *The Goon Show* that pointed the way forward and established a very new way of doing things. Indeed, the programme broadcast on 18th March had been the first with a full half-hour plotline: Spike's version of H. Rider Haggard's *She* – entitled 'Her'. Life would never quite be the same again. Not for Sellers. Not for anyone!

However, although Bentine may have bowed out, at least in his own head, he was still a Goon in the Summer of 1952 when he reconvened with the gang to shoot a feature film. As with *London Entertains*, it was E.J. Fancey Productions who: "have the misfortune to inflict . . . The Goons" in *Down Among the Z Men*. Harry Secombe, Michael Bentine, Spike Milligan, Peter Sellers and guest femme fatale Carole Carr then introduce themselves and the characters they play within the action. It's that kind of film, folks.

Importantly, for the first time in Peter's film career, he only plays one character, as opposed to multi-roles or appearing as himself . . . but what a character! Basically, for the Sellers-phile this is Bloodnok the movie. It's certainly not *The Goon Show* film it wants to me, despite Sellers bringing Bloodnok to visual life, and Spike galloping around the place as Private Eccles. Bentine brings his beloved loon, the absent-minded Professor Pureheart to the party, and he's at the heart of the fun, or at least his chemical formula is. Spider, a lightweight heavy played reassuringly by Graham Stark, is certainly after the secret, and convinces gullible lummox Secombe that he's a high-ranking policeman. Harry's character is obsessed with law-enforcing, you see, having got rave reviews as Bats of the Yard in the local amateur dramatic society. Jimmy Grafton, co-writing (with Francis Charles) and disappointingly keeping the whole Goon family on lengthy, rather lacklustre leashes, delivers some stonkers and stinkers in the one-liner department. All are played with great charm and spell-binding enthusiasm. To everyone's eternal credit. It's as if the lads can scarcely believe they are getting away with all this. They do. Just. Simply for the sheer historical clout of having all four of them in a feature film romp. Well, it's almost feature length, at just over an hour, and that's with pit-stops for Carole Carr's songs.

There's also the diversion of a ramshackle army camp variety show, which at least indulges Sellers in a brilliant burlesque. It's a little snippet of his own music-hall routine at the time: the reconstruction of an American war movie with the squeaky-voiced lieutenant eagerly outlining his plan to his bluff commanding officer. All too late, of course, for the invasion happens in mid-sentence. That's the joke, folks.

Apart from this slip into red-nosed clown, it is Sellers who is most controlled throughout the film. Or the most laudable considering it was a two-week schedule and the majority of first takes were the ones that were printed.[1] Peter's the usual silly old buffer but without the flights of surrealism that Milligan's scripts lent the character. The closest is a brief briefing of military personnel as Secombe hovers round their legs and obliterates the all-important orders. One hopes the script mistakenly read that 'Secombe hoovers', and that that prime corny gag was thrown into the mixture. There's certainly a sense that the Goons are thinking on their feet, and exercising their funny bones, within and without the screenplay. Certainly the whole thing has that glorious feel of on-the-hoof invention about it, although it was very much scripted. Honestly!

Sellers has some playful moments of bewildered insanity with Bentine, but is at his acting best opposite Carole Carr. Away from his usual Goon chums, Sellers is even more reined-in; enjoying the interaction with this sexy military mole masquerading as his attractive daughter, and throwing in all the expected "By gad!" and "By jove!" exclamations around the most bland of utterances. He certainly likes the idea of being the young lady's sugar daddy. Fine . . . fine . . . fine. The square-bashing and espionage overtones are

---

1 It was shot in and around the military premises of Warwell Camp, and at the Maida Vale Studios. Once again it was distributed by New Realm Pictures.

fun too; while the unexpected unleashing of Bentine's laughter and tear gas combination allows the comic turns to mug away happily. Although, here also, there is a nicely-played moment of Sellers shock at the barked army orders. The frantic climax, with both Harry and Spike also dressed up as a hairy Bentine, has a pleasing sense of the Marx Brothers about it.[1] The bottom line question is though: is *Down Among the Z Men* funny? Yes, it's alright, mate. Historical artefact, for sure, and worth enduring just for that closing moment when all four Goons chant the title like some wanton ritual for shared laughter. It's iconic and vital.

---

1 The following year, the same director and producer were at work on the New Realm Entertainment film *Forces Sweetheart*, starring Secombe, Bentine, and Freddie Frinton, fresh from *Penny Points to Paradise*, as three inept servicemen. Sellers would have doubtlessly loved to have been involved. 1953, for him, started with a *Workers' Playtime*, recorded from St. Giles' Hospital, Camberwell, on Monday 25th January, for a Home Service broadcast the following day. Subsequent broadcasts that spring included *Show Band Show*, on 8th February, and *Midday Music-Hall*, on 12th February.

Chapter 3

"I just remembered the clever idea I had!"

Henry Crun

Down Among the Z Men was released or, more fittingly, it escaped, in October 1952, just a month ahead of the third batch of radio episodes. The programme was now simply and forever dubbed *The Goon Show*. Despite the complete non-appearance of Bentine in the series, a move was made to reinforce *Down Among the Z Men* as the official *Goon Show* film, by enlisting Carole Carr for the forty-five-minute Boxing Day pantomime 'Robin Hood'. Still, Spike was absent from this show too, as well as a great chunk of the series. Although Dick Emery and Graham Stark alternated as pit-props in the cast, it was Sellers who would often super-substitute for the ailing Milligan and, on occasions, play a three-character scene all by himself. The zenith of Peter's dexterity and mental agility was required. And he delivered. Boy, how he delivered.

Peter became so adept at doing these all-character sequences that he began capitalising on it for his live variety appearances. Bob Monkhouse and Denis Goodwin would write him special five-minute Goon scripts in which he would play everybody: not just his own Bloodnok and Bluebottle et al., but Eccles and Neddie too. Tailormade for variety bills, a broadcast example of this, and still thankfully in the BBC archives, was heard in *Calling All Forces*. Our 'Forces Sweetheart' Carole Carr was also on call to belt out some popular tunes. Aimed at serving personnel stationed at home and in Germany and transmitted on the Light Programme, the genial host of the show was peerless fast-patter merchant Ted Ray, a star comedian who Sellers, naturally, greatly admired. He was also extremely grateful to him, even though that October of 1953 would see Peter start his final batch of *Ray's a Laugh*, leaving at the end of series five.[1] *Calling All Forces* was still a relaxed, welcome environment then, for Sellers to show-up and show-off. In the best possible way.[2] Of course. With multi-tracking or just deep breaths Sellers could have performed every radio episode solo, but where would the fun for him be in that?

Spike, even winded and flying on a broken wing, certainly lifted Sellers in confidence and performance. Even more so than Ted Ray. Spike was a pal, a contemporary, a brother-in-arms. And Spike was certainly fit enough to rally round in order to join Peter at the Princess Theatre, in London's glittering West End, for *Don't Spare the Horses*. This was a BBC Television presentation, produced by W. Lyon-Shaw, and co-starring the comedian's comedian Jimmy James, for three live broadcasts from Saturday, 1st November 1952. Spike would also notch up a few Goon episodes from the following Sunday, but would not return, full-strength, until the March of 1953.

The series rolled on until the broadcast of 'The Story of the Plymouth Hoe Armada', on Sunday, 5th May; with a special, forty-minute Coronation edition, with guest star Graham Stark, recorded on 1st June 1953 for transmission on 3rd June. This was the day after Queen Elizabeth II had been crowned in Westminster Abbey, thus allowing the reverence to hold sway, before the anarchy took over.[3] The previous Christmas Sellers had also joined the all-in radio comedy jamboree of *The Santa Claus Show*. An hour-long variety

---

1 Kenneth Connor, that versatile voice-man and gold medal-winning graduate from the Central School of Speech and Drama, was on hand to fill Peter's shoes; along with Charles Hawtrey, late of *The Will Hay Programme – The Diary of a Schoolmaster* and still the oldest school boy around on the *Children's Hour* serial *Norman and Henry Bones, the Boy Detectives*, with Patricia Hayes, who stayed with *Ray's a Laugh* until the sixth series. It was on that series that portly Alexander Gauge, later to achieve small-screen stardom as Friar Tuck in *The Adventures of Robin Hood*, joined the Ted Ray repertory company.

2 *The Goon Show Compendium* compact disc collections from the BBC are an essential trove – for all sorts of reasons. Volume 2 features the un-broadcast remake of 'The Phantom Batter-Pudding Hurler', in which pre-show warm-up chat with Sellers reveals he will be playing all Spike's characters too. And rather wonderful he is.

3 Stark kept hold of his script. His proudest achievement. The three Goons were all credited as Lords, while his own fourth billing, above the title credit, was Dame Graham Stark.

romp, scripted by Alan Simpson and Ray Galton. Sellers was on hand to give his beloved Soppy schoolboy from *Ray's a Laugh*, and Graham Stark was in it too.[1]

It was all a perfect prelude for a short film subject *The Super Secret Service*. Sellers plays both Sir Walter Smood and Reuben J. Crouch in a Goonish twenty-odd minutes mucking about with the make-up kit and playing high-octane film noir espionage on a miniscule budget. Ray Ellington and His Quartet are even on hand to offer a musical break. Although Spike had a massive hand in the scripting of the film, it was shot during his ill-health sabbatical from *The Goon Show* and, with great logic, his radio replacements Dick Emery and Graham Stark stepped into the breach. To be honest Sellers could have played his parts and everybody else's parts too. He had become an all-round comedy engine. Practically a limited company of laughs. He was a family-friendly sketch comedian and the anarchic Goon. Peddling silly voices for both cosy domesticity and the intelligentsia. At the core of this comedic mechanism was still Peter's profound skill for impersonation. For chum and cohort Eric Sykes, Sellers was: "number one . . . uncanny . . . any character he chose to play he would be that person . . ." It was not just the voice. Once, when impersonating *Educating Archie*'s first tutor, comedian Robert Moreton, "Peter had changed for that moment his metabolism." It was that chilling authenticity that Peter's old agent Joe Collins had found so clinical. Peter's performances were elevated from mere impressions to exact recreations of the actual person. Disturbing, even. Much more telling was Peter's twisting of this perfect mimicry for when he played his own vocal inventions. Peter

---

1 It was produced by Dennis Main Wilson who, less than two years later, would launch Galton and Simpson's *Hancock's Half-Hour* on radio. *The Santa Claus Show* was transmitted on Boxing Day, from 2.p.m. on the Light Programme, Hermione Gingold was Mother Christmas, Bernard Bra.den and Barbara Kelly were the parents, and Beryl Reid contributed her saucy school kid Monica, from *Educating Archie*. Fellow *Educating Archie* alumni Hattie Jacques was recruited alongside Sellers, Stark, Braden and Kelly for another edition, on Christmas Day 1953. In between these festive frolics, Peter's bit of comedy business on *Music Hall*, broadcast on BBC Television, on 2nd May 1953, for producer Richard Afton, was particularly well received. Graham Stark was his stooge. While his six minutes of schtick on shows like *Everything Under Control*, *Join in and Sing*, and *Northern Lights* was now earning him a twenty-five guinea pay cheque.

would metamorphose at will, becoming diminished and wizened for Crun; expanded and bloated for Bloodnok. For *Me and My Shadows*, a special Light Programme showcase for an impressionist to entertain, Sellers delighted in subverting his sublime talent and presenting shades of well-known broadcasters alongside his favoured Goon characters. Here was a comedian at ease within many, many skins.[1]

Certainly, when *The Super Secret Service* hit cinemas for Christmas 1953, Peter was happily slap bang in the middle of the fourth series of *The Goon Show*. It had started on Friday, 2nd October, with the Spike Milligan and Larry Stephens scripted 'The Dreaded Piano Clubber'. By now the gloriously insane characters were inextricably becoming part of the fabric of British life. The dedicated audiences at the Paris Theatre recordings were totally in tune and in awe and, at times, insane, with the madness unfurling before their very eyes and ears. 'The Missing Prime Minister', recorded on Sunday, 3rd January 1954, for transmission the following Friday, has Peter offer a rather strangulated version of Bluebottle. Even at this embryonic stage, that first appearance gets a huge round of applause. His comic pay-off, concerning the analysis of a pair of gloves found at the scene of the crime, and reporting that they are the sort you wear on your hands, gets a borderline manic reaction.

Bluebottle, having developed from the cheeky *Ray's a Laugh* schoolboy Soppy, had truly found his inspiration in a giant of a man, eccentric scout-leader Ruxton Hayward. Sellers would delight, nay insist, on relating the tale. It was all Michael Bentine's fault. He had a gloriously encouraging habit of considering everybody a genius, and, as he was the educated Goon, the others always believed him.

---

1 *Eric Sykes' Comedy Heroes*, by Eric Sykes, Virgin Books Ltd. 2003. *Me and My Shadows*, which was recorded at the Aeolian, on Wednesday 31st March 1954, really was, in practice, Peter's one-man Goon show, with Bluebottle introducing it as Radio Bluebottle. Moreover, it lovingly sends up the impersonator's art. Henry Crun is there, as Cheerful Charlie Crun. There is no pretence to do radio comedian Cheerful Charlie Chester. Bloodnok is on parade, while an amalgam creature called Spike Eccles proves Milligan was in Peter's comic soul. Sports heroes (Stanley Matthews), sports commentators (Raymond Glendenning, or Raymond Goon-Denning as he is called here), distinguished orators (Gilbert Harding), all are fair game, with little to no attempt at the accuracy that was supple in the Sellers speech. Produced by George Inns, and broadcast on 9th April 1954, this tour de force was made available as a rare bonus on the, now itself, rare *The Goon Show Compendium Volume One*.

Hayward was sent round to the variety theatre Sellers was playing, instructed the bemused Goon that: "Michael Bentine says I'm a genius!" and, boom, Bluebottle. This anecdote was a favourite for Sellers to relate in the 1970s. At a time when the Goons were comic deities to be celebrated and resurrected for special occasions. Before this lengthy, intellectual and historical digging, contemporary comments from Sellers and Secombe would make Bluebottle's source that breed of faceless, irritating "fringer!": a term of less than endearment for one of those stage-struck idiots who hung round the stage door of theatres in which the Goons frequently played. Courteous, ingratiating even, but with no social skills filter whatsoever. A Herbert, to be frank.

The adenoidal-whine, the knobbly knees, barely concealed by the boy scout shorts; the, at turns heroic and cowardice glee in reciting his stage directions: he was a gift to Sellers. No wonder the character hailed from Peter's neck of the woods, of East Finchley. Bluebottle was the comic gremlin in Peter's subconscious. He remains, arguably, his most personal and endearing comic character.[1]

Bluebottle certainly gave Peter a comic voice he never tired of; and crystallised his fast-growing position as the star of *The Goon Show*. Not that the others minded that much. Indeed, such was their celebrity that all three Goons joined such fellow wireless luminaries as Joyce Grenfell, and Terry-Thomas, live, for *The Hundredth Boat Race*. This was, unsurprisingly, a towpath comic commentary on the 100th annual rowing contest between Oxford and Cambridge, with *Take It from Here* stars Jimmy Edwards and Dick Bentley ad-libbing and fibbing their way through it. Sellers, in character as Bloodnok, interacted with his old chum Jimmy Edwards. Blooknok, having come to see the Grand National, believes that the horses will still run despite the course being flooded! In actual fact, the Goons beamed their contribution from the comfort of the Langham Hotel, Portland

---

1 Indeed, Bluebottle's characteristics ricocheted around comedy long after Peter's death, his habit of being "deaded" every week being picked up by Stan and Kyle of Trey Parker and Matt Stone's *South Park* for their continually ill-fated chum Kenny, of "Oh, my God! They've killed Kenny!" fame!

Place, immediately opposite the BBC.[1]

National fame on radio may have increased their weekly earnings and marquee value on variety theatre billing matters, but Sellers, in particular, was quickly becoming disingenuous about the circuit. The relentless and tedious ritual of shabby theatrical digs and half-empty theatres: "some godforsaken hole, and dying"[2] were no fun. Still, the joy did come when Sellers shared the bill with a fellow Goon which, with canny promoters and managers arranging, happened on a fairly regular basis. It was still a trial but at least there was a chum along for the agony. Harry Secombe recalled a particularly tough week at the Coventry Empire. Sellers, sick of his repertoire of impressions, and sick of a lacklustre house, simply set up a gramophone player, settled himself down and played the A side of a Wally Stott Orchestra extended play recording of Christmas carols. All Sellers did was hum along to the familiar tunes. Delighted with the nonplussed reaction of the audience, he gleefully flipped the disc over and muttered: "I knew you'd like it . . . so let's hear the other side shall we?"[3]

Sellers would often meet with Bentine on the variety circuit too. Indeed, the post-Goons Bentine was invariably the comedy top of the bill, while Peter's gallery of impressions would languish somewhere in the first half – between the 'Aerial thrills' of the Two Angelos and the 'Glamorous singing personality' Pearl Carr.[4] The two were still firm friends though. Bentine recalls one hilarious incident in his book *The Shy Person's Guide to Life*:[5] "Once on the stage of the Empire

---

1 This ambitious show was written and produced by John Bridges, and heard on the Home Service, from 7.45 p.m. on Friday, 2nd April 1954. The same day that Anne gave birth to their son, Michael Sellers. *The Goon Show* had recently been shifted to a Monday evening slot, with the Boat Race frolics being heard between the episodes 'The Saga of the Internal Mountain' and 'The Invisible Acrobat'.

2 Sellers, in conversation with comic genius follower Marty Feldman, for *One Pair of Eyes*: 'Marty Feldman: No, But Seriously . . .', 7th June 1969.

3 *Strawberries and Cheam: An Autobiography* by Harry Secombe (Robson Books, 1996). For Secombe, the experiences of boarding houses and booing audiences also informed his brilliant novel *Twice Brightly*, which had been published by Robson Books in 1974.

4 This variety bill played the week commencing Monday, 19th July 1954, at the Bristol Hippodrome. Peter was heralded as "From Radio's 'Goon Show' and 'Rays a Laugh'" (sic); Bentine, who followed Max Geldray "The Harmonica Virtuoso from Radio's 'Goon Show'", was simply "The Missing Link". He was second only to the star of the show, Teddy Johnson "Outstanding Columbia Recording and singing star" and husband of Pearl Carr.

5 Granada Publishing Limited, 1984.

music-hall at Leeds, and to Peter Sellers's hysterical delight, my flies split open in the middle of my ultra-energetic 'chair-back' routine – and I didn't know. I just thought that the act was going particularly well and put even more energy into it. Deaf to all warnings and blinded by what I believed to be my brilliant comedy success that night, I was only brought to my senses by Peter finally writing the word 'Balls' on a piece of card and holding it up in the wings."

Peter wouldn't have to play the variety circuit for much longer though. Things were beginning to move quite swiftly in the film world but, true to loyalty and the sheer fun of it all, he gladly continued to add layer upon layer to his fast-establishing characters within *The Goon Show*. The fifth series began on Tuesday, 28th September 1954, with 'The Whistling Spy Enigma'. Recorded on the previous Sunday, with suitable fanfare and, announcer Wallace Greenslade, with tongue in cheek, proclaiming it the start of a series of one, it proved a pivotal run. It ended on 22nd March 1955, and included at least one indelible instalment, 'China Story', which had been recorded on Sunday, 16th January for transmission two days later. This immediacy, almost spontaneity, was infectious. And the seed of 'Ying Tong' had been planted.

During *The Goon Show* series 5 came another stagger forward into celebrity, with Sellers guest-starring alongside his old mate Dick Bentley in *And So to Bentley*. Scripted by *Take It from Here*'s Denis Norden and Frank Muir as a television showcase for their *Take It from Here* comedian, the first of six shows went out on 1st October 1954. Shirley Eaton and Alma Cogan added glamour, while character support was offered up by Charlotte Mitchell who appeared in every episode. "God, is it your ambition to remind me of every failure I've ever been involved with?" chuckled co-creator Denis Norden. "Sellers was a mate, and his star was still very much in the ascent then, of course, so he did us a favour and turned up for some silly sketches. We paid him too, so it wasn't that much of a favour."[1]

That pantomime season Shirley Eaton would give her Margery Daw,

1 Interview with the author, May 2009.

in *Mother Goose*. In a return to the London Palladium, Sellers was cast as the Squire, with David Dale supporting him with traditional comic business, as the Squire's Bailiff. Dale would also double-up as King Goose; while the actual headlining comedy turns were Max Bygraves as Sammy, and Mr. Pastry himself, Richard Hearne, as Mother Goose. The show opened on Saturday, 11th December 1954, for the season. It was Val Parnell's 7th Magnificent Christmas Pantomime and, as Shirley Eaton remembered: "it was a tremendous workload, often three shows a day, but it was the most valuable comedy lesson of my life. I honed my skills in front of that packed house, every performance, at the world's greatest variety theatre. It was thrilling. And every single show I learned something new about comedy timing. Peter was at his zenith. He even invited me to a recording of *The Goon Show*. More comedy education! It was scripted but they all seemed to be ab-libbing all the time. Particularly Peter. The audience never stopped laughing. As for me, I just ached from laughing. It was relentless. Glorious. As was Peter. Every time."[1]

This more traditional, matey matey, let's do each other's shows mentality, may seem like something of an antithesis to Peter's subsequent, international career but, of course, it wasn't. Pantomime was in his blood. He was, and would remain, a red-nosed clown, albeit one with lunacy in the genes. For sure, despite his preference for radio comedy at this time, the pantomime assignment was not only appealing but irresistible. This was the London Palladium: the world's greatest Palace of Variety. Sellers was at the top of the tree, and his interpretation of the frosty Squire would drip with Goonish overtones. There would be a burst of Bluebottle on occasion. An assured laugh. Certainly by *The Goon Show*'s 'The Case of the Missing Heir', broadcast on the very day that Shirley Eaton was celebrating her 18th birthday at the London Palladium, on 11th January 1955, Bluebottle's only line of dialogue, a belated "You rotten swine!", brings the house down. There's a literal roar from the crowd. True fame. And fame that crossed our modern perceived

---

1 Interview with the author, August 2023.

boundaries between Goon and Panto, simply because there were no boundaries. The traditional audience participation certainly rested extremely easily with the more experimental spin-off avenues alongside *The Goon Show*.

One such fringe project was *The Starlings*, which was broadcast on 31st August 1954. The self-contained radio broadcast had recruited the team, alongside announcer Andrew Timothy, under the production of Peter Eton. His comment that: "any resemblance to a *Goon Show* is due to the laxity of the producer", was fooling nobody who read the *Radio Times* that week. For the vast array of fans *The Starlings* was *The Goon Show*. Naturally. And then again, it wasn't. The basic premise – that of various, bizarre methods of local councils trying to control flocks of starlings – had been ripped straight from genuine headlines at the time. It was *The Goon Show* reflecting the insanity of reality, which is what *The Goon Show* did best. And, indeed, the familiar Goon characters were deployed. In slightly twisted ways. Sellers has the most fun as Jim 'Tigernuts' Bluebottle, who invents a special exploding bird lime. To rid the world – at least Woolwich Arsenal – of the starlings. However, recorded without a live audience and with no musical interludes, it was pieced together in a very modern way, with a very modern sound. What it lacks in hysterical, group response, it certainly makes up for in polished, controlled performance . . . of utter madness.[1]

A couple of months earlier, the Goons had indulged in a rather more establishment fringe project: a blurring of the edges between two well-loved radio shows. *Paradise Street* was an attempt to make Goons Sellers and Milligan more like family entertainers. Just like that nice Harry Secombe! Secombe had been in *Educating Archie* earlier in 1954, and *Paradise Street* was a spin-off series. Without Archie Andrews! Instead *Educating Archie* writer, Eric Sykes, united Archie's tutor Max Bygraves, and comic foil Hattie Jacques, with the two wayward Goons. Spike's unreliability dictated that Sellers

---

1 Little wonder it was so polished. The programme was recorded across two days, on 11th and 12th August 1954, and provided much needed respite from variety dates. That first week of August had seen Sellers complete a week at the Bradford Alhambra.

would often have to deputise, which usually meant doing the Eccles voice as well as his own characters. The producer of both *Educating Archie* and *Paradise Street* was Roy Speer. Yes, the same Roy Speer who Peter had phoned, and gleefully conned, with his Henry Hall and Dicky Murdoch impersonations. So Speer knew vividly that Sellers was more than able to fill the dual assignment. *Paradise Street* ran for thirteen episodes on the Light Programme, from 20th April 1954, and proved successful enough for an even more intriguing experiment. *Archie in Goonland* was recorded, during the run of *Paradise Street*, on 6th May 1954 for transmission on 11th June and was, as the title suggests, an opportunity, at long last, for the wooden-headed rascal Archie Andrews himself to meet the Goons. Yes! All of them. Not just Sellers and Milligan, but a reunion with Secombe too. As the *Radio Times* put it: "Peter Brough[1] and Archie Andrews enter Goonland via a mousehole and are immediately involved in a fantastic adventure involving the destruction of London – and mice!" Peter initially popped up in the guise of Dick Barton – Special Agent, whose adventures had run on the Light Programme until spring 1951 – although Bloodnok and Bluebottle and Crun got on the mouse trail too. What larks!

All three Goons threw themselves into the adventure, of course. As Sellers maintained decades later, "we worked like one person".[2] Besides, the Beeb were paying them, folks, and all were part of the glorious Light Entertainment brigade at the Corporation. Hattie Jacques, concurrently appearing as Agatha Dinglebody in *Educating Archie*, was back, present and correct and in character. And indeed, Harry was in *Archie* mode, as Doctor Harold Secombe. Also back

---

1 Peter Brough was the ventriloquist with a hand in the dummy. Peter Sellers was booked as Spike's replacement for *Paradise Street* shows recorded from Sunday, 11th July 1954, although it did little to halt the fading out of the series. It was merely a, quite literal, footnote in Peter's talent, and thirst for exposure. Indeed, that July also saw Sellers chalk up another edition of *Show Band Show*, on the Light Programme, on Saturday, 24th. The following day he was in Brighton for another *Workers' Playtime* too; followed by a recording for the Home Service's *Home and Away*, on 29th July. In the immediate wake of *Paradise Street* a further *Educating Archie* spin-off was attempted. This time with Peter Brough and Archie in the cast. With Benny Hill as the star comedian, *Archie's the Boy* fared better, albeit slightly, running for twenty episodes from November.

2 *Parkinson*, BBC1, 9th November 1974.

was Eric Sykes, co-writer of the *Archie* show, with Sid Colin. Eric co-wrote the crossover show with Spike, and became a regular co-writer for the fifth series of *The Goon Show* and beyond. Apart from keeping Spike on a semi-sane straight and narrow, Sykes was on hand to curb and exorcise Milligan's counter-productive love of a joke at the expense of *Educating Archie*!

Although, even in his dotage, Sykes always maintained *The Goon Show* was categorically Spike's universe, Eric's stability of structure and stringency was paramount to the programme's development.

Already infuriating and infiltrating the brains of Britain's intellectuals, some thought *The Goon Show* was pure radio, impossible to be conveyed on any other media. Others insisted that pictures were needed to fully capitalise on the humour. And not just Michael Bentine, either. Whatever side you found yourself on, there was no denying the Goons had become national figures, albeit as a collective and not yet as individuals. Even so, the trio had starkly defined personas: Milligan was the handsome Goon from Rangoon; while Secombe was the normal one. Forever modest, Harry would continually admit to having a moderately successful variety career, before much preferring to salute Peter's unique ability to make all his characters "completely different". Sellers, typically, was swift to turn the praise back away from himself or, at the very least, use it as fuel to build up his own bland mystique, claiming that unlike Secombe: "I've got no one to go onto the stage and be . . ."[1] All the characters of the Goons were abstract, with real-life hooks or riffs to hang Peter's own fevered imagination and vocal brilliance upon. Arch villain Hercules Grytpype-Thynne was, as Sellers said, "the only one I've borrowed . . . the only one that fit" – from Hollywood's arch villain and dashing detective George Sanders.[2]

---

1 *The Lid off the BBC*: 'The Variety Department', recorded Tuesday, 3rd May 1955, for broadcast on the Home Service, from 7.30 p.m. the following day. When interviewed, Sellers was in the company of Secombe, and Goon producer Peter Eton, so had a friendly audience, used to his usual pat answers.

2 *The Lid off the BBC*, 4th May 1955. Sanders was at his best as an arch villain for Alfred Hitchcock's *Rebecca*; and at his dashing peak as amateur sleuth and man about town the Falcon; ironically Sanders is best-loved now as a voice, that of Walt Disney's arch villain of *The Jungle Book*, tiger Shere Khan.

Peter's success as part of the Goons certainly secured him an invitation, ahead of Panto, from Val Parnell to perform before Her Majesty the Queen, Prince Philip, and Princess Margaret, at the 25th annual Royal Command Performance, held at the London Palladium, on 1st November 1954. Bob Hope was the headlining comedian that night, but Peter was safe within a bill that bristled with familiar BBC Radio funnymen including Max Bygraves, Jimmy Edwards, and Frankie Howerd.

The attempt to turn Sellers family-friendly had reached its optimum clout, and the *Educating Archie* factor can not be overstated. Peter had swum in that ken as far back as December 1951, when he joined Peter Brough and the dummy on the bill of the variety show *Christmas Crackers*. Also on the show were Richard Murdoch and Kenneth Horne, Cyril Fletcher, and Sellers radio lynchpins Ted Ray and Kitty Bluett. By 1954 Peter had those two big toes in the Archie Andrews universe. And, from Thursday 15th July until 23rd September 1954, he enjoyed a fortnightly run in *Happy Holiday*. Sellers played the Mayor of Littleton-on-Sea, determined to put the resort on the map, in this all-star comedy musical on the Light Programme. It starred Dennis Price and Bill Owen (who was replaced by Arthur English halfway through the series); as well as old mate Dick Emery. With a script co-written by Jimmy Grafton, Wally Stott as musical director, and Dennis Main Wilson producing alongside Jacques Brown, *Happy Holiday* was a real home from home. So much so that Sellers was indulged in a wacky, secondary character too. That of the small town's brash landlady – usually in debate with her daughter, played by opera singer and future *Up Pompeii* doyen Elizabeth Larner. The following spring, from 16th March to 4th May 1955, Peter joined the cast of *Calling Miss Courtneidge*, the second Home Service series for the redoubtable Australian entertainer Cicely Courtneidge, who had been a West End sensation since she was sweet sixteen. Phew. That's a lot of radio, even for a vocal chameleon like Sellers. Unsurprisingly, the powers at the BBC thought Peter was getting dangerously close to saturation point. Indeed, a plan to spin a series from his Home Service showcase *Sellers At Your Service* was abandoned for this very reason. It just proves that nothing ever changes. So, when you next catch yourself saying: "That Romesh Ranganathan is on everything!", just remember curmudgeons, seventy years ago, we were saying the same about Peter Sellers! Still, this big, friendly pool of talent at the BBC of the mid-'50s would throw up all sorts of lovely favours and connections for our main man. None more so beam-worthy than what happened at the dawn of *Hancock's Half-Hour*. The episode in question was 'The Marriage Bureau', the penultimate show from the first series, recorded on Monday, 7th February 1955, for broadcast the following day. Filling in for an indisposed Kenneth Williams, the end announcement thanks an: "on leave from *The Goon Show*, Peter Sellers." Oh, yes. First heard as jobsworth Mr. Bush – who refuses to employ Hancock as a caretaker until he is married – Peter gives a subtle, northern burr to the role. There's a touch of the monotone Robb Wilton about him too: dogmatic, fair, but easily distracted in the art of folding a paper aeroplane. More obviously Sellers, Peter is the sexually-desperate Granny Higgins. This old crone is pure Crystal Jollibottom, who through strangled giggles and lustful screams bags her man at the end.

These early Hancocks were very much stand-alone affairs, with only the interior logic of the particular half-hour at play. Hancock was single again and Granny was forgotten about by the following week. Still the juxtaposition of shows is fascinating, and in particular the meshing of styles between Sellers and Hancock in the opening dialogue. Hancock was rather high-pitched and erratic in this first series. He still is, rather, as he crusades toward the finishing line of series one. Sellers, on the other hand, had been a firmly established Goon for several years. 'The Marriage Bureau' clearly showcases Sellers as a master character actor at work. Sid James, too, is as rock solid and reliable as ever.[1]

---

1 Despite the musical connection of Wally Stott, *The Goon Show* and *Hancock's Half-Hour* were so familiar and so separate that the fact they co-existed so tightly was a moot one – until, that is, this episode was discovered on a reel-to-reel tape by radio archivist Richard Harrison, and repeated, for the first time since its original transmission, on the 100th birthday of the BBC, Tuesday, 18th October 2022. In April 1955 an absent without leave Hancock would be replaced by Harry Secombe for three episodes – a fourth, with Hancock reappearing and thanking Secombe, was also found by the sainted, resourceful Harrison; while Milligan had guest-starred as himself in an erratic, brief interlude in the meta first radio series *Hancock's Half-Hour* episode 'The Hancock Festival', from November 1954. The nation awaits Mr. Harrison to do the triple and find this one too!

Besides, Sellers, Sid and Hancock had already worked together. Even before the concept of *Hancock's Half-Hour* had first been heard. The occasion had been the Group 3 Film *Orders Are Orders*, a wonderfully ramshackle army comedy that pits the British military against the might of micro-budget Hollywood film-making. Sid James is loud-mouthed American director Ed Waggermeyer who, typically, uses fair means and foul language to commandeer the base for the setting for his Ed Wood-styled science-fiction epic, *Devil Dogs*. Sellers is Private Goffin, personal valet and batman to Captain Harper, played by Radio's PC 49 Brian Reece. Sellers, Brylcreemed and chirpy, is a cockney conscript who is continually on the fiddle. His partner in comedy and crime is Bill Fraser who, two years later, would finally become a comedy star – back in khaki – in Granada Television's *The Army Game*. In *Orders Are Orders* Sellers is introduced as a bored squaddie, sluggishly sliding an empty beer glass across the barrack bar. He's semi-smart and sycophantic though. Immediately on his toes as soon as he spots an officer; flustered and ill-at-ease when faced by confident women or hard cash.

Although he secures fifth billing in the opening credits – demoted to sixth in the closing credits, after Tony Hancock, who enjoys an 'introducing . . .' build-up and even a cheeky case of breaking the fourth wall at the film's end – Sellers relishes his moments of Uriah Heap-styled subservience. And he looks fetching in a makeshift Martian costume, complete with long johns! It's in this ungainly garb that we last see his character: standing to attention and under caution, alongside an uncredited and unscripted cameo from Peter's real-life R.A.F. cohort and dear chum David Lodge. Not that Sellers would have had much clout on this production. Even though Eric Sykes pops up too, and contributed to brushing up the elderly play on which the film is based upon. It is a more grammatically correct re-working of the 1933 comedy *Orders Is Orders* by Ian Hay and Anthony Armstrong.

Reassuringly, as Bluebottle is kind of Sellers and Sellers is most definitely Bluebottle, there's an air of Bluebottle about Sellers in *Orders*

Are Orders. He's all wide-eyed wonder and frantic attempts to ingratiate himself. There's a childlike respect too; and an air of duplicitousness. Even more interestingly, this is Sellers the tubby screen comedian, desperate to impress, and eager to grab what little opportunity he can. Thus, there's a boyish enthusiasm to his intricate moments of slapstick. In this art, Peter utilises everything from beer crates to bar snacks in order to inject extra bits of business. It's a jolly, little performance, with elements of gleeful corruption and ridiculous behaviour. His addressing of the American Sid James as "Buddy!" is particularly endearing. Suitably enough, after an elongated post-production period, the film was released on Sid's birthday, his 42nd, on 8th May 1955.

Then Sellers was back with Sid, for the third time within a year, when both were, once again, signed up by economic independent film company Group 3, at Beaconsfield Studios, for the delightful *John and Julie*. It's a charming tale of the two titular children, played adorably by Colin Gibson and Lesley Dudley, who make their way to London to see the Queen's Coronation. Shot in glorious Eastmancolor, and with Eddie Calvert's golden trumpet blaring at pivotal moments, and a glut of familiar faces doing their familiar thing – from Wilfrid Hyde-White's benevolent Field Marshal to Moira Lister's tart with a heart – it's perhaps the most fifties British comedy film of all fifties British comedy films. Sid James is the killjoy, anti-royalist father of John; Peter Sellers the kindly Police Constable Diamond. There's a tinge of Goon, and a pinch of Jack Warner's PC Dixon,[1] which makes for a lovely little study of friendly authority: competent, dependable, and kind. That distinct Sellers twinkle lifts the role too. His affable, dogged country copper is benignity itself with the kids, while his officious petulance is effortlessly deployed when squaring up to the angry dad: and who can blame him? Sid continually moans about authority throughout, and even sends up Sellers by dubbing him Sherlock Holmes. Sellers has the last laugh though. Quite literally, as Sid is forced to spend

---

1 The character had been shot dead, by Dirk Bogarde, in the Ealing Studios classic *The Blue Lamp*, only to be resurrected in the July of 1955. He'd be saying "Evening all!" for the next twenty years.

the night in the cells ahead of the big day. While Sid rants and raves, Sellers smiles and sleuths. Anxious character acting versus subtle underplaying. A bickering partnership born out of experience and mutual respect.

Sellers enjoyed eighth billing in the opening credits of *John and Julie*, fifteenth during the final roll-call, and it's the last of those chubby character actor film cameos. Peter was about to become a chubby comedy film star. In the spring of 1955 he was up a rung or two of the ladder, at Ealing Studios, and sparring on screen with his hero, his idol, his inspiration, Alec Guinness. The production was *The Ladykillers*.

As with *Orders Are Orders*, Peter's source for his character of Harry was his best-loved and his personal favourite weekly fall-guy Bluebottle. In those *Goon Show* outings of early 1955 the pimply, young fantasist had become even more self-aware and meta. Now, not only would he read out his stage directions with a breathy excitement, but, in 'Yehti' he even, rather petulantly, questions the fairness of his getting 'deaded' every week. The boy even bemoans the fact that Eccles seems to have got away with it this episode. Cue sound effects of said 'deading', and the dumbfounded reaction from Eccles: "You rotten swine, you!"[1]

In *The Ladykillers* Sellers takes the essence of Bluebottle – a youngster out of his depth – and makes him an adolescent, a rocker, a comic cipher who is not merely pretending to be a dangerous criminal but is a dangerous criminal, for real. The joke is that this thug is still, fundamentally, a child, and without a clue as to what he is doing. One can imagine on that first day of filming, that the twenty-nine-and-a-half-year-old Sellers, the actor, felt rather the same. For not only was Alec Guinness starring as the cunning mastermind Professor Marcus, but the rest of his faux string quintet of ruthless crooks were made

---

1 Scripted by Milligan and Sykes, recorded Sunday, 6th March 1955, for transmission the following Tuesday. By the sixth series episode, 'The Lost Emperor', from 4th October 1955, Sellers himself is shining through. The "Aardvarks never killed anybody . . ." line is repeated. Twice. The sheer desperation and nervousness breaks Sellers, who lapses into his own, monotone voice, and, with a giggle, mutters: "It's going to kill *us* if we use it anymore!"

up of familiar, reliable screen players. There was hulking character actor Danny Green, as the ultimate Gentle Giant, muscle-for-hire 'One-Round'; Ealing and drawing room comedy maestro Cecil Parker (perfectly flustered and cowardly as the major); and Herbert Lom as Louis, sinister, silent, and every inch the escaped convict.[1]

Brutalistic film-maker Alexander Mackendrick – Sandy to his chums – was directing *The Ladykillers*, from a wickedly bleak screenplay by American in Britain William Rose. Mackendrick himself would head off to Hollywood immediately afterwards. The little Britian of *The Ladykillers* is cynical and corrupt and, as such, perfectly in keeping with the fading embers of the original Ealing Studios at the end of its day.

Sellers gives his breakthrough film role, his first truly iconic characterisation for the big screen. It is a faded youth of fledgling rock 'n' roll culture. More Brighton riots than Elvis cool: a comic-book Teddy boy, the brothel creepers, and greased-up, duck's-arse haircut simply part of his uniform. His signifiers of rebellion. They are a mask for the chubby and confused and cherubic coward he really is. A chap completely out of his depth. Sellers, in tandem with such an exhilarating director as Mackendrick at the top of his game, gives a performance of bleak desperation. The touches of naive joy are moot indeed. We, the audience, sense he is doomed from the get-go. That cocky, cockney swagger is fooling nobody. Not even himself.

There's the nervous ticks; the impromptu giggling at nothing; that Warner Brothers cartoon-like "GULP" when he gets the short straw and has to act on behalf of the group. The act, of course, is the completely unenviable and, as it turns out, completely impossible task of bumping off Mrs. Lopsided![2] More than that. It's pure *Goon Show*, and Peter's overplayed panic doesn't jar. Not one bit. It fits

---

1 The hardened criminal image is heightened by the actor having shaved his head for his October 1953 debut in *The King and I*, at the Theatre Royal, Drury Lane. The production would run, concurrently with the Ealing Studios filming schedule, and beyond, clocking up 926 performances, and closing on 14th January 1956.

2 Katie Johnson, who had been a bit-part player at Ealing for an age, got her one and only opportunity to shine as a film star as the redoubtable Mrs. Wilderforce. Indeed she had given yet another 'Old Lady' in *John and Julie* over at Group 3. *The Ladykillers* won her a BAFTA for Best Actress in 1956 but she was back to bit parts by the time of her death in May 1957, at the age of seventy-eight.

the moment perfectly. This is Sellers utilising his bag of vocal tricks in order to ground this performance, and make him absurd. Real *and* absurd.

When crook turns on crook, the real Harry is revealed. The brute force of Danny Green is not a fun comrade when provoked. Believing Sellers to actually have done the deed and killed the old lady, he loses control of his temper. Sellers, genuinely terrified, has to turn to comedy. Even at the end. That strangled cry of: "Where's your sense of humour 'One-Round'?" is all he's got. And it's not enough.

This flippant, playful treatment of death runs through the whole film. The dank colour platter; the backdrop of war-torn, depressed London, reflected in the condemned gang; the stoic eccentricity of the old lady; the familiar faces – both within and on the cusp of fame: *The Ladykillers* is an endlessly fascinating time-capsule for mid-fifties British cinema, and mid-fifties Britain.[1]

In 1999 the British Film Institute compiled its list of 100 Best British Films. *The Ladykillers* nestled in nicely at position number thirteen. There is something so satisfying about that, that it leaves a dull ache; a crooked smile.

---

1 Dependable Jack Warner is the policeman behind the desk. Of course he is. He may have been killed in *The Blue Lamp*, but he was on his way back, on BBC Television, and had already influenced Peter's copper in *John and Julie*. Peter's radio chum Kenneth Connor pops in as the frantic cab driver too; while Frankie Howerd, a character acting riff on his stage and radio persona, steals a scene as the brow-beaten barrow boy.

Chapter 4

"How dare you change your voice from mine to his for one joke only!"

Peter Sellers, 1957

When *The Ladykillers* was released, as a kind of murder pantomime for the season, on Thursday, 8th December 1955, Peter was very much in the thick of life as a Goon.

The Ladykillers may have set him off on the path to film stardom, but in November he had completed the whistle-stop shoot of the Goonish short film subject *The Case of the Mukkinese Battle-Horn*; and the previous three-quarters of the year had been awash with high-octane Goon activity.

On 3rd May 1955 Sellers joined Spike and Secombe, Ray Ellington, Ray's pianist Dick Katz, and writers Frank Muir and Denis Norden, to record the fourth episode of *The Lid off the BBC*, for transmission on the BBC Home Service. Produced by Alan Burgess, for transmission the following day, the subject was 'The Variety Department', "the giggle mill", with the interviewees revealing some secrets – in a silly way – to presenter Wilfred Thomas. The three Goons and their producer, Peter Eton, took it much more seriously. And whilst the Goons were still appearing, separately, in weekly variety, Eton makes the point that, now, for the show, they had all developed from "a music-hall at the end of a microphone" into fine radio actors, within a play of "inspired lunacy". It would have been music to Peter's ears.

It was still all about silly characters though. A one-man repertory company. This was certainly the case when Sellers had recorded a double A-side single. Doing all the voices, naturally. 'Dipso Calypso' and 'Never Never Land', while very separate songs, segway into each other so perfectly that Sellers could have whipped them off in an hour . . . and did. Fuelled, as they are, by gloriously ancient jokes, and enlivened by a relentlessly hilarious catalogue of Peter's silly voices and impressions, 'Never Never Land' puts big-nosed American vaudevillian Jimmy Durante to the fore. The comedian was currently hosting the hit NBC variety show *The Jimmy Durante Show*, while in Britain, his larger-than-life stage and screen persona was well loved. In 1955 he even released a couple of singles himself, on the Brunswick label, including a duet with Patty Andrews, 'It's Bigger Than Both of Us'. The 'It' being his nose, of course.

Thus Sellers eagerly throws himself into the gravel-voiced razzamatazz of the performer, although he's keen for his listener to know that it is actually him and not simply Durante slumping it on a throwaway fable. At one point, hilariously frazzled, he mutters: "This is Peter Sellers doing an impression of Jimmy Durante, doing an impression of me, all you've got to do is guess who I am and let me know coz I'm getting worried." It's a tongue-in-cheek summing-up of the split personality of the mimic, and none the less powerful for that. Whilst in Durante mode Sellers even introduces a surprise – a sort of even more manic – if possible – variation on Peter's old Crystal Jollibottom character from the *Ray's a Laugh* days. Peter's closing, and most telling, comic character here is Fred Clink, the Singing Undertaker: a breathless, occasionally vulnerable cove, who brings sober gravitas to the song. It's all a treasurable testament of Sellers both as mimic and man of his own manic voices.

The flip side is mostly all this fresh Sellers vocal invention, with only a cameo from his Jimmy Durante popping over from the other side, during the upbeat send-up of the current musical trend, the 'Dipso Calypso'. Apart from that, it's the jolly calypso singer who tackles the bulk of the comedy. What's more he even apologies for the old jokes with a carefree, couldn't care less attitude because he's "getting paid". It's the seed for Monty Python's brilliantly blatant comedy for cash attitude. Sellers throws in an English cricketer shouting "Howzat!" at the close, pre-echoing the Test Match rivalry of his own 'Boiled Bananas and Carrots'. Underscoring the ancient gags of 'Dipso Calypso' is a social commentary reference to chronic Caribbean alcoholism. It's a less than jolly premise for a genuinely jolly track. Even the suggestion that cinematic celebrities allegedly with a panache for very young girls being the only ones not welcome – with the line about not letting in Charlie Chaplin and Errol Flynn – can't stop the flowing fun of the song. It's pure madness. In a good way. There's real gusto in his: "last verse coming up . . . good luck everybody!"

Goons at play together brought Sellers that exact same unashamed joy. Just a handful of days before his thirtieth birthday, Peter guest-starred, live from the Radio Show at Earl's Court, on the 3rd September 1955, BBC Television edition of *Secombe Here!*[1]

Although Goon producer Peter Eton would often reflect that the early programmes – before his tenure – were, in the main, overly reliant on the tried and tested variety personalities of the comedians with little or no plot, it is undeniable that after 125 shows, the Goons had been honed into highly esteemed music-hall performers who could function perfectly within these surreal flights of fancy. As the opening gambit of 'The Secret Escritoire'[2] rather beautifully had it, *The Goon Show* was now: "a Three-and-a-Half Act Dream."

Series six was transmitted from Tuesday, 20th September 1955 to 3rd April 1956 which, apart from the one that fell on Christmas Day, enlivened Peter's Sundays off from filming with the madness of recording *The Goon Show*.[3]

For Peter the impact of *The Ladykillers* was immense, and *The Goon Show* that lingered in the ears of listeners that week of the

---

1 Transmission was from 8.45 p.m., with other special guests including Irish ballad singer Ruby Murray, and supporting actors extraordinaire Sam Kydd, and Johnny Vyvyan. ITV was just three weeks away from starting, and *The Goon Show* series six, beginning just one day before ITV launched, would layer joke after joke around the fact that Secombe was also working for the commercial network!

2 Broadcast 29th September 1955.

3 That Christmas episode, 'The Hastings Flyer – Robbed' had actually been recorded the previous Sunday, 18th December, on the same day as the recording of the wonderful intertextuality of 'The Greenslade Story'. That year also saw an extra special special, 'The Missing Christmas Parcel – Post Early for Christmas', a fifteen-minute burst of Goonery, recorded on 27th November, for inclusion in the 8th December edition of *Children's Hour*. It pays to get those Goon fans early, you know!

Ealing comedy classic's release was 'The Terrible Revenge of Fred Fu-Manchu'. On 28th December 1955 Sellers was straddling film exposure and *Goon Show* fame when he hosted the live record show *The Listening Room*, produced by Michael Bell, for the Light Programme. Peter couldn't resist enlisting the help of some critics, including Grytpype-Thynne, Bloodnok, and Crun; as well as interacting with recorded interventions from Spike; a rendition of 'I'm Walking Backwards for Christmas'; and a rare spin of 'Dance with Me, Henry', which remained unreleased by Parlophone during Peter's life.[1] With the sixth series of *The Goon Show* completed, an exhibition of Goon script scribblings was unveiled in the BBC's press room in Cavendish Place. Peter and Spike were interviewed – well, John Ellison tried – for the 28th April 1956 edition of *In Town Tonight*. Typically Spike is more concerned about the lack of fee; while Sellers goes into a bombastic American film-maker act. Both rally round to perform – Spike on vocals, Peter on piano – 'I'm Walking Backwards for Christmas'. Harry, freshly home from a holiday in Bermuda and nursing a broken arm, was not on hand to comment.

Usually it was Sellers and Secombe who would happily leave Spike to his five-day intensive writing schedule, simply turning up at the studio at 3 p.m. to spend an equally intense four hours rehearsing the script; discussing sound effects; and sharing their own, childlike Goonish language to warm themselves up for the studio audience. For fifteen minutes before recording commenced, the trio would even warm up the theatre, metaphorically casting their insane comic runes over the very bricks and mortar in readiness to reverberate with laughter.

In the immediate wake of series six, the spring and summer of 1956 saw a glut of spin-off Goon recordings. Spike and Sellers were recruited – separately – to perform an anthology of Anglo-American humorist writings for *Curiouser and Curiouser*, recorded in June of 1956 for broadcast on Tuesday, 14th August. Peter got perfectly

---

1 The disc finally was heard by the great unwashed when it was released as a bonus track on the 4-CD 1990 collection *A Celebration of Sellers*, and the pilot fish sampler single CD and double cassette *EMI Comedy Classics Peter Sellers: The Peter Sellers Collection*.

pretentious for Robert Benchley's 'Der Meister-Genossenschaft'; while Miriam Karlin joined him as the nagging wife of Mr. Preble, destined for an ill-fate down in the cellar. Peter's aged and determined Yankee is a delight. For the British-geared extracts, he teamed up with June Whitfield for a bustle-bursting, earnest reading of Daisy Ashford's *The Young Visiters*; while a beloved cohort Beryl Reid – who Peter would often delight in giving filthy material to say – aided in a merrie moment from the Charles Dickens novel *Nicholas Nickleby* – no source for fresh filth here. For his performance as the Stranger, Peter channels his strong, inner Alec Guinness.

That iconic and relentless song 'I'm Walking Backwards for Christmas' was recorded in May. It had come about by glorious accident. The February *Goon Show* 'The Great Tuscan Salami Scandal' had been hit by a musician's strike.[1] In the end the Goons and Greenslade provided musical stings and numbers. One such stop-gap was Milligan, warbling 'I'm Walking Backwards for Christmas', which is introduced by Sellers – as Reuben Croucher, a typically money-obsessed, Jewish theatrical agent – who calls his boy the "North Korean Johnnie Ray". Genius born from necessity, after a moment of suppressed nervous laughter, the resulting recital clearly delights and intrigues the studio audience in equal measure. Sellers accompanied his singing chum on the piano, and rather good he is too. In the May session that saw the yuletide ditty professionally recorded in studio, the Goons also laid down 'Bluebottle Blues'. The tracks reference each other so can be played on and on and on with never a dip in continuity . . . although the same probably could not be said for the listener's sanity. The disc was released by Decca Records in August of 1956.[2]

Later that month, on Friday, 24th August, Dennis Main Wilson produced a reworked version of 'China Story' at the National Radio Show, for transmission on Wednesday, 29th August 1956. August too saw another couple of songs recorded over at Decca Records. 'Bloodnok's Rock 'n' Roll Call', credited the Goons featuring Major

1 No black legs were allowed, which gave Ray Ellington no leg to stand on!
2 Serial number: DECCA F.10756

Dennis Bloodnok, Roland Rockcake and His Wholly Rollers. Ray Ellington had brought rock 'n' roll to the nation via *The Goon Show* for years – pioneering in many ways – while this recording indulged his comedy co-stars in an affectionate pastiche of Bill Haley and His Comets, and their 'Shake, Rattle and Roll', from two summers previous. The embracing of Americana was further heightened with the reference to Marilyn Monroe, the blonde bombshell who during this August of 1956 was in Britain, at Pinewood Studios to be precise, filming with acting royalty Sir Laurence Olivier, in *The Prince and the Showgirl*.[1]

Despite all this glorious topicality, the other Goon track would be *the* Goon track. Clearly inspired by the prevailing wind of 'China Story', the 'Ying Tong Song', came from the fevered vocals of the Goons with Maurice Ponke and His Orchestra Fromage. Released in October of 1956[2] the disc was plugged, on BBC TV's *Off the Record*, on 10th December 1956, with Sellers and Spike miming to the 'Ying Tong Song'.[3] The future King of England was just one amongst millions who fell under the song's spell, admitting that: "almost at once I knew it by heart – the only song I do know by heart. I plagued everybody with its dulcet tones and 'Solo for Raspberry Blower' to such an extent that when my small brothers heard a recording of the Goons for the first time they thought it was their elder brother!"[4]

'China Story' was broadcast slap bang in the middle of the seventh series of *The Goon Show*, which had kicked off with 'The Nasty Affair at the Burami Oasis', recorded on Sunday, 2nd October 1956, for transmission the following Tuesday. *The Goon Show* reached a zenith amongst zeniths with the Boxing Day 1956 show.[5] 'Six Charlies in Search of an Author' was meta beyond meta, with

---

1 Bloodnok had been obsessing about Monroe since the third series of *The Goon Show* by which point, in 1953, Marilyn had made career-defining films *Gentlemen Prefer Blondes* and *How to Marry a Millionaire*. Monroe would also cause stirrings in Bluebottle's loins. Earlier, in 1949, she had bewitched Groucho Marx, a favourite Sellers impression, in *Love Happy*.

2 With the serial number: DECCA F.10780

3 Jack Payne presented the show, and sales went through the skylight!

4 The foreword by HRH The Prince of Wales, *More Goon Show Scripts* (Woburn Press, 1973).

5 Recorded 22nd December 1956.

Spike playing the crazed interjector Adolphus 'Jim' Spriggs, the actual writer of the script, as played by the actual writer of the script. Confused? No, you'll be delighted. The Goons had used their heads to crack the nut of mad logic within *The Goon Show*.

Still, Sellers wasn't established enough to simply wallow in the safely insane and insanely popular confines of *The Goon Show*. That summer of 1956 he had teamed up with his old chum Sid James for another Frank Muir and Denis Norden comedy show, *Finkel's Cafe*. A one-letter riff off of *Finkel's Cave* it was, as Norden recalled, "a direct request from the BBC. We were asked to do it because a series in America, starring Ed Gardiner, and called *Duffy's Tavern*, had been very popular. This was our version. The banner tag for the US show was 'Where the Elite meet to Eat'. Over here, we made that 'Where the Posh Squash to Nosh', so you can get an idea of the quality of the thing! That series was a bit of a disaster for us really, so, again, thank you for reminding me of it!" chuckled Norden. Sellers was perfectly cast as the seedy manager of the cafe: "and was a joy", remembered Norden. "You have to remember we were all mates, learning the craft of radio comedy together. Sellers wasn't a star at the time. Not by a long way. Oh, forget the Ealing comedy, and the Goons. If anyone was the star of the group it was Harry Secombe, because he had the mums and the grans with his fabulous singing voice. We were all just larking about trying to make a living out of making you laugh. Sellers was brilliant though. And he truly loved the microphone. He was a natural-born radio comedian."[1]

Despite Secombe's absence, Sellers and Spike had relished the opportunity to perform Goonish comedy – visually – with the mini masterwork *The Case of the Mukkinese Battle-Horn*. The film had been the brainchild of Michael Deeley and his editing partner Harry Booth who had a desire to turn *The Goon Show* into a television series. The duo sought out Larry Stephens to write a pilot show. The result – a skilful pastiche of the *Scotland Yard* cinema shorts – was *The Case of the Mukkinese Battle-Horn* – filmed in the wonder of

---

1 Interview with the author, June 2000.

Schizophrenoscope (the new split screen). Distributed and funded by Archway Film Distributors, the entire budget was just £4,500; and Sellers bagged £900 of that to star in the film. He was already aware – as were the producers – of his cinematic ascent. *The Ladykillers* was doing an awful lot of heavy-lifting for Peter's reputation, but the film was more than equipped to do just that. With or without Danny Green.

Peter Weingreen produced *The Case of the Mukkinese Battle-Horn*. He was an American currently working as Assistant Director on the commercial television smash hit *The Adventures of Robin Hood* and, in turn, he was gainfully employing both Deeley and Booth on the Lincoln Green action adventure serial starring ever so slightly faded Hollywood heartthrob Richard Greene. He still looked great in tights though; and Weingreen embraced the enthusiasm of Deeley and Booth in their mission to mount a television-styled *Goon Show*.

The final part of the jigsaw puzzle was Joseph Sterling, who pitched in with a contribution of £1,500 to the budget, just so long as he could direct the film. Which he did! Filmed at Merton Park Studios, near Walton-upon-Thames, and the home of many a quota quickie, it was wrapped in a speedy shooting schedule of just five days. According to Deeley: "Sellers was clearly ambitious and well disciplined."[1] He was also on sparkling form.

Peter's central role – that of Superintendent Quilt of Scotland Yard – is played with dead seriousness and respect for the mad crime at the heart of the plot. This detective clearly knows nothing about the 19th-century musical instrument, and even less about human nature, but he guffaws, and fidgets, and misdirects his way through the case with a rock-solid air of feigned authority. There is, of course, oodles of Grytpype-Thynne about the silky charm of Assistant Commissioner Sir Jervis Fruit – bouffant-haired, languid, and confident. The character also gifts the production one of its most filmic jokes too, when Sellers, as Quilt, lights the cigarette of

---

1 *Blade Runners, Deer Hunters and Blowing the Bloody Doors Off: My Life in Cult Movies* by Michael Deeley (Faber and Faber, 2008).

Fruit over the phone and through the receiver. You can almost hear a muffled cry of Secombe shouting: "Try doing that on the radio."

There's also a delightful burst of Henry Crun for the true Goon aficionado; while Spike pitches in with cameos for Eccles and – an off-camera – Minnie Bannister. Pamela Thomas as the peroxide love interest is flagged up as the producer's girlfriend, and Milligan breaks the fourth wall to mutter into our ears: "You think I'm joking!" It's that kind of film. Thankfully. If anything guest star Dick Emery very nearly nicks the whole thing as the relentlessly cheerful Maurice Ponk; bulbous of nose and whining of voice. I found his scene so funny when I first saw this film as a kid that I, literally, almost choked with laughter. Comedy that can nearly kill you. That's powerful stuff, folks.

As was the original plan, *The Case of the Mukkinese Battle-Horn* was shot and edited as a television show: twenty-six minutes, to be precise, just ripe for a commercial half-hour slot; and fully intended to debut on American syndication. Such was the intent that a test audience of United States television executive movers and shakers was assembled, and this pilot film was screened . . . to complete silence. Not a titter. Archway had a Plan B though. Swiftly re-edited to thirty-three minutes, it was almost as swiftly sold as a support picture for British cinemas. The name attachment of Peter Sellers helped, of course.

Milligan's too, naturally, and the sideways shift from television to cinema was a natural one and, even though Deeley and his cronies had been usurped in their attempt to transfer the humour of *The Goon Show* to the small screen, 1956 was smothered in television Goonery.

From 10 p.m. on 24th February, Associated-Rediffusion broadcast the first episode of *The Idiot Weekly, Price 2d*. Six editions were screened, until 6th April, with the loose – very loose – idea of the show being a Victorian newspaper, of which Sellers was the editor. Spike popped in for the bookending episodes; with Graham Stark and Kenneth Connor as sketch show support. Eric Sykes and June

Whitfield appeared in episode one; while Goon harmonica maestro Max Geldray was there in a sparkling vision of black and white in the last instalment. Dick Lester directed the madness, with good grace, wit, and undoubtedly a bottle of aspirin!

Not even a month after, Associated-Rediffusion Television tried again – with much of the same personnel – with *A Show Called Fred*, which, in the merry month of May, 1956, chalked up five incredible episodes.[1]

Sellers and Spike were, once again, to the fore, with such delicious flights of weirdness as choirboys leaping about in dustbins.[2] Regular Goon guest villain, Valentine Dyall, was on hand to intone with sinister meaning the odd non sequitur; Max Geldray was back for harmonica breaks; while like-minded comic souls Kenneth Connor and Graham Stark were, once more, intrinsic parts of the ensemble. As Stark remembered: "all of us accepted whatever we were asked to do . . . We broke all the rules but we were also a palpable hit."[3]

A second batch, this time entitled *Son of Fred*, burst forth from Associated-Rediffusion, from 17th September 1956.[4] The inspired insanity went even further with the Goons as visual comedians,

---

1 It was transmitted on Wednesdays, from 9.30 p.m., from 2nd through to 30th May. It was a monumental month that also saw John Osborne's *Look Back in Anger* open in London; the 1st Eurovision Song Contest held; and Elvis Presley hit the British Hit Parade for the first time, with 'Heartbreak Hotel'. May 1956 also saw the release of the latest Goon single, 'Eeh! Ah! Oh! Ooh!' coupled with 'I Love You', DECCA F.10885. In 2023 Jasmine Records released a glorious ragbag of associated Goon rarities, including some lovely incidental music from Peter's feature films. The two-disc collection was entitled *An Album Called Fred*: JASMCD2764.

2 A fragrant or two of this insanity survives in the archives, oft dusted down and included in retrospectives as a way to illustrate Peter's bizarre television antics of the fifties, because, well, it does!

3 *Remembering Peter Sellers*, by Graham Stark (Robson Books, 1990).

4 It was broadcast on Monday evenings, from 9.30 p.m., over eight weeks, concluding on Bonfire Night. Eric Sykes, who had made a guest appearance on the 15th October edition of *Son of Fred*, fronted a couple of Sellers television showcases early in the following year, with *Saturday Spectacular Eric Sykes Presents Peter Sellers*, transmitted on 5th and 12th January 1957. Eric was a guest on *The Lord's Taverners' Ball*, transmitted on BBC Television on Monday, 2nd December 1957, and was joined by Secombe and Sellers. This spot was pure anarchy. However, Sellers, despite his vocalised loathing of variety gigs, would still pop up in star turn guest spots on BBC Television, notably *The World Our Stage*, on 3rd May 1958, narrated by Trevor Howard, and featuring such distinguished actors as John Gregson, Jack Hawkins, and John Neville; and playful chums Ian Carmichael, Dilys Laye, and Terry-Thomas. Later that year, on 2nd August, Peter was back for even lower Light Entertainment, when he appeared on *The Marguerite Piazza Show*, on the same bill as singer Ronnie Carroll and puppet pigs Pinky & Perky!

with the exact same gang of comedians recruited to partake: indeed, Valentine Dyall would make several guest appearances in the seventh series of *The Goon Show* which started the following month.[1]

In November 1956 Spike Milligan and Larry Stephens gave voice to Harry Secombe, who was nowhere to be seen in these TV ventures. In *The Goon Show*: 'The Mystery of the Fake Neddie Seagoons', and ranting away at the top of the show, Secombe insists he is the funny one. On radio, he gets a huge laugh, before announcer Wallace Greenslade insists he pull his trousers up at once. "This is not ITV television . . ." he intones. It was indeed the kind of thing Sellers and Milligan were getting away with in between the commercials.

Despite the fact that the *Fred* shows and their ilk are now mere footnotes in the history of *The Goon Show*, at the time they heightened the appeal and national standing of the principals. As Graham Stark commented: "To re-create in words visual comedy is a dreadful risk but a risk one has to take if only to stress the extraordinary chances that Peter, as a performer, took in those shows."[2]

Much of this televised madness was running concurrently with the mid-week broadcasts of *The Goon Show*. That seventh series ended on Thursday, 28th March 1957. The episode was 'The Histories of Pliny the Elder', with an Ancient Roman setting that saw Bluebottle as a whining galley slave; Bloodnok – or Bloodnokus – accused of being a turncoat and leading a rebellion; and Grytpype-Thynne moonlighting as Julius Caesar. All in a plot that revels in glorious old jokes. They were new back then, folks! As Sellers, out of character and with the joy of spring upon him, mutters at the end of 'The Fake Neddie Seagoons': "I don't know how we get away with it . . ."

In actual fact, not only was Peter getting away with it, but as a frequent face on television, and something of a National Treasure

---

1 He is in the second of the series, 'Drums Across the Mersey', 11th October 1956; the Transcription Services special 'Robin Hood', and the most Valentine Dyall-suited show of all, 'The Spectre of Tintagel'. Dyall would also return for the August 1957 special 'The Reason Why', produced by Jacques Brown, without a studio audience. In November 1957 the group released a second EP of old Goon songs, featuring 'Whistle Your Cares Away', and 'A Russian Love Song', credited to Igor Blimey and his Romanoff Cafe Fred Players, with Zym Balist on his Collective Farm.

2 *Remembering Peter Sellers*, by Graham Stark (Robson Books, 1990).

on the wireless, he was about to add another layer to his standing in British cinema.

As befitting the next rung of the ladder after *The Ladykillers*, there was an essence of Ealing comedy about *The Smallest Show on Earth*; a quaint, tongue-in-cheek though affectionate kiss to the glorious days of twenties British film. Like *The Ladykillers*, *The Smallest Show on Earth* emerged from an idea by William Rose, who co-scripted with John Eldridge, and like *The Ladykillers* it cast Sellers in a heightened caricature of a supporting role. Here he is Percy Quill, the alcoholic, aged film projectionist, with repertory theatre make-up and wizened gait.

The premise is indeed pure Ealing comedy, with a young and beautiful married couple (played by young and beautiful, and on the verge of marrying, couple Bill Travers and Virginia McKenna) inheriting the dilapidated Bijou Kinema. Along with the responsibility for the crumbling edifice, comes the added responsibility of the decrepit three-strong workforce: Margaret Rutherford in the box office; Bernard Miles on the door; and Sellers in the projection booth. Although a crucial film performance for Peter, it is, undoubtedly, in many ways, an extension of a radio performance. Certainly the characterisation of Quill is a toned-down, only slightly more under-played, contextualised shade of William Mate from *The Goon Show*.

Sellers deploys vocal tricks and ticks throughout, with a succession of comedic gurgles and giggles and gulps. It's Sellers shorthand for a guaranteed laugh, and there's nothing wrong with that. Moreover, for a riff off of radio, he displays a loving sense of slapstick too: the pratfall through the ramshackle cinema screen being the most dramatic; the delicate, almost fearful starting up of his ancient cinema equipment the most joyous. You can also see Sellers is enjoying himself hugely, throughout. There's an almost Chaplinesque back of the head walkaway moment as he leaves the cinema in high spirits. A skip in the air adding to the overall feeling of happiness, and a job well done.

However, right slap bang in the middle of this, albeit treasurable, performance of pantomime proportions, is the sheer love for film that radiates throughout the whole production. While Old Tom (Bernard Miles) watches on, and Mrs. Fazackalee (Margaret Rutherford) pounds out a sentimental tune on the Wurlitzer, Sellers gazes wistfully as he screens the 1923 British film melodrama *Comin' Thru the Rye*.[1] It's a moment of pure beauty, and pure performance, as Sellers explains to the new owners about his collection of bits and pieces of old film, and the collective pleasure the aged trio glean from running them when the place is dark. As he watches, there are real tears in Peter's eyes; real acting, and, if you have a heart full of classic cinema, the viewer won't be far behind him. It's an especially lovely moment. There's something true about that scene which gives Peter's portrayal a heart above and beyond the written page.

The Smallest Show on Earth is a Frank Launder and Sidney Gilliat film, the only assignment they offered Sellers. The film was released by British Lion on 9th April 1957, in between the film-makers' first two *St Trinian's* comedies. Third billed, below the romantic leads and crucially, the spearhead for the character actors, Sellers had just completed work on series seven of *The Goon Show* at the time. That Rome Antic 'The Histories of Pliny the Elder', recorded on Sunday 24th March is proof-positive that Sellers could lapse back to pure Willium Mate if the occasion called for it. Gone are the subtle moments within Quill, and again to the fore is the sheer joy of larking about within a pseudo-historical setting. Here Mate is William Hannibal, transporting elephants to the Colosseum, and receiving a nasty lump on the bounce, there. The work of a dirty great club, mate. The joke upon joke dialogue building to the play on club: "Would you care to join us?" results in the further extension of word-play. The counteracting: "Why are you coming apart?" isn't

---

1 One of my all-time favourite film facts is that producer Basil Dearden was clearly as sentimental as old Percy Quill, for the leading lady of *Comin' Thru the Rye*, Alma Taylor, once Britain's brightest screen star, can be spotted, as an extra, in the cinema scenes when the perennially popular westerns are running, some thirty-five years on from her heyday. Liz Fraser, soon to be Peter's on-screen daughter and then on-screen girlfriend, auditioned for the role of Marlene Hogg – which eventually went to June Cunningham. However, Liz was kept on as an extra. You can spot her, in a striped top, as the late-coming, gum-chewing blonde, who grabs a seat second to the aisle.

greeted with a groan; nor a comment. There's just pure silence from Sellers. On the radio. A delicate acknowledgement that this is his Sunday playground.[1] The films are where the reality lies.

Also between wrapping on *The Smallest Show on Earth* and its premiere, Sellers had indulged in yet more television Goonery in *Yes, It's the Cathode-Ray Tube Show!* Yes, those little negative electrodes that made telly possible, folks. From 11th February 1957 six editions were broadcast by dear old Associated-Rediffusion, in one last nibble of the small screen surrealist cherry.[2] Michael Bentine performed and wrote, with David Nettheim, but the undisrupted headliner Sellers was drafted in to play everything from a Chelsea pensioner to a television reporter giving the nation the four-minute warning before a collision with Mars. These apocalyptic and wacky sketches happily rubbed shoulders with film and theatre pastiche; animated interludes; and distorted filming techniques.[3]

If nothing else, this six-week *Cathode-Ray* exposure in a variety of guises was the perfect dress-rehearsal for the feature film Sellers was preparing to shoot. *The Naked Truth* was a Rank Organisation film, dreamed up by that jet-black humorist, Mario Zampi, who produced and directed this original screenplay by Michael Pertwee. For the first time on the big screen Sellers was seen as himself, without ridiculous character make-up or outrageous vocal inflections . . . at least for some of the time. The role of beloved television personality Wee Sonny MacGregor is introduced by the on-screen announcer (Peter Noble) as: "the King of Good Hearts"; an affable people person presenter of kindness. We first meet MacGregor as the kilted, soft-brogued darling of light entertainment; sending

---

1 The episode also indulges Sellers in a frantically Jewish talent-booker – for the Colosseum, you see. Not to mention an extremely camp galley-slave oarsman. I told you not to mention the extremely camp galley-slave oarsman!

2 Again in that half-hour slot from 9.30 p.m. on Monday evenings, the series was produced and directed by Kenneth Carter. Running until 18th March, the series was, all in all, just another brick in the wall that inspired those teenage, future Monty Python members.

3 Bentine had been referenced in *The Goon Show*: 'Drums Along the Mersey', broadcast on 11th October 1956. Within the convoluted and completely irrelevant plot, Neddie Seagoon's Welshness is in question. By gad, he's Peruvian. As Sellers notes, Mr. Bentine has provided the inside information. Now there's meta. Once a Goon, always a Goon, right Michael? Even in the 1957 special 'The Reason Why' Lord Bentine is referenced in the plot concerning Cleopatra's Needle. It is, indeed, all very Pureheart from the early days.

love to the old folk, and gently sending-up aged Chelsea pensioner (Wilfred Lawson) and his talent with a penny whistle. The television programme within the film is a feel-good talent show, with gifts aplenty for the ordinary person in the street, and Sellers delivering his saccharine, patronising script with wide-eyed charm. The satirical twist is swiftly revealed, however. Sellers, off-stage and puffing on a cigarette while the old boy blows his pipe on stage, is a cold and calculated charlatan. His factotum (Kenneth Griffith) looks after his every whim and gently guides him away from being too greedy and, thus, exposing himself as the monster he really is. Peter's Sonny MacGregor is a master of disguise and also a nasty piece of work. Perhaps the closest Sellers ever got to playing a shade of himself on screen. Even in front of the cameras he momentarily loses the sweetness of his screen persona to appreciatively eye up the show's hostess. MacGregor too has used and abused his fame, investing his money in buying up shoddy accommodation in Eastditch. As the reality of his being a slum landlord is hinted at, he has a near violent breakdown on air when a jovial contestant (Wally Patch) cheerfully goes on about the poor living conditions there. Moreover, as Sonny leaves the theatre from which the show is broadcast live, he kisses the ancient Edie Martin on the cheek, and signs an autograph for a smouldering brunette whilst whispering his private phone number into her shell-like ear. This is Sellers revealing the fiend behind the adorable characters. A maxim for Sellers and *The Goon Show*. Peter's own naked truth and, laudably, an exposure that he seems very happy to endorse.

Whereas Percy Quill in *The Smallest Show on Earth* is Willium Mate made flesh and fleshed-out for film, the character nearest to Mate in *The Naked Truth* is all-too fake; all-too obvious. Indeed it is his closest associate (Kenneth Griffith) who voices the stark fact: his characters are over-acted. The bumbling buffoon here wheezes and puffs for full radio recognition of *The Goon Show* creation, while there is no pretence that this is anything more than an absurdist character dropped into reality. It is a comedian playing a role. All of Peter's lapses into character are thus treated. With bombastic ridicule. The moustache of the Willium Mate clone drops off; while an Irish schemer is quickly identified as a sham by the hard-hitting, hard-drinking clientele of a Belfast boozer. Peter's stage nose is punched, squashed, and dripping off by the scene's climax. It's Clouseau incompetence in an embryonic state. An actor playing a comedian, rather than a comedian acting in a film.

Moreover *The Naked Truth* is testament of the film cache of Sellers in the ascendancy: he is second billed under Terry-Thomas, while the trailer made a virtue of Peter's multifaceted performance, bellowing that it's: "Starring Terry-Thomas . . . and Peter Sellers and Peter Sellers and Peter Sellers and Peter Sellers and Peter Sellers . . . the man of a thousand crazy characters." The beauty of the work is that it's not really a gimmick. It's the, dare I say, naked truth behind a comedian's gallery of comedy characters.

Terry-Thomas and Sellers are united as victims. Both are being blackmailed by Mr. Dennis (Dennis Price) a publisher of scandal magazine, *The Naked Truth*. There's a murder mystery authoress (Peggy Mount) and Peter's *Mother Goose* co-star Shirley Eaton, playing a glamorous model cum starlet – a reflection of her own identity akin to Peter's. She's engaged to an oil magnate. The desperate need all of them have to eliminate Price is the crutch of the comic plot. It's dark indeed. Within the first thirty seconds Price's campaign of intrigue has resulted in the gun-shot suicide of a distinguished scientist (a lovely, uncredited bit for Arnold Marlé). Price's character is shown to be intuitive too. While all around him an adoring audience watches Wee Sonny MacGregor's sentimental schtick, the blackmailer gives the merest shake of his head in recoiled disgust.[1] It's all the sweeter because we, the audience, already know what an appalling person MacGregor is. He's a crook and a fraud.

---

[1] This notion of exploiting elderly members of the general public on a feelgood television programme had been pin-pointed and sent-up by *The Goon Show*'s most ambitious and prescient episode, '1985', originally broadcast on 4th January 1955. In the programme it is suggested Neddie can age himself up in order to get on to the show hosted by Wilfred Pickles. This was a jib at *Ask Pickles*, on air from the May of 1954. This was the television transfer for the Pickles-presented radio success *Have a Go*, in which the host gleaned a new catchphrase when asking elderly players the cheeky question: "Are you courting?"

And a clever one. Later, while in conference with his confederate Kenneth Griffith, Sellers reveals the character as a borderline insane megalomaniac too. Plotting the demise of his tormentor, he realises that one of his characters could do the deed. It would be murder by: "a figment of my imagination." Griffith represents the viewer here. He senses the madness taking hold. Sellers enjoys himself hugely. Waxing lyrical, quoting poetically, and shouting theatrically like the wannabe Alec Guinness he was. It's his moment. His full-blooded opportunity to show what he can do. That effortless gear-shift from his normal voice to a tight-eyed, exuberant Irish lilt is pure alchemy. The rest is glorious comic characterisation and split-second slapstick. There's even an Oliver Hardy-like glance into camera, having spent the night, in old codger guise, under the bed of a newly-married couple. Ooh, and in this guise he encounters a policeman on the beat, played by good pal and lifelong acolyte David Lodge. One for the Lodge ledger, there.

With the deliciously bleak touch of master film craftsman Mario Zampi, *The Naked Truth* still stands out as one of Peter's greatest films of the pre-super stardom British era.[1]

Before our very eyes, the actor creates the very essence of Mate and makes him so loveable and convincing, within a fabricated, real-life environment. It's arguably Peter's most personal and multi-layered film moment, with Sellers exposing himself so completely. And he really does – wittingly – take on the mentality of exactly how a star would, and in his own head should, behave and adapts the personality traits accordingly.

With its intertextuality as a cuddly character comedian with a guilty secret, it's the most potent key to the real Sellers he ever

---

1 Fifteen years later that friend and shallow-water Sellers Dick Emery pulled off a similar feat in his only starring film vehicle *Ooh, You Are Awful*. His leading role, con artist Charlie Tully, deploys a myriad of guises in the pursuit of the tattooed numbers on the rear-ends of a load of dolly-birds. Well, it was the seventies! Emery's film follow-up was to have tried to out-do those multi-character Sellers comedies by making the impossible remake: that of the Alec Guinness eight in *Kind Hearts and Coronets*. It was never made. More immediately, in the wake of completing work on *The Naked Truth*, Sellers was joined by Dick Emery – stepping in for Secombe, in 'Spon', the first episode of the eighth series of *The Goon Show*, transmitted on Monday, 30th September 1957; just at the time Peter's recording of 'Any Old Iron' peaked at number seventeen in the charts.

committed to his comedy legacy. It's also very, very funny. Sellers sparks off of Terry-Thomas with a whiz-bang of panicked energy and reluctant criminal collaboration.

T-T would certainly relish a swift reunion filming with Mario Zampi the following year, for the equally black, funeral farce *Too Many Crooks*. Sellers was less keen to be loyal to Zampi. Having been offered the lead role of 'Fingers', the inept criminal mastermind, Sellers pleaded exhaustion, and turned it down flat. The cold fact was, the role was just too superficially silly for his current tastes. George Cole was cast in his stead, and did an admirable job as the head of the gang comprising streetwise Sid James, provocative Vera Day, hulking Bernard Bresslaw, and whispering Joe Melia. Sellers could have done it in his sleep.

Chapter 5

"Tell us who we are!"

Grytpype-Thynne

It was nothing personal with Zampi, and certainly nothing personal with Terry-Thomas, it was simply that Sellers was aiming higher, and internationally. Certainly, when *The Naked Truth* premiered, on 3rd December 1957, he was already back at work with T-T. Although the role was, of all things, an inept crook, this was no black and white romp for the British market; this was *tom thumb*, a lavish, high-profile and colourful fantasy, for American producer George Pal. A family audience was in mind too for, on 16th October 1957, Peter and Anne welcomed daughter Sarah Sellers.

Although shot at MGM Britain, in Elstree – utilising all seven sound stages at the studios, from November 1957 – *tom thumb* was very much a step-up to Hollywood for Sellers. Indeed, much of Russ Tamblyn's scenes, as the diminutive hero, were filmed in California.

The project had long been a pet one of George Pal and his Galaxy Productions. As early as the late 1940s he saw it as the perfect fantasy fare in the desolate post-war era. Still, it wasn't until 1952 that he succeeded in floating the notion to a major studio. At the time Pal had expressed a desire to cast Stan Laurel and Oliver Hardy as the baddies: in the roles subsequently taken by Terry-Thomas and Peter Sellers. Sellers, of course, had dubbed for Hardy already, and his whole being was in tune with the master of slapstick. The knowledge that, once upon a time, Hardy was in line for Peter's role just gives it an extra weight, if you follow me.

When *tom thumb* hit American cinemas for the festive season of 1958, it was a palpable hit: with a budget of $909,000, the box office take was three and a quarter million dollars. The success was compounded for the British release of the film, on Christmas Eve 1958.[1]

The timing was perfect, for it is a pantomime. And Peter clearly knew this. His Antony is a barrel-like, black-hearted baddie, in cahoots with Terry-Thomas. Antony's sole interest is the accumulation of wealth, as is usually the case with these kinds of baddie. The *Time* review, published early in 1959, summed up the appeal perfectly, considering the film: "fresh and appealing; it is kids' stuff, but it will probably sell a lot of popcorn to the grownups, too."

Imagine, if you can, Walt Disney's arch villains from *Pinocchio*, theatrical fox J. Worthington Foulfellow and befuddled feline Gideon, dropped into a Three Stooges slapstick short. In fact. No need. That's exactly what T-T and Sellers deliver in *tom thumb*. Padded out and shamelessly mugging as a simpleton, rather sinister side-kick, Peter is far more transparently evil; far less duplicitous. T-T is devious, of course, while Sellers is horrible and heartless. He even suggests dispatching their tiny cohort just as soon as the treasure is in their nasty mitts.

And there was certainly something of *The Goon Show* about the pairing of Sellers and T-T in *tom thumb*. Something very Moriarty and Grytpype-Thynne; and while Sellers was relishing a whiff of Hollywood, he was still very much a Goon.

For once a Goon, always a Goon, and, indeed, while filming at Elstree, Peter was still eager to dispense with his Sundays off and continue with *The Goon Show*. However, Sellers was certainly not about to immerse himself in Spike's battles with depression and the Corporation. Sellers didn't need or want to get involved in internal

---

1 Unsurprisingly George Pal immediately announced the making of at least three more *tom thumb* films, to be released once a year up to and including Christmas 1961. These were never made. Pal did produce *The Wonderful World of the Brothers Grimm*, for the summer of 1962, with Terry-Thomas paired this time with Buddy Hackett as a couple of fairy tale rogues. Pal's original casting for the Brothers – eventually played by Laurence Harvey and Karlheinz Bohm, was, wait for it, Alec Guinness and Peter Sellers. Sellers would have to wait another fifteen years – for *Murder By Death* – to reunite with his gang leader from *The Ladykillers*.

politics. Brand new episodes were being recorded; alongside re-written classic *Vintage Goons*, and Sellers was more than happy to pop in on a Sunday, put on the funny voices, and go home.

On 3rd October 1957, just a month before starting work on *tom thumb*, Sellers was hard at it, guesting on *The Wakey Wakey Tavern*, the Jimmy Grafton scripted television showcase for Bill Cotton and His Orchestra. Three days later Peter was reunited with Spike and Secombe for the recording of 'The Mummified Priest', the first in a batch of *Vintage Goons*, specially reheated for the BBC Transcription Service.[1]

While filming *tom thumb* Sellers was very much an active guest-star Goon too. On 14th December 1957 he joined Spike for an appearance on *Six-Five Special* promoting a jelly-detecting device!; while the following January Peter was a guest on Harry Secombe's *This Is Your Life*.

The essence of the team – if not the team itself – was also back in the recording studio; with Sellers laying down two reworked and reheated music-hall numbers from the songbook of Harry Champion, 'Boiled Bananas and Carrots', a calypso variation on 'Boiled Beef and Carrots', that credited Sellers as presenting Alfred the Grate and His Kings of Collapso; and 'Any Old Iron', which allowed William Mate a major moment in the singalong spotlight, with a cameo from a temperamental Fred Spoons and his rhythmic Melody Spoons. Sellers, as Bloodnok, had previously performed 'Any Old Iron', in a duet with Spike's Minnie Bannister in *The Goon Show*: 'The Booted Gorilla', while, here, he is clearly pleased with himself at his ad-lib: "You look nice . . . dressed in ice!"; and even his running out of breath three-quarters of the way through the song is laudably left in the recording, amidst impromptu laughter, and interaction from a sultry lady of the night: Sellers, of course. The disc peaked at no. 17 in the British Hit Parade, in June 1957. It's a perfect, silly summer season single. Even now.

---

1 Six of these beauties were also selected for transmission on the BBC Home Service immediately ahead of the start of *The Goon Show* series nine. In 1974 two of these, '10 Downing Street' and 'The Red Fort', were released on a Special Added Value Edition EMI Records LP, *The Very Best of The Goons-1* (EMC 3062). There was never a Vol. 2.

Peter was also indulging his passion for truly abstract comedy. *The April 8th Show ('Seven Days Early')* was a case in point, even with its 'wink to the audience' title. The show, written by John Antrobus, Ray Galton, and Alan Simpson was, of course, transmitted on April Fool's Day. Sellers was headlining but he was ably supported by a gang of chums, notably Graham Stark and David Lodge, of course, alongside Alec Bregonzi, Harry Fowler, Patricia Hayes, those experts in the pompous, John Vere and Totti Truman Taylor, and hilarious, diminutive gargoyles Ronnie Brody and Johnny Vyvyan. As if to further embrace small screen subversion, as the closing credits ran, Sellers broke the fourth wall, grabbed the caption roller and, while tearing the sheets to shreds, yelled: "It's all lies! It's all been Tom Sloan's fault, him and his liniment!" Sloan was the producer and, needless to say, the programme was a one-off, never to be repeated.

Equally obscure were three short films, designed as cinema time-fillers, in which once again Sellers was abstract and abrasive in a slapstick, silent two-reeler scenario. Made and distributed by Park Lane Films, *Insomnia Is Good for You*, *Dearth of a Salesman*, and *Cold Comfort*, all starred Sellers as Hector Dimwittie, a Jacques Tati-like figure at odds with the world around him. James Hill directed *Cold Comfort*, from a script by Lewis Griefer and Maurice Wiltshire, while *Insomnia Is Good for You*, and *Dearth of a Salesman* were directed by Leslie Arliss, and written by Griefer with Mordecai Richler.[1]

Still, Peter had a cinema hit in *The Naked Truth*. At the exploding hot air balloon climax of that film – don't ask! – 'The End' flashes up on the screen . . . with the never resolved – so far – codicil 'or is it?' In terms of Peter's screen career it most certainly wasn't the end. And, it certainly wasn't the beginning, either, which rather undermines the oft-quoted opinion that Val Guest was the first film-maker to give Sellers a leading screen role. If not a veteran, Sellers was without doubt in the ranks – and the Gamounts, and the Plazas – of British film character stars by the time he worked with Guest. For Val Guest the opportunity

---

1 Long thought lost, in 1996 the only known copies in the world of the Arliss films were found after being dumped in a skip outside the old premises of Park Lane Films in, surprise, surprise, Park Lane, London. The prints were subsequently restored and screened at the Southend Film Festival, on 1st May 2014.

arose, over at Hammer Films, with a naughty, nautical comedy *Up the Creek*, with Sellers landing yet another second billed credit. While in *The Naked Truth* it was Terry-Thomas, in *Up the Creek* it was under another moustachioed English gent, David Tomlinson: "I was fascinated by him. He was in his early thirties by this time . . . He was in great demand doing provincial variety but he hated it. It brought back memories of the constant movement and hard cold sheets and the landladies telling him, 'Don't touch anything, Sonny.' He was being tipped as a very rare talent. Peter had done television, but his work in films had been only in supporting roles. He was determined to be taken seriously as an actor – a character actor and not just a clown who did funny voices."[1]

In Tomlinson – a theatrical farceur who had been a leading light in British films since the early 1940s – Sellers had a screen mentor.

The back-up casting of Sellers opposite Tomlinson was a safety net for Hammer boss, James Carreras, who had baulked at the idea of starring Sellers in one of his films. According to Val Guest: "Jimmy wasn't convinced when I explained that Peter was a big deal on the radio and on television. Jimmy said: 'Television audiences don't go to the pictures!' So the compromise was that I had to get a proven film star to appear in the film. Then I could use Sellers. David Tomlinson was a popular and successful light comedian. He agreed to do the picture. It was Tomlinson and Sellers in *Up the Creek*. Hammer were happy . . ."[2]

It's a just about sea-worthy naval comedy, proudly shot in Hammerscope by Byron Film Productions and our enterprising, triple threat film-maker Val Guest. As writer, director, and producer Guest had already turned radio laughs into cinema success with a couple of Hammer comedies based on *Life with the Lyons*; while he had also spearheaded the company towards its brand gold standard of horror with the first two Quatermass sci-fi romps and the big screen adaptation of another Nigel Kneale television play

1 *Luckier Than Most: An Autobiography*, by David Tomlinson (Hodder & Stoughton, 1990).
2 Interview with the author, September 2000.

The Abominable Snowman. Its star, Peter Cushing, had already shot *The Curse of Frankenstein*. Bingo. Still, comedy would be part of Hammer's schedule until the early seventies. While the basic plot of *Up the Creek* – a crafty Chief Petty Officer utilising the Royal Navy's supplies for his own nefarious schemes – would inform BBC radio's *The Navy Lark* for the next eighteen years.

Even after the intervention of Carreras, Guest continually claimed to have given Sellers his first starring film vehicle, but, as Carreras wished, Peter is in fact very much second fiddle and, yes, very much, second billing to silly ass officer David Tomlinson. Tomlinson's fine line in up-standing toff, whose incompetence is a liability, was certainly a known quantity. In 1957 he had done very much the same in Val Guest's *Carry On Admiral*. In *Up the Creek* he's obsessed with inventing his own rocket. As a plot point it keeps his mind off and nose out of the dodgy dealings on board.

And, again, despite Guest's faith in Sellers, according to Guest, Sellers himself was, initially, fearful of sustaining one characterisation throughout an entire film: "Peter was nervous at the prospect. He was a big star on radio, mostly through playing lots of different characters in little sketches. Very funny, but not a fully-rounded performance. He came to me in a quiet panic, explaining that, yes, he understood his role was this Bosun,[1] with fiddles on the ship, but 'what accent do you want?' I said: 'Well, what accents can you do?' With not an ounce of big headedness he candidly said: 'I can do them all, but who is this character?' Anyway, one day I was trying to park round the back of the Shaftesbury Theatre in the West End of London and this very officious guy came over to me and, in the nicest possible way, explained and apologised about the fact I couldn't leave my car there. He was a Uriah Heap sort of character, wringing his hands together and expressing profuse sadness at the fact I would have to move on. Anyway, he was an Irishman and I thought he would be perfect for Peter's character in *Up the Creek*. I went round to Peter's, picked him up and drove him straight to this

---

1 Chief Petty Officer Doherty.

spot. Sure enough, the guy came out again, and again and laid on the sorrow. After about a minute Peter shouted: 'That's it!' Turning to this guy Peter said: 'Thank you! I'll send you two tickets to the premiere!' and we whizzed off, leaving this guy in a whirl. That was the character, and Peter played him brilliantly."[1]

Indeed, Sellers does give his first major, fully sustained screen performance here. No funny voice gimmicks or multi-characterisation, just a one-note Irish Liverpudlian wide-boy. Sellers fully gets to grips with the mounting panic and fast-talking backchat. He is borderline Sergeant Bilko at times, galloping through dialogue and barking orders in the finest Phil Silvers fashion. The ship, HMS Barkeley, runs a same-day laundry service, while keeping the local pub, the Pig and Whistle, in rum and eggs and cigarettes.

With eyes flashing with conceit and invention behind his spectacles, Peter's performance is at fever-pitch throughout, but at his very best while calmly trying to keep Tomlinson away from the cooked books of the pay ledger. You can almost hear his brain whirling, in desperate attempts to sidetrack and bamboozle his superior officer. He repeats and enforces his concern for Tomlinson's "hard day!" It falls on deaf ears, of course. This is a comedy of flimflam. Only when Sellers baffles him with fantasy figures does the situation cool. It's a battle won, not the war. While there's nothing really remarkable about *Up the Creek*, it is a fun example of the services comedies that were rife in British cinema for a handful of years from the late fifties, when National Service was dying in the embers. Moreover, Sellers enjoys himself hugely, and there's few more fun spectacles to witness than that.

It paid dividends too, for as David Tomlinson remembered: "[*Up the Creek*] cost very little to make and was one of the year's successes when it was released."[2]

However, akin to his leg-up with Mario Zampi, clearly Sellers was not enjoying himself enough to stay loyal to Val Guest. The film's

---

1 Interview with the author, September 2000.
2 *Luckier Than Most: An Autobiography*, by David Tomlinson (Hodder & Stoughton, 1990).

micro budget and quick return upon its release on 13th May 1958 saw Hammer rush in a sequel, *Further Up the Creek*. Tomlinson was back; as were many of the actors playing the ship's corrupt crew, including Sellers satellite David Lodge. There was no Sellers though. He was keen to move on to something different, so in his stead Guest cast Frankie Howerd, the camp comedian and close friend who he *had* launched in films, with *The Runaway Bus*.

With both *tom thumb* and *Up the Creek* under his belt by the end of the eighth series of *The Goon Show*, Sellers was still noticeably heightened in performance – both for the cinema and, most assuredly, for the radio.

On Sunday, 16th March 1958 – for a broadcast the following day, folks – distinguished old eccentric A.E. Matthews – eighty-eight and a third, and still acting – was the guest-star in 'The Evils of Bushey Spon', concerning his distress and inconvenience over a lamp-post being placed outside his house.[1] Matthews was the kind of actor who didn't need to stick to the script. Moreover, he didn't want to stick to the script. He was a glorious personality; an ancient deity of a thespian; a seasoned scene-stealer who, in *The Chiltern Hundreds*, had overshadowed Peter's current screen chum David Tomlinson, without seeming to try. Such was his force of charm, bluff, and polished dithering, that, opposite the Goons, he simply wandered in and muttered for the last few minutes. Matthews doesn't have to try hard, Matthews just is. His mild temper can hit home though, with deadly accuracy. At one point – rather like Kenneth Griffith in *The Naked Truth*, but for real – Matthews harshly points out Peter's over-acting. At the end of his fuse, Matthews turns to Sellers and says: "I've told you, you act too much!" Ouch!

One longs to see Peter's facial reaction to the barb. He is rather stunned into silence, momentarily. One can surmise that at that precise second Sellers had a flash of a thought about what he had just committed to celluloid for George Pal, and Val Guest, and thought: "Never

---

1 The actor was, in actual fact, in stern conversation with regards such an item – made of concrete – which had been erected outside his home, much to his chagrin. The elderly gent had even camped outside in protest. So newsworthy was it that the previous edition of *The Goon Show*, 'Tiddleywinks', had also made reference to it.

again, mate!" Fred Kite, and a West End play were just around the corner. Arguably the throwaway observation of A.E. Matthews instilled, even more so, in Sellers the determination that pastures new must be challenging . . . and, as much as possible, career-defining.

Having professed, as early as 1951, that he would love to make the grade as a serious stage actor, Sellers took on the role of the Sultan in *Brouhaha*. A comedy, for sure, but a French one – a frantic farce written by George Tabori, and staged at the Aldwych Theatre: the historical and hysterical past home of the beloved romps written by Ben Travers. Besides, it was directed by Peter Hall! With press and public intrigued, the play opened, on Wednesday, 27th August 1958.

Still in those seven years between throwaway quote and quality theatre the itch to get off the variety stage had segued into a profound dislike of live theatre – of any kind. In a mixture of emotions that was seven parts total boredom and one part impish subversion, Sellers soon dispensed with his allotted stage costume – all silk robes, jodhpurs, and a turban atop his head – in favour of anything he fancied, even his own civvies off of the Soho streets.

Brouhaha's plot – that of a wry, duplicitous potentate of a small, impoverished principality – tapped into the zeitgeist of Cold War politics and international intrigue that Peter's bookending films *Carlton-Browne of the F.O.* and *The Mouse That Roared* also addressed; while the Yankee end was kept up by popular, though fading, Hollywood and Broadway musical star Jules Munshin. It's a fair bet that he and much of the audience had no idea what to expect, and that was part of the appeal from Peter's point of view. Indeed, he relished his on-stage allies Lionel Jeffries and Leo McKern who gleefully went along with whatever theatre convention-twisting or plot amendments Sellers felt in the mood for any particular performance. Avant-garde experimental shenanigans were not what playwright George Tabori had had in mind, but once a Goon always a Goon and if that was the Sellers you had paid your money to see, then this would have been a West End evening to cherish.[1]

Indeed, Peter's successful six-month run in the play rather fanned the flames, and then unceremoniously undermined, an offer from Bernard Miles, who had approached the three Goons with unlimited use of his Mermaid Theatre. This would have been for a six-week season, in which the team: "could do whatever they like." Miles continued in his admiration, waxing lyrical that: "their humour . . . is pure and inspired lunacy, but sometimes it takes a leap over the boundaries of lunacy and lands itself into a staggering sense."[2] *The Goon Show* broadcast just the week before that interview was published was 'The Treasure of the Tower'. It had featured Sellers giving his gnarled Long John Silver – a favourite Bernard Miles part – and one that Harry Secombe flags up as Peter Sellers and his Bernard Miles set of teeth there, folks.[3]

The six-month run of *Brouhaha* was certainly a pivotal half year for Peter. Not only would he begin a fruitful and long-lasting association with the Boulting brothers but, in a glut of contemporary and delayed releases, some of his pioneering film performances would be seen in America for the first time. This was the spearhead to international stardom.

In the autumn of 1958, some eighteen months after its British release, *The Smallest Show on Earth* got a limited cinema release across the United States. Two things had changed: the billing and the title. Despite the poster concentrating on Virginia McKenna pulling on her silk stocking, the tagline proclaimed Peter Sellers & Margaret Rutherford as *The Big Time Operators*. Not only did America not endorse the small time, Sellers and Rutherford were clearly bigger names to conjure with. Certainly bigger than Goon

---

1 Such was the buzz around the production that, less than a month after opening, BBC Television presented extracts within their *Theatre Night* segment, on 18th September 1958. What Peter got up to on that particular performance is, alas, lost to the cathode-ray ether.

2 'The Goons – as others see them' by Gale Pedrick, *Radio Times*, 31st October 1958.

3 Miles would stage *Treasure Island* often and, in 1961, and into the early 1970s, ragged old Ben Gunn would give a plaudit-winning, often ad-libbed role for a certain Spike Milligan. Fine, fine, fine . . .

champion Bernard Miles.[1]

American audiences had also seen Peter's virtuoso catalogue of characters in *The Naked Truth* although, again, the title was changed, to *Your Past Is Showing*, with certain touchy states in the United States being unable to cope with the word 'naked'.[2]

Even more incongruous was the release of that primitive Sellers screen gem, *Orders Are Orders*, which had emerged in the States, from Distributors Corporation of America, title unchanged. However, billed as "a great British comedy in the tradition of *Private's Progress*" it was now starring Peter Sellers. Whether the Yanks obeyed the "Laugh is the Command!" strapline is debatable.

After three black and white, rather parochial comedies, America had certainly warmed up and warmed to the colourful, larger-than-life Sellers of *tom thumb*, which opened that Christmas of 1958. Back at home, meanwhile, with the security and the street-cred of a stage success, in October 1958 Peter found time to record his breakthrough long-playing album, *The Best of Sellers*. His first studio album, it was produced by George Martin, arranged by Ron Goodwin, and released on the Parlophone label for the Christmas market.[3]

In his comic and gushing sleeve note, recording manager Doug Geddes, with tongue firmly in cheek, ends in a chummy manner: "in closing, Peter Sellers wishes me to acknowledge his recording manager, without whose help this LP might have been produced much more easily!" Still, Geddes seems deadly earnest in his opening gambit that: "it does, at long last, demonstrate the many facets of his delightful humour and his uncanny ability at character portrayal". Geddes goes on to be rather sycophantic too, when he states that

---

1 Indeed, the film's romantic lead is credited as Bill 'Wee Geordie' Travers to capitalise on the financial success of another Launder and Gilliat film from British Lion. It had been released as plain *Geordie* in Britain. Sellers would join co-star Margaret Rutherford on the New Year's Day celebration, *The 1959 Show*, from Associated-Rediffusion Television.

2 In the late 1950s at least for, by the mid-sixties, at a time when Sellers was the biggest comedy star in the world, the American magazine *Naked Truth* was a notorious, best-selling scandal publication.

3 Serial number: PMD 1069. As befitting his comedic usurping of the recording industry and as a result of the popularity of *The Best of Sellers*, Peter happily attended the fourth Ivor Novello Awards, held at the BBC Television Theatre, in London, on Monday, 25th May 1959.

Sellers: "today . . . stands unchallenged at the top of his profession, and a popular person both within and outside it." Certainly the brief factual but satirical summing up of each track suggests that all the lavish praise is deliberately sweet and deliberately silly. That notwithstanding, the actual album is indeed a masterwork . . .

Not to mention a showcase, and a playground; an oasis for Sellers the actor to stretch his muscles within audio sketch paradise. There's the gloriously macabre 'Auntie Rotter' – written by Bob Monkhouse and Denis Goodwin – which allows Peter a moment of Alastair Sim-like ghoulish drag – in sound only, folks! Playing the cheerfully malicious headmistress, Sellers farms kids for the slaughter of their parents. Instant orphans. Well, I told you it was macabre. And it's certainly glorious. There's the relentless, poverty row travelogue of 'Balham – Gateway to the South' too: a reheated skit, written by Frank Muir and Denis Norden, and originally performed by the full cast of *Third Division – 'Some Vulgar Fractions'*. On *The Best of Sellers* it is totally Sellers, front and centre, with just one friendly concession to producer George Martin, who cameos as the grave funeral director. It was a favour; an in-joke; a warm embrace. It certainly wasn't beyond Sellers. Regardless, the track is nothing short of miraculous. And there's a shade of Bluebottle in the pathetic chap who whittles away at Toothbrush Holes-Manship.

The banal rambling of everyone sitting in the House of Commons is mercilessly mocked in 'Party Political Speech', written by Max Schreiner: "what about the workers, indeed sir!", while 'The Trumpet Volunteer', co-written by Sellers himself, mocks the trend for modern pop songs to plunder classical music. Other tracks range from the tongue-in-cheek 'Suddenly It's Folk Song' (which not only allows Sellers to travel three, only Wales is missing, of the four corners of the United Kingdom – in the studio at least – but also indulge him in his own passion for the very technique of recording itself) to the strangled sentimentality of 'All the Things You Are'. The impoverished aristocracy are mocked in 'We Need the Money' (again Sellers co-writing, with Ken Hare, this comic expose of a silly ass who is bare-faced canny enough to exploit the tourists. He is unrepentant, proud even, with a braying laugh). Everybody is sent-up on *The Best of Sellers*, in fact, but none more beautifully and timelessly than the youth-obsessed pop industry in 'I'm So Ashamed'. Suitably enough it was the track selected as the single from the album.[1] The singing infant – one of Peter's most treasurable vignettes – has tried everything to stay at the top of the Hit Parade, from humming to hot strumming. It's a mini masterpiece; so concise; so hilarious; so damned right. A funny satire on the late fifties industry, musically fun, and still relevant. In fact, it's the benchmark that other comedy records must be judged against.

Peter had also been busy in the film studio, collaborating with those most intuitive of film-makers John and Roy Boulting. The brothers would coax the most important and pivotal screen performances of Peter's British cinema years; arguably of his entire film career. The safety net on the first venture, *Carlton-Browne of the F.O.*, was Peter's old screen sparring partner Terry-Thomas. T-T was the cement, and already something of a veteran of the Boulting brothers' oeuvre – having played everything from an ineffectual country copper (*Happy Is the Bride*) to a snivelling spiv (*Brothers-in-Law*) – but he was in definitive terms as Carlton-Browne, the inept British diplomat, sent to a Pacific outpost on the verge of a political coup. With his stage mindset focused upon the Sultan in *Brouhaha*, Sellers is another foreign potentate here: Senar Amphibulous, Prime Minister of Gaillardia. He's a caricature, for sure, but there's a shading there which is fresh and new. He's not just another funny cipher but much more a swarthy pen-picture of otherness, with elements of subtle subterfuge and slimy soporific sub-plot. T-T under-plays Peter's villainy by referring to him as "rather tricky" and even more damning – a politician. There is a wonderful moment when T-T and Sellers, being pampered on the beach by gorgeous suntan lotion-rubbing girls, share the political crunch moment. Sellers quite literally draws

---

1 Serial number: Parlophone R4491, with 'A Drop of the Hard Stuff', the Irish folk song segment from 'Suddenly It's Folk Song', on the B-side. 'I'm So Ashamed' is a little piece of Sellers that my dad would play often and, as a result, it comically crept into my DNA. It's stuck there. Forever.

a line in the sand, planting the seed for the island's segregation and, naturally, putting himself in pole position. The wealth of the people is in Calbat. Enough to blow up the entire world, and thus establishing the Goonish deconstruction of Armageddon that *Dr. Strangelove* and *The Bed-Sitting Room* would map out. Oh, yes!

Here, overweight, greasy, and duplicitous, this manipulative Prime Minister fits the name of Amphibulous like a dripping-wet wetsuit. Whispering niceties and sweating at the armpits, this is a man of the people if only the people keep him in the lap of luxury. Unlike T-T who seems a tad backwards when it comes to the local lovelies, Sellers indulges in the pleasures of the flesh as if to the manor born, and eagerly pushes the island beverage too: "not a drop is drunk until it's three weeks old!" he proudly leers.

His brother-in-law (Mario Fabrizi) and cousin (Marne Maitland) have high-ranking positions too: the only other authoritarians Sellers deems worth mentioning. Every sneer, every scheme simply adds fuel to the fire of this corrupt characterisation. Throughout the performance, Sellers radiates the knowledge that he, finally, has his feet under the Top Table of British Film. In tandem, and with the encouragement of the Boultings, he adds elements of slapstick and visual playfulness to the role: the bongo-like tapping on the table at the feast; the skating chair, pushed away by the Grand Duke (John Le Mesurier), with Sellers gurning to perfection in anguish. There's also dexterity with his hat: both using it to emphasise his applause at the British fraternity leaving the airport and – spoiler alert here – to momentarily mask his handcuffed state at the film's end. The movements are fluid and funny. Sellers is enjoying himself again. Nowhere more so than during his final moment of glory: the impending explosive climax and, the perceived, end of his clodhopping nemesis.

This being the satire of the Boultings, of course, blind British bluster is rewarded with decoration. Bullish diplomacy and cast-iron stupidity are the very bedrocks of bureaucracy in the Boultings' universe. Still, the swinish smirk of Sellers is rich in comic creativity.

This is a despicable man, with absolutely no redeeming features. Sellers gives backstory to this crook without backbone. The fact that we smile as he sneaks is testament, wholly, to Sellers as a comic colossus. Perhaps the greatest trick Sellers allows his Amphibulous to pull is that the audience actually have a grudging liking of him.

And not simply because they liked Peter Sellers. Although, admittedly, an Indian Summer of *The Goon Show* was being relished in the few months immediately before *Carlton-Browne of the F.O.* was released across cinemas in Britain, through British Lion, on Tuesday, 10th March 1959.

Perhaps the most fascinating programme of that ninth series is 'Who Is Pink Oboe?', an episode that Sellers *didn't* record on Sunday, 11th January 1959.[1] Nearing the end of his six-month run in the West End, Sellers dropped out of the recording at the eleventh hour, complaining of a severe sore throat. Whereas Sellers could effortlessly step in and play Spike's characters in his absence, with Peter out of the studio, producer John Browell was forced to recruit four – count 'em – four actors to substitute: Kenneth Connor (not only as his own *Ray's a Laugh* character Sidney Mincing – "I fit into this programme . . ." but William Mate, mate), Valentine Dyall (as Hercules Grytpype-Thynne), Graham Stark (as various subordinates including an Irish Minnie Bannister-type; with Connor as his Crunesque counterpart), and the mighty Jack Train (returning, from beyond the grave, as Chinstrap in lieu of Bloodnok). That's an awful lot of talent to replace just one actor. Testament, if any was needed, of Peter's sheer breadth and skill. And he could do Sidney Mincing too. And had . . . much to the joy of Spike and Secombe in *The Goon Show*: 'The Treasure in the Tower'.[2]

Still, there was a break imminent for *The Goon Show* and, in many ways, it couldn't come soon enough for Sellers. It was a full

---

1 The title was a suitably naughty genitalia-geared gag. Just fifteen days later, chum and scribe Larry Stephens died, at the age of thirty-five.

2 Later in that series, in 'The £50 Cure', the very last of series nine, in fact, Connor came in to replace an indisposed Harry Secombe. Once Sellers, as his Jewish agent and promoter, actually addresses him as Neddie Seagoon, before the rest of the script has been amended to 'Kenny Connor'.

ten months away from Bluebottle and Bloodnok and the others; a mental and physical break from the studio madness of the BBC; and, most practically, forty-odd sainted Sundays off. Actually off, folks![1]

The break was also in the wake of *Brouhaha* closing in the West End. So, yes, from 23rd February through to 19th December 1959, Peter was free to concentrate almost exclusively on his film career. It was an opportunity he grabbed with both hands. Besides, the words of A.E. Matthews were probably still echoing round his noggin. There was now a determination not to over-act; to get to the truth of a character rather than the comic outer-layer. In that ten-month stop-gap Sellers made the two films that made him: one, *The Mouse That Roared*, made him an international star; the other, *I'm All Right Jack*, made him an actor of integrity. A bankable name and an award winner.

Carlton-Browne of the F.O. had found favour in America, under the title change of *Man in a Cocked Hat*. Confused audiences were none the wiser, really, for the film screamed little Britain through and through. They loved Sellers though. Of course. And the American audience was about to love him even more. With wonderful irony, it would be in a film that trod very similar terrain to *Carlton-Browne of the F.O.*, but, this time, in full colour, and with lashings of reference to the United States of America.

The Mouse That Roared was based upon Leonard Wibberley's 1955 novel of the same name – the first in a series of satires based around the fictional and microscopic European country of the Duchy of Grand Fenwick. An apocalyptic satire, it had appealed to, of all people, ageing matinee idol Tyrone Power, who had read it whilst in England filming *Seven Waves Away* – or *Abandon Ship!* as the States got it. You see even Power wasn't immune to a title change! The film star was so enamoured of *The Mouse That Roared* book that he gave a copy to producer Walter Shenson. In turn, producer Carl Foreman of Highroad Productions, picked it up and together with Shenson, took it to Columbia Pictures who immediately got behind it. Studio

<hr>

1 Although, on 7th June 1959, Peter was a guest on *Val Parnell's Sunday Night at the London Palladium*.

The Ladykillers:

Harry, the child-like spiv in *The Ladykillers*, was Peter's first major breakthrough in cinema. The last of the truly great comedies from Ealing Studios, at the time it was a sea change from the old order. The cynical, war-weary working classes were taking over.

STUDIOCANAL FILMS LTD / Alamy Stock Photo

Valentine Dyall:

Charles Dickens, a fine mimic himself, admitted that he loved: "feigning to be somebody else", as it allowed him to: "blow off my superfluous fierceness." Dickens would have adored Sellers: undoubtedly the greatest pretender of them all, here as chum and cohort Valentine Dyall. *Trinity Mirror / Mirrorpix / Alamy Stock Photo*

The Mouse That Roared:

In costume, as the mild-mannered warrior Tully Bascombe, relaxing during *The Mouse That Roared*. Always a voracious reader, on the look-out for source material, this one was already in production, also by Columbia Pictures, with his acting hero, Alec Guinness in the lead role. *Cinematic / Alamy Stock Photo*

I'm All Right Jack:

The BAFTA-winning performance of Fred Kite in *I'm All Right Jack*. The Union leader, with his Hitler moustache, obsession with Russia, and ineffectual domestic life, showed the general public and the film industry that Peter Sellers was much more than just a silly voices comedian. His opening cameo, as dinosaur of industry Sir John Kennaway, shuffling off and ushering in a new age, is telling indeed. *Classic Cinema Archive / Alamy Stock Photo*

Mr. Topaze:

Actor as Auteur: While still in the guise of his moralistic schoolteacher, Peter calls the shots on *Mr. Topaze*. At the time Peter said: "what I am really hoping for is that I will be able to achieve sufficient success as a director to give up acting entirely." As a film director he preferred both comedy and drama in full-length long-shot. Frequent cinema colleagues Blake Edwards and Joe McGrath shared his vision.

Everett Collection Inc / Alamy Stock Photo

The Wrong Arm of the Law:

The cockney arch-criminal 'Pearly' Gates in *The Wrong Arm of the Law* is arguably the most slick and polished of Peter's British cinema star turns. The rapid wit, the sophisticated facial hair, and the gear-shifting dexterity of the performance remains a benchmark of quality. *Everett Collection Inc / Alamy Stock Photo* contract player Jean Seberg was cast as the ingenue Helen Kokintz. Everybody's favourite military authority figure William Hartnell enjoyed third billing as Will Buckley, a wonderfully efficient, rather redundant army sergeant who had done his bit in the last war.[1] Top billing – three times – was undoubtedly the prerogative of Peter Sellers.

It is more than fitting that at least two of his three roles (four, if you count the statue-likeness of Sellers as the English Knight who founded the entire country) have firm roots in his radio creations of old. The Grand Duchess Gloriana XII takes on more of an aged Queen Victoria in Peter's interpretation of the script; as opposed to the original novel in which the Duchess is far younger, modelled upon the fairly recently crowned Queen Elizabeth II. Within the Sellers gallery of grotesques, however, there is more than a whiff of Crystal Jollibottom about the Duchess. Not in the quivering caricature but in the gravitas and grandiose of her presence and status. Her continued grieving for her lost love, Leopold, is never once mocked, but always played with sensitivity and understanding. Her embrace of the nuclear race, with a quiet but room-shattering "boom!" is played with such poise; such subtlety.

The Prime Minister, Count Rupert of Mountjoy, fittingly, has the air of one of Victoria's Prime Ministers, Benjamin Disraeli, but, aptly enough as the villain of the piece, he is much more George Sanders and, as such, by default, Grytpype-Thynne. This bearded bureaucrat has the air of a pantomime baddie, for sure, and in cahoots with the leader of the opposition (Peter's *Brouhaha* co-star Leo McKern) there's even an embrace of silent movie skullduggery, emphasised by a slightly speeded-up camera and a plinky-plonky piano accompaniment when their dastardly deeds are at their most dastardly and duplicitous. Still, this is no cardboard crook. There

---

1 On screen, Hartnell had indeed become the definitive army sergeant – in the 1944 film *The Way Ahead* – while, in 1959, he was back on television, in *The Army Game*, following a brief sabbatical that had included the leading role in the inaugural *Carry On Sergeant*. There's barely a cigarette paper between that performance and this. Indeed, he bellows that oft-used military phrase "Carry On!" towards the end of *The Mouse That Roared*, and his casting certainly helped box office business in Britain.

is a weight and logic behind his devilish plan. Indeed, his wicked intelligence is the very source of the plot. His plan is to fiendishly exploit the fact that, whereas once America had been the biggest importer of his country's major product, the Pinot Grand Fenwick wine, now a company in the United States is producing Pinot Grand Enwick, a much cheaper imitation. As an excuse reaction, in actuality a way to escape obscurity and impending bankruptcy, Grand Fenwick declares war on America. The plan being to surrender, and subsequently wallow in the financial assistance of America upon a defeated enemy.

The Duchess and the Politician are pawns in this plot, but arguably Peter's most impressive turn in *The Mouse That Roared* is the hapless hero Tully Bascombe. A bland, blank canvas, he is as anonymous as Fenwick itself.

Bascombe is bespectacled and clad in medieval chainmail military uniform as he and Sergeant Will lead a twenty-strong army invasion of America – well, New York City. The Big Apple is eerily deserted, with the populace underground due to a drill for a new bomb – the Q-Bomb, which is 100 times stronger than hydrogen! Tully Bascombe is evenly spoken, borderline boring, with his hands in his pockets, sidestepping, lagging behind, and being horrendously seasick. This is Sellers as Sellers. The nobody. Without a character. He even adopts his own, distinctive spectacles for Tully, as if to emphasise the point. Sellers presents a hero made of nothingness; the foreshadow of *Being There*; a Field Marshal cum Grand Constable fresh from his own, tiny field. He is a man of the forest, caught in his own tender trap – quite literally – when terrorised by a frantic fox. It would have been this role, and this role alone, that Sellers would have latched on to and, metaphorically, wished A.E. Matthews could be witnessing unfolding on the sound stages at Shepperton Studios. All that obvious 'back-projection', overawed sightseeing of New York works amazingly well, because of and not despite its rudimentary special effects. Genuinely, Sellers looking skyward to a skyscraper that really wasn't there is more than enough. The acting here is that good.

Indeed, during production of *The Mouse That Roared*, on the very last day of November 1958, Sellers recorded *The Goon Show*'s 'The Mountain Eaters', for broadcast the following day. Here it is Sellers who throws away a comment on Milligan: "his over-acting is becoming apparent to us all." Even in gloriously silly caricature, Peter was now injecting truths, even home truths. In your lovely old face, Matty. And, indeed, in his naive and gullible action hero in *The Mouse That Roared* there is an intricate beauty within the ordinary; a deceptive depth of a canyon within the perceived pothole. And the face of Sellers as Tully was the one that adorned the poster. No outlandish comic character seemed to be needed to promote this film. Sellers was enough.

Chapter 6

"He was funny in that, let's get him to be funny in this!"

Peter Sellers, 1960

Peter's popularity was undeniably on the ascent and, quite rightly, Adelphi Films felt justified in capitalising on the film stardom that they had launched. In 1959 David Dent dusted off *The Slappiest Days of Our Lives*, that creaky old compilation that Sellers had narrated six years earlier. Dent had a vision of chomping up the film into even tinier, bite-sized chunks, for exploitation on commercial television. Peter's narration would be retained and promoted, for full publicity clout, and these pratfalling nuggets were to have bathed under the glorious title of *Movie Mirthquakes*. The idea stalled at the planning stage . . . For Sellers it was perhaps just as well.

Rather than celebrating Hollywood's past, Peter was at the sharp end of contemporary satire. He was snappy; he was modern; he was a comedian for the Atomic Age. Certainly *The Mouse That Roared* is steeped in the threat of nuclear destruction, and the absurdity of international diplomacy. It's the very light and shade of the film. Peter's lovesick sap even mutters: "My Girl! My bomb!" as his victorious bargaining tool is whisked away. At that very moment the screen explodes into a mushroom cloud – in a foreshadowing of the upcoming *Dr. Strangelove* – although, as our friendly narrator intones, this is not the destructive end of the film, merely a chilling reminder of something that could happen at any moment. So, prepare yourself . . . It's that kind of film.

This is not only a send-up of the current situation but another, very sharp, shard of ice in Peter's stock as the ultimate Cold War comedian. He is the jester who can take the mickey out of mass destruction. There's a lovely line, near the end of *The Mouse That Roared*, when Peter's beautifully naive Tully, realises he has the upper hand. He quietly mutters about the fact that the world is in a worse state now than it was before the last war, with "all these bombs and things!" Again Tully *is* Sellers here. It's almost Peter's mission statement.[1] Tully, at the close, is a slightly happier man. Gone is that bland awkwardness, and his serious ship-bound inability to take advantage of the girl of his dreams. That's all a ruse on her part anyway, compounded by Peter's natural timidity and a touch of mal de mer. However, by the end, he has made an asset of his quiet truthfulness to calmly win her heart.

At the close, with a wedding day set and, supposedly, the bomb exactly where he wants it, it's his ultimate happy ending. The crafty closing credits 'The End – We hope . . .' – not only harks back to the tongue-in-cheek pessimism of *The Naked Truth*, but means the story is open-ended. To an extent. As the novelist had proved.

Sellers, however, would bow out of Fenwick with a cheery grin, and a hasty winked eye. Well, who can blame him? Jean Seberg is an elfin honey. And he's got her. Yes, it's the Boulting brothers satire with a transatlantic shine: Sellers as Prime Minister even lists off malted milk and hot dogs as fringe benefits of the war; and Sellers as the meek invader steps in bubble gum. Even the inanimate central McGuffin – the bomb itself – is shaped exactly like an American football. A brief vignette of play takes place, with Tully breathlessly scoring the touchdown. This is a Little Britain air kiss to the Great White Way. And America fell under its charm. Indeed, its $450,000 budget was quadrupled within weeks of its release, on Friday, 17th July 1959.

---

1 The codes and conventions of cinema are not spared. English subtitles of French films are mocked, with Peter's English punchline of not being able to speak French even presented in English subtitles. Moreover, Columbia Pictures itself is sent-up by *The Mouse That Roared*. The opening credit animation, designed by Maurice Binder, added a cartoon mouse who, yes, roars in spite of himself, and thus mocks MGM's roaring lion. Immediately beforehand a real mouse has been more than enough to put the wind up the torch-holding Columbia lady, who lifts up her skirt and runs off in terror. Meta movie-making, there.

Not that Roy and John Boulting were bothered. They were as in love with Peter Sellers as the United States were. What's more, they had another collaboration up their sleeve. Arguably their finest collaboration. A Charter Film Productions for British Lion, it was all set for a general release, following a Leicester Square premiere on Thursday, 13th August 1959. Indeed, while *The Mouse That Roared* did only moderate business in Britain, *I'm All Right Jack* was a colossus of biting political satire.

Based on Alan Hackney's 1958 novel *Private Life*, *I'm All Right Jack* is contemporary and cutting. It lifts up Ian Carmichael as Stanley Windrush, the anti-hero of *Private's Progress*, and plonks him down, a decade or so after those war years, and slap bang into industry, union problems, and the ethos of the worker in 1950s Britain. A lot of the old guard are back on parade: corrupt young pal Richard Attenborough; corrupt manipulator Dennis Price; bamboozled military authoritarian Terry-Thomas. And then there's Peter Sellers. New to the mix, although hardly new to the Boulting brothers. In a comedic masterstroke, the brothers don't just blame the poor old workshy workers, they don't just blame the management, they don't even just blame the union bosses and the union. No, they blame everybody!

The seed of the satire, for the Boultings at least, was the interminable and intrusive union structure in British Film Studios. It was a thinly veiled attack but one which, at least, provided Peter with the hook on his bombastic union leader, Fred Kite. Roy Boulting recalled that: "when he was given it he read it and said he didn't want to do it. So we asked him: 'Why Peter?' and he said: 'Where are the laughs?' Then we had to explain to him, as best we could, that we didn't regard him as a Goon for this film, but that he was going to be playing a real character. And there were laughs aplenty if he played it.

"Once he got into the wardrobe, once he had put on that little Hitler moustache, and then, above all, as the cameras were about to turn, the door of the studio stage at Shepperton opened and in walked the works committee. All the unions: carpenters, electricians, camera, and so on. They stood there silent, because I had put up the bell, but when he started to play the scene, as Fred Kite, the shop steward, they immediately recognised the man. They didn't see it as themselves but they did the inexcusable thing in a studio when the camera is turning: they burst into laughter, which they couldn't contain. Immediately we cut, but then I saw the change in Peter's face. He hadn't thought it was funny himself but now he knew it was funny. And from that moment, he was convinced."[1]

Once Sellers had relaxed within the skin, and accepted the in-built humour of the man, he was free to give one of his career-defining performances.

For all his perceived power and clout Peter's militant shop steward Fred Kite is a weak man; an ineffectual man. Used and abused by the people with real power and clout, he crumbles like an undercooked biscuit while embroiled in the live television debate. He even crumbles when his naive and misinformed passions, nay obsessions, with communism and the pleasures of Russia ultimately alienate his family. There is a wistful romanticism, as Sellers intones that glorious line of dialogue about Mother Russia: "All those cornfields and ballet in the evenings . . .". Nobody says anything, but the eyes roll, and the heart sinks a little, for this silly small man, with his tin-pot empire. His idealised dreams of a system that, like every other, has that single flaw at its centre: the people. Kite's ideal is sweet and naive but ultimately doomed. His vision for mankind and how mankind operates is his downfall. His wife, played with steely frothiness by Irene Handl, and his daughter, the whistle-worthy leading role film breakthrough for Liz Fraser, up sticks and leave him to his own devices. It was this plot point, this moment, that Sellers seized upon to give his cardboard dictator a real soul.

That pivotal scene, as he struggles to darn his thread-worn socks, and forms a most unlikely alliance with Major Terry-Thomas, lifts the lid on this lonely, rather likeable idiot. Moreover, it was that scene that cemented his winning all the prizes and plaudits that

---

1 *Best Sellers?* Lucida Productions, Channel 4, 1992.

resulted once the people saw *I'm All Right Jack*. It is also part of the Sellers mythology, as co-star Ian Carmichael remembered: "Peter Sellers was a strain for Terry and vice-versa. The reason was that Terry would love a lot of takes to get his performance right, whereas Peter always felt that his performance was deteriorating with each fresh take. Professionally and personally they got on wonderfully well, it was just this difference in acting technique. But then, maybe it helped that intense scene. Somehow they got through that scene and it remains very, very funny indeed."[1]

It still does, Ian. It still does. In many ways it was the end of an era for, although Sellers worked with the Boultings again, he would never again support T-T on film. He had been such an intrinsic part of Peter's film education. Awards and avenues anew were to come, but first Peter was committed to a thoroughly brilliant if unchallenging crime caper.

It was to prove a speedy reunion with Liz Fraser – this time as Peter's girlfriend rather than offspring – and Irene Handl, who was content to play Liz's loving mum. Again.

Sellers and Handl were something of a comedic item at the time, for Peter's difficult second album was anything but. *Songs for Swinging Sellers* enabled Peter to explore the codes and conventions of the recording studio even more, enlisting cool and gloriously self-deprecating chum Matt Monro to croon the opening number 'You Keep Me Swingin''. Contemporary audiences may well have been convinced that this was actually Sellers singing and been suitably impressed. To conceal the identity of the singer that even Sinatra considered perfection, Monro is credited as Fred Flange, with Sellers, to his own opening number at one minute forty-seven seconds, voicing his admiration: "I wish I could sing like that!", and attempting his own version.[2] Irene Handl, who wrote the sweet,

---

1 Interview with the author, October 2001.

2 The term 'flanging', meaning to mix two identical recorded pieces of sound to make a unique effect, is still used in recording today. Producer George Martin maintained that it was a John Lennonism but, with Martin having produced this record for Sellers, and recorded like-for-like takes of both Peter and Monro singing 'You Keep Me Swingin'', coupled with Lennon's well-documented obsession with *The Goon Show* and the Sellers recordings, this use of the word has to have been an influence on the Beatles and, thus, recording technology from then on.

park bench encounter 'Shadows on the Grass', plays her role with giggling flirtation and working-class gaucheness. Sellers, as the gentle, romantic Frenchman, is the skilled and selfless comic feed here, allowing his beloved female co-star, after all the scribe of the piece, to shine. Both Sellers and Handl are wonderful as the pretentious and often bewildered and misinformed orators in 'The Critics', written by Max Schreiner and Denis Goodwin. Sellers does a lot of the heavy lifting here – as the whining, upper-crust Newton Teesdale, and the professional Scot J. Wallace Hardwood, but Handl's crisp interjections and flights of reverence are a precise counterpoint. Schreiner and Goodwin also wrote 'Lord Badminton's Memoirs', a colonial monologue, 'In a Free State', a Sellers two-hander, with himself, as a ranting, drunken Irish playwright and timid interviewer, and 'Face to Face', the spot-on pastiche of John Freeman's television interview show, which had been a controversial watch since February 1959. Peter's fascination with popular culture is further embraced with 'Wouldn't It Be Loverly', the Indian take on Lerner and Loewe's *My Fair Lady* hit which directly points towards *The Millionairess* and the rest; as well as Frank Muir and Denis Norden's 'So Little Time', an aggressive satire on the booming British pop market. Peter gives a three-way virtuoso performance here: as the breathy female journalist, the gruff upper-class manager, and the adenoidal, idle teenage rock 'n' roll idol. While it's a different chart sensation, an illiterate and arrogant skiffle star – modelled after Lonnie Donegan – who sends up and insults the erudite interviewer – in 'Putting on the Smile'.

'I Haven't Told Her, She Hasn't Told Me (But We Know It Just the Same)' was an old music-hall number taught to Peter by his father, and such a part of his musical DNA was it that he resurrected it for his scruffy variety artiste in *The Optimists*, and even performed it in his 1974 *Parkinson* interview. The essence of William Mate is present and correct in a gentle and charming rendition of 'My Old Dutch' which is simply there to build up to the Scandinavian interruption; and 'Peter Sellers Sings George Gershwin' is similarly a one-joke track – albeit an hilarious one.[1]

All that tireless characterisation was a satisfying contrast with that film commitment of Peter's, with Irene Handl a fun and free-wheeling bridge between the two.

The film was Peter's first attempt to play a copper-bottomed, albeit corrupt, charming, dashing, leading man. It was the prison romp *Two-Way Stretch*, dreamed up and scripted by John Warren and Len Heath, with additional dialogue by *I'm All Right Jack* scribe Alan Hackney. It was very much cut from the same cloth, but this wasn't satire. It was a pure, undiluted comedy heist romp. One of the jewels in Peter's British cinema crown.

From those few jaunty, jazzy tones of the Ken Jones opening musical score,[2] and, despite Sellers enjoying top-billing status alongside Wilfred Hyde-White, above that seemingly never-ending roll-call of the great and the good of British character actors, this is comedy as community. *Two-Way Stretch* is a joyous, relentless roller-coaster of one-upmanship; crafty criminality, and getting one over on the man. Shot at Shepperton Studios and certainly an ensemble piece, there is no doubting that Lionel Jeffries – as no-nonsense prison warder Sidney 'Sour' Kraut – is on scene-stealing form throughout. Indeed, there are times when our trio of prison inmates simply stand in a row and allow Jeffries to vent his sadistic instructions and ranting observations. So much so that Sellers cannot resist sending up the performance, even within the sending up of authority at the very heart and soul of *Two-Way Stretch*. The high-pitched delivery is gleefully mocked during the Wooden Horse tunnel-digging scene and, back in the cell, Sellers, Bernard Cribbins, and David Lodge all have a bash at the screeched whine, right into the face of Jeffries. One imagines the gang were having huge fun during the shoot.

---

1 On this track it is Peter Sellers acolyte John Junkin who provides the strangulated introduction and the recording session also resulted in 'A Right Bird', a post-booze-up conversation with dimwit Junkin and confident cockney Sellers. This joyous, improvised sketch – which ends with Junkin's uncontrollable laughter – remained unreleased until the EMI compilation *The Peter Sellers Collection*, in 1990.
2 Incidentally, not the actor Ken Jones who played 'orrible Ives in *Porridge*. More of which in the footnote on page 108!

Undoubtedly, Peter was at his most confident and assured when he was safe in the knowledge that a strong support system was in place. It was key to his pitch-perfect, measured, and relaxed screen performance. Peter's old chum David Lodge is his right-hand man throughout, and there's even a moment of such laid-back, natural interplay that screams ad-libbed fun, as Sellers observes that Wilber the pigeon is getting fat. There's a pause from Lodge, as if their director Robert Day is going to shout 'Cut!', but Sellers grins, ploughs on with the scripted dialogue, and a moment of genuine charm remains. It's that kind of film. Wonderfully . . . and Sellers warmed to the gentle friendliness of Bernard Cribbins immediately. Naturally. Cribbins recalled that: "the film was a joy. Funnily enough, I remember that first day of filming as if it was yesterday. It was the filming of the very first scene of the film, which is very, very rare in this business. So, it was myself, Peter Sellers, and David Lodge, in the prison cell together. Now, we had all made a fair few films, even back then, and it was very unusual for the first day of filming to be the very first scene of the script. We were all used to shooting everything out of order, but Robert Day, our director, thought this would establish the dynamics of this trio of criminals and it really did. Then Lionel Jeffries turned up, as the no-nonsense, bastard of a prison warden, and we had the conflict that was the engine of that film's comedy. It was a total hoot from start to finish, and Peter Sellers was one of the lads, you know. He mucked in with everybody else. It was a real team. A team of kindly ruffians. Great fun."[1]

Peter's Dodger Lane is a banged-up wrong 'un, of course, but he oozes cool and accepted ease of his incarcerated lifestyle. That introductory scene is indeed pivotal. Sellers is coaxed awake by a gentle nudge from David Lodge, slowly gets to grips with the hangover resulting from Lodge's trifle from the previous evening, and steamrolls over a crestfallen Cribbins as he switches off the radio just before his mum's request is played. The request is 'Don't Face Me In', with Sellers deliciously dismissive and resolute in his

---

1 Interview with the author, October 2017.

spat-out comment: "Very subtle sense of humour!"

During the tour of the female welfare committee – including beloved BBC playmate and Goon acolyte Beryl Reid – Sellers embraces his natural cockney delivery to a heightened, almost music-hall reading of the lines. This is Peter dipping a toe back into grotesque, comic characterisation, almost giving the visitors what they want, what they expect: a caricature of the London criminal. The over-played niceties are counterbalanced by his playfulness (stroking the leg of ugly-beautiful male model, Ted Carroll, and making the crook think it's the haughty Miss Prescott, as played by Noel Hood). Moreover when Sellers first encounters old law-breaking colleague Hyde-White, in heavy disguise as the Reverend, and in – of all places – the governor's office, there is an expression of such unease, such disgust, such distrust. The whole stitch up from their previous job – resulting in our loveable trio being behind bars in the first place – is played out in those seconds. No dialogue is needed. We feel the contempt Sellers has for this man fairly pulsating in every pore. The ingenious plot – Sellers and his gang escaping from prison, committing a two-million-pound diamond robbery, then breaking back inside, on the eve of their release, and thus securing the perfect alibi – is the brainchild of Hyde-White, but it's the verve of Sellers that pulls it off. The fact that the screws are as contemptuous and lazy and lacklustre as the inmates merely adds to our admiration and adoration of Sellers.[1]

After the smooth criminal of *Two-Way Stretch* it was back to character acting, as mild mannered, reluctant murderer, Mr. Martin, for *The Battle of the Sexes*. The first production out of Bryanston Films, the company signed off on the project in May 1959, having bought the rights to American humourist James Thurber's novel

---

1 The filming location for H.M. Prison Huntleigh was actually the gates of South Cavalry Barracks, in Aldershot. The premise is, of course, the huge seed that grew into the Dick Clement and Ian La Frenis situation comedy *Porridge*. Sellers is the model for Ronnie Barker's Fletch, and his little victories inside. Cribbins would become the naive Gober, as played by Richard Beckinsale. There is much of Lionel Jeffries in Fulton Mackay's prison guard; and Maurice Denham in Michael Barrington's governor; and George Woodbridge in Brian Wilde's prison warden. So strong a sitcom blueprint is it, that the 'alternative' set referenced *Two-Way Stretch* in Ben Elton's *Happy Families*.

The Catbird Seat, from Hecht Hill Lancaster. Burt Lancaster was originally to have starred, with direction by no less a screen giant as Billy Wilder, in the director's catbird seat. However, Constance Cummings recalled that: "it was Peter Sellers all the way, from when I got involved. I had seen *The Mouse That Roared*, like most people I knew, but, I'm ashamed to say, that was all! I was half expecting a whirligig of a comedian but Peter wasn't a comedian, not really. He was an actor who played comedy really well. There's a huge difference. He was quiet, methodical and good at his job. A lot like the character he played, really."[1]

Still, at the time Sellers was very much a fully-fledged Goon too. Indeed, Christmas 1959 was a very happy one. Within the last eighteen months Peter had put four landmark films in the can, and had made that joyful return to *The Goon Show*. So enamoured with the absurdism of it all, that Peter, even now, happily got involved with yet another attempt to film the essence of the Goons. Thus, he was very content to lark about in a field for *The Running, Jumping & Standing Still Film*. The credits proudly scream that the film was devised by Peter Sellers; he also had some thoughts on the matter of how it should be shot. Although Spike Milligan claimed creative inspiration for the film, it was Richard Lester who fully oversaw the project, edited it together, and received sole directorial credit – much to Milligan's chagrin.[2]

The result was ten minutes of surreal madness. There's certainly running – including Sellers, dragging along a bike as he rushes back and forth between musical stands with sheet music and violin . . . and telescope! There's an awful lot of standing still too, but absolutely no jumping. Unless of course you include jump cuts, physical knocks, and slow burns just off camera. Peter too is a trilby-wearing chap, complete with snorkel and shotgun, who engages with photographer Mario Fabrizi; and stone-faced lunatic Bruce Lacey.[3] As this local

---

1 Interview with the author, April 1998.

2 Although, when Spike hit the West End big with *Son of Oblomov* Lester ruefully saw adverts for Spike Milligan's *Running, Jumping & Standing Still Film!*

3 Who, in a career of glorious eccentricity, constructed and animated bizarre props for Michael Bentine's *It's a Square World*.

yokel runs round and round a gramophone record, Sellers jigs and jerks to the ancient recording of gibberish: authentic Goonish gibberish, to boot.

Often to be seen screened in the Cartoon Cinema on Waterloo Station, this wondrous snippet of Goonish nonsense was nominated for an Academy Award for Best Live Action Short Subject.[1] Not bad for a film that had a budget of £70 and took all of 36 hours to film. Everything that Lester captured on film went into the final edit: and then some. Sellers, who had shot some footage on his personal 16mm zoom Bolex camera, threw his material in too. With props purloined by our loveable loony local Bruce Lacey, from his work over at Granada Television, and an edit job of two hours, the finished product was accompanied by a scat jazz musical score composed by Lester. It's a nutty, nuanced, and naturally hilarious flick made with affection and Goonish camaraderie. It pointed the way towards Lester's Beatles films too: but that's another story in Peter's screen journey.

All in all the film was also a warm fuzz for Peter around the tenth, and sigh it with sadness, final series, of six editions of the wireless-type *Goon Show*, which were broadcast over the preamble and deflation of the holiday season. What's more, and beyond Peter's control, an element of Goonish fun was to be found under many a Christmas tree in the shape of the 1960 *Film Fun* annual. Peter's weekly column was pure *Goon Show*: Carry On Mate! wallowed in his bespectacled and shabby over-coated depiction as William Mate, a hapless, helpful soul who wanders through the streets of *Film Fun* land assisting attractive ladies and being sent-up by snotty toffs. Typical *Film Fun*, indeed. Despite not getting a penny piece for the comic strip, it is a measure of Peter's popularity, with children of all ages. The annual for that year even featured a colour portrait of

---

1 Disappointingly, it lost out to Jacques Cousteau's *The Golden Fish*, which doesn't have any jumping in it either!

Peter's Wee Sonny MacGregor from *The Naked Truth* on the back.[1]

Another Christmas treat, wrapped up expectantly for the fan in your family – and one that Peter did get a few bob for – was the Parlophone long-playing record *Best of the Goon Shows*.[2] Producer John Browell, who had just steered through the final batch of episodes – and it was conceived and performed, knowingly, as the final batch – wrote the energetic sleeve note for the album. Perceptive and intimate, they are a valuable window into the dying embers of *The Goon Show*, and the playful insanity of Sellers: "On stage the script gets its first rehearsal. A phone message says Peter will be late. I am baffled by this as Peter is just walking through the stage door. It seems he made the phone call from his car parked outside . . . Beaming all over and bursting with good nature, Harry giggles his way into the script. Peter, more serious, studies his character closely, while Spike, to whom this is all real and earnest, ranges between ecstasy and agony . . . This is a hilarious show, an exhausting show, a show with sheer genius mixed with lunacy. To me, it's a great deal more satisfying and closer to reality than anything else I have ever produced."

Peter was on hand, with his latest car, to give stressed and troubled Spike a lift home if he missed his last tube train. For Sellers it was the least he could do, for he needed *The Goon Show* despite the mental anguish it caused Milligan: "We used to look forward immensely to those Sunday meetings. Every Sunday was a reunion, when we could meet at the Camden Theatre to record the shows. *The Goon Show* would then set us up for another week."[3] Spike readily explained that the team all helped in the development of the series: "We all helped to create the characters. They just happened. There was no family planning for the Goons. The list of characters grew

---

1 Goon chum Harry Secombe was a *Film Fun* favourite too, as was film pal Terry-Thomas. Laurel and Hardy, now dropped just after Olly's death, had long been the *Film Fun* stars. During their legendary 1952 tour of England editor Frederick George Cordwell forbade cartoonist Terry Wakefield from visiting the boys backstage, just in case they asked for money!

2 Serial number: PMC 1108, which featured 'Dishonoured', just nine months after its original transmission; alongside the February 1956 episode 'Tales of Old Dartmoor'.

3 *Radio Times*, interviewed by Ray Connolly, 28th September 1972.

just like a family." To the very end. It was family.

Harry Secombe spoke for every Goon when he wrote: "for we three *The Goon Show* was a chance to get together on a Sunday and indulge in our private fantasies. It was a time for hysteria and brandy, for soaring upward on the thermal currents of Milligan's imagination, a time for wishing every day of the week to be a Sunday."[1]

The last *Goon Show* of all . . . for now . . . was, suitably enough, entitled 'The Last of the Smoking Seagoons',[2] and was recorded on Sunday, 24th January 1960, for transmission the following Thursday evening. It was the end. Honestly. There's real bite in Spike's sending up of Peter's passion for cars, noting: "he's not heard of one of those . . ." in character!; while Wal Greenslade, with comic lump in throat, wrapped it all up with: "Yes, that was it. The last of them. So bye now . . ." The audience clap along to the final play-out; the last drop of brandy was consumed round the old back there, and then the three Goons were out of the loyal commitment to communal comedy for the corporation, to enjoy dinner at the Czech restaurant on Edgware Road. Comrades, comrades . . . ever since they were Crazy People; and, as I can't help to keep making clear, once a Goon, always a Goon . . .

Indeed, Sellers joined Spike, as well as Peggy Mount, on a London-taping of *The Tonight Show*, with Jack Paar.[3] It was only to be expected that Peter made himself so readily available for he had two – count 'em – two major films to promote. *Two-Way Stretch* was distributed by British Lion Films, with a premiere at the Warner Theatre, London, on 11th February 1960, followed by a general

---

1 'Backword' by Harry Secombe in *The Goon Show Scripts* (Woburn Press, 1972).

2 At least, that's how dear old Wallace Greenslade announced it, although Spike's script had it down as 'The Last Smoking Seagoon'.

3 Broadcast on 29th March 1960, under the direction of Hal Gurnee, Peter had also joined the variety fun of *Saturday Spectacular: The Anthony Newley Show*, 30th January. He particularly enjoyed Newley's conceit of getting all the special guests to reconvene at the show's climax. As Snappy-Fingers Sellers he provided drum beat backing for 'It Takes a Worried Man to Sing a Worried Song'. It was glorious pop music pastiche while, naturally, being really rather good!

release on Valentine's Day.[1]

A mere eleven days later, on 25th February 1960, *The Battle of the Sexes* made it a very strong Sellers spring across Britain. The film was swiftly released in America too, on 18th April 1960, prompting a swift return to *The Tonight Show*, two days later. The following month, in a ceremony at the Dorchester Hotel, on 22nd March, Prince Philip presented Peter with his BAFTA for *I'm All Right Jack*. This royal seal of approval did Sellers no harm stateside, even though *The Battle of the Sexes* is pure British film terrain.[2]

For a production made at the very end of *The Goon Show* and released in the immediate wake of its slow, first death, *The Battle of the Sexes* is the perfect bridging of outrageous comic characterisation and a plot with more prolonged, evocative satire than sketchy silliness. The hair and make-up for Peter's gentle and simple Mr. Martin is no less repertory theatre dress-up basket than *The Smallest Show on Earth*, although the performance is even more rounded, even more determined, and even more profound. This old man is part of the Edinburgh establishment. The battle is not a romantic one – not until the final scene, that is – but more a battle of homespun Scottish industry against modern, American business. It's Peter Sellers versus Constance Cummings, with that bulbous manchild Robert Morley in the middle, as the young pretender to the throne of McPherson textiles. Cummings, with those gorgeous cheekbones set to stun, was an anglophile who had already once touched British film greatness, as the nagging second wife in Noel Coward's *Blithe Spirit*. She remembered Sellers with acute affection: "he was an absolute darling. And so modest. That – now – very famous scene when his meek and mild character is attempting to murder me in my apartment was a sheer delight to shoot. It was a kind of slapstick ballet that Peter and our director Charlie Crichton worked out between them, really. I

---

1 *Two-Way Stretch* would creep into America, early in 1962, when *New York Times* critic Bosley Crowther noted that: "Mr. Sellers is still on the rise." It would subsequently appear on American television, at least once a year, for years and years and years . . . and certainly well beyond Peter's death. And giving David Lodge chance to comically grumble about lack of residuals.

2 That same month, on 10th March to be precise, that same performance of Fred Kite won Peter the Variety Club of Great Britain Award for Best Film Actor.

mean it was on the page, in the script, but the timing was all them. I just had to walk round it and try not to get in Peter's way. Watching the rushes the following day I was bewitched by how fluid Peter's movements were. I told him that he had glimpses of Charlie Chaplin in the ease of comic movement he put into that scene. He just looked at me, dumbfounded. I don't think he believed me, but I meant it. Absolutely. After that he rather sheepishly and sweetly came over to me to ask about the time I made a film with Harold Lloyd.[1] He was besotted by the great screen comedians. And very knowledgeable."

There is certainly a slapstick truth at play in Peter's work here. Only on occasions does he allow his calm, monosyllabic Scots persona to dip into vocal insanity. And it is when the plot dictates that he crusades into totally unpredictable territory that he does it. At these times it seems right. Justified. The first hint of controlled insanity is when he deliberately smashes Morley's pre-Columbus artefact. The deed done, and safely outside the door of his boss's office, Sellers allows himself just a pause; a moment to enjoy his act of rebellion. The gulp is the prelude to the planned anarchy to come.

The night of sabotage, as Sellers skips and parries his way round the unwatchful eye of the night watchman (James Gibson) reveals a childish wonder in playing the baddie. Sellers uses his walking stick as a sword, while the little snippy-snippy business with the scissors is heightened to perfection, and the double-takes and overplayed physicality is silent comedy technique learned by heart and absorbed by passion.

That murderous attempt on the life of Cummings – the American who comes into the business and disrupts it completely – is a Hitchcockian hymn to slaughter.[2] "It never works out how you plan it," Martin laments. The kitchen knife is lost and an egg whisk is the useless replacement; the whiskey bottle misses its target by a mere

---

1 *Movie Crazy*, in 1932. Constance Cummings interview with the author, April 1998.

2 Like *Torn Curtain*, a few years later in 1966, Sellers finds it is not as easy to "rub out an error" as the movies make out. Indeed, the point is rammed home as the Sherlock Holmes film within a film spells out just how easy murder can be – and be deduced, of course – with a quite superb Holmes and Watson cameo from Michael Goodliffe and William Mervyn.

matter of inches; the thought of pushing the helpless, albeit annoying, woman out of the window is halted by the beauteous choral singing of 'All Creatures Great and Small' on the television.

Still, for all the farcical black comedy at the heart of *The Battle of the Sexes*, Sellers is at his most impressive when he reigns in the comic clout and inwardly reflects on his mission to get rid of the American influence. Martin is clearly very proud of the tradition of his work, and lovingly respects the legacy of the senior McPherson – a touching cameo by Ernest Thesiger – which radiates influence throughout the film via a startling portrait which hangs in the office of his son. The final nod to the old gentleman, when Sellers has achieved his goal, is moving indeed. There are real tears in the eyes of Sellers; real emotion. This is much, much more than an Ealingesque comedy now. This is a parable for the little man beating the big corporation. Every thought process is played out with subtle skill. Peter's facial reactions are self-contained, and determined. When the notion of implying his American nemesis is insane hits him, the idea dawns in those deep, calculating eyes of his. As Constance Cummings flutters around, with her non-stop chatter intoning that his office colleagues would never swallow the idea of Mr. Martin as a murderer, the final solution hits him. "I don't think they'd believe you!" he ruminates, almost to himself. It's a moment of fine screen acting. Comic and chilling.

The film too is a little wobble towards making Sellers an international star. Ealing was still a watchword for quality comedy film-making in the States, and that Sellers had had a part in the – albeit declining – legacy of the studios was enough to give this film a tangible link with Ealing's still sparkling reputation. Moreover, distinguished actor and theatre-maker Sam Wanamaker provides the bookending narration for the film. Here was the American voice to reassure the potential American audience; the correct tones to soften the joke concerning the loud-mouthed American tourist (Althea Orr) who wants synthetic materials.

The clout of Ealing was one thing, but the BAFTA was

revolutionary. If nothing else it allowed Sellers to branch away from comedy, and certainly added gravitas to his gleeful desire for brave filmic experiment. While still an active Goon he had accepted and submerged himself in a thoroughly unpleasant, deliberately unfunny big-screen role: the ruthless Liverpudlian gangland boss and used-car salesman, Lionel Meadows, in *Never Let Go*. Directed and co-written by stoic and dogmatic John Guillermin, with a brisk, take-no-prisoners screenplay from Alun Falconer, the film was shot at Beaconsfield Studios, and hit London cinemas on 7th June 1960.

That opening scene could have come from *Two-Way Stretch*: the tense synth-heavy jazz musical score by John Barry; the furtive looks from petty criminal Fred Griffiths as he jemmies a licence plate off of an abandoned car; the deliberate, mannered movement as henchman John Bailey pays him for the log book; the knowing, wordless inclination of the head as hood David Lodge ushers him in to see the big man . . . Peter Sellers. John Le Mesurier is in the mix as a stern, humourless potential customer; Peter Jones is the waspish, blunt boss; Marianne Stone the cheery pub barmaid; Cyril Shaps the Eastern European cafe owner. However, despite this company of familiar comedy supporting actors, this is no joke. Peter and this beloved repertory company are the signifiers for a jolly romp. It makes the hard-hitting drama of *Never Let Go* all the more powerful. Poor hapless, ineffectual cosmetic salesman John Cummings (Richard Todd) has his Ford Anglia pinched by obnoxious youth Tommy Towers (Adam Faith). It's all the seed for the drama. And Sellers, like a smiling, moustache-twirling, hoary melodrama baddie, is at the heart of the corrupt web.

Initially offered the role of John Cummings, Sellers begged for the role of the heavy and, as he told a National Film Theatre audience that year, although a few grey hairs resulted and some film distributors dropped out, for "gimmick value only" it was agreed. For Sellers it was "a nice change to get away from the comedy parts."

It's certainly an uncomfortable watch. And, yes, despite the black-hearted, dark-under-the-eye make-up being a little stagey, Sellers is sublime. You totally believe his character. It's just a palpably disturbing experience to spend time with this snarling, hand-crushing, terrapin-crunching gangster. In the first act he hardly has any screen time at all. His brooding presence is all over it though: a smirk as he sets the heist in motion; a determined blast of his car horn as he summons blonde bombshell Jackie (Carol White) from the centre of attention of the seedy, young gang. Then Sellers storms in, perpetually grinning through his anger. Before his trapped, unshaven descent into boozer foolhardiness, Peter's performance as Lionel Meadows is a powerhouse of barely suppressed rage and corruption. An unblinking cobra in the bosom of English moral values. Even that air kiss to Carol White is horrible, malicious, controlling, and calculated. A prelude to his determined exploitation of the kid. In the same way he calls his car mechanic, played by Nigel Stock, "boy!" It's all undermining. With not a laugh in it. Wonderfully. "Peter was chuffed not to get a laugh. Not one", remembered David Lodge. "He revelled in playing this complete and utter bastard. You know, I've heard all these stories since Peter's death that he became the character he played on screen, well I can tell you that's cobblers. After a day of playing this horrible crook, focused, brilliant, Peter was then straight back to being Peter again. He thoroughly enjoyed the day's work, and then we laughed and laughed and laughed, until the next day's filming!"[1] For Peter, having his old mate David Lodge, as Cliff, at his right-hand side throughout had been reassuring. A talisman of reality. And I can only imagine the crowds leaving their local cinemas, grim and scared, with a sense of shuddering disquiet. A sight that would have sent Sellers into fits of giggles, for that was why he did it. So, having proved himself an actor of sheer sinister serious realism and, what's more, not under any control or expectations of public tastes, Peter took a deep breath and returned to comedy.

And the next project was *the* comedy.

---

1 Interview with the author, August 2003.

Chapter 7

"Wanted – Money! No reasonable offer refused."

Bloodnok

That comedy was *The Millionairess*. There is nothing new under the sun, for it was happily adapted from the creaky 1936 play by distinguished Irish playwright George Bernard Shaw. Still the sparked ignition of Britain's favourite character comedian and the most gorgeous Italian on film was more than enough to shove Sellers into the topper-most echelon of cinema celebrity. No less an international goddess as Sophia Loren was coming to London to star opposite him.

On and off the connection was clear and, certainly, judging on just their on-screen association the Sellers–Loren chemistry was electric. The infatuation that Loren's millionairess has for Peter's doctor in the film was pretty much mirrored by Peter's infatuation for Sophia Loren off. So much so that the debate concerning a romance has raged ever since. It was undoubtedly another straw on the camel's back for Anne Sellers, although not the one that finally broke it. Certainly Graham Stark forever maintained that the Loren affair was the peak of Peter's internal sexual fantasy. Sellers himself was more than happy to labour the point during his 1974 appearance on *Parkinson*. Naming no name but simply lapsing into a little boom-boody-boom. Milligan was adamant that Peter orchestrated an Elstree Studio get-together of the recently ex-Goons totally in order to allow Spike to walk in on the two stars of *The Millionairess*.[1]

---

1 "Rather than meeting me in the bar, Sellers had asked me to meet him in the Dressing Room. Odd, but OK. The door is ajar, and there's Sellers and Ms. Loren . . . not going through their lines, I can tell you. Sellers looks up and says through his Cheshire Cat grin, "I'll meet you in five minutes!". We had lunch and he never mentioned it. He just couldn't stop smiling." Spike Milligan, interview with the author, July 2000.

Whatever the truth, the tabloid speculation has successfully overshadowed Peter's sublime performance in *The Millionairess* for over sixty years. The Indian accent and mannerisms are perfect at a time when no Indian actor in mainstream Anglo-American cinema could have secured the budget and estimated box office for the project. More crucially the sentimentality and mawkishness of the play and the part is handled with care and subtlety by Sellers. The portrayal of Doctor Ahmed el Kabir is both humane and humorous, and not in any shape or form in a caricatured, silly voice sort of way. At all. He is a truly good man, a sympathetic and understanding physician, a man of principle, and a man of the people. He also falls in love at a steady, believable pace. Faced with the most beautiful woman in the world, the Doctor, unlike the actor playing him, does not lose control of all of his faculties. Instead he is admiring, and desirous, while remaining staid and professional.

So, yes, Sellers delivers a performance that is far, far better than he has ever been given credit for. The reason is simple. The press coverage, at the time of the Twentieth Century Fox release, on 18th October 1960, was wallowing in the Sellers–Loren inferno, while the feverish speculation, ever since, dominates a lovely, quiet, and still interpretation of the role. More than anything, of course, is *that* song. Even today audiences are occasionally shocked and not a little disappointed that Sellers and Sophia don't break into 'Goodness Gracious Me' during the preliminary medical examination scene.

And that song and that album speaks, or more over sings, volumes of that glorious working relationship that Peter and Sophia shared. It wouldn't end with the record, either, but the sheer verve and cheerful willingness to muck about and send herself up opposite the people's best-loved chameleon, paints Sophia as a self-aware icon and clever comedienne.

The album, *Peter and Sophia*, was released in November 1960 for the huge Christmas market,[1] and basked in the popularity of the

---

1 The serial number was PMC 1131. Parlophone and George Martin were really making it a bumper yuletide for Sellers on vinyl, for their *The Best of the Goon Shows No. 2* was also on the shelves, featuring 'The Scarlet Capsule', from February 1959, and 'Tale of Men's Shirts', from December 1959. Both shows were edited of their musical interludes.

film, with a still from *The Millionairess* on the cover. Still, despite solo Sophia tracks, the album is very much another Sellers long-player: he's joined by dear chum Graham Stark for 'Smith', an interview with the illustrious explorer Sir Eric Goodness, penned especially by Leslie Bricusse; while Munro and Smith wrote three cuts, 'Why Worry?'; 'Africa Today'; and 'Setting Fire to the Policeman', a nostalgic tour-de-force for Peter, as he embodies an elderly gentleman's playful memories of igniting his local bobby and swiftly running away.[1] Peter enjoys a couple of solo songs too: the faux romantic rendition of George Gershwin's 'Oh! Lady Be Good', which quickly and gloriously lapses into pastiche; and the gravelling, gargling, ghoulish 'Grandpa's Grave' which channels both a Willium Mate-alike, as well as a toffee-nosed bloke from the council.

However, it's the four tracks that Sophia and Sellers recorded together that spearheaded the album's success. Indeed, it was all part of Twentieth Century Fox's massive publicity push. The album ends with the dulcet tones of the duo warbling 'Fare Thee Well'; while Leslie Bricusse was back for the lyrical missive of passion 'I Fell in Love with an Englishman'. Loren once more proves herself a fine comedienne, and almost Peter's equal, on 'Bangers and Mash', when her typically Italianate wistfulness gives way to a cockney knees-up. Peter matches her, in reverse, with his Italian: "What'sa the matter Soph!" making his leading lady literally snort with delight. Sellers even has a third part to play, as the soppy squaddie mate of Peter's cocky, cockney charmer. This smooth-talking chancer, all wideboy confidence, chats up this Italian beauty and gets the red signal: "Droppa dead!" "There," the never-say-never, and ultimately getting-in-there soldier chuckles, "you can't say fairer than that!"

Topping them all, though, was, of course, 'Goodness Gracious Me', a song that, as planned, did much to keep the box office takings

---

1 In latter years this track became unwittingly controversial. I well remember a broadcast of it on Ray Moore's *The Saturday Morning Show* resulting in a stream of complaints that were addressed amidst much apology the following week. Still, quite possibly that very exposure of the track's wistful weirdness seeped into the subconscious of the adolescent creators of *The League of Gentlemen*, to help fuel their twisted view of the world.

of *The Millionairess* rolling in. The song has come to, unfairly and unrepresentatively, embody what the film is about. Certainly for those who haven't actually seen it. The passion is there, of course, but the Shavian grandeur uses love as a cipher for honourability. Indeed, the jolly, throwaway quality of the song, naturally, is a very different beast from the film. And certainly the two Sellers performances are very different too. Sellers recorded 'Goodness Gracious Me' as very much a jaunty music-hall number. Both he and Sophia are very much in character, but Sellers, gleefully, just cannot control the gusto of his old variety theatre days. This is a comedic three minutes. A very heightened Indian caricature, taking that under-played calm of the film as a shading, and injecting nylon lights, comic gulps, and delicious mugging, for comedy admirers in need of an instant fix.

It's glorious, of course, and the single entered the British Hit Parade on Thursday, 10th November 1960, reaching a peak of number four in the charts – Peter's highest ever position.[1] It got an awful lot of airplay. It was a fizzing champagne of a ditty, taking the playful fun of the film and cranking it to eleven.

Such was the impact of the marketing campaign that even contemporary comedians referenced it. In June 1961, when the inaugural episode of *Hancock*, Tony Hancock's solo starring television vehicle, was first transmitted on BBC Television, the lad himself was alone in his Earls Court apartment. Talking to himself, struggling with intellectual reading, and doing impersonations, Hancock muses on an Indian doctor: "What was his name?" he reflects. "Peter Sellers!" Hancock makes himself laugh. Even qualifying the joke: "No it wasn't . . ." before happily musing: "good film though!" Such was the popularity of *The Millionairess*. During the production of the film, in 1960, Sellers had been quoted that his

---

1 'Bangers and Mash' was rushed in as a follow-up, in January 1961, stalling at number twenty-two. Still, the *Goodness Gracious Me* team – lifting the hit song inspired by but never in *The Millionairess*, were originally determined to call their BBC sketch show *Peter Sellers Is Dead*. Brilliant, but contentious. Not in that Sellers was dead. He was. It's just the material shouldn't have been controversial.

favourite comedian was Tony Hancock, so the feeling was mutual.[1]

Such an instant key factor in popular culture was *The Millionairess*, that Sellers was recruited to play a starry cameo as an Indian neurologist in the British-filmed comedy reunion *The Road to Hong Kong*. Reviving a comic partnership that had been running, on and off, since Peter was in his early teens, Bob Hope and Bing Crosby gamefully staggered through this far better than it ought to be romp. Peter's popularity is clear, bearing in mind the other top names who lined up to take part included Frank Sinatra and Dean Martin as a couple of Italian astronauts; original *Road To . . .* girl Dorothy Lamour; and David Niven, as a Tibetan Monk caught sniggering at *Lady Chatterley's Lover*.[2] Less starry, but no less impressive, Sellers joined Katie Boyle and Russ Conway as a panellist on the Christmas Eve 1960 edition of *Juke Box Jury*. And he was still gleefully taking the corporate pound with one of the earliest chimpanzee-centric campaigns for PG Tips teabags, providing a frightfully English voiceover through playful tea-slurping. Not that he needed the money . . .

The Millionairess had put Sellers in the super-rich bracket. Soon after the film was released, film-maker Joe McGrath recalled: "going round Peter's place, and I just happened to look out of his window and saw five or six cars on the road outside. I said: 'My God Peter, how do you ever park here?' and he, rather sheepishly said, 'That's

---

1 Although it emphasises the ever so swift passing of a scant few years since both Sellers and Hancock were merrily struggling through the filming of *Orders Are Orders* together. *Hancock* creators Ray Galton and Alan Simpson co-wrote the Peter Sellers film *The Wrong Arm of the Law*, featuring Hancock's old mucker Bill Kerr, and many years later, in 1979, wrote *Le Petomane* for Sellers. It was the biopic of the legendary French music-hall performer who broke wind, without smell and in tune. Leonard Rossiter ultimately played the role. Peter's success as a film star would later rankle with Hancock, whose two attempts met with muted success, although it was Hancock who beat Sellers to the front cover of that 1960 *Film Fun* annual, in a shot from his finest starring vehicle, *The Rebel*, also written by Galton & Simpson. By the time of Hancock's suicide, in June 1968, he would have seen Sellers achieve what he himself had always wanted to achieve: to break Hollywood, currently riding high at the Box Office in *The Party*.

2 The Penguin Books publication in 1960 had provoked much public disquiet and a notoriously lengthy legal battle. Just twenty months earlier Sellers had beautifully mocked Bob Hope – and Steve Allen – as a couple of men who can read ancient scripts. Boom! – in the inaugural *Vintage Goons* presentation 'The Mummified Priest', transmitted on 22nd September 1958.

alright, Joe. They're all mine!'"[1]

The phenomenal popularity of *The Millionairess* certainly made Sellers one of the world's most bankable stars. As a result, spectres from his screen past were ripe for re-release. Indeed, *Penny Points to Paradise* re-emerged. Now tailormade as a Peter Sellers vehicle in light of his increased marquee value over the previous decade since it was made, it was lopped of great swatches of the original print for a shorter, more Sellers-centric film. In an even cleverer move to capitalise on the already existing multi-characters of Sellers in *Penny Points to Paradise*, these butchered prints were occasionally supplemented, and extended back to feature length, by adding even more Sellers eccentrics plucked from Adelphi's *Let's Go Crazy*. This gleefully shambolic mixture was released as a fifty-five-minute support picture. Called *Penny Points* and exclusively for the Australian market, it was now undoubtedly starring Peter Sellers, for better or worse. As far as Sellers was still concerned it was definitely for the worse. While desperately wanting to plug his latest release, and frustratingly reminded of this skeleton from the furthest recess of his comedy closet he considered it "a terrifyingly bad film".

Still, even this out-of-his-hands shade from his murky screen beginnings couldn't dampen the buzz and popularity of *The Millionairess*. Sellers embraced the clout the film gave him with Twentieth Century Fox. The result was the opportunity to satisfy his desire to direct his next starring film role. Fox readily agreed. Initially Peter favoured a film of *The Memoirs of a Cross-Eyed Man*, by James Wellard, the 1956 American novel of ugliness, disillusionment, and obsession – for a beautiful but horrid film star: "a bitch", as Peter saw her. Sellers was set to direct and play the haunted, lonely man with this destructive desire, but the budget proved exorbitant, and the casting of the female lead impossible. Versatile bitches were clearly hard to find in British film. Even an international search proved fruitless. Instead, his attention turned to an almost Chekhovian project. Peter's directorial debut would, in

---

1 Interview with the author, July 2003.

the end, be his only directorial credit, but the post-production of *Mr. Topaze*, was, at least, a thrilling time for him. Not least because just three weeks before the film was released, and, for the second year running, at a Variety Club of Great Britain ceremony held at the Savoy Hotel on 14th March 1961, Peter was named the Best Film Actor of 1960. *Mr. Topaze* was rather bluntly re-named *I Like Money* on its American release – from the cabaret song belted out by Nadia Gray and used as an exposure of Topaze's moral dilemma. The film hit British cinemas on 4th April 1961. Alas, few found the joke of a contented, poor nobody finding wealth and inner-satisfaction by dropping his integrity in favour of corruption, palatable – despite the presence of Johnny Speight as script associate. Gainfully employed as the chief writer for *The Arthur Haynes Show* on television, Speight would create Alf Garnett for BBC situation comedy *Till Death Do Us Part*. Sellers was first in the frame to play the loud-mouthed bigot in the *Comedy Playhouse* pilot, before Warren Mitchell landed the role of a lifetime.

The joke of *Mr. Topaze*, of course, was painfully close to Peter's own career path and mentality. Hungry for fame and position, it is all the more potent and powerful that *Mr. Topaze* was the first – and ultimately – only film Sellers would direct.[1] That he was prepared – eager indeed – to put his own anonymity and integrity to the sword for a glittering, international film career embroils the plot with a fizz that fairly pulses off of the screen. The bookending of Sellers leading a crocodile of kids through the streets of Paris, which is then reflected in his lowly ex-cohort and chum Michael Gough doing the self same thing at the film's end, is a body blow to the audience, to Gough, to everybody, in fact, save Peter's corrupted character. He puffs out his chest; walks away from true companionship; and faces the bright skyline with a determined air of building his business empire. That Sellers, as director, has encouraged Gough's performance to be in bright and garish and brilliantly over-played strokes, is shown to be

---

1 Despite Peter's active behind-the-camera involvement in *The Bobo and the Panthers*, students should file it along with *Night of the Hunter*, from Charles Laughton, and *One-Eyed Jacks*, from Marlon Brando, as excellent one-off film directing credits for supremely good film actors.

a master film-maker's twist here. At the end, Gough is crushed by the transformation of his colleague. Gough's performance is now subdued, quiet, and disinterested. While his friend has become a worshiper of wealth, he still retains his dedication to life as a humble schoolteacher.

Sellers also coaxes an over-wrought and over-ripe turn from Leo McKern. As the bulbous headmaster, the performance is pure caricature: all frantic hand-wringing, time-checking, and agitated mannerisms. There is no redemption for this pompous jobsworth either. He dismisses Topaze's love and offer of marriage to his daughter – Billie Whitelaw – and reveals himself as only interested in money money money, when he runs back to his dismissed, and now well-off, schoolteacher. McKern now offers him both re-employment, and instant membership of his family, by accepting, on his daughter's behalf, that offer of marriage. Whitelaw too – having used and abused Topaze's devotion in order to skip marking the school books of the class she teaches – flaunts and throws herself at the newly wealthy gentleman. In this regard Sellers still retains his dignity and integrity, ordering the wanton woman to leave, despite still longing for her feminine charms.

Herbert Lom, an Ealing pal from *The Ladykillers* gang, also wallows in an eye-rolling, eye-popping performance, that of continental corruption, injecting flecks of landed gentry power within the larger-than-life canvas of bully boy baddie. Sellers, himself, is content to be the passive and pastel central figure within the narrative. The foolish fool to which things happen rather than the anti-hero who moves the plot along . . . until the final reel, that is. Topaze is a quiet, awkward, intimidated, and resolutely sweet innocent, who tries and fails to keep his head above the waters of power and position. As film-maker Sellers populates the supporting cast with surprisingly few other familiar faces from his previous life as supporting film actor. There's Joan Sims – coquettish and quaint – as Topaze's secretary, resplendent in yellow gown and flirtatious giggles. And best of all, Sellers orchestrates one of the most scene-stealing and cynical cameos ever from John Le Mesurier. Duplicitous, sly, and utterly unscrupulous, this blackmailing blaggard is only on screen for a matter of minutes, but the performance is subtle and succulent. This totally dishonourable figure is the Ying and Yang contrast with Peter's complete honourability. The scene when Lom's dapper mover and shaker fixes the problem, and Le Mesurier cowers in the corner, framed next to a wooden effigy of a horned devil, is Peter's mise-en-scene at full pelt.

As director Sellers favours long shots, memorably in order to emphasise the lovesick romance that has clearly plagued Topaze for months. Whitelaw's Ernestine plays Topaze like a fine string instrument. She encourages the sexual foreplay, and pouts with disappointment when her ruse to seduce him by borrowing a bottle of red ink merely climaxes in her borrowing a bottle of red ink! When Topaze, eagerly lumbered with her stack of school books, parries and pirouettes around her, as she strolls purposefully away from him, the long shot Sellers employs enforces the angst at work. As Keaton and Tati knew, the long shot works beautifully for pratfalls and slapstick too. Sellers deploys it for a tentative trip, a moment of self-doubt, or a nervous shepherding into a chorus-line theatre dressing room.

The long shot is at play in reclination too: whether it is Sellers, in love, and in poverty, stretched out, philosophical and excited, in his shabby attic bedsit; or Herbert Lom, in elegant splendour, frantically nursing an anxiety headache with an ice pack.

The script, by the film's producer Pierre Rouve, is based very lovingly on Marcel Pagnol's play *Topaze*, and is applied to Peter's need for a fundamentally flawed but fundamentally good character. That character, Gaston Topaze, may end up happy and lost, but his path is both fascinating and fastidious for an actor desperately trying to prove himself as Sellers was desperately trying to prove himself at the end of 1960. It had been a year in which he had, for now, kissed *The Goon Show* farewell and had both international cinema success with *The Millionairess* and directed himself in a further Twentieth Century Fox production. Astronomical scarcely covers it. With

Topaze, this breathless, altruistic, comic-tragic figure, who "loves teaching", and clearly loves people, and then obsessively loves money, Sellers saw a mirror image of himself. It was a vehicle to impress his peers and, hopefully, and ultimately, in vain, a character to appeal to the general public. It was also a film for Sellers to appeal as an actor and not just a man of seemingly endless silly voices. However, as if to give his loyal Goonish crowd one nod to the good old days Peter's steady and unflappable teacher cracks, just once, while he berates a problem child who continually undermines his lesson with the playing of a musical box. This child, inevitably, lives up to the expectations that he will, once again, play the infernal machine. This unleashes Topaze's "glove of steel" that rests, forever, waiting, behind the languid facade of the timid schoolteacher. At that instance, Peter's voice ventures into the high-pitched, frantic insanity of a Goon character. Just for a split second. It's as if to prove that, yes, it really is our loveable radio comedian, behind that genuine beard, those cheap spectacles, and that endearingly and frustratingly vulnerable character of Mr. Topaze. That its relative box-office failure caused the film to be semi-forgotten is nothing short of tragedy. As it is, *Mr. Topaze* can hold its head up as high and proud as the titular character does at the film's end.

Mr. Topaze was a brave attempt; akin to *Never Let Go*, the film gave Peter a challenge and an opportunity to prove himself. In the end, though, Peter happily accepted that there was nothing wrong in having fun with gloriously silly comic voices, and the audience certainly preferred seeing Sellers skipping with dexterity from one gloriously silly voice to another.

Still, if Peter could play comedy on his own terms, with great swathes of pathos, even bathos, and lots of romantic leading man status, then all the better. He may have been straight back into comedy off the back of *Mr. Topaze*, but *Only Two Can Play* had similar weight and gravitas. Cast as Welsh lothario librarian John Lewis, the film was based on the Kingsley Amis novel *That Uncertain Feeling*. The novel, first published in August 1955, is told in the first person, from John's point of view, with this revealing self-portrait: "My face is a round and rubicund one, and a girl I once knew used to say it looked cheerful, but that was before I got this job." Very faithfully written for the screen by Bryan Forbes, produced by Leslie Gilliat, and directed by Leslie's older brother, Sidney Gilliat, the film was most definitely for adults only. It was, at the time, the most adult of British comedies. When it was premiered on 11th January 1962 it was the first X-rated comedy film released in Britain, although the controversial asides mainly add up to Virginia Maskell discussing her bra – sticking it to her revealing dress to avoid a society wardrobe malfunction; and Peter readily admitting that there was no affair and "I didn't go to bed with her" when the married couple reunite at the film's end. Still, the mere suggestion of an extramarital dalliance was enough. Certainly in 1962.[1] Sellers relished the opportunity to present a terribly flawed romantic leading role, a lady's man who forever uses his position as a librarian in the library of the fictional South Wales village of Aberdarcy to pick up women. Well, anything to relieve the boredom. That, and a sideline career as the drama critic for the local newspaper. While the love triangle between his downtrodden but lovely wife (Virginia Maskell) and the blonde continental bombshell (Mai Zetterling) is the heart of the story, it's the script's mockery of artistry pretension which really enlivens Peter's performance.

It's a worthy case of extreme talents at the very top of their game – the sparkling, sultry and sexy script by Forbes skilfully retains the social upheaval and disappointment of the novel, while allowing Sellers to give a stunningly truthful performance of jaded husband, father (of three, if you count the imaginary friend, whose invisible bottom he kisses goodbye, with a warm, wry look to his wife) and frustrated lover. There is a real sense of the clock ticking on his perceived masculinity. Even at home, from his own daughter Gwyneth. While he is miserable and semi-snug in bed, she disturbs his snatched sleep with a playful knocking on his cranium, and the

---

1 And it was a trend Sellers would actively embrace with *There's a Girl in My Soup*, and *Where Does it Hurt?*

crushing, cheerful enquiry: "Were you attractive to women?" This is a niggling thought rammed home when, spying a couple of virginal, but very sexy, tennis players (the very sexy Marie Devereux and Eve Eden) he takes his chance and flirts with one as he retrieves their out-of-reach ball. Those eyes light up, the grin becomes predatory, and he enters the game: "You're winning!" he smirks. The young girl only thinks of tennis, not vital statistics, and the final insult before getting on with the set is that she smiles and says: "Thank you, sir!" The pain of defeat on Peter's face is palpable. Thank heavens hot and happening Mai Zetterling roars up in her sports car to stroke his ego.

The film, in the main, strokes the ego of Sellers too. It comes at the very tail-end of that immediately pre-heart attack, British movie puppy fat era, and the actor fare smoulders with mean, good health. There's that Italian lover that beats within the chest of many a red-blooded Welshman. As his eyes lock with a brunette across the paperbacks in the library, here's a man on a mission, and a mission he, invariably, has won. Up to now. His cosy domain is a hot bed of hotties: brunettes, in the main, within his place of work, and tied up with his luscious brunette at home; and blondes outside of work – notably Marjie Lawrence on the bus – twice – and, of course, the exotic war bride of Mai Zetterling. Her revelation that she misses the war – because of all the handsome military men on her tail – is perhaps the most shocking moment of all. Sex conquers battle. It was a common attitude to hold for people who had got through the war and made the best of it. The early sixties may have been the dawning of a new age of love and peace, but this generation wallowed in memories of love and war.

That moment as she willingly submits to the sexual situation, sensually mutters "carry me!", and opens herself up to the affair, is the key to the relationship and the key to the film. As Zetterling freely admits when the actual deed of sex is interrupted, at least the man has committed to the affair. That is enough. For now. Of course, this being a comedy, and a British comedy at that, the sexual antics always end in hilarious disaster – from an inquisitive cow poking its head into the gadget-strewn motor car to the burning down of the theatre presenting the turgid play. The pre-show piano recital is so excruciating that Sellers, quite literally, eats his theatre programme. The early abandonment of the performance of the play is also key to the exposure of Peter's subterfuge. The local paper publishes his impossible theatrical review regardless, and blows his alibi with the wife. It is the very meat and potatoes of farce convention. And it is extremely Peter Sellers.[1]

Although *Only Two Can Play* remains one of Peter's most satisfying, grown-up performances, there is also ample opportunity for the clown to clown. The high society party, very much pre-empting Peter's Hollywood bash in *The Party*, has moments of lavatorial playfulness, with his sneaky library colleague (Kenneth Griffith) hiding away in shame. You see, he has let down Mr. and Mrs. Lewis in babysitting duties in order to attend the party himself. Peter's frustratedly aggressive pounding on the door of a ridiculously long, engaged toilet: "Somebody dead in there!" is a moment of mastery comic angst. A pre-echo of *The Party* is even more clearly evoked in the waiting room for the job interview. Sellers pulls at a towel dispenser and the towel keeps coming and coming and coming. If this isn't Tati in terms of the Taffy I don't know what is.

Only Two Can Play reaches its zenith of frantic farce when the illicit couple of Sellers and Zetterling are – almost – caught with their proverbial pants down by her husband, a typically officious and bumptious turn by Raymond Huntley. Sellers goes full-on bedroom romp here. Even the vocal characterisation gets a little more strangulated; a little more zany; a little more Goonish. This is particularly evident when he is desperately making his escape, and assumes the role of the household's butler cum doorman. Here his performance lapses into the only truly Goon-like line in the film. Well the line isn't Goon-like, it's a mundane exclamation to cover

---

1 This neat comic conceit isn't in the Amis novel at all. John and Elizabeth simply get bored of the performance and leave. What is in the Amis novel is lots of slapstick vignettes – trouble with a rolling parked car; multiple hats falling; business with a kettle and a kitchen sink too small to fill it – that Blake Edwards could have pulled an entirely different film out of. In the spring of 1986 Denis Lawson starred in a faithful four-part series from BBC Wales. Reverting to the original title, *That Uncertain Feeling* cast Brenda Blethyn as Jean and Sheila Gish as Elizabeth.

his exit, but it is Peter's delivery that slips. Gloriously. This is Goon-like. Pure Light Programme!

The encounters with that ever-dependable repertory company of British film actors are also at a peak in *Only Two Can Play*. Graham Stark is, of course, exemplary as the slightly seedy, slightly odd, book borrower in the library, clearly fancying Peter's character or, at the very least, wanting to be his best friend in order to gain access to the most controversial and stimulating literature. Peter's disgust is clear. He looks at Stark as if a nasty smell has invaded his nostrils. Sellers is the top dog here, shifting him out of his eyeline as he gazes at Zetterling, fuelling Stark's desire while disliking him intensely.

Rather more socially awkward is the hilarious vignette with John Le Mesurier. All in the course of getting away with his affair, Sellers assumes the role of a plumber and inspects the boiler, much to Le Mesurier's chagrin. It is an unforgettable moment, not least for Le Mesurier who obsesses about Peter's personal or family connections with plumbers during the job interview later in the film. Surely if this isn't the same man, it must be his brother!

It is this sniff of promotion that underlines Peter's affair. Zetterling knows it and so does he. She has the power to get him the job and, in turn, she has the power to provide his family with more money. Even though Peter's character has little interest in it. He is even reluctant to post off the application at that first breakfast table conflab with his wife. Still, the thrill of the chase of the skirt is what gets the fires within John Lewis flamed, and if he gets a bit more in his pay packet each month as a result, so much the better. The fact that his moral code – both martial and literal – wins in the end, is the measure of the man, and the fact that we root for this funny, overly sexed librarian.

Richard Attenborough, playing pompous and self-important playwright Gareth Probert, is not only an old boyfriend of Peter's wife, but also the writer of the play that Sellers had unwittingly, prematurely reviewed: it's the play that should have played before the theatre burned down, you see. A neat plot twist to lumber Peter, and let in his chief rival with his wife.

Unsurprisingly, the friction between Sellers and Attenborough is brilliant. Brief, but brilliant. These are stags at dawn, sizing each other up, one taunting the other. Peter's performance goes up a gear when the two are trapped together at that swanky party. There is a pressure-boiler anger just about to explode, a fundamental distrust and dislike. Attenborough puts down the librarian with a biting: "Still peddling rubbish to the masses?" Sellers comes straight back with: "Yes! Still writing it?" Wow! As a subtext, Peter's recent film directorial shortcoming adds to his passionate playing of all this pretension-popping. Conversely, Mai Zetterling, having been a glamorous breath of Swedish fresh air in British film from the late forties[1] would make her first documentary film later in 1961 and go on to be a director of distinction.

Sellers as an actor reaches another level here. This is a sex comedy, for sure, but there is absolutely no childish sniggering-behind-hands sex comedy: although it baulks at John and Elizabeth actually having sex, as they do in the Amis novel. Still, it's a truthful, sexually-charged, often heart-breaking domestic love story. With all the rough edges left in. It's also uproariously funny.

The role of John Lewis undoubtedly points in the right direction, towards those dysfunctional romantic leads that Sellers craved. Still, as was so often the case, the insecurity of the actor dictated that he make himself go two steps forward and then one step back. Amidst brave experiment his mind would often turn to the comfort blanket of a full-throttle comic character role, an easier, sillier character to play. This trait was twofold. It would reassure his sensibilities as an actor, and reassure him that his faithful audience were reassured, that those glorious, silly voices and that outlandish eccentric make-up were never too far away.

So, if you didn't like *Only Two Can Play* or, more likely, weren't old enough to get in to see it, Peter had his General Leo Fitzjohn in *Waltz of the Toreadors* for you. It's a repertory theatre curmudgeon. Indeed,

---

1 Notably the title role in the 1947 film *Frieda*; as Teresa Guiccioli opposite Dennis Price in *The Bad Lord Byron*; and alongside Tyrone Power, while he was reading a copy of *The Mouse That Roared*, on the set of *Seven Waves Away*.

Peter's performance makes perfect sense when you consider that the role had been played in the original 1957 West End stage production by Sir Ralph Richardson. The Rank Organisation premiered the film version, in London, on 12th April 1962, and in that year since his one and only film as a director, and the two years since *The Goon Show* had ceased to be an ongoing concern, Peter was back to over-frisky whiskers, and batty, wide-eyed over-acting. Indeed, there's much of Bloodnok about his aged military buffoon. Totally intentional too.

Speaking in 1972 Sellers revealed that *The Goon Show*'s Bloodnok was very much a product of Milligan's childhood in the Raj but the light and shade of the character came from Peter's own time: "in India during the war." He was a "very strong character; a dreadful character, who would do anything . . . for money, [but was] always worried he's going to get caught out." This is the essence of Fitzjohn too, a character that piles layer upon layer of backstory, grief, frustration, and humiliation onto the radio will-o'-the-wisp. As an actor Sellers ladles truth and heartache onto his military madman and, as a result, it's a most misunderstood screen performance.

Certainly, this is Sellers having the time of his life, fleshing out a familiar, lost friend. Despite initial reluctance to hide behind old-age make-up – the very essence of the veteran soldier premise, after-all – this is Sellers back in the dressing-up basket in which he felt safe, contented, and, despite himself, his most creative. That remnant of French frolics Dany Robin has a ball in it too. And, with Peter filing for divorce from Anne on 11th November 1961, Dany was that final straw! The latest international glamour co-star that Sellers fell for, amused, and failed to take any further than the screenplay allowed!

Although it could be assumed to be a lazy return to stock characterisation, *Waltz of the Toreadors* saw Sellers reunite with a talent he greatly admired, *Never Let Go* director John Guillermin.[1]

---

1 Both *Waltz of the Toreadors* and *Never Let Go* were selected for the 2002 Carlton DVD box set *The Peter Sellers Collection*, along with *The Wrong Arm of the Law*, and *Soft Beds, Hard Battles*. A moment from *Waltz of the Toreadors* was also plucked, from the concurrent compilation series *Best of British*, to include Sellers in the roll-call of departed stars at the end of the Terry Wogan-fronted chat show *Wogan's Film Fun*, in 1986. When the showreel of late greats was introduced, Kenneth Connor, representing the Carry Ons, feigned a fatal heart attack. Anything for a giggle. Sellers would have approved.

Working, once again, for Independent Artists, Wolf Mankowitz adapted the Jean Anouilh play, and the film proved to be a massive hit. It gave the people what they wanted. Sellers being funny and saucy. With no fuss. Or so it would seem at first. However, although very much Bloodnok the Movie II, the film is much more than a resurrection of a weary, albeit fruity, old stage romp. The love triangle at its beating centre does provide Sellers with many comedic opportunities. None played with more relish than his sword versus umbrella battle with a wily and wiry doctor cum car mechanic (Cyril Cusack) who inspires forthright jealous rage at the thought of a dalliance with Peter's bonkers, bedraggled, bag of bones wife (played by distinguished stage actress Margaret Leighton, at her most bonkers and bedraggled). The object of the retired old General's passion is a French Mademoiselle Ghislaine (the role played with ravishing elan by our European screen goddess Dany Robin). The interminable wait to consummate their love – seventeen years since an impromptu fling round the dance floor to the 'Waltz of the Toreadors' – is the frantic and farcical heart of the action. It is funny, of course, but more than that, it is painfully poignant. The flashbacks to a youthful, dashing Sellers, full of words of love and adventurous plans are the first hints that there is a dashing romantic lead within the tired old military figure. The rampant horse statue at the fountain during the love at first sight romance is a bristling, sparkling echo of things to come: namely the rather pathetic, murky figure that the retiring General cuts as he reluctantly bids farewell to his regiment. The flashback to his glory days adds sentiment and poignancy to our anti-hero. We see him fall apart and fall into step with the environs of his dusty, private quarters at home.

Like a comedic *Citizen Kane* he is the reluctant prisoner of his own great wealth, and his own loveless marriage. It is a union that has descended into hatred, and, thus, Peter's overall performance itself is more pathetic than comedic. There is a powerful moment, again opposite Cyril Cusack's calm and collected medic, in which Sellers looks wistfully into the dead embers of a fire. Director Guillermin shoots his actor from the side, his pained eyes averted from the camera. The delivery is sombre, one-note, muted. "I'm empty, my friend," he mutters. And he is. Emotionally and spiritually done with life. Later, when his youthful rival in warfare and wedlock (John Fraser) is court-martialled, Sellers is a red-eyed, teary-eyed mess.

Interestingly, during the film's production, Peter returned to his grass comic roots of BBC Radio, guest-starring on the Light Programme, on Christmas Day 1961, for the prestigious broadcast of *The Bob Hope Christmas Show*. Hope was a Showbiz pal in the wake of Peter filming his bit for *The Road to Hong Kong*, set for its British release the following March. The radio revue was scripted by Denis Goodwin, and support came from horror icon Boris Karloff, mellow, Bing Crosby-admiring, crooner Michael Holliday, and super stooges Jerry Desmonde and Warren Mitchell. It was yet another ratcheting up of Peter's comedy credibility, and it's a strength that shows in *Waltz of the Toreadors*.

Even the slapstick elements of the film have a tragic twist to them – most of the principals end up getting a soaking (at least once) with Sellers dropping, along with a collapsing balcony, into a water barrel at the local inn. It's the final, heart-breaking chapter in his lady love's desperate attempt to finally bed him. She is a vision: angelic and desperate, but Sellers is waylaid by a horde of cheery fox hunters (uncredited cad Guy Middleton and burly wag Howard Marion Crawford, among them). Indeed, this baggage of familiar faces: Cardew Robinson as a chirpy undertaker; Raymond Huntley as a gruff Military Judge; John Le Mesurier as a tentative reverend, merely adds to the power of Peter's performance. It's a staggering essay of old-age wanderlust, peppered with pals from jollier films. Even a lustful bound through the window of the wrong room is more inevitably a moment of despair than bedroom farce.

It is certainly not a comical character, merely a flawed, broken man with comic interludes. Indeed, the only chinks of light in the shade; joy in the maudlin; is when the General spots a pretty female face – from the buxom, mature dressmaker Mrs. Bulstrode

(Vanda Godsell) to the pretty, and willing new chambermaid (Claire Marshall). Indeed, the marketing campaign vigorously sold the film as a sex romp. Across the English territories the chief poster image was that of crusty old Sellers pinching the extremely naive but willing bottom of the saucy new chambermaid, Rosemary (Catherine Fuller). However, Peter's character is cruel to his two daughters (delightful early turns for Prunella Scales and Denise Coffey), calling them ugly and forever dismissing them from his sight; while he is introspective and wistful whenever he hears the haunting refrain of a solitary bugle. The sound pricks him back to the knowledge that he has left his army career behind and is now, seemingly, condemned to be at home with his wife for a lacklustre eternity. His resigned, annoyed reactions to her continual need for attention escalates to the point that his insincere cry of "my love" is spat out of the corner of his mouth. This is his purgatory. His penance. Dark, hooded, haunted eyes mark this out as a truthful, deep, tragicomedy performance. It is a farce with an iron heart, and Peter's performance is arguably his most unsung and sensational. Well, not completely unsung. Not at the time, at least, for he won the Best Actor award at the San Sebastian Film Festival.

With that one step back, or at least two feet treading water, proving popular, Peter felt confident to dive into waters new, and waters deliciously dangerous. Stanley Kubrick hove into view, and Peter was keen to swim in his ken.

Chapter 8

"I like a director to allow me to extemporize and be spontaneous.
Now it's all about having fun."

Peter Sellers, 1965

It was Stanley Kubrick who was to direct the ever-controversial novel of *Lolita* into the ever-controversial film of *Lolita*, with the full blessing of the novelist who had written it, Vladimir Nabokov. Indeed, Nabokov is credited with the adaptation although Kubrick wrote his screenplay out of existence. Nabokov's was dripping with material from the book that would have got the film denied distribution. Besides, apart from that it was over 400 pages long. At the time Kubrick's producer partner and trusted script-puncher James B. Harris muttered: "You couldn't make it. You couldn't *lift* it!" Kubrick's version was a blessing for Sellers, for sure. In Kubrick's script, Peter's role, that of chameleon and slimeball Clare Quilty, benefitted from a far more multi-layered characterisation and, as a result of Kubrick's re-shuffling of vital plot-points, gave Sellers an early opportunity to impress. Opposite James Mason as Humbert Humbert, no less. All of this story massaging was purely as a vehicle to indulge and exploit both the popularity and versatility of Sellers, which Kubrick relished almost as much as Sellers. Although Kubrick was keen to have Sellers deploy a New York accent for Quilty, the director had been made all too aware that a precise vocal hook was not only what his actor needed to get interested in the role, but also to stay interested in the role. In the end Sellers incorporated elements of Kubrick's own voice, although it was a recording the director played, of jazz impresario Norman Ganz, that provided

Peter with the key to the character. In the speaking voice of Ganz was the far-too loud, lisping otherness that gave Sellers the seed to plant and water and grow. Thus, Peter starts the film as the clipped and pretentious intellectual, matching the suave James Mason ping for pong in the table tennis match. His lacklustre: "Gee, I'm really winning here!" not enough to deter or undermine the singularity of Mason's hatred and disgust. Humbert is not here to play games with this creature. He's here for revenge. Sellers, hungover, dishevelled, and beleaguered, is wrapped in a curtain – Roman Emperor-like. He's the tinpot despot of his own faded mansion. Those first five minutes would remain among Peter's own personal favourite glimpses at what he thought he was capable of on screen. He really thought that scene worked. It was that sense of joy: "at the time when you are doing it, doing the take on the floor . . ."[1] that by some miraculous coming together of Sellers, Mason and Kubrick, retained the glee and energy of the moment of creation. This was rare for Sellers. A comedic fusion that he loved at the time, and that still resonated with his high standard of quality five, ten, even fifteen years later.

Off the back of this imperishable beginning, the story of Lolita is told in flashback, casting Sellers as the annoyingly relentless terrier snapping at the heels of Mason's infatuated and doomed Humbert. Sellers morphs into the dogged policeman at the hotel in which Humbert and Lolita are staying. Then he is the High School psychologist Doctor Zempf, then the personification of intrusive press journalism at Lolita's play, and finally an anonymous phone-caller with a survey. Sellers is omnipresent bedevilment. A grinning irritation.

Fresh from the comic controversy of *Only Two Can Play*, *Lolita* was very controversial indeed. Internationally distributed by MGM, from 13th June 1962, it was an X-certificate. Although both in looks and actions Sue Lyon, as Lolita, is twelve going on twenty-eight, the actress was in fact fourteen at the start of filming, and fifteen when the film wrapped. By the time Lolita hits that age in the novel Humbert refers to her as his: "aging mistress". At both suggesting this extreme

---

1 *Parkinson*, BBC Television, 1974.

youth and capturing the attractive sexuality of Lolita, Sue Lyon was perfect casting. She is assured, and confident, as Humbert Humbert crumbles in her hands.

Between filming *Lolita* and the release of this pivotal and prestigious production, Sellers had readily accepted the role of Wilfred Morgenhall in *The Dock Brief*. It was something of a one-set, character-driven piece. Pretty much Peter's sole reason for taking it on was to allow a gleeful on-screen jousting with Richard Attenborough, whom he had relished working with – all too briefly – within the satirical world of the Boultings and, most recently of all, *Only Two Can Play*.[1]

The Dock Brief was shot at Shepperton Studios, in March and April 1962. However, for all the sheer, anticipated joy of working closely with Attenborough, this passion project initially proved a problem for Sellers. During pre-production he struggled to get a feel for his character of the hopeless failure of a barrister. For writer and associate producer John Mortimer it was conceived and written as a rather faded southern chap: part Oxbridge education, part Thames estuary loafer. For Sellers, there was nothing in the script to give him the key to unlock this character. Taking lunch together at Shepperton Studios, scribe and star chatted idly about this and that until, as Mortimer remembered: "Mr. Sellers unfortunately ordered a plate of cockles. He had been desperately uncertain as to how to play the part, but the shellfish came to him with a whiff of the sea and the memory of a scrappy moustache. He felt he had been thrown the lifeline of a voice and work could begin."[2] Under gentle pressure from Mortimer, the beleaguered director James Hill ultimately dragged Sellers away from a desire to adopt a north country accent toward something like standardised 'posh English' which would be more easily digestible by the Americans. If indeed anything in this gently off-kilter courtroom fantasy could be described as standardised.

There's certainly a touch of *A Christmas Carol* about the ability

---

1 Just two months after *The Dock Brief* was released, Peter would make a surprise appearance on Richard Attenborough's *This Is Your Life*, on 18th December 1962.

2 *Clinging to the Wreckage: A Part of Life,* by John Mortimer (Weidenfeld and Nicolson, 1982).

our two protagonists possess: both the fading, failed barrister, and insignificant wife-murderer, able, as they are, to eavesdrop on their pasts. Sellers is most Scrooge-like, as the youthful student, surviving on herrings and strong tea, while he studies his Latin Law in a gloomy bedsit and his fun flapper friends whoop it up within the frivolous glamour of the late 1920s. While Richard Attenborough is matter-of-fact about his guilt, Sellers, as the pathetic legal representation, is at turns furtive and jittery; and then energised and enthused. A lonely, lowly life of crossword puzzles and patiently waiting to be called to the bar, tangibly evaporates as his glee for criminal law takes over. There is a high pitch in his voice; a clenched fist of ruthless determination. In the fantasy playground that is the deserted courtroom of the imagination, Sellers and Attenborough play out possible scenarios, with interjections from the lost wife (Beryl Reid) and the laughter-fuelled lodger (David Lodge). The close-up two-hander conversation between Sellers and Attenborough may rely on heavy, repertory company theatre make-up, and bask in an engaging, if wafer-thin premise, but the subtle pauses, and the agonising exchanges, are rich indeed. Sellers has moments of painful beauty during the domestic flashbacks. At a suggestion that the wife and lodger are sexually entwined, this man of law turns away from the scene. He actually inspects the wallpaper, so consumed is he with awkwardness, when there is nothing awkward going on. At the point of the actual trial Sellers is incompetent, and invisible. Simply a mess of clumsy slapstick with his legal papers.

Even the playfully absurdist camera of James Hill cannot fully linger on his embarrassing display. We withdraw, only to see the disconcerted and beaten man wander from the court, a thoroughly defeated man. Sellers the actor, of course, triumphs. He trumps everybody. He even, rather wonderfully, over-dubs the few lines of dialogue delivered by Eric Woodburn as the aged Judge.

At the, as joyous as possible denouement, Sellers is crest-fallen; quietly-disgusted even at the reason for his one and only client's release from prison. There is a closing, Chaplinesque fade-out of shared skipping over Westminster Bridge which, with something of a pre-echo of *Being There*, has bushels of sentimental friendship pulsating in every frame.

Premiered at the Plaza Theatre, London, on 20th September 1962, *The Dock Brief* was a product of Metro-Goldwyn-Mayer's stake in British film-making, a leg of the business which, at the time, was happily churning out colloquial films with the hope of a strong pay-back in America. This Sellers effort, as with Spike Milligan in *Postman's Knock* and Eric Sykes in *Village of Daughters*, did not break the *Goon Show* generation en masse stateside. Although it notched up profits of $141,000, it yet again divided the transatlantic audiences, with a title change. Across America *The Dock Brief* was released as *Trial & Error*. Still, there's something very Sellers about a comic murder case that revolves around the victim's passion for laughing uproariously at "radio jokes . . .", and the ultimate crime seemingly to rest on an ordinary little man with absolutely no sense of humour at all. Once a Goon, always a Goon.

So much so that Peter eagerly indulged himself in his love of multi-character productions with *Bridge on the River Wye*, a long-playing record project which saw Spike Milligan lovingly pinch from his own script for the December 1957 *Goon Show* 'Africa Incident'. The original had been transmitted when *The Bridge on the River Kwai* was extremely prevalent, but five years later the Oscar-winning David Lean war epic was still a touchstone for stoic courage in the face of enemy atrocity. The disc was produced by Sellers favourite George Martin, and released in November 1962 – the third year on the bounce that you could find some Goon comedy under your Christmas tree. Just a month earlier Martin had scored with a certain beat group from Liverpool, and 'Love Me Do' and the Beatles shifted Martin's career from novelty nonsense to world-conquering pop. However, for the comedy connoisseur, the irresistible gimmick of *Bridge on the River Wye* was the casting of two Goons, Sellers and Spike, alongside two of the new kids on the comedy block, *Beyond the Fringe* Cambridge smarties Peter Cook and Jonathan

Miller. The humour is pure Goon though. Pre-Pythonesque in the way the story is recorded and unfolds. "For best results, play this record in a circular fashion," quips the sleeve note, but the play itself is literally a circular story. On a loop. Almost. You could play it forever, continually flipping the disc and starting again. And it would kind of work, despite Peter's salute to variety punchlines and Goon composer Wally Stott's music-hall styled closing sting.

For Sellers the appeal of the production was clear. He could play Alec Guinness. For real. His Major Barbara is pristine Guinness. There are even some speeches almost exactly culled from *The Bridge on the River Kwai* dropped into the script to allow Sellers to be quiet and reflective and military-minded . . . before gleefully defusing the tension with some silliness and send-up. There's room for a Willium Mate cameo too, while his Brigadier Startling-Grope is Bloodnok in disguise. There's the Scottish Doc and U Bai Dung: a lovely, subservient Indian characterisation which is subtle and kindly and played with gentle heart and dedication. It certainly proves that Sellers could play a more convincing Indian than Alec Guinness, a feat he attempted in David Lean's *A Passage to India*, while Sellers could pretty much out-Guinness Guinness in the hail and hearty, British stiff-upper-lipped stakes too.[1]

As a punctuation mark between the World War II survivors and the Oxbridge generation, *Bridge on the River Wye* is a comedy crossroads indeed. Some ten years later even Sellers had made the connection: "You know, our humour was really way ahead of its time. All those satire boys, *Beyond the Fringe*, *Private Eye*, they took on what we had started."[2] With Cook and Miller just about to take *Beyond the Fringe* to New York, this was the young pretenders acknowledging the debt they owed to *The Goon Show*. Cinema audiences in the summer of 1962 had also had the opportunity to

---

1 Spike Milligan, while gleefully at ease as 'Field-Marshall' Eccles, mugs and splutters his way through the Japanese oppressor General Itchikutchi. None of the subtlety of Peter Sellers is considered necessary nor attempted. Jonathan Miller and Peter Cook, who also narrates the whole epic with gusto, are joined by Peter Rawley and Patricia Ridgeway in the cast. The disc was issued on the Parlophone label: PMC 1190.

2 'Goons let loose on air again', by Peter Waymark, *The Times*, Monday, 1st May 1972.

revisit the Goonish pioneering of Sellers and Spike, for *The Case of the Mukkinese Battle-Horn* was playing in American theatres, as the support picture to *Very Important Person*: the James Robertson Justice and Leslie Phillips and dual-acting Stanley Baxter prisoner of war camp comedy that was re-titled *A Coming-Out Party*, in America. Of *Battle-Horn* no less a respected orator as Bosley Crowther of the *New York Times* got the premeditated slapdash point by writing: "This little item is winging from the moment it begins ... His style is that of the familiar Peter Sellers crossed with Groucho Marx. As it happens, the comic quality is not superior, and the jumble of travesty and farce, showing definite influences of Mack Sennett, soon wears redundant and thin. It is a good thing Mr. Sellers and his helpers didn't try to stretch it for longer than a half hour ..." Clearly nobody told film-maker Blake Edwards for he was about to sign up Sellers and stretch that Mack Sennett business to breaking point and beyond. Bosley Crowther further noted on *Battle-Horn* that Sellers: "plays a blase and bilious inspector ... [who] goes through a wild and inane business of scratching around for clues." Bingo!

On Monday, 19th November 1962 filming started on *The Pink Panther*. As well as under the shadow of the death of Peter's Dad Bill, in October 1962, it came in the wake of two crunch decisions. Peter Ustinov – still clutching his Best Supporting Actor Oscar for *Spartacus*, from April 1961 – had turned down such Franco frippery. Ironically, 1962 saw Parlophone release the extended-play platter *The Two Peters* which paired a couple of humorous classical musical Ustinov tracks with Peter Sellers and Graham Stark's 'Fuller's Earth' routine, written by Peter Munro-Smith in which Sellers, as Jeremiah Fuller, frantically defends the International Flat Earth Association and the end of the world: "So, I'm a day out ... what's a day!?"[1]

---

1 The EP boasted a glorious caricature cover by Tony Hart, featuring Sellers cranking a phonograph's handle while holding a false moustache in the other hand. A subtle nod to his man of many faces reputation. The Parlophone serial number is GEP 8853. Sellers and Stark had performed as a seventy-thirty double act on *The Jo Stafford Show*, transmitted by ATV on 9th September 1961. Ostensibly a British showcase for the American songstress the episode, sub-titled 'The Language of Language', featured a comedy sketch explaining how relentless mishaps can result from the simplest misunderstanding in conversation. Along the way jolly Jo warbled such seemingly contradictory – but not really! – classics from the Gershwin and Berlin Great American Song-Book 'A Foggy Day' and 'Isn't It a Lovely Day'.

Again playing with recording conventions, Stark's beleaguered interviewer halts the track by screaming for his engineer, the listener, anyone, to turn the sound off. This brings Peter's rant to an abrupt end. It was a performance that Charles Fox's sleeve notes called a: "brand-new addition to his gallery of British characters." For Blake Edwards, it certainly wasn't a case of if we can't have that Peter, let's have this Peter, but it was a record that most assuredly twined the two comic performers, Ustinov and Sellers, together in the hearts and minds of the public. Grains of sand, my friends. Grains of sand.[1]

The desperate Blake Edwards offer – of ninety grand for a long month's filming – was one that Sellers couldn't refuse. And didn't! Still, he was only in a free mindset to accept the last-minute invitation to play Inspector Clouseau because he had turned down another film opportunity. The reason being that he remained reluctant to return to the scene of a cinematic crime. Ironic, considering the career-defining, oft-resurrected, role he was about to take on. Leonard Wibberley, who had written the original novel of *The Mouse That Roared*, had published a novel and a direct Grand Fenwick sequel, *The Mouse on the Moon*, in 1962. It was filmed from September that year for a 1963 release. Even with the brief raffish support of old pal Terry-Thomas, and the madcap direction of old pal Richard Lester, Peter was well out of the film. Crucially out of it, of course. As with Peter's absences from *The Goon Show*, a starry cast of seasoned film headliners were recruited to play the Sellers roles: Margaret Rutherford as the dithering duchess; Ron Moody as the devious politician; and Peter's old screen pal Bernard Cribbins playing the blank canvas leading man: "It took three actors to almost get close to how good Peter had been . . . And I was one of them! No false modesty. He could do something with nothing that was nothing short of miraculous. That's what I had. Nothing. I did my best. It was a popular film. But I wasn't Sellers."[2]

---

1 In 1968, just before shooting started on *The Party*, Sellers announced that he was to star – opposite Ustinov – in a film of Eugene Ionesco's *Rhinoceros*. To be directed by Alexander Mackendrick, of *The Ladykillers*, studio allocation was found in Munich, Germany, but the film was shelved, going into production six years later with a re-teaming of *The Producers* stars Gene Wilder, in Peter's role, and Zero Mostel, in place of Ustinov. The film was directed by Tom O'Horgan.

2 Interview with the author, December 2021.

Cribbins certainly had had the opportunity to study the original creator of the role, for the two actors had been recently reunited for an equal rather than a sequel to *Two-Way Stretch*. *The Wrong Arm of the Law* was just one pivotal element of Peter's 38th year. It was quite a year. *The* year, in many ways. It was also very nearly Peter's last year.

Sellers had two films, both for British Lion Films, in the Top Ten Box Office winners in the shapes of the aforementioned *The Wrong Arm of the Law*, and a new collaboration with the Boulting brothers, *Heavens Above!* Not only that, but the first *Panther* was in the can and, by the very end of 1963, set for release. Sellers was also back with Stanley Kubrick, filming the ultimate Cold War comedy *Dr. Strangelove*. Moreover the Goons had reunited – once a Goon always a Goon, you know – to record abridged scripts for *The Telegoons*. Thus, Sellers went back to group mentality, made the last of his cosy, British films, and became truly international within the space of a few months. It's putting my head in a spin at the very thought of the speed Peter's life was going at. Heaven knows how he was feeling. Elevated, no doubt. Under mental and physical pressure, certainly.

Shot on location at Beaconsfield Studios and on location around Uxbridge and Ealing, in the summer of 1962, *The Wrong Arm of the Law* is a masterpiece of plotting. The tight comic construction and laugh-out-loud one-liners are hardly surprising, coming from Ray Galton and Alan Simpson (fed-up and freed-up following the abandonment of Tony Hancock's *The Day Off*), and aided by Milligan collaborator John Antrobus. The Crooks versus Crooks, with the British fraternity teaming up with the British police to beat the Australians, is nothing short of inspired. As with *Two-Way Stretch* it is undoubtedly an ensemble piece, although Sellers is very much the star attraction here, reuniting with Lionel Jeffries and Bernard Cribbins, as the top-lining, above-the-title, names. All three are on a high plane of characterisation. Not to decry *Two-Way Stretch*, but Jeffries is more subtle than ranting, more likeable in his inefficiency than detestable in his sadism. There's a mutual respect in both positions in society between the characters: and multi-layered performance in the acting out of the piece. That showdown when crook Sellers spins the plot of collaboration is a masterclass in cat and mouse interplay. The ridiculous disguise, adopted by cop Jeffries when joining the criminal gang – for the good of the police, of course – is all the more impressive in that Sellers doesn't go over-the-top in reaction. It is muted. Disbelieving. There's no fuss, no protest as Jeffries swiftly removes the disguise. Sellers is simply unimpressed: "I'm not very strong on it, no," he mutters.

Premiered at the Warner Theatre, London, on 14th March 1963, for many Pearly Gates in *The Wrong Arm of the Law* is the greatest Peter Sellers film performance. Certainly up to this point in his illustrious career. The gear-shift from flamboyant French fashion designer to crafty cockney criminal is seamless. Perfection. This man is a success too: both in the rag trade; and the lag trade. He's a clever cookie. At one moment of business crisis he taps his head and says: "I've got things going on in here that'll make Maigret drop his pipe!"[1] A great gag, lads, beautifully delivered. Heavily-lidded; charismatic; calm and collected, with that Ronald Colman moustache suiting him down to the upper lip, Sellers goes from Charles Boyer to Michael Caine in a split second.[2] This Frenchman is not the Clouseau that Sellers was about to launch himself into, but a heightened reality; as near as genuine as a good cockney lad would be able to do. This criminal is clearly a master of accents too! One moment, when the henchmen of Nervous O'Toole (Bernard Cribbins) apprehends him, Sellers moves from Paris to Bow Bells, on just the one repeated word. Dexterous, and delightful.

Cribbins, like many, considered the performance one of his old pal's finest of all. *The Wrong Arm of the Law* is very much in a

---

1 Rupert Davies, as the French detective, was a contemporary on BBC Television.

2 Michael Caine, on the verge of superstardom, can be spotted as a police constable; while much more starry, hilarious, uncredited guest spots are given by old Sellers cohorts Dick Emery – as a beleaguered adulterer; and Dennis Price as confidence trickster Educated Ernest. It would be in the character of Pearly Gates, as photographed by Bill Brandt, that Peter would adorn the 17 pence stamp in the October 1985 British Films postal collection. Other luminaries so honoured were, in ascending monetary value, David Niven, Charlie Chaplin, Vivien Leigh, and Alfred Hitchcock.

parallel universe to *Two-Way Stretch*: a companion piece; the perfect second film in a Sellers double-bill for folk organising a Best Sellers Festival out there. Indeed, *Two-Way Stretch* creators John Warren and Len Heath had a couple of hands in polishing up the idea of *The Wrong Arm of the Law*, for the same producer, M. Smedley-Aston. However, much had changed for Sellers in the previous year or so. Bernard Cribbins was swift to notice this: "There was maybe a slight shift in Sellers, since we had made *Two-Way Stretch* together. This was a semi-sequel, I suppose, although we were playing different characters. Another crime caper, with Lionel Jeffries as our nemesis. Sellers was the perfect technician by now. Giving, for my money, perhaps his finest film performance. He could shift from this cockney wide-boy geezer to the cover character of this sophisticated Frenchman, without showing his workings out, if you follow me. The gear shift between characterisations was seamless, seemingly effortless. Breath-taking. I remember one scene, when I was giving my all as this frustrated Irish crook, and Sellers didn't seem to be doing anything at all really. Then I saw the rushes, and, my God, Sellers was doing everything. The truth of his performance was incredible. Too little and the camera would miss it. Too much it would come across on that huge screen as mugging a performance. He was fully engaged with the camera, which was the medium he was working in, of course. A master craftsman of film acting, was Sellers." Cribbins, thinking for a moment, added: "I wouldn't want you to think Peter was difficult on the film. He really wasn't. Just focused, I supposed. His mind seemed to be on other things than it had been on a few years earlier. That's not to say he wasn't fun. He was. He was tremendous fun. We had such laughs during the fun fair sequences. Sellers could be the best of company, particularly when he was as relaxed and happy as he was on that film. There, write that down!" he chuckled.[1]

Fun is the optimum word here. Fun and respect. Two words. Respect for the sparkling story and script, conjured up by the finest,

---

1 Interview with the author, December 2021.

most bankable comedy writers in the business at the time. Fruity for the time too. Sellers complains of being "knackered" and points out that the visiting German explosives-expert (Tutte Lemkov) is a "spare dick at a wedding!" There's fantastic backstory too. Sellers wistfully reflects on his mother, as a Bluebell Girl, and suddenly there's real depth to the character. This is no one-note crook; this is an actor and script in perfect unison.

The fun came in the company of a bunch of mates who Sellers knew could do the job, and make his path to a dual-performance of exquisite timing all the easier. From that first bungled Post Office job Sellers is surrounded by the cream of the crop: his trio of lackeys being played by Graham Stark, John Junkin, and Davy Kaye. The rival mob from Down Under are no slouches either: Galton and Simpson favourite Bill Kerr, Reg Lye, and Ed Devereaux. Most scene-stealing of all is Mario Fabrizi – a Sellers favourite, not long for this world – as the genuinely terrified wrong van-driver in the criminal-police faux robbery. Sellers seems visibly to glow in Mario's company, genuinely to melt as Mario really goes for the hands-up moment. Sellers too had at least two things in common with his crafty crooked character. Firstly he fell for Nanette Newman, and who can blame him? The heat that director Cliff Owen puts into the seduction scene is intense indeed. Newman fairly smoulders, as Sellers, in a breathless, throwaway line mutters: "you're getting a bit fresh". Sellers and Pearly also shared a passion for the Aston Martin DB4 GT. Sellers fell in love with the car during the production and as soon as the film wrapped, he bought it! Yes, the actual one in the film. Glorious.

So. 1963. The year Britain started to swing, according to Philip Larkin and everybody else who was there. And for Sellers, there was that giant leap between English comedies and international stardom. *The Wrong Arm of the Law* was swiftly followed into British cinemas by the latest – and for getting on for a decade – the last collaboration with the Boultings.

Premiered at the Columbia Cinema, Shaftesbury Avenue[1] on 23rd May 1963, *Heavens Above!* certainly was the last hurrah for that safe and colloquial, pseudo-Ealing comedy romp Peter had come to personify. As the American narrator announces during the prologue, this is "England's green and pleasant land", and, although he would gleefully return to the warm waters of the Boulting Brothers twice more, never again would the union be as cosy, reassuring, and just plain subtly written as *Heavens Above!* The seventies would be a different country, for sure. The early sixties still had a foot in the pre-war class system, with this tail-ender, elegantly subversive parable recruiting a lip-smacking rooster of the Boulting repertory company in reassuringly familiar settings: Thorley Walters is the businessman; Eric Barker is the banker; Irene Handl is the fiddling traveller; William Hartnell is the bumptious military type. A countryside idyll, the satire here has real bite, and wrapped up and right at the heart of it all, is a subtle, poised, gentle, and truthful Sellers performance.

With light Birmingham brogue, a silver fox crew cut, almost pebble-glasses, and a gentleness of spirit, Peter's Reverend John Smallwood is a quiet wonder. It's a stark, deliberate contrast with that other Boulting brothers favourite Ian Carmichael's toothy, outlandish performance as the Other Smallwood: the clerical error that sets up the whole plot. Sellers – who, having been told the truth, earnestly says, "I think I'm the right man!" – is kind, gingerly awkward, eternally forgiving, upbeat to the point of saccharine, and calm to the point of radiating hope. To all. He is treated like a fool – by everyone – and he knows it. God is his boss and his business. Tolerance and understanding his clean and loving watch words. At the beating heart of the performance is a cheering friendship and working relationship with that mercurial black actor Brock Peters, as Matthew Robinson, dustbin man and child of God. His faith is so pure; so uplifting, that few on-screen partnerships retain such warmth and truth as that which Sellers creates with Peters. A naive happiness is never to last, but it's magical while it does. And, of course, free

---

1 Now the Curzon Soho.

food and services will always be separated from pure charity and corrupted by the wry and greedy. It's the worm at the centre of this satirical apple. Sellers senses it from the outset. As a prison chaplain fooled, tied-up, and impersonated by one of his imprisoned flock (a scene-stealing early turn by *That Was the Week That Was* satirist Roy Kinnear as prisoner number 181) the innocence of Peter's character is abused. It is a trick pulled on Sellers again later in the film; while Sellers himself mirrors the subterfuge in his substitution for the petrified, space-bound astronaut at the film's end.

Upon first seeing Sellers, Miriam Karlin – as one of the travellers, and thrice-blessed wife of Roy Kinnear – condemns him as a "devil dodger" but throughout *Heavens Above!* Smallwood's resolve and faith do not flounder. Not once. Even when faced with the power of wealth (Isabel Dean) and ecclesiastical establishment (Peter's distinguished cohort from *The Ladykillers*, Cecil Parker). One of the traveller kids, lovingly feeding her cuddly toy donkey – a religious symbol if ever there was one – innocently asks Sellers: "Do you like donkeys, mister." Having just dealt with the obstinate and obnoxious figures of authority, he pauses, grins, and warmly says: "I try to, love. God knows, I try to." It is just one of countless examples of Sellers and scriptwriters (Frank Warren and John Boulting) bonding over the dream of goodness conquering all. Peter's performance is arguably the most assured and reigned in of his entire career. There is no wonderfully crazy continental business; no gimmickry of other-worldly propheteering. This is a gentle man faced not with outrageous comic obstacles, but the everyday battle of faith against television, bingo, hatred, and a thousand and one other distractions of modern life. The Boultings allow the film to reflect, even meander somewhat – with a glorious self-serving turn from Bernard Miles as the decrepit butler Simpson – and this, in turn, allows the viewer to witness, first-hand, the double-crossing and industrial upheaval going on behind the back of Sellers. It all sets up the inevitable crossroads he faces at the end.

Moreover there are a handful of pure slapstick vignettes too: the dog biscuit-eating social faux pas that is never addressed, has the awkward, fall from grace call-back when the dog urinates against the Reverend's leg. Most pratfalling of all is the trip into the open grave. A pre-echo of the kind of sight gags that Clouseau would thrive on, Peter's reaction to this embarrassment is to smile it off. He tries to cover the moment by brushing himself off, and nonchalantly carries on in the face of disapproving looks from the crusty church committee. Not for one second does he send up his own stupidity, or milk his comic misadventure. Indeed, his initial recovery from the dank pit is off camera. The horror of the situation – a dark graveyard, on a rain-sodden evening – is played for the scream of terror rather than the scream of laughter. All the more important as the crux of the small village mentality is about to be tested: with the nervous appearance of black Brock Peters as the appointed church warden. His lowly position as a dustbin man is enough to ruffle feathers, his ethnic background is an unspoken step too far. Interestingly it is the working classes who use his colour as a weapon: the feuding housewives who fight over the free meat given out by the church, turn on Matthew. One tells him to go back to where he came from; the older, even more harsh, orders him to keep his black face out of her business. The angry mob who react to falling profits for the local factory, and closing shops put out of business by Smallwood's misguided charity, once again throw racist slurs. This is the final straw. Matthew leaves Smallwood to face the music alone. The final, crushing defeat is when his soulmate throws his friendship and faith in the face of Peter's character. Although it is the end for this most devout and devoted man, love must be seen to still win in the end.

Moreover, *Heavens Above!* is another brick in the wall of Peter Sellers: Atomic Age comedian. The religious rigour, capitalism satire, and simple, rather depressing message, that giving always leads to greed, is spiced-up with a denouncement straight out of science-fiction and science-fact. Although the heavens above and holy smoke references in the dialogue only come in the last ten minutes, when our hapless hero has become embroiled in the Space

Race, the Bishop in a spaceship spoiler was emblazoned all over the film's publicity posters.[1]

All that subtly needed a release and, between the launches of *The Wrong Arm of the Law* and *Heavens Above!*, in the March and April of 1963, Sellers took a break from cinema promoting to reunite with Harry Secombe and Spike Milligan to record those familiar voices for *The Telegoons*.

The scripts were shortened to fifteen minutes: compact, concentrated chunks of original Goonery, edited and reheated by writer Maurice Wiltshire. The glorious Goon puppets, inspired by Spike's original doodles, were designed by Ralph Young, the father of Toby Young, who produced these micro delights for Grosvenor Films, on behalf of the BBC. No musical interludes, and intensely funny, *The Telegoons* was an easy burst of insanity for Sellers. Apart from being a much-needed break from intensive self-promotion, in the busiest year of his life, it was a blessed opportunity to reunite with his two closest comic allies. Goon humour was and would remain the backbone of his comedic life. This was the real thing. These two were his brothers-in-comedy-arms.

The trio had revisited past glories before, of course, with the highly polished, highly esteemed *Vintage Goons* of 1958. However, *The Telegoons*, a child-friendly world of Goonish surrealism and cheese-nightmares, was something eagerly anticipated. The first episode, 'The Ascent of Mount Everest', was broadcast on Saturday, 5th October 1963. Weird and wonderful – often both at the same time – *The Telegoons* is now merely remembered as a footnote, coupled with the beginning of *Doctor Who* and the ending of John F. Kennedy that November.

However, for the tireless and relentless comedy career of Sellers, *The Telegoons* was a suitable full stop to the past. He was about to enjoy his first taste of working in America, having signed up as the titular star of *The World of Henry Orient*. In May 1963, he was

---

1 Sellers had put a toe in the comic world of astronauts already, of course, with Bob Hope and Bing Crosby swapping the Orient for Outer Space in the final act of *The Road to Hong Kong*.

immediately jetting off to the States after recording the soundtracks for *The Telegoons*.

The World of Henry Orient was produced by United Artists, with Peter's first stop-off en route to Hollywood stardom being a commitment to join the judging panel for the Miss Universe contest in Miami – he even visited the delectable Susan Pratt in hospital on 21st July 1963 after she had to withdraw from representing England after fracturing her leg in a car crash!

The role of Henry Orient, a pretentious and pompous concert pianist living in luxury in New York City had, as Sellers saw it on the page, "a dreadful Brooklynese accent but in an attempt to appear cultured and charming he hides it with a phoney French accent". There were subtle shades of the still, as yet, unseen Inspector Clouseau too. United Artists had originally wanted Rex Harrison to play the part but he had swiftly turned it down.[1] The central premise: a couple of fourteen-year-old girls who fan obsess over Henry Orient, was something of the candyfloss flipside of *Lolita*. The girls are played by Tippy Walker and Merrie Spaeth, with the sexual tension less important to the story than the nature and abuse of fame itself. Nora Johnson, whose idea and story the film was based upon, co-wrote the screenplay with her distinguished writer father, Nunnally Johnson. The level of fabulous famousness was based around singer Tony Bennett, and comic maestro and professional grouch, ivory-pounder Oscar Levant – hence Orient. Frankly, the story was secondary to Sellers. It was simply this flattening and financially securing chance to make it big in American pictures. Filming started on 29th July 1963 and was well and truly wrapped by that October.

The World of Henry Orient was so important, so precious to Sellers that he was absolutely adamant that he was not, absolutely not, taking on any other work during the shoot. Absolutely not!

---

1 Harrison had played in a similar, pretentious world of classical concerts, in the 1948 Preston Sturges jet-black comedy *Unfaithfully Yours*. The script for the 1984 remake, starring Dudley Moore, had been sitting around Hollywood for years and, indeed, had been offered to Sellers for consideration in the spring of 1980.

Chapter 9

"Time can't stand still for you, you know."

Bloodnok

So determined was he that Sellers expressly forbade any more press interviews or publicity photograph sessions to be planned in the two weeks leading up to the start date of *The World of Henry Orient*. Instead, that fortnight was to be spent exclusively discussing the all-important project, in private, and in a lengthy conference with the film's director George Roy Hill, and the film's producer Jerry Hellman.

Still, Sellers was very much aware that he had two films with international appeal under his belt: *The Pink Panther*, and *Dr. Strangelove*. Both films opened in London in January 1964. That was quite a month for the thirty-eight-year-old. While he was still hawking round his British-centric successes *The Wrong Arm of the Law*, and *Heavens, Above!*, Sellers had his mind firmly set on the world market. Peter's second Stanley Kubrick collaboration, and his first with Blake Edwards, were both ready to conquer the cinema-going world. And, yes, it was the world. Not just the home counties. Sellers was undoubtedly the current muse of great film-makers, the contemporary screen darling of these two world-beating directors, directors who had kick-started the sixties with *Spartacus* and *Breakfast at Tiffany's*. No slouches, these two film directors. No cream puffs. And Sellers was swimming in their kens. Without water-wings.

So. Peter Sellers broke his own rules. He agreed to just one more fringe project, and one that would only enhance and improve his international standing. As well as the strength of his position as a finger-on-the-pulse, satirical comedian.

That two-week conflab under wraps at United Artists, with George Roy Hill, and Jerry Hellman *was* interrupted for the recording of *Fool Britannia*. Sellers could hardly refuse. He rather admired the fact that Anthony Newley and Leslie Bricusse had written great chunks of the material with Sellers particularly in mind, simply because they knew he was in the area and knew he was blocking other commitments. As a result of this media-silence Newley and Bricusse reckoned he would be free and willing. And Sellers was a chum. He read the script, loved it, and said: "Yes!" immediately.

Thus, Sellers had, very willingly, been roped into a production of Mr. Anthony Newley and Mrs. Anthony Newley, who was Joan Collins at the time. Newley too was supposed to be taking it easy: relaxing with his song-writing partner Leslie Bricusse, and Joan too, of course, in Long Island, after an exhausting West End run of *Stop the World, I Want to Get Off*. That Sellers and Newley were collaborating on a secret project was a great surprise to John Springer, Head of the Rogers and Cowan's Public Relations Company, which dealt with both Sellers and Newley. Springer was the direct publicity man for both of them, and it was he who wrote the gushingly enthused sleeve notes for the project in-question: a politically explosive, long-playing album entitled *Fool Britannia*.[1]

As Springer noted: "Peter Sellers brought it up first – very casually, just in passing. 'Oh, by the way, I'm recording something next week – something Tony Newley and Leslie Bricusse have written. I'll play a part or two – quite a few, I should imagine. Yes, I know I said I didn't want to do anything once the picture started but I think it's really quite a clever thing.'"

And it really was slap-bang in the middle of filming for *The World of Henry Orient*. *Fool Britannia* was recorded at the R.C.A. Victor Studios, in New York, from midnight on Tuesday, 6th August 1963:

---

1 Ember Records (International) Limited: CEL 902, 196. Seven years later, Sellers was desperate to perform more Newley and Bricusse material, when he begged for the role of the mad chocolatier in *Willy Wonka & the Chocolate Factory*. Sellers even badgered the writer Roald Dahl by phone, but the producers insisted on Gene Wilder.

the lateness of the hour certainly suited cast member Daniel Massey, who was currently playing at the Eugene O'Neill Theatre, in the hit musical *She Loves Me!* For everybody else, *Fool Britannia* was very timely too. Certainly it was time-centric. Every topical joke had to hit the mark, and hit the mark immediately. Basically, it was a poke in the ribs of the Profumo case, which resulted in the resignation of Prime Minister Harold Macmillan, who had already been ribbed mercilessly in *The Goon Show*: 'The Red Fort'. Sellers and Spike had got a big laugh when Grytpype-Thynne and Moriarty, feasting on scraps from a dustbin, said: "We've never had it so good!", Mac's political catchphrase and a touch of the zeitgeist. *Fool Britannia* starts with Sellers as Macmillan in 'The House That Mac Built'. He is a drowsy, recently-awoken politician, befuddled and bemused to find himself caught up in the scandal and, as a result, reluctantly, all over the newspapers. Internationally. A release date for the record in October 1963, was timely enough to reference Macmillan's impending-departure . . . and the cheeky emergence of Harold Wilson . . . for the Christmas market. Ching! It is a comic newspaper. A trait that Beatle John would absorb and rekindle for his breakthrough post-Beatles Lennon single 'Cold Turkey'.

Sellers, of course, wasn't done with just portraying the Prime Minister. Of course not. He's Peter Sellers after all. And, in this controversial maelstrom of satirical barbs, Sellers pops up as Russian Eugene Ivanov: the Assistant Naval Attache at the Soviet Embassy; as well as various Hooray Henries, streetwise Americans (very much akin to, the still in the White House, Kennedy); an Indian newscaster; disreputable press barons and, hilariously, a Jewish Soho underground film-maker ("I'm 16 and I'm Not Ashamed of My Body"). There's more than a touch of Fellini there, not to mention a skating round the edges of Stanley Kubrick. Sellers the Goon is very much to the fore too. There's a wheezing, port-fuelled General who is filtered through the prism of Bloodnok. William Mate even makes a cameo, cleaning up at the Old Bailey. And from the lowest to the highest, Sellers even takes on the Queen, with Daniel Massey as a gloriously petulant Prince Philip: "Darling, we're at home now, you don't have to keep smiling and waving!" Sellers hums the National Anthem, referring to it as "Our tune!" The inmates had truly taken over the asylum, and when the audience stood to attention, there were some very starry people on their feet: the recording being witnessed by Stanley Baker, Sammy Davis Jnr, Vivien Leigh, and Beatrice Lillie.

By the time the album hit the shelves, in the autumn of 1963, Sellers was back in Britain. By the end of the year, Macmillan was political toast, and Kennedy had been blown away. Less than a month later, on 18th December 1963, *The Pink Panther* finally enjoyed its first commercial exposure, premiered to great hype and expectation, in Italy. Far more colloquially and quietly, the last episode of the first series of *The Telegoons*, 'The Choking Horror', was broadcast on Saturday, 28th December 1963.

And so to January 1964. Spring was in the air, and Sellers was, quite literally, on top of the world. It would prove to be the most pivotal month of his life. And the prelude to the darkest of days.

It's safe to say *The Pink Panther* had a lasting impact on Peter's career; on everything, really. Everyone close to it knew. A sequel was already on the boil.

A Shot in the Dark offered up the irresistible joy of Sellers working with the real Grytpype-Thynne in the effortlessly urbane shape of George Sanders. A French farce of bedroom hopping; great swathes of comedy of embarrassment with a naked Sellers and leading lady Elke Sommer in a nudist camp; and beautifully constructed ballets of slapstick, *A Shot in the Dark* is, ironically as the only Sellers one without 'Pink Panther' in the title, the definitive *Pink Panther*. Oh, alright, the definitive Clouseau. It's certainly that, for never again would Sellers completely reign in his love of the absurd and the abstract to keep an, almost, controlled, pressure-cooker performance in the role. This was a reheating of a screen character that, for once, fascinated Sellers. It gave the actor ample opportunity to extend, expand, and experiment with the seed he had nurtured in the original film. The basic joke was simplicity itself. Beautifully so: "He is very serious but completely hopeless at his job." A lover too, of course. He is a Frenchman. "The size of his moustache is to give him – in his own mind – masculinity. He's a very romantic man but, again, hopeless at that too".[1] Clouseau *knows* he is hopeless, and it is this desperate masking of inadequacy that Sellers riffed off. That first re-introductory shot, in *A Shot in the Dark*, is masterly, as the big build-up ends with Sellers, calm, self-confident, steely, his eyes full of pride and pluck in the face of the crime case ahead . . . and then that pratfall into the ornamental pond. Boom! Clouseau in microcosm.

Despite David Niven being the top-billed star attraction in the first one and – you heard it here first! – the Pink Panther actually being the stolen diamond and not the crime-busting dullard who pinched every scene, the film and its direct sequel, the continuation of the franchise a decade later, and the feuding friendship between creator Blake Edwards and comic catalyst Peter Sellers would dominate both men's lives for the next twenty years and beyond. Certainly beyond the death of Sellers and, as it turned out, the death of Edwards too.[2]

The Mirisch Company had naturally been quick to feel the oh so pleasant breeze of the box office turnstiles spinning round. Inspector Jacques Clouseau was an instant classic. That voice came from a Paris hotel concierge Sellers had encountered. A smart man who would deal with American tourists in an accent that wasn't French but sounded French to the English-speaking ear. The trench coat was in homage to Hollywood's greatest gumshoe Humphrey Bogart. The spiralling, often improvised, invention was pure Sellers. It was Peter's signature role and he was out of the traps and winning the race. Things would never be the same again, for Clouseau was

1 Interviewed by Barry Norman, on location in Gstaad during the filming of *The Return of the Pink Panther*, for *Film '75*.

2 When Blake Edwards collected his Honorary Academy Award in 2004 – from Jim Carrey introducing with a mosaic of Hrundi V. Bakshi and Clouseau quotes – the celebrated film-maker entered stage right in a motorised wheelchair. Grabbing the statuette and bursting through a canvas stage left, Edwards proceeded to explode and pratfall his way through an hilarious acceptance speech. Overseeing, albeit from a well-paid distance, the two Steve Martin performances, in *The Pink Panther* in 2006 and *The Pink Panther 2* in 2009, Blake's name is still posthumously connected with the reboot of the franchise, with Eddie Murphy and a tangible pink panther in the buddy-movie mix.

never going to go away. Blake Edwards knew it too. A sequel, with Clouseau at its heart, and the fabulous diamond out of the limelight, had been rushed into production – even before *The Pink Panther* had opened in America. *A Shot in the Dark* would be *the* Clouseau. Polished and primed. For Sellers too, his world was about to spin out of control and out of his reach. He had willingly looked back, to where it all, almost, began, when he filmed a tribute to his old gang leader Ralph Reader, for inclusion in his *This Is Your Life*. Fellow comic comrade Dick Emery was on hand, in the studio, for the recording on Monday 11th November, with the tribute being broadcast, on BBC Television, on Thursday, 21st November 1963. *The Dick Emery Show* had only started that July, but for Sellers 1963 had been an even more monumental year. 1964, however, was about to top it, and almost end it.[1]

On 29th January 1964 *Dr. Strangelove or How I Stopped Worrying and Learned to Love the Bomb*, premiered in London. January 1964 was also the month Peter first met Britt Ekland. Both professionally, and personally, it was a new beginning. *Dr. Strangelove* was a New Year film. A time of rebirth and optimism. Of a cynical sort. An era when the decade really was swinging, and all around was a feeling of hope. It was a perfect time for a comedy film without any hope at all. Resolutions were futile. Even Vera Lynn singing 'We'll Meet Again' couldn't stop the tide of the end of humanity, the end of civilisation as we knew it. It was the ultimate destructive farewell for Sellers, the Cold War comedian. As Kubrick perceived the film at the time: "everywhere you turn there is some version of Peter Sellers holding the fate of the world in his hands."

Columbia Pictures were smiling all the way to the fall-out shelter too. With Stanley Kubrick having picked away the sheer dread of

---

1 Peter bookended this BBC Television appearance with a couple of further stints on *Juke Box Jury*. Hosted by David Jacobs, from June 1959, the format was simple: a panel of four celebrities listen to the latest chart releases and vote them a 'Hit' or a 'Miss'. Peter joined Juliette Greco, Jean Metcalfe and his trusted medium Maurice Woodruff, on 15th June 1963. All nine discs were considered hits! Sellers returned to the programme on 4th January 1964, with Dora Bryan, David Gell, and Cilla Black. Latest platters from Billie Davis ('That Boy John'), Helen Shapiro ('Fever'), Gerry & the Pacemakers ('I'm the One'), the Ronettes ('Baby I Love You') and Ray Charles ('That Lucky Old Sun') were voted hits. Both broadcasts were produced by Neville Wortman.

the nuclear drama *Fail Safe*, this comedy twist on Armageddon clocked in at a budget of $1.8 million, and picked up a more than satisfying, although ironically, not earth-shattering $9.2 million on its first release. If only Peter had rodeo-ridden that bomb at the end. The ultimate Atomic comic image. For Kubrick stretched and stretched and stretched again. He stretched so much that Sellers broke: relinquishing his fourth role of bomber pilot King Kong to Western veteran Slim Pickens. Originally Sellers was down for just three – just three! – characters in *Dr. Strangelove* in any case. Kong was offered to the biggest cowboy star in the world John Wayne American, but John Wayne American, and fierce patriot, turned it down flat. Sellers tried and tried again. It was just too much for his head space at the time, so ever dependable Slim was cast. There was no acting required here. Slim was perfect for the role. He was the role. Slim dressed like a cowboy and talked like a cowboy anyway. All the time. With little interest or indeed awareness of the satirical context, Slim played it straight. Brilliantly. As Slim later reflected, after *Strangelove* the parts and the dressing rooms and the pay cheques all got much bigger!

For Sellers too. This was his first one-million-dollar movie. Over half of the entire budget. At the time, Stanley Kubrick quipped that he had got three performances for the price of six, but, having been bewitched by Sellers on *Lolita*, the director was visibly in awe of his master-craftsman actor during the shooting at Shepperton Studios: "To me it's like having three different great actors."[1]

And *Dr. Strangelove* was a hot and happening opportunity, not only for another glorious wallow in the dressing-up box, but also to put Peter's uncanny skill for characterisation under the microscope. Group Captain Lionel Mandrake is a delight. An easy delight, for Sellers, but a delight nonetheless. Strangelove himself is a grotesque, an unforgettable, nightmarish vision of science gone mad. Inhumanity in human shape. Sort of. The plum of the trio, though,

---

1 *Queen* magazine, interview Elaine Dundy, 13th March 1963. That the collaboration with Sellers ended at *Strangelove* is a disappointment, to put it mildly. One can only daydream of the ghoulish giggles Peter could have offered to *The Shining*; or of the frightfully English eccentricity to *Barry Lyndon*.

is President Merkin Muffley. Balding; bespectacled; bewildered, this is an elder statesman completely out of his depth. The awkward telephone conversations with his Russian counterpart are memorable indeed. The dexterity of Peter's vocal and physical performance is a masterclass in desperate diplomacy. Based, as Muffley was, on the former Illinois Governor Adlai Stevenson II, there is a precision and perfection to the subtle Americanisms that Sellers deploys here. For a boy from Hampshire, there is a cleverness, and a geographically ambitious core to Muffley. It is an impeccable performance. The American accent is not some cod, generalised drawl. The trained ear can pinpoint the very state that Muffley hails from. The very district. The very street even. It is a mind-blowing, ear-haunting performance. The one that Sellers was most proud of, and who can blame him? Crucially, of all the myriad characters he created over the course of thirty years, his simple starting point, the voice, resonates here: "I start with the voice", Sellers explained. "I find out how the character sounds. It's through the way he speaks that I find out the rest about him."

Of course, in terms of poster publicity and column inches, it was Strangelove himself that captured the world's imagination. Loosely inspired by the New York photojournalist Weegee, this crippled figure of insanity hardly appears in the film at all. Still, he has the mad, masterplan of the survival of the fittest . . . and himself. Sellers remained proud of the collaborative and organic quality of his Strangelove too. It was a characterisation matured on set, in discussion with Kubrick. Artiste and actor. As one. Peter Sellers: the actor as auteur. Peter, of course, couldn't analyse his work for long, memorably lapsing into jokery when discussing *Strangelove* at the National Film Theatre and reflecting: "Ah, they don't write hands like that anymore!" Strangelove is a sinister throwback to the Third Reich, and, in turn, a gleeful throwback to Peter's own war. As the twisted brain overrides the twisted body, and Strangelove rises from his restrictive wheelchair, is arguably Peter's most unforgettable screen moment. Stark, chilling, and hilariously funny. All at the same time. Strangelove certainly taps into Peter's shading of a characterisation, for after the voice, he explained: "I establish how the character walks. Very important, the walk. And then, suddenly, something strange happens. The person takes over. The man you play begins to exist." Something Strangelove, in fact. Little wonder then that Robin Williams said: "For me the most influential actor in films was Peter Sellers . . ." and, despite the sheer comic joy of *The Pink Panther*, it was *Dr. Strangelove* that sealed it.[1]

Peter Sellers was happy and in love too. He had moved out of the Manor House, Chipperfield, in Hertfordshire, and into the slightly more modest Brooksfield House, near the village of Elstead, in Surrey. Sellers constructed a cinema room above the garage, and imported a new front door from Italy. Pumping £80,000 into the place, he transformed a rough piece of land leading down to the River Wye into "elegant parkland with trees, ornamental lakes and shrubberies. Dams were built, waterways constructed and lawns created on a base of imported chalk."[2] Sellers loved his garden. When he finally moved out, in 1968, it was the one element he said he missed. Years later he returned to Brooksfield House, and asked the owner if he would mind him wandering round the garden, one last time, to see how his work had fared in the intervening years. It was a place of memories, both fond and bitter. It was here that the whirlwind romance with Britt Ekland flourished, and where the couple got engaged.

Within a month the two were married, on Wednesday, 19th February 1964; as Peter's thrice-time screen cohort Richard Attenborough recalled: "on a snowy day . . . at Guildford Register Office".[3] The following morning Peter jetted off to America. Duty called.

For Britt too, who was beginning filming on *Guns at Batasi*,

---

1 Interview for the American Film Institute's *100 Years 100 Laughs*, June 2000. *Dr. Strangelove* came in at third place. Beaten by *Tootsie*, and topped by *Some Like it Hot*. *Being There* was at no. 26, with *A Shot in the Dark* at 48. Robin Williams found himself represented by *Mrs. Doubtfire*, at no. 67 and *Good Morning, Vietnam*, sneaking in at 100.

2 'The Goon Showcase' by Ronald Payne, *The Times Weekend*, Saturday, 10th October 1998.

3 *Entirely Up to You, Darling*, by Richard Attenborough and Diana Hawkins (Hutchinson, 2008).

at Pinewood Studios, playing opposite Richard Attenborough. Ironically, as with Peter's *Kiss Me Stupid*, Britt's work on *Guns at Batasi* was hastily curtailed – ostensibly because Sellers was getting jealous of the dashing good looks of her pop idol co-star John Leyton. Mia Farrow was drafted in as Britt's replacement, for Britt was bound for America. To be with Peter.

For Peter, the duty was even more important and fun than *Fool Britannia* had been: the home-based recording assignment he had readily, and rather hastily, agreed to. With *The Telegoons* still a fond and recent memory, Sellers was eager to get back with Spike and Secombe in the studio as Rex Berry, who came up with the original idea, recorded in his sleeve note: "Lunch was arranged at the Pickwick Club before going to the studio. Fatal. Peter Sellers not only couldn't make the meal but also the actual session. He was married the day before and was going to Hollywood in the morning (Thursday, 20th February 1964). Harry Secombe and Spike Milligan made the restaurant but not having seen each other for over six months soon forgot the business of the day." They reminisced and laughed, before finally remembering to work on and tape: "their personal message recorded to Peter, who put his voice on in Hollywood and flew them back, [it] was classic. After black coffee and more red wine the session got under way".

Rex Berry remembered, the notion came about from a musing as to who would win the election. A musing within earshot of his client Leslie Bricusse, and Leslie's wife, Yvonne Bricusse. Three weeks later, that idea had blossomed into a concept album which basked in the zeitgeist success of *Fool Britannia*, which Bricusse had co-created. Along with fellow producer David Platz, Bricusse hoped that the satirical barb could hit the target twice within the same year. By embracing the assured glee that Sellers, and the other two Goons, would have a ball and be spontaneously hilarious, *How To Win An Election* was put into orbit, and green lit. As Bricusse gloated, he had: "the three finest comedy voices in the land to record it."

While much of what Spike and Secombe were doing was ad-libbed under the influence of a buoyant Bricusse, bursts of infectious laughter, and copious bottles of Rioja, Sellers, away from the London-centric madness, and newly married, stuck very much to the script. He recorded his bits for *How to Win an Election (Or Not Lose By Much)*,[1] to give it its full title, in comfortable isolation, in Hollywood. As Rex Berry noted: "Peter duly recorded his bits and put the tapes back on a plane. One of the funniest moments came when we played back the unanswered questions being sent to Peter. Many editing hours later the whole thing was complete."

The opening track, 'What's It All About', spotlights Sellers as a rather straight character. Himself, for all intents and purposes. He is bemused and confused as he sets out the stall of the album: why you vote for who you vote for or why you don't vote for anybody and the reasons behind that decision. Sellers, as close to himself as he ever was, is heckled by Sellers as a fledgling Socialist Bluebottle who, reluctantly, decides he's a "Twit". Willium Mate gives his opinion as a Man in the Street Vox Pox.

The album was impeccably timed, with its release coming on 15th October 1964, the day before the country went to the polls. Harold Wilson narrowly beat the serving Conservative leader Alec Douglas-Hume, after thirteen years of Tory rule: Smart Alec versus Dull Alec as David Frost had dubbed the battle, and a notion Sellers repeats here. Indeed, Sellers does a wonderful Wilson: all pipe and slippers, and papers. An ordinary, working-class bloke. A man of the People. Rex Berry celebrated "Peter's 'Man of the People'", convinced that the sketch "should give the Leader of the Opposition a lot of laughs or . . . something. And his 'To Home It May Concern', gives the whole Housing issue a chaotic slant." In the sketch Sellers and his wily architect beautifully slot together with Secombe's gullible home-buyer. Comic hands across the Atlantic. Still, there was no need for skilful editing for the Bond meets Beatles pastiche 'On Her Majesty's Swinging Service', in which Sellers interviews himself, as a scouse rocker. 'I Want to Hold Your Hand' was number

---

1 The album was released on Philips Records, serial number: Philips AL 3464.

one in the US billboard chart when Sellers recorded the routine. The British Invasion was spearheading throughout the States. Indeed February had seen the Beatles make their debut on live American television with the pivotal appearance on *The Ed Sullivan Show*, that proved so popular even the criminals stayed home to tune in. The 'Swinging Service' skit is politics meets pop with the suggestion of a *Sunday Night at the House of Commons*. It's canny and clever. 'I'm So Ashamed' raised to the World Stage.

Indeed, while Harold Steptoe's working-class philosophy in *Steptoe and Son* did affect the election, this last-minute vinyl reunion of the Goons may well have tipped it over the balance. Maybe. As quoted in the sleeve notes, Leslie Bricusse hoped the listener wouldn't be swayed by the offering: "Not unless you want anarchy for the next five years!"[1]

Peter's sixties was about to be anarchic and enviable. Even Nunnally Johnson, the co-writer of *The World of Henry Orient*, who considered his performance far too broad for the material couldn't dampen Peter's mood . . . or popularity. Although Johnson's opinion mellowed over the years – and over the box office receipts – at the time he thought the actor was just not pin-point sharp enough for the complex plotting of the film. Rather overawed by the American spotlight, Sellers does paint his Continental Stallion in rather broad strokes: the slump into slum talk does, brilliantly, expose his roots in the Bronx, while the lyrical piano score accompanies his every move – a little like the "little punks" that relentlessly follow his every move round a lyrical, luscious New York City. The Ronald Colman moustache quivers – very fresh from *The Wrong Arm of the Law* – and once more bristles with over-blown splendour. The concert hall sequence has an under-rehearsed and arrogant Sellers muffing and miming his way through the avant-garde drone of the piano piece, while it's borderline Goonish comedy as he outlandishly and operatically sings to himself as he lounges like

---

1 The month after the record's release, on 8th November 1964, to be precise, all three Goons contributed to the BBC Light Programme's *Forces Gala Night Twenty-First Anniversary*. It was written by Gale Pedrick, and produced by Bill Worsley.

a lounge lizard on his luxurious bed. It's all a pompous personality to fever-pitch. One can see Johnson's point. To an extent. But only through the eyes of a writer who had envisaged an Oscar Levant or a Rex Harrison. Sellers, as a film actor, was almost as excited as Peter's Henry Orient character is around the sniff of a female conquest. He giggles and jerks and fidgets with anticipation. While he is alone. When the woman is in his sites – usually married and nervous Paula Prentiss – the rebellious rogue rises to the occasion. He is in a gladiatorial mood. All set for the battle. So much so that the bird has flown from the Italian restaurant as the conqueror hails a cab. When she is entrapped in the apartment, she mutters that she is frightened. Peter's Henry Orient is a Sex God who only shows his true, overly-sexed and overly-excitable colours while alone. The bedroom romps are played out in long strides and flailing arms, literally grasping at the curtains to conceal himself and his intended sexual conquest. He struggles to move a heavy objet d'art in his apartment. It is the pantomime grace of a Keaton or a Chaplin. One feels the weight of this pretentious statue.

Moreover, he can never pass a mirror without looking into it, and he can never spy a female without setting his cap at her feet. His charm and grace and chat – dropping in lusty, half-remembered knowledge of John Sargent portraits – is even deployed, and succeeds, with the frosty mother of Boyd, one of his young fans. The mother is played by Angela Lansbury. British-born, but with Hollywood and Broadway in her soul for the previous two decades, Lansbury is subtle where Sellers is heightened. Throwaway where Sellers is try-hard. In the restaurant showdown the contrast of acting styles works wonderfully. Lansbury does nothing and steals the scene. Sellers helps rather than hinders with dramatic pauses, theatrical gulps, and facial tics. He is gleeful at the scent of a new woman to track. His hormones rage as he sees this fur-clad Ice Queen melt. He knows the signs. He is a professional Casanova. Vain he may be, as he sullenly dismisses the first grey hair his hair-cutter locates. It's as if his posh front from *The Wrong Arm of the Law* has landed in the Mean Streets. This is a caricature in a universe populated by proper New York types – John

Fielder, in a similar assistant cum Jiminy Cricket turn as Kenneth Griffith gave in *The Naked Truth*, is pure White Way, while Al Lewis – familiar on television at the time in showy supporting bursts in *Car 54, Where Are You?* – is achingly authentic as the ranting, fawning shop assistant. The sweeping, swirling musical score is by Elmer Bernstein. Enough said. The soundscape is sheer New York. Indeed, the first time we spy Sellers – in a Hollywood film – he is in Central Park. Still, you can take Sellers out of England but you can't take England out of Sellers. He is seen snogging Paula Prentiss. The wannabe ultimate comical lover is here, loud and proud. Those staring, blazing eyes – the eyes the two young female heroes of the piece fall for – are alive with passion and anxiety. It is a bombastic turn, but a powerful one. Sellers the actor knows that this character is a buffoon. A fake. An Emperor's New Clothes kind of pianist, and a cowardly cuckolder to boot. Sellers plays it with just the right amount of pomp and circumstance. He's a guest star in a foreign climate, but he means to leave his mark *and* stand out. The sheer pratfall as he hits the sidewalk – the result of a fast fleeing from fanatics – is a moment of sensational slapstick. The clown is in town. In bristling colour and filling the wide screen in Panavision, it is a garish frolic of adolescent silliness and obsession and near hysteria. Sellers is the maddening and madly fascinating ogre in the centre of this grown-up fairy tale. What's more Sellers is the eponymous anti-hero of fun. There are speeded-up pratfalls up the steps to his apartment, pretentious facial grimaces, and gloriously over-blown comic mannerisms. He is Henry Orient. Megastar in his own mind. The megalomaniac. Frantic and funny and over-the-top, for sure.

Still, it followed *Dr. Strangelove* into American cinemas less than two months later, with *The World of Henry Orient* premiering, suitably enough, at the Radio City Music Hall, in New York, on 19th March 1964. Again, unsurprisingly, it was a massive hit in New York. It's something of a wry love letter to the city. And it's a sort of Christmas film too. Shots of New York City looking splendid in the snow would fill the emotional cup of any New Yorker to overflow. Still, the film struggled to make such an impact across the States. That fact notwithstanding, it was the entry from the United States at the Cannes Film Festival which began five weeks after the film had opened.

On 18th March 1964, the day before *The World of Henry Orient* had enjoyed that premiere, Sellers was being even more broad, with *The Pink Panther* making its debut in cinemas across America. *A Shot in the Dark* was in the can and in the schedules for the summer. New York was at Peter's feet, with three of his films in the Top Ten: *Strangelove*; *Panther*; and *Orient*. Sellers was the toast of celluloid Broadway. As a comedy star and cultural icon Sellers was rather on top of the world. Look at him, Ma!

And he met his comedy idol Stan Laurel, at Stan's apartment at 849 Ocean Avenue, Santa Monica, California. In the bewitching, life-affirming photograph Stan looks delighted, Sellers beams like the cat who has all the cream. Indeed, few photographs show Peter Sellers looking as happy as this one. Whether he discussed *The Slappiest Days of Our Lives* remains unrecorded!

Certainly, it's unlikely he had tuned in to watch the Jack Arnold TV version of *The Mouse That Roared*, with Sid Ceasar repeating the Sellers triple. It was not a success, and subsequently not picked up for a series. Sellers wasn't interested in any case, or bothered for that matter. He was a few days into working with Hollywood royalty, Billy Wilder,[1] on *Kiss Me Stupid*, a romantic comedy with Dean Martin and Kim Novak. Sellers was playing Orville Spooner, an eccentric pianist who bumps into Dino – ostensibly playing himself – and invites him back to his pad. Trashy beauty Polly the Pistol – Novak, of course – distracts them both.

Sellers was not only the world's most famous comedy actor, he was one of the world's most famous people. And his reputation as not so much a naughty comedian and more a thinking comedian for grown-ups was complemented by his appearance in the April edition of *Playboy* for which he had recreated a cavalcade of legendary Hollywood figures: 'Sellers Mimes the Movie Lovers'. The stars

---

1 Wilder, you will remember, had once been attached to what became *The Battle of the Sexes*. Before Sellers though.

emulated were Peter's own choice. On the inside pages he is Bela Lugosi's Count Dracula; he is Francis X. Bushman in the silent *Ben Hur*; he is comic hero Groucho Marx in *A Night at the Opera*. He is his own, contemporary Hollywood lover, Henry Orient, with December 1961 *Playboy* playmate Lynn Karrol, draped over his piano. While on the cover he poses as Rudolph Valentino. Or Fred Valentino, as Peter preferred, in character as *The Sheikh*. Although an alluring Karen Douglas, in his arms, was the news stand attraction – and revealed rather more within the magazine – Sellers was the first male to be on the cover of Hugh Hefner's hymn to the female form. Sellers was *that* famous.

Then. Boom!

That first, near-fatal heart attack hit on Sunday, 5th April 1964. The Beatles were at number one, on both sides of the Atlantic, with 'Can't Buy Me Love'. Clouseau and Strangelove were international hits too. The nations were united. As Sellers fought for his life.

Cared for and saved by the skilled staff at the Cedars of Lebanon Hospital, it was reported that Sellers had anything up to thirteen heart attacks that weekend. Unlucky for some. In actual fact it was only – only! – eight: "I don't do things by half!", Sellers would quip for the press. In serious moments he would reflect that this was "extremely rare". Extremely rare to survive, at any rate.

It had been an unbelievably busy year, with a workload of staggering depth and complexity. Not only that, but there had been a divorce, a family split asunder, house move, a marriage, a Goon reunion, awards both won and lost, total financial security and beyond, and ditto cinematic success. Peter's last pre-heart attack film, *A Shot in the Dark*, was released on 23rd June 1964. Plans to team up with hot and happening *Zulu* actor James Booth, in the film *Barbu*, were shelved and then completely abandoned. Billy Wilder re-cast Orville in *Kiss Me Stupid*, with Ray Walston, and released the film for Christmas 1964. By which time, Sellers – with Britt in tow – was already back at work.

Chapter 10

"You do it because it gives you enjoyment and you've fulfilled something within yourself. Never in an attempt to break new ground. That would kill it."

Peter Sellers, 1969

BAFTA-winning for *The Pink Panther*, and Oscar-nominated for *Dr. Strangelove*, Peter had marked his thirty-ninth birthday in convalescence. Quite incredibly, the previous month had seen him with a smash hit double-bill of *The Pink Panther* and *Dr. Strangelove* opening in New York City, on 19th August 1964. The fact that this cinematic treat – proudly heralded as a Peter Sellers fest – was a celebration and not a tribute was something of a miracle. Indeed, if that string of heart attacks had proved fatal, Sellers would have bowed out at an absolute peak. The Elvis Presley of comedy, he had nurtured and moulded Milligan's unique vision of Goonish, looney comedy, and conquered the world with it – well, America, which in 1964 was pretty much the same thing in terms of Light Entertainment.

Quite literally back from the brink of death, Sellers was a new man; a different man; with a mission to conquer even more. On 3rd June 1964, after a good month in hospital, he was accompanied by Britt when he contributed his handprint to the legendary Grauman's Chinese Theatre, on Hollywood Boulevard. A milestone honour for any movie star, Peter made cheeky reference to his condition by adding a heart alongside his signature. He was back in business, and, by that yuletide of 1964 he was well and truly back in the show business saddle. On 1st November, on the telephone from his hotel room in Paris, Sellers rejoiced in another swift reunion with Spike Milligan and Harry Secombe for the recording of an eight-minute, abridged version of the old adventure 'I Was Monty's Treble'. As with *How to Win an Election*, Spike and Secombe were together in the flesh, this time recording from the stage of the Victoria Palace in the West End. The skit was broadcast exactly one week later, on the Light Programme. Sellers sounded thrilled and thrilling.[1] He was certainly ripe and ready for a return to fully-fledged acting work, teaming up with the heavily-pregnant Britt Ekland (Peter's very own Victoria was born on 20th January 1965) for Rod Serling's magical and miraculous and mysterious *A Carol for Another Christmas*, which went out on 28th December 1964, from the Michael Myerberg Studios, in New York City. Sterling Haydn, fresh from *Strangelove*, is Mr. Grudge – a Scrooge for the unkind America of the 1960s. With the same world-hating insanity but with a cold chip on his shoulder, this is another element in Peter's position as the Atomic Comic, for it is Charles Dickens for the Cold War era. Produced and directed by Joseph L. Mankowitz, with a musical score by Henry Mancini, Sellers was surrounded by allies. Britt knits as the world goes to hell in a handcart, and gets top billing in the alphabetical order the show received, but it's Peter's moment. He is the star of the section set in the near-future, introduced by the Ghost of Christmas Yet to Come – a haunting portrayal by a cowled and bearded Robert Shaw. With an insane grin, and a humongous hat emblazoned with a glittering 'Me', this performance as the Imperial Me was another Peter Sellers, for sure. Intelligent, intimidating, and illuminating, it is a wild, unreserved, and unforgettable embrace of seasonal sadism. That moment when the madness brims over and he cheerily dismisses the thought of kindness toward anybody other than his clan is chilling, indeed. In full close-up. You can see the demons of delusion in Peter's eyes. It is the after-war aftermath of selfishness and isolation. Of the glory of the self. Played with a manic Southern states accent, with the air of a bonkers evangelist, this grinning megalomaniac with the Cult of Me, needed a comedy actor going slightly mad.

---

1 In a glut of press and television interviews, including *The Eamonn Andrews Show*, ABC Weekend Television, on 20th December 1964, Sellers would chat about his upcoming projects and near-death experience. His favourite phrase was that he wasn't "booked for the old wooden overcoat quite yet!".

It is the death knell of reason. Debate and understanding is made a mockery. Laughter is all. Evil guffaws in the face of compassion. Sellers, as the potential last human, will be laughing all the way to the brink. It's a perfect, largely unheralded Christmas treat for the cynic amongst you.[1]

Britain was really rather great in 1965: BBC2 had burst forth late in '64 with Peter Cook and Dudley Moore injecting verve into satire in *Not Only . . . But Also*. Sellers was delighted to endorse their first series, in particular as aged, bath chair-confined Major-General Wingly-Spoons in 'The Gourmets' sketch. Pure Beyond the Goons. So, on 20th March 1965 it was Not Only Peter Cook and Peter Sellers But Also Dudley Moore and Barry Humphries. *Not Only . . . But Also* was just another example of Sellers as the personification of cool comedy, for John Lennon and Norman Rossington popped in as well. Rossington had played the manager of the Beatles in the previous year's smash hit film *A Hard Day's Night*. United Artists had a vested interest in both Sellers and the Beatles. It was a match made in heaven. Lennon's first book of nonsense poetry *In His Own Write* had been published to great acclaim, and whenever asked about influences, Lennon would always drop in an intelligent nod to Lewis Carroll and a laughter-fuelled finger-point to *The Goon Show*. It had been Sellers who had presented the Beatles with the Grammy – or "Grandma" as he insisted on calling it – for 'Best Performance of a Vocal Group' for the year 1964. The ceremony took place at Twickenham Studios, on Wednesday, 28th April 1965.[2] With such a connection with the coolest cats on the planet, Sellers would eagerly put his Laurence Olivier as Richard III spin on 'A Hard Day's Night' for *The Music of Lennon & McCartney*, on 16th December 1965. The Beatles and EMI Records themselves, already sensing the huge value of their past, had sanctioned a greatest hits package, *A*

---

1 Peter also eased himself back into the saddle with some laidback voiceover work, narrating *Tales from Hoffnung*, a 1965 series of animated shorts in celebration of the absurdist musical expression and hilarious grumblings of the late comic genius raconteur Gerard Hoffnung.

2 The filmed insert was broadcast within *The Best of Record*, on NBC, on Tuesday, 18th May 1965, a full celebration of all the awards handed out on behalf of the National Academy of Recording Arts and Sciences.

Collection of Beatles Oldies . . . But Goldies!, which cleaned up the following Christmas. No wonder exports were booming and business was good. Peter had been doing the Laurence Olivier as Richard III impersonation since the film had come out, in 1955, and would perform his rendition of 'A Hard Day's Night' again on *Top of the Pops*, on 30th December 1965. Peter was still giving his Richard III nearly a decade later when he enjoyed a full interview with Michael Parkinson. It was this long game of comic dependability, coupled with Peter's dreaded boredom during theatre runs, that saw him turn down Olivier's serious offer to play the great Shakespearean roles – seriously – at the National. It was all about the fun. Instant karma fun, at that, and that was exactly what the Beatles Songbook gave him. Peter's Lennon & McCartney sessions gleaned over half a dozen hilarious in-tune and drop-out tracks, all produced by his faithful and funny producer George Martin. It was a visceral connection with the output of the Beatles which makes these Sellers recordings not only musically brilliant and achingly amusing but three-minute time capsules that can summon up the sixties in sixty seconds. As well as the spin on the Bard – which inspired an, at the time, unreleased, Sellers warm-up Scouse reading of the 'Now is the Winter of Our Discontent' speech – the B-side recording, of 'Help!', indulged Peter in a heavenly ecclesiastical characterisation with the earnest plea: a cry of "Help!" from the heart for the church's collection plates. At the number's close Peter alerts the congregation that "the church Beatle will pass among you!" Not Beadle but Beatle. It's that meta, man. 'Can't Buy Me Love' heard Peter resurrect Crystal Jollibottom from the *Ray's a Laugh* days and in conversation with an upper-crust gentleman (Peter again, obviously) leaves no doubt in the listener's mind that she had been a lady of easy virtue all these years! Her strangulated giggling mutter of "Balls!" at the close shows this was not intended for release at the time! No rarer were Peter's various takes on 'She Loves You'. One featured a couple of Hooray Henries. These two chaps – both Sellers, of course – discuss attachment and all its problems. One is a mumbling moron, the other in deadly earnest: "She Loves You, Nigel!", he barks. It's known as the Twits Version or the Chinless Wonders, for good reason. It's glorious to boot. There is a cockney version too, and an Irish one, inspired by Phil McCafferty – The Irish Dentist, but the stand-out cut resurrects the aggressive angst of Doctor Strangelove to make the romantic lyrics borderline sado-masochistic! Not to mention a resurrection of the fascist zeal of the Nuremberg rallies in its relentless storm-trooping crowd chant of: "Yeah! Yeah! Yeah!"[1]

Such was the joy the Beatles gleaned from Peter's work, not to mention his unique interpretation of a handful of their spearhead hit singles, that the group had hit upon the wheeze of inviting him to guest star in their next film, *Help!* Having embraced Sellers producer George Martin for their Abbey Road recordings, the Beatles had also teamed up with Peter's old chum and cohort Richard Lester, as director for their first feature film *A Hard Day's Night*, as well as the follow-up *Help!*, a script originally conceived as a Sellers film, thus it was a shoo-in that Sellers would jump into the colourful romp in the hunt for Ringo's sacred ring! In the end Peter was far too busy coming down from filming *What's New Pussycat?* and gearing up to film his own heist epic *After the Fox*. It would have been futile in any case. The cameo Sellers would have played was to teach the Fab Four elocution. Frankie Howerd took on the role of Sam Ahab, but the scene was cut from the final release print.

Besides, Sellers was loving life. He had just forked out a cool £11,500 on a Ferrari fresh from a London showroom, and with Britt in tow, and newly-born Victoria, of course, Tony Curtis came along for the ride too. It was that kind of high life, folks. So Sellers!

The Beatles bonding notwithstanding, Peter Sellers had very much joined the coolest cool set himself. This was the jet-set, the sexy set. United Artists, thankful to have the world's most popular clown back to fighting-fit strength, had offered him the wild and

---

1 The 1993 *A Hard Day's Night* EP gathered together the original single, coupled with 'Help!', alongside the first official release of the Twits Version of 'She Loves You', and 'Can't Buy Me Love': Parlophone EM 293. All Peter's Beatles recordings, including the previously unreleased 'Yes It Is', and the ultra-rare Liverpudlian 'Now is the Winter of Our Discontent', are available on the definitive *Celebration of Sellers* box set.

wacky and wonderful role of Doctor Fritz Fassbender in *What's New Pussycat?* Perfectly of the zeitgeist this was the swingingest, sexiest sex comedy of the era. With the Tom Jones title track, the garish and groovy Richard Williams cartoon title sequence, the edgiest of cool kid chat and catchphrases, and the turbo-charged warmth and wit from Woody Allen's screenplay, this was the living end of cool comedy.

Sellers was aware of two things: this was going to be a big and breezy smash hit; and secondly he was a big star, *the* big star, and would not relinquish his well-earned top-billing to anybody. Not even Lawrence of Arabia himself. Peter O'Toole wasn't fussed.[1] He was delirious at the thought of locking comic horns with Sellers. Besides, the hottest girls in town were in the cast: from girlfriend Romy Schneider to psychotic nymphomaniac Capucine – fresh from *The Pink Panther* – to sky-diving pioneering Bond girl Ursula Andress. Indeed, Sellers taps into Ursula's hipness, fresh from *Dr. No*, and pre-empting their soon to come Bondian parody *Casino Royale*, by wrapping up *What's New Pussycat?* with an almost-into-camera aside: "she's a personal friend of James Bond!"

And, despite O'Toole's beautiful blue eyes never being more beautiful, it is Sellers who grabs up this neo-French sixties sex romp and shakes it into bonkers life. Wild, long, dark, luscious hair; thick, black, authoritative and intellectual-looking spectacles; and a strangled, Germanic, cod-Albert Einstein way with clever-sounding nonsense, gobbledegook, and psycho-babble, makes Peter's Doctor Fritz Fassbender so sixties, so cool, so of his time and so of a slapstick past. Fassbender is also very much of Peter's past too. There is an edge of Bluebottle about his offer to be the man who helps O'Toole out with his irresistible attractiveness to gorgeous women. Their hilarious sex chats indulge Sellers in Goonish sounds and gurgles. His gleeful admission that he: "likes thighs. Do you like thighs?" generates a very Goonish giggle indeed. Sellers also interjects with

---

1 The comic banter was still fresh a decade on when Sellers guested on *The Muppet Show*. His Strangelove-like physiotherapist gives a brutal massage to cleft-chinned matinee idol Link Hogthrob who says: "That Peter O'Toole is good!"

"You know!" – a lot. Very Goonish. And very funny. The playful physical business too is born of years of madcap expertise in this kind of outlandish and outrageous comedy. Whether it is getting the telephone receiver caught up in the hair; the emerging with a rose clenched between his teeth; or the Wagnerian tussle with his blonde battleaxe wife Anna (Eddra Gale).

Peter's is a larger-than-life portrayal. A hip and happening personification of sexual freedom of expression in Hollywood, and, without doubt, a pivotal role in his international stardom.

When the film was released on 22nd June 1965 it was a wow. It clearly had its saucy finger on the pulse of the in-crowd. It took just shy of twenty million dollars at the box office, and Peter Sellers was bankable beyond belief. He was the biggest comedy export of the sound era, and he could snigger, stumble, and over-play in over-the-top wig and costume. And get away with it. None of it mattered. He was hilarious. The world looked on and laughed. And dropped out. Glorious.

It was when promoting *What's New Pussycat?* that Sellers gave that oft-quoted remark about not being a Cary Grant: "I could never be a real star," he explained. "I am a character actor. I couldn't play Peter Sellers – the way Cary Grant plays Cary Grant, for instance – because I have no concrete image of myself. But I could do one helluva Cary Grant."[1]

Peter's Doctor Fritz Fassbender is very much a character acting part. It's a crazed romantic lead, of sorts, but in broad, brash terms. It's a heightened, insane comedy roller-coaster of lust. Certainly not Cary Grant. Still, having planted that seed in his own head, Sellers seemed hellbent on becoming a type of Cary Grant. A *Goon Show* twist on Cary Grant. It was a notion that would take a full-on five years of concentrated film work to reach full fruition. And it would take every inch of his comic genius.

Sellers was a comic genius, of course, and in 1965 a comic genius

---

1 It's a slightly different variation on that *ABC Film Review* quote, from June 1965, but like the real Peter Sellers having been surgically removed, it was a handy observation that he found a lot of mileage from when questioned by the press.

again by Royal Command too. On Monday, 8th November 1965, Her Majesty Queen Elizabeth II attended the Royal Variety Performance, at the London Palladium. It had been a full ten years since Peter had previously been on the regal bill, and boy what a difference a decade makes! Along with Spike Milligan, the roll-call of hip and happening talents included not only . . . Peter Cook and Ken Dodd and Tony Bennett, but also Dudney Moore and Jack Benny and Shirley Bassey.[1]

Peter had been merrily swimming in the Cook and Moore ken for a while now. Indeed, he had joined them in the cast of *The Wrong Box*, a dark satanic Victorian comedy melodrama from Bryan Forbes: actor cum film-maker cum good chum and old guest-starring cameo gag-player from *A Shot in the Dark*. Forbes had gladly sent himself up and shredded his clothes to play the nudist camp attendant. To keep the pleasant surprise, he had been credited as Turk Thrust. It had been a fond favour. Something that even thirteen heart attacks in the interim couldn't erase. Thus, Sellers was cock-a-hoop to take a Hansom Cab down to Pinewood Studios for an hilarious couple of days for Forbes's all-star re-working of Robert Louis Stevenson's jet-black novel *The Wrong Box*. Theatrical dignitaries John Mills and Ralph Richardson star as aged, feuding brothers, the last two survivors of a tontine which decrees the one that out-lives the other will inherit a fortune of £20,000. It's a breakneck, macabre farce, and Sellers has very little narrative importance. Indeed his character doesn't even feature in the original novel. That doesn't stop him pulling out every facial trick and slapstick schtick to effortlessly dominate his one scene. Even his name kind of lingers: Doctor Pratt.[2] With the endless supply of cats. The felines are everywhere. *What's New Pussy Cat?*, indeed. At one point Sellers even uses one as a blotting pad. For Bryan Forbes, "Peter's freedom and relaxed confidence in comedy was at a peak on *The Wrong Box*. He was so inventive. All that business about eggs not making good pets. They're too quiet! That was all Sellers'

---

1 And that's the last time I'll do that *Not Only* bit of business. Promise!

2 One likes to think that Sellers made the macabre connection with doyen of horror films Boris Karloff. Real name: William Henry Pratt.

invention. The entire crew cracked-up. Peter Cook cracked-up. Even I cracked-up. All rather fitting for comic ramblings on eggs. All Peter needed was a clue or two. Like a crossword puzzle. Give him a clue to his character and he would fill in the rest. For me, the good doctor is the perfect distillation of what made Sellers so uniquely funny."[1] The rather ponderous prose is given a brash New York make-over by scriptwriters Larry Gelbart and Burt Shevelove, while the showy casting of hip sixties icon Michael Caine – who enjoys a boxed-out credit under the two leads – certainly helped Salamander Film Productions and Columbia Pictures with international distribution after the film's British premiere on 27th May 1966. A minor but important point. It was the first film Sellers completed after his 40th birthday. Life, if cliche is to be believed, was just beginning. His prominent star guest billing certainly didn't do the film any damage in America either and, almost inevitably, it engendered praise from our old friend and trustworthy Sellers champion Bosley Crowther of the *New York Times* who singled out Peter after this fashion: "Perhaps the best of the clowning is the little bit Mr. Sellers does drink-sodden, absent-minded, skip-jack, fumbling foolishly and a little sadly among his cats." It's that "little sadly" that is the key for, although the sequence and Sellers is sublime slapstick, there is a profound melancholy at work here. A richly layered slice of silliness.

Sellers would play out 1966 as a special guest turn for Jonathan Miller: Cook's old Cambridge pal, Moore's *Beyond the Fringe* playmate, and a bright young thing that Sellers had sparked off of on the album *Bridge on the River Wye*. Three years on, now Jonathan Miller was wielding creative clout at the BBC, and his all-star adaptation of Lewis Carroll's *Alice in Wonderland* was a costly treat for the holiday fortnight. Being aired on 28th December 1966, Peter

---

1 Interview with the author, October 2007. Bryan Forbes was appointed Head of Production at Elstree Studios, in 1969, and the following year welcomed Sellers, and co-star Sinead Cusack, at the start of production on *Hoffman*. Forbes was also married to Peter's screen squeeze Nanette Newman. Although not in any scenes together, *The Wrong Box* marks the last film roles for glorious scene-stealers and notorious drinking buddies Wilfrid Lawson, as the aged butler, and Tony Hancock, as the befuddled detective. At the time plans were still afoot for their dream production of *King Lear*, with Lawson as the King and Hancock as the Fool.

fairly twinkles as the benign and bonkers King of Hearts.

The assignment came in the wake of an earnest and, in the end, unsuccessful attempt by the BBC to pump renewed vigour back into *The Goon Show*. It had all come about because of the relentless interest in the team following *The Telegoons*. A ratings-winning, mini-repeat season had hit the screen from the September of 1965, and in the wake of the triumph of Sellers and Spike at the London Palladium for the Royal Command that November, the talks of a revival series were at fever pitch. The plan was to relaunch *The Goon Show* as a television series on BBC2, and the continued interest, and schedule availability of the three principals, was in discussion until the spring of 1966. In the end it would be down to Milligan's various *Q* shows to reignite Goonish comedy at the Beeb Beeb Ceeb, for the Goons, at full-strength, finally got back, on screen, over at dear old Associated-Rediffusion. It had been nearly a decade since Sellers and Bentine had last been seen larking about for Associated-Rediffusion and, as has already been noted, what a difference a decade makes.

This time Sellers and Spike happily agreed to join in the fun for the 16th October 1966 edition of *Secombe and Friends*. The treat, dusted down from the vaults, was a newly-recorded vignette from *The Goon Show*: 'The Whistling Spy Enigma'. Ray Ellington even popped in for a chat. That's nice!

Harry Secombe was instrumental in getting the band back together again, in the March of 1967. This time, however, the occasion was tragic. ATV's *The Heart of Show Business* was broadcast on Easter Day, 26th March 1967. Under the direction of Alan Tarrant, it headlined great Welsh talent – including Shirley Bassey and Stanley Baker – contributing to a benefit in aid of the Aberfan Disaster Charity Fund. Aberfan was the beleaguered Welsh mining community whose village school had been engulfed by a slurry slide. Dreadful.

That this springtime showing of compassion from the showbiz fraternity should herald the summer of love is painfully beautiful. It also heralded Peter's full embarkation into the Jet-Set Years.

Peter's glut of international, hip and happening comedy successes were both personal and popular. They were the ABC of fashionable: *After the Fox*, *The Bobo*, and *Casino Royale*; and the very fabric of world-wise traveller. In the first he was an irritable Italian; in the second a sultry Spaniard; and finally a revealingly bland Brit in the most glamorous of settings.

Shot in the summer of 1966, back at the Cinecitta Studios, for the first time since *The Pink Panther*, and for the distinguished director Vittorio De Sica (who had played Joe in *The Millionairess*), *After the Fox* was the perfect pilfering pantomime for its 15th December 1966 release. Cast as master criminal Aldo Vanucci, there was an air of Peter's British-based heist classics *Two-Way Stretch* and *The Wrong Arm of the Law* about it; (even Maurice Denham, who was the prison governor in *Two-Way Stretch* bookends the action as the head honcho of Interpol): with an additional Yankee twang courtesy of scriptwriter Neil Simon, who delivered the screenplay in tandem with an uncredited Cesare Zavattini. The plot – using a film location shot to smuggle a haul of gold – is fabulous. A clever subterfuge for a film within a film within a plot. As a loving mockery of the art of film-making it's an absolute hoot. Sellers, with the wind in his international sails, and healthily post-heart attack scare, is in full, funny force.

United Artists lavished care and money onto the largely Italian cast and crew, with beautiful Bay of Naples locations, and a meta love letter to the nature and nurture of film-making by the neo-realist genius of *The Bicycle Thieves*. All with a swinging sixties kick. Having spearheaded *What's New Pussycat?* Burt Bacharach and Hal David wrote the catchy *After the Fox* title song, with the Hollies selling it alongside interjections from Sellers himself. He is the master chameleon in the film. The master criminal. A crook so cunning – like the fox – that he even fools himself at the end. Peter's performance switches from flamboyant, gesticulating, pretentious film-maker to impassioned, calm, collected, and belittled family man: "I'm the Poppa and the brother!" he yells at one point. Not with the over-the-top theatrics of his faux film director, but with the heart and soul of a true Italian. Intriguingly, it is at the moment that this jailbird decides to return to crime – for the good of the family – that Sellers is at his most calm; his most collected: "the fox is out of the tree", he says. It's this vital and pivotal phone pronouncement that sees Sellers sway from steely determination to childlike gentleness, when he realises that the person on the other end of the phone is not his criminal cohort but a youngster. It's gear-shifting, character-building, endearing, and believable . . . all in a matter of seconds of screen development.

The animated credits – with the cartoon fox removing his mask to reveal a smiling black and white visage of Sellers himself – is the perfect metaphor for this multifaceted, multi-characterisation turn. In a myriad of designs Peter is a bearded prison doctor, a troubled Catholic priest (who denounces movies as sinful!), a rigid military official, and, most throwaway and mumbling of all, a gum-chewing American tourist. It's a cartoon caricature, which somehow sums up an entire nation on holiday. Sellers dubs another doctor too, of course, which only adds layer upon layer to the confusion.

All that venting of feelings merely allows Sellers to impress even more in the subtle, imploring courtroom speech. You cheer for the invention, and you cheer for the honesty, and you cheer for the dishonesty. It's quite a feat of characterisation. And within all the intertextuality and cinematic pastiche there is the dull and lifeless reading of "Wonderful!" as his actors do their thing: running from themselves, and all that mockery of movie-making motivation. The almost turn to camera with the simple, dismissive "Lunch!" is spot on. And what of the actors starring in Peter's film within a film for the fantastical and fictional Italian genius Federico Fellini . . . sorry, I'll write that again Federico Fabrizi . . . : well, talk about self-aware send-up. Fading Hollywood matinee idol Victor Mature is a sensation as film star Tony Powell. He is dumb, vain, and steals scenes by doing very little but playing gullible and naivety with the gentlest of touch. His cry of, "I'd rather get laughs than sympathy!" could be a watch-phrase for the entire film. For Peter's entire career. Martin

Balsam, as the Hollywood publicist and agent, is an intricate pen-picture of the cinema mover and shaker, and played with delicious relish. If only for his snap assessment of what neorealism is – "no money!" – this is a personification of the cynicism of cinema. Loyalty also saw Peter secure chum David Lodge a small role, as a British policeman, confronted with Timothy Bateson's short-sighted petty crook. Peter wasn't even in the scene; not even in that narrative vignette. Friendship, you see.

Playing Peter's sister is Peter's wife and, yes, Britt Ekland is jaw-droppingly terrific as Gina, who simply wants to get into movies. There is a juvenile gaucheness to this beautiful woman, an innocent who overplays street-walking wisdom just right, tears up when her movie breakthrough is revealed as the criminal byproduct it has always been, and is just not impressed when the crazed film critic erupts with superlatives. This is De Sica sending up his own industry. Sellers is his clownish conduit. The perfect match. So much so that on-screen director and real director form a synergy. When Sellers, amateur and in extreme close-up, shooting nonsense, shooting anything, yells "Cut!" and the scene cuts to an evening serenade, it is a slice to celebrate. The playful toing and froing between rival criminal consortium is skilfully constructed too, greatly aided and abetted by the wry experience of Akim Tamiroff and statuesque glamour girl Maria Grazia Buccella. The hand-kissing, necking, and general flirtations to cover up the criminal chat required absolutely no acting on Peter's part at all.

What's more, the location filming afforded Sellers the opportunity of accepting a guest starring role opposite his squeeze from *The Millionairess*, for the television spectacular *With Love, Sophia*. A telling reunion with the lovely Loren, and while madcap American comedian Jonathan Winters was cast as a 16th-century sculptor, Sellers was a World War II British officer, in a comic travelogue filmed in and around Miss Loren's scrumptious villa in Rome. It's why Sophia endorsed and laughed along to the mock telephone conversation gag – used twice in *After the Fox*, with heightened success – as the faux film director desperately tries to convince all and sundry that Sophia Loren is eager for a part in the film. It's sly winks amongst friends taken to the maximum. And it works.

The August of 1966 saw Sellers in Barcelona, for *The Bobo*. Britt had a five-film contract with producer Jerry Gershwin and was assigned this project, picked up by Gershwin and partner Elliott Kastner, in May 1966. Britt was the chick that attracts the bullfighter maestro of Peter's character Juan Bautista. *The Bobo* was originally set to be Peter's second directorial effort, but in the end he decided to bring in Robert Parrish to oversee the film. Sellers did, however, direct several sequences.[1]

In the October of 1966 Peter had taken half a week off to nip along to Paris to film *Woman Times Seven*. It was a favour to Vittorio De Sica who had been a demi-dream of a director to work with. Plus the pivotal, titular star of the film was Shirley MacLaine, someone who Sellers adored and would adore even more at the bookend of his life on *Being There*. In seven very different personas – from cultural nymphomaniac interpreter to a faithful lover with a crush on Michael Caine – it's that kind of film – it is a showcase for a multi-talented screen actress. Peter's bit, the very first of the seven vignettes, is a deliciously dark eight minutes set during a Parisian funeral procession. Indeed, 'Funeral Procession' is the title of this opening segment. The dead is Shirley's husband. Shirley is Pauline here, clad in her widow weeds, accompanied by an earnest, bearded, rather furtive doctor, John – Sellers, of course. Within a few hundred yards in the rain-filled puddles of Paris, Sellers goes from loyal friend to besotted suitor. Sellers has all the heavy-lifting here: waxing lyrical about his French farmhouse, the delights of raw milk, and the subservient and sexy way he will treat this lady he has adored since first sight. Shirley is a model of subtle, tearful resolution, Sellers the anxious, abrupt and awkward romantic. Interrupted by motor cars whizzing by, and aghast fellow mourners putting him off his stride, Peter's continual opening and closing of his mouth, thinking better

---

1 Based on Burt Cole's 1959 novel *Olimpia*. It had originally been adapted for the screen in 1961, with Norman Jewison set to direct comedian Shelley Berman in Peter's role.

of yet another lavish expression of love, display the clear cogs of this man's scattergun mind played out in a ballet of facial tics and fumbled elegance. He wins in the end though. The two – Pauline and John – are so wrapped up in thoughts of a foreign getaway together that the hearse and the rest of the mourners go down one fork in the road, the fledgling lovers down the other.

For Sellers afficionados it's one of the rarest, sweetest and easily digestible slices of his mid-sixties gallery of continental lovers. For Sellers himself it was a brief but blessed break from the upheaval of filming *The Bobo*. Still, the rest from the film, and the break from Britt, clearly did him good and put him in such a lovely place that, somewhat surprisingly, his discernment abandoned him. For, returning to *The Bobo* set, and watching all the rushes of the footage so far shot, he declared to anybody who cared to listen that it was a masterpiece. The best film he had ever seen.

Whether Peter was being delusional or not, the first few months of 1967 were eventful, indeed. On 30th January, Peter's mother Peg died, at the age of 75. His last completed film, *After the Fox*, had at its domestic heart a fiery, truthful relationship with an overpowering mother (played with gusto by Lydia Brazzi). A few days later, on 2nd February, Peter was a guest on the *ABC Stage 67* show *David Frost's Night Out in London*. He starred in two sketches: one as a pompous person at a pretentious wine tasting, and the other as a befuddled television interviewer chatting to a supposed deep-sea diver, portrayed by his old chum and fellow funny voice man Kenneth Connor. He's actually an insurance agent! The comedy skits were written by Tim Brooke-Taylor, John Cleese, and Barry Cryer who recalled: "Sellers was brilliant. He just seemed to turn up and do it. Kenny Connor was an old mate of his, of course, so the two just clicked. After a bit of argy-bargy over the sketches, Peter was very affable to everybody, showed no sense of stage fright whatsoever, and certainly no sense of personal loss. I certainly didn't know at the time that his poor old Mum had just died. He was professional and as warm and funny as you could hope."[1] Still, the gilt may have been off the ginger bread of the investiture of his CBE, at Buckinghamshire Palace, on 7th February. It was the highest of accolades, although Sellers would have preferred a Knighthood. Quite right too.

As regards the quality of his latest film, Peter Sellers Commander of the Order of the British Empire, *was* being delusional, of course. The lukewarm reaction to *The Bobo* proved it. The actor didn't seem that bothered anymore. Without the clinging approval of Peg, what did critical approval matter?

Things were certainly not good with Britt either. Having played brother and sister in *After the Fox*, Mr. and Mrs. Sellers were now playing the potential lovers: Britt as a tantrum-throwing baby doll blonde attraction, with Peter's own, borderline and beyond, sexual fascination with fast cars. With fire in her belly, and wistful sensuality when Sellers seduces her with an impoverished love song – with lyrics actually concocted by maestro of the Great American Song Book, Sammy Cahn – the wooing and conquering of the manipulative ice queen is romantic indeed.

Sellers, well on the road to beautifully playing every nationality under the sun, is as affectionate and understated as he was when essaying Italian the previous year. Here, as a simple and gentle singing matador from a little Spanish village, this cheese-sandwich-obsessed entertainer merely wants to prove himself in the eyes of the local theatrical impresario – a wild-eyed, vindictive supporting role of gargantuan appetite from Adolfo Celi.

There is no mockery within Peter's performance; no comic characteristics. Just pure humanity, and pure desperation in having to do whatever it takes to perform and keep him in those cheese sandwiches . . . even if that means to deceive and bewitch the fair Olimpia, as a ways and a means to live his dream life. The plot dictates that Celi is eaten up with jealousy and bitterness over the young woman, so much so that he wagers Peter's wandering troubadour, Juan Bautista, a week's paid residency at his theatre if he can bed

---

1 Interview with the author, March 2021.

her. The revelation that it is merely for the sum of two thousand peseta pay is a shock to the girl. It is also a moment when Sellers gives the most touching realisation of what he has done. The shame, the humiliation, and the humble pity for putting the woman through such subterfuge. There are real tears in his eyes. Real remorse.

The blue dye revenge of Britt's character – overly used in promotional materials, and rather giving the game away to cinema queues – has, over the decades, rather overshadowed the central good-heartedness of Peter's performance. He is an honourable man, forced into behaving dishonourably. The fact that all can laugh at his ultimate misfortune – even Juan himself – is proof that within the core reasoning of Peter's accepting of any given role was the fundamental pay-off of shared humour. Like Juan, Sellers simply wanted to entertain.

Britt's character may be unpleasant, and uncaring, but we still, ironically, care for her. Sellers may be focused to the point of tunnel-vision but we still will him on. The star-crossed lovers don't get hurt, just blue. There is certainly an air of carefree continental travelogue about these swinging sixties international vehicles for Sellers: screen space is made for a moment, always, for reflection on local colour, local customs, and local entertainment. A sort of *International Cabaret* built into the story. There is too a fantasy reality at play within the on-screen courtship. One could not guess that the marriage was on the rocks, and that Sellers had already instructed his solicitors to file for divorce. Both are terrific actors, for sure.

The audience were, of course, fully aware that Peter and Britt were husband and wife in real life: the marriage generated acres of column inches in contemporary newspapers and fan magazines. That the bickering and bantering and bludgeoning desire is played so forcefully, and so convincingly, is testament to the skill and precision of both actors. From pompous put-down through wide-eyed wonderment, and finally disgust, resentment, and comic ultimatum, it is a roller-coaster relationship indeed. For Sellers, alongside a truly likeable, anti-hero of maturity and resolve, are treasurable touches of slapstick clowning: the exploding champagne bottle resulting in a dab of fizz behind both ears; the playful incoherence with the modern telephone; the enchanting, staccato dancing blending into heightened bull-fighting with Britt's modern, groovy gyrating.[1]

His absent-minded chomping upon the flowers is not so absent-minded as it seems. It is the root of the natural calmness within the Juan character. His life mantra being, that if a thing looks good and smells good it will taste good also. Far more than just metaphorical love chat with an on-the-verge of love reaction from Britt's character Olimpia, it sets up the line of dialogue that provides the mission statement for Juan's life. The mission statement for Peter's life too: "I like to enjoy life with all my senses."

The globe was turning on and tuning in and dropping out to *Sgt. Pepper's Lonely Hearts Club Band* when Warner Brothers released *The Bobo* on 28th September 1967.[2] Critically it was greeted with a mixture of disinterest and dismissal. Even Peter's journalistic champion Bosley Crowther was left cold by it, rather shockingly considering the Sellers performance a lacklustre one. The most positive spin came from Richard Schickel, of *The Times*, who opinionated: "There comes a time in the life of every screen comedian when he urgently feels the need to have the adjective 'Chaplinesque' applied to his work. It is a dangerous moment, with the pitfall of pretentiousness yawning on one side, sentimentality on the other and all the psychological hazards of overreaching buzzing in the back of the mind. It is a pleasure to report that Peter Sellers – that excellent fellow – has not only endured this trial, but has mostly prevailed over it."

Indeed, there is a pinch of Chaplin about the bookended arriving and leaving of Juan in Barcelona. We first meet him as a name imprinted

---

1 There is even a spirited "Yeah!" from Sellers in this scene which, lock, stock, and smoking cloak, could have been dropped into an Austin Powers film some thirty years hence. It's the sixties, baby!

2 The Beatles, now having moved on from Peter's Goon-film chum Richard Lester, had, apparently, set their sights on Peter's critically-acclaimed cinema collaborator Stanley Kubrick. The proposed starring of the Fab Four in a film version of *The Lord of the Rings* went unmade, and my learned friend Patrick Humphries, author of *With the Beatles* (Great Northern Books, 2024) believes the rumour is apocryphal. Peter Jackson would take on Tolkien . . . and the Beatles, but that's Patrick's story.

on a tatty trunk, then with his back to the camera, walking away, dejectedly, with his guitar-case slung over his shoulder. The musical sting of plaintive Spanish strings is enough to paint this character as a loser, a vagabond, a little tramp even. He is an innocent, a waif; a character not quite in step with the rest of the world. However, as Schickel asserts, Sellers does avoid the pitfalls of pathos and bathos in *The Bobo*. There is a jollity within his comeuppance, and a spring in his step, even if his future, at the film's close, is inevitable and dispiriting.

Even so Sellers *was* momentarily tempted to indulge his inner slapstick clown, when Eric Sykes came a'calling with a very noisy silent comedy for the big screen. *The Plank* would star Sykes and Sellers as a couple of hapless carpenters, and their hilarious battle with a six-foot piece of plywood. The marquee value of the two old Goon pals was required for the film to get distribution, according to Sykes, who, in turn, desperately courted his international box office guaranteeing chum over three weeks of intensive lunches. With every mouthful of good food and fine wine Peter's glee mounted. The intricate, beautifully constructed series of mishaps and mistakes would not so much be Laurel and Hardy, as Laurel and Laurel. The great Stan had died, in 1965, just over a year after Sellers had finally met him. *The Plank* would be Peter's affectionate salute to this titan of comedy. But, in the end, Sellers dropped out of the project, and Tommy Cooper, with even bigger feet, stepped in. Not before Sykes had secured the budget on the back of Peter's promise to appear though. For Peter it wasn't his inner Chaplin or his inner Laurel he now wanted to prove, it was his inner Cary Grant, or more pressingly, his inner Sean Connery . . .

Chapter 11

"Send in our highly skilled mysterious whistling espionage agent."

Grytpype-Thynne

The James Bond franchise was the biggest blockbuster in the world. Out of Pinewood Studios, and with lavish locations across the globe, Sean Connery as James Bond 007 Licence to Kill was the very definition of film star. By the summer of 1967 Connery was starring in his fifth James Bond smash hit, *You Only Live Twice*. During production it had been announced that Connery was relinquishing the role.[1] Thus a pastiche, playing around with the title of Ian Fleming's very first James Bond novel, was not only inevitable but a box office powder keg.

Casino Royale – the spoof – cast the great and the good as James Bond: from David Niven as Sir James Bond, the original you might say, to Woody Allen, as weedy, duplicitous Jimmy Bond. As the poster tagline screamed: "It's not much . . . for one James Bond!" Quite! Still, as far as MGM were concerned their proper James Bond was Peter Sellers, as Evelyn Tremble, codename James Bond 007. From that very first scene – displaying his credentials in a Parisian pissoir with dour Duncan Macrae, Sellers is every inch the cool face of espionage. It's funny too. When Sellers gets on his tip-toe to check out what's been boasted about, it's beyond double meaning.

Still, not only the expected funnies, but also lean, mean, super-fit and super-famous, this is Sellers as a professional heart-attack survivor on a mission to prove himself a matinee idol.

Much later in the film, in stripped swimming suit and cavorting

---

1 Although he would return twice more, officially in *Diamonds Are Forever*, and unofficially for *Never Say Never Again*.

with Ursula Andress and play-acting in front of her new-fangled cine camera, this is post-heart-attack Sellers in reality as well as fun. The bespectacled coolness is replaced by Sellers, sans glasses, with a performance of the ultra-coolness of James Bond proper. In this guise he bumps into old chum Graham Stark, as a star-struck casino receptionist.[1] Stark even asks the suave, supposed spy for his autograph. Upon and beyond the obvious, fumbled moments – notably opposite Colin Gordon as the Head of the Casino and a hilarious reaction to a lolling tongue emerging from a stuffed tiger – Peter's action hero has a Goon at its core, of course. Notably whilst relishing a wacky five minutes in the dressing-up basket with Ursula Andress: at turns Sellers disguises himself as a General, a gay Hitler – of course – and diminutive powerhouses Napoleon and Toulouse-Lautrec. Naturally it's all to impress the beauteous ex-Bond girl; the proper Bond girl; as well as indulge the madcap comic swiftness of Sellers, the performer. The voices of these mini-impersonations are impeccable, naturally, as are the Indian and Chinese sayings Peter lapses into during the pivotal and tense Baccarat showdown with Orson Welles. Even though there are these little concessions to Goonish folklore, to his screen credit Sellers doesn't crack once, not once, in the 141 minutes of running, jumping and standing still time. Although, to be fair, after that opening urinal gag spot, Sellers doesn't appear again for nearly an hour. That pre-title sequence in the pissoir is tacked on at the front to give the punters Sellers: what they want. Immediately. It was actually lifted from the narrative just before Sellers wanders into the casino, in full James Bond mode. The scrawled graffiti of Les Beatles beds the film in the psychedelic sixties as well as making it timeless. Now and Then, indeed. However, how David Niven's agent justified his third billing in place of pole position I'll never know; although considering Niven, like Sellers, was represented by Dennis Selinger, the agent got both his clients a very good deal! Still, for Sellers up there and Niven somewhere in

---

1 Sellers' chums, outside of Sellers' scenes, in *Casino Royale*, also number Burt Kwouk as a Chinese ambassador; Bernard Cribbins as an undercover agent posing as a London cabbie; and John Le Mesurier, as a silent and belligerent chauffeur – just days away from the career lifeline of *Dad's Army*.

the middle, it had been quite a three years since *The Pink Panther*.

Being surrounded as he is by pals and adversaries, only heightened the intensity and the truthfulness of Peter's performance. In the lengthy roll-call of directors on *Casino Royale* was Joe McGrath – of television's *Not Only . . . But Also* – who steered Peter through most of his important scenes, including the showdown with Orson Welles. Sellers and Welles were at loggerheads throughout. A rather fitting situation for Bond and the big Bond baddie. McGrath orchestrated the casino scene in such a way that Welles would film his scenes on one day and then, the following day, Sellers would be brought in to film his scenes. Never the twain shall meet. Almost. They do appear, very fleetingly, in the same frame. And Sellers holds his own extremely well. While he is doing the occasional silly voice alongside the steely confidence of the super spy, Welles is engaging in one-upmanship, enjoying himself with an array of self-indulgent and typical magic tricks and cigar-chomping put-downs. He even injects an "Old man . . ." to resurrect memories of Harry Lime from *The Third Man*.

On first meeting, at least, Sellers had warmly greeted Welles in pre-production, and greatly looked forward to sparring with the mercurial talent on film. In the end, when the physically diminished Sellers and the exuberantly expanding Welles met it was a knock-out: "Welles, arriving for work every day, made a habit of pointedly asking, 'Where's our thin friend this morning?'"[1] Much more than bulk though, it was a severe case of Mr. Topaze coming face to face with Citizen Kane. With the best will in the world, that was Featherweight vs. Heavyweight. No contest. McGrath works wonders to give the scene dramatic tension and humour. McGrath was no slouch in the pugilistic art either: "Sellers and I came to blows during that film. Peter punched me. And I punched him back! At that moment that beautiful stunt man Gerry Crampton stepped between the two of us and said: 'I can't hit either of you. I love you both!' That broke the tension with warm laughter. Later I told

1 *Orson Welles: The Stories of His Life*, by Peter Conrad (Faber & Faber, 2003).

Spike Milligan what had happened and he looked amazed and a little impressed. He said: 'You hit Peter! I hit him once. I tell you Joe, he's your friend for life!' And he was!"[1]

That friendship certainly shows in certain, post-battle, sequences in *Casino Royale*, where McGrath's lens makes Sellers look and feel like James Bond. Notwithstanding the plot devices. Indeed, the notion of multiple Bonds and the bequeathing of the name and number was prescient too. Sellers even gets to punch-out an innocent customs officer. In a moment of pure cinema action hero, Sellers looks the part. It's a seriously good, well-sustained performance in a madcap romp which allows Sellers to be heroic; obstinate; and very, very funny. Often all at once. And, apart from the aforementioned and absolutely stunning Miss Andress, there's young Jacqueline Bisset, billed as Jacky Bisset in those days, as the perfectly Bondian-named honeytrap Miss Goodthighs. Sellers gets to get off with her too. It's a tough assignment, for sure! The aftermath of the seduction is another cold and calculated moment of pure action hero for Sellers: he is genuinely angry and aggressive, in the drugged fug, as Andress revives him. His bitterness that the secret service anecdote pill failed is tangible indeed.

That he goes out in a machine-gun attack within a Scots mist is certainly not the weirdest scene in this gloriously unhinged film. There's a mad dream sequence – after he has drunk the drugged champagne proffered by Jacky Bisset. This is a trip to end all trips, with an orgy of card games and Ursula Andress snogging. It's hell in there, I tell you. In the Scottish sequence Sellers even bumps into *What's New Pussycat?* chum Peter O'Toole who asks him whether he is Richard Burton. Sellers replies, to O'Toole, that, no, he is Peter O'Toole, and the Irish adonis waves his sporran in glee. It's that kind of film. Wonderfully. It's even the kind of film in which ex-Man in Black and Goon favourite Valentine Dyall can voice – spoiler alert – Woody Allen as arch villain Doctor Noah. Oh, yes.

The Bobo director, or as far as Peter was concerned, co-director,

---

1 Interview with the author, July 2003.

Robert Parrish was also in the mixed-up mixture of *Casino Royale*; while Peter's old mentor and champion Val Guest oversaw much of the establishing shots and backstory material with David Niven and Deborah Kerr. Ken Hughes and John Huston – who also appears, under Val Guest's direction – had a bash at directing sections of the elephantine romp too. The screenplay was written, in the main, by Wolf Mankowitz, who had contributed to and then hated the original screenplay for the inaugural James Bond film *Dr. No*. Even more importantly, for Sellers, Mankowitz had also written *The Millionairess*. The rest of the glorious muddle of *Casino Royale* was fleshed out by writers more familiar with television: with *The Frost Report* sketch guru John Law pitching in. Law had a hand in the hilarious, non-Sellers vignettes with Joanna Parrit as the daughter of super spies James Bond and Mata Hari, and the Bond nemesis Polo, played with Peter Lorre-like conviction by Ronnie Corbett. Corbett, a talisman from *The Frost Report* too, of course, had also been a close friend of Sean Connery. Both were Edinburgh-born, in 1930, and would hang out while finding their feet in London's West End. John Law's contributions sat comfortably alongside Michael Sayers, who had cut his teeth on ITC historical serials like *William Tell*, and *The Adventures of Robin Hood*. *Casino Royale* was his last writing credit. What a way to go!

Donald Zec, the distinguished film critic for the *Daily Mirror*, called *Casino Royale*: "the worst film I ever enjoyed!" and I know exactly what he means. It's a glorious smorgasbord of trendy fashions and pop culture; a wacky time capsule from when Carnaby Street was the centre of the known universe and Britannia was well and truly cool. It's a colourful, noisy, exhilarating mess, but it's never boring, never not eye-catching, and never not one of the most gleeful and life-affirming credits in the cinematic CV of one Peter Sellers.

Peter had been in ultra-serious, ultra-cinematic hip mode, when he accepted that starry cameo in the funeral procession segment of *Woman Times Seven* . . . but he was happiest in his position as the playboy of the pratfall that Blake Edwards had gifted him.

While United Artists were badgering and badgering for their dream team to reunite on the third instalment of the Pink Panther series, Sellers and, to a lesser extent, Edwards, was reluctant to oblige. United Artists couldn't bear to wait so, with Alan Arkin donning the trench coat in the lead role, and with Bud Yorkin directing, they ploughed on regardless. Mirisch Films released *Inspector Clouseau* in the spring of 1968. To something of a damp squelch. Joe Public was no mug, and they knew that this was a desperate attempt to keep the series going without the talents that gave it its spark.

United Artists need not have worried though, for that spring schedule of 1968 also included the aforementioned and much-desired Sellers and Edwards, alongside composer extraordinaire Henry Mancini, having been gleefully busy conjuring up what is – arguably – their finest slice of full-throttle slapstick fantasy of all. The mercurial; the unique; the utterly-adorable; and relentlessly-hilariously *The Party*. Originally entitled *RSVP*, the film started shooting on 15th May 1967.

As Indian actor and fledgling Hollywood leading man Hrundi V. Bakshi, Sellers throws himself into the wildest, most physical star comedy vehicle since the glory days of 'Buster' Keaton and Harold Lloyd some forty summers previously. And this was 1967. The Summer of Love. In the All-Fools April that followed, on 4th April 1968 to be precise, United Artists proudly unveiled the latest Sellers and Edwards comic masterpiece. Edwards, himself, of course, had, post-*Pink Panther*, delivered an epic, all-star comedy chase, in the vein of Stanley Kramer's *It's a Mad, Mad, Mad, Mad World*, from 1963: a film for which, in what would have been his first Hollywood assignment, Peter had been first choice for the frightfully British J. Algernon Hawthrone before old cohort Terry-Thomas put it on like a perfectly tailored Savile Row suit. The Blake Edwards film, *The Great Race*, had pitted Tony Curtis opposite Jack Lemmon and been lovingly dedicated to Mr. Laurel and Mr. Hardy. The fact that this Edwardian romp had swiftly made back double its 12-million-dollar budget had been more than enough to keep Mr. Edwards in the very good books of United Artists. The fact that Sellers was willing to work with the film-maker for the third time was lip-smacking to executives indeed. Whammo. A sixty-three-page script was approved, green lit, and in every way, eagerly endorsed by United Artists. So what if Sellers was playing Indian this time and not French, it was a bumbling idiot at odds with the world at large. It was Sellers. And Edwards. Yes.

The Party was largely improvised between Sellers and Edwards. If they had one inspiration to reference and latch upon it was Jacques Tati: much admired by Sellers as the greatest laughter-making talent of contemporary cinema, he was the masterful French clown of the comedy of one man at war with all he encounters, particularly inanimate objects. All in the nicest, most silly, and frustratingly relatable way, of course. *The Party* is really a nothing kind of a movie. No, wait, hear me out. It's not a nothing kind of a comedy, but it's certainly a nothing kind of a plot. It doesn't need to be anything else. The premise is the slenderest of all. Sellers is an Indian actor; a one-man accident-prone disaster area for any Hollywood budget. Although never referenced as such in the film, the movie in crisis stars Sellers, as the Son of Gunga Din. The tone is set from the outset. Even in this most heroic of moments, as Din makes a din of his bugle and saves the British troops, Peter mugs and over-acts and demonstrates that, once again, it takes a genius of an actor to play a bad actor. Bakshi himself is a hero though, of course. Following the catalogue of set-pieces, slapstick vignettes, and high-society faux pas, Bakshi is a hero to wane and wistful French starlet Michele Monet (played by the wane and wistful, and totally enchanting Claudine Longet). However Bakshi does not arrive on a white charger, but in a pair of white loafers. This is the essence of *The Party*. Although this heart, this detail, is there in the two-reel comedies Sellers loved; the full-length feature allows the depth and truth of the clown to bloom. No story to speak of; no change of location for the most part. Just pure Peter Sellers. Stripped of his good-natured nervousness, he is gallant, respectable, sweetly charming, and oh so ever so nice. It is the bread and butter for a comedic actor of Peter's instinct and skill, this seemingly effortless ability to switch from guffaw-inducing goon to gentle gentleman. It's catnip for the ladies, particularly in the Hollywood of late sixties excess that *The Party* holds up to the prism and then proceeds to prick out its pomposity. Still, it is those crazy, self-contained moments of heightened sight humour that makes *The Party* such a delirious and dizzying comedy experience. It's a fabulous, fragmented time capsule of a Hollywood that never was: a pastiche of the orgies of the twenties, that Timothy Leary mentality of the sixties, the never never land of La La Land.

For Sellers he hatches out his inner silent clown to squeeze every drop of hilarity out of the lost white shoe – aided and abetted by Steve Franken who as the increasingly drunkard waiter almost walks off with the picture, stealing several scenes right from under Peter's nose. Not that Sellers was threatened. He was delighted. Franken even works wonders with a nothing kind of role, in foil to Sid Ceasar, in Peter's final, completed film, *The Fiendish Plot of Dr. Fu Manchu*, twelve years later. That Sellers gathered Franken close on that project speaks volumes of comedy reassurance.

In *The Party* there's the water closet with a mind of its own too, with a completely unfurling toilet-roll dispenser, and collapsing cistern-lid. There are, of course, mild traces of Goonish terminology as well. As always with Peter. His childlike delight in encountering an – at first – frosty, and irritated Denny Miller as Hollywood's Western hero 'Wyoming' Bill Kelso is charming. The actor who had played Tarzan in the late fifties and, indeed, became a go-to face for big and small screen horse operas, had already guest-starred in *Have Gun, Will Travel*, and notched up 106 episodes on *Wagon Train*, before *The Party* gave him a self-referencing, affectionately self-parodying role: his favourite in a long, long career.

All this familiar, name-on-the-tip-of-your-tongue, but not real big star casting for *The Party* achieves something of a plus . . . in that we become Sellers, thrown into an unfamiliar world of a Hollywood Party, with faces we may recognise. A real, tangible Hollywood

Party, with us as the dumbstruck, awkward outsider . . . within. The play-acting gunfighting, and misplaced firing of a toy arrow, from Peter, full of awkward, star-struck love, doesn't undercut Kelso's undiluted love for the little fellow. At every opportunity Sellers calls the hulking macho man his buddy, and you believe it. So does the film. At the end of *The Party*, the big man upgrades the autographed scrap of paper to an 8x10 photo . . . not to mention a Stetson hat. Neatly, it is this Stetson hat that gives Peter's character the excuse to return to his fair French lady love. He gifts the hat to her, during the morning after the night before, and almost immediately admits that he would like his hat back. Bingo. Not a cute meet, but a cute semi-farewell, a cute reason to continue the relationship, and continue the romance.

It is the calmness and underplaying of these moments that allows Sellers the freedom to embrace the pure slapstick, and allow those moments to breathe, thrive, and sit happily within this garish reality. It was this skilful walking of a tightrope that made Sellers completely at ease during the making of the film. *The Party* was such a joy in production that, on those very rare occasions he looked back on his work, it was a very pleasant memory. That pleasure still radiates. The "Birdie Num Num" line is one of the momentous moments in his screen career. Done with sheer love and laughter, it is the innocent in a world of wealth. The idiot in an idiotic universe.

Sellers was particularly delighted to learn that *The Party* was at its most successful and lastingly popular in India. And that Indira Gandhi was a fan. In the film, when Sellers is asked, "Who do you think you are?" he proudly but never smugly answers, "In India we don't think who we are, we know who we are!" Gandhi would often repeat this line. Glorious.

It puts to rest the question of racism. For the baby elephant in the pool has become the bull elephant in the room. Not a fault of *The Party*, but because of good-intentioned, received revisionism. That line of dialogue that Gandhi was so enamoured of, and which inspired praise of Peter's performance from none other than the father of

Indian Cinema Satyajit Ray, is all the more profound and powerful because of the context of the scene. Sellers, being Sellers, knows not to play any moment in that scene for laughs. It is his big moment as the hero of the party within *The Party*. He rescues the damsel in distress. And this is the real revisionist subtext that *The Party* is keen to reveal. It tackles the casting coach and the future of Me Too and women's place within Hollywood with more clout and understanding than simply being a mere fringe benefit of the slapstick. Sellers, as the outsider, both in terms of an Indian actor in Hollywood in the plot and a British comedian in Hollywood in reality, undermines the lascivious advances of the Filmland hoodlum in a thousand-dollar suit. We have seen this Executive Producer, played with single-minded unpleasantness by Gavin MacLeod, blow up at Bakshi's wrecking of the film within a film and, moreover, callously have on tap a bikini-clad blonde bombshell who, reluctantly puts down her pulp novel, and dutifully follows him into his trailer. It's sex on tap, and although this Hollywood hick is ridiculed – his toupee wearing is just one of the guilty secrets stumbled upon by Peter in search of a vacant toilet – he is a forceful man, pinning Michele to the bed with promises of Hollywood stardom. He certainly doesn't take rejection well. Or mockery. There's the drug culture too: peppering Western popular culture, and subtly exposed as rife in Hollywood. A gaggle of geezers are caught puffing wacky baccy in one toilet, while, most telling and subtle of all, a couple of young ladies touch their noses in nervousness, as a line of Colombia's finest hits the spot. The fact that the chief protagonist in this little slice of social commentary is the blonde bimbo stooge (Natalia Borisova) of Peter's dinner-table comedy – with the flying roasted fowl; the painfully tiny chair – merely drives the point home with additional force. It's a throwaway moment but the very heart of *The Party*, and the very heart of Peter's pure performance. No drugs; no debauchery; no drink. The fact that medicinal brandy is – reluctantly – taken not only gives Peter's performance the excuse to behave outrageously, but also paints him even more as the innocent; the child; in a horrible, grown-up world.

For me, you only have to run *The Party* to palpably see the joy and affection that beats within its comic heart.

Despite the Indian musical stings during the pre-title sequence of Peter's next film, *"I Love You, Alice B. Toklas!"*, set for release in the summer of 1968, this one was all about the drugs . . . and debauchery . . . and a little bit of drink. It is all about embracing the essence of the new age. All about the peace and love. The film, in which Sellers was cast as American attorney Harold Fine, knowingly cottoned on to George Harrison's Inner Light spiritualism, and passion for India. Directed by Hy Averback for Warner Bros.-Seven Arts, the film's Los Angeles preview screening took place on 29th August 1968, with a general release across America from 18th October. Once more it proved that not only was Sellers the most bankable clown in the world, but that his film choices were right on the pulse of contemporary thought and understanding. *"I Love You, Alice B. Toklas!"* is so 1968 it hurts: a psychedelic sex comedy whose sole ambition is to bring peaceful thoughts to the police, while spreading the mantra of make love, not war, via the relentless on-screen bed-hopping of the young members of the cast. Sellers, as the rather humourless figure of authority, merely has to look on with a weary shake of the head. *Then* he gets it, with a Legalise Pot badge, a bandana, and the full freak out and get it on mentality. The poster tagline screamed: "Peter Sellers explores new territory . . ." as the image shows him closely examining the thigh tattoo of a butterfly on the young girl (Leigh Taylor-Young). To get the punters in – unaware – the poster illustration is that familiar chat show personality Sellers, with nice shirt and thick-rimmed glasses, rather than the happy, clappy, hippie Sellers that dominates the film. Within the film he is the progressive and sexually-pioneering screen comedian of *Only Two Can Play*, but with added Hollywood money and added late-sixties permissiveness. That kissing of the butterfly thigh is one thing. Even more daring is his demand to kiss my eyes, kiss my neck, kiss my ankh. Yes, his ankh! When Taylor-Young, as Nancy, touches her lips to the religious symbol round his neck, the camera flips onto his white-clad back. An image of peace and purity, but Peter's back of the neck acting is pure indulgence, pure orgasm. There's also the lovely detail of a huge, framed portrait of Laurel and Hardy above his fireplace. This is Peter Sellers stamping a character with lots and lots of himself.

It's not just the nod to Stan and Olly that screams classic comedy in a groovy setting. There's a delightful cameo for Grady Sutton, ageing Hollywood Mummy's Boy who, nearly thirty years before, had bamboozled W.C. Fields in *The Bank Dick*. Moreover, the final revelation that the beatnik lifestyle is not for Sellers – wallowing in a bubble bath and invaded by fellow peaceniks – is pure Marx Brothers . . . with a spliff. The insanity of thirties slapstick meeting sixties hallucinogenics creates the ultimate swinging sixties sex romp and, boy, in sixties Hollywood there were plenty of those. The fever for square, middle-class, middle-aged businessmen dropping out of commercialism and discovering the ways of the peace Guru was everywhere . . . even as early as 1963's *It's a Mad, Mad, Mad, Mad World*. Here Dick Shawn's hippie ways may dismay his brother-in-law, Milton Berle, but the besuited, and befuddled Berle has an attractive trophy wife (Dorothy Provine) and bravely faces the British brickbats of Terry-Thomas who succinctly sums up America's obsession with breasts. This obsession is personified in *"I Love You, Alice B. Toklas!"* in the guise of Peter's office chronic Murray (Herb Edelman) who spends a quiet few minutes ogling every hot, mini-skirted girl that walks past.

Typically this mature, over-sexed, very married dinosaur blames the females for flaunting it. It's a theme covered by Gene Kelly's *A Guide for the Married Man*, the previous year. Sellers doesn't tap into this anarchic mentality. He's intrigued, then enraptured by the far-out Timothy Leary-inspired ethos of the hippie community. At once going from a groovy comparison of it with communism, to embracing it fully, he ultimately moves out of his swish apartment, and goes all out for free love in the back of his swish car. The multicoloured status symbol may undermine his hippie transformation, but we, as an audience, like Sellers. And we root for him, mainly because the source of his transformation is a comic mistake. Ah yes, of course, it's the hash brownies that the plot spins upon. Those hash brownies, which are lovingly prepared by the tempting youth and unwittingly consumed by Sellers and his very proper fiancee and the very proper, very Jewish parents. It's this scene that set the box office turnstiles spinning too. Tickets were sold simply to see these solid pillars of establishment, dropping out, getting high, and enjoying life. For finance Joyce (Joyce Van Patten) it merely makes her uber-horny; for the parents (Janet Clark and Salem Ludwig) it rekindles fun and frolics; for Sellers, it reinstates a faith in humanity, a spark of love for his mother, and a moment of peace for the reawakening of his often-overshadowed father. This is true happiness. Mere possessions don't matter. Love is the word. Peter's performance is pure love too. Escaping the strait-jacket of business and respectability, this legal eagle goes full white figure of peace and love. Understated, calm, focused, and more than happy to allow Jo Van Fleet – as his overbearing, fussy mother – to get the lion's share of the laughs, Peter's comedy comes from the situation, and the dumb-founded reaction to the American society norms around him. Tellingly, in the years immediately after the death of his mother Peg, mothers were now a staple of Sellers comedy.

In the shadow of the serious character Sellers plays at the start of the film, the hip and happening Sellers – forty-three playing thirty-five – could be a caricature, a send-up of the hippie movement. Rather winningly, he is the American spin on his Doctor from *What's New Pussycat?*, and that the hair, make-up and wardrobe department summon up respect and likability speaks volumes. All this to a life soundtrack from Harpers Bizarre . . . and, indeed, even though it could all be a bad trip, man, Sellers, at the end of the day and the end of the film, wants and needs to believe that life is beautiful. Somewhere. Sellers keeps his past pretty much to the past too. The only really funny, Goonish, trip occurs when in conversation with Louis Gottlieb, as his poetic Guru on the beach. Barefoot and skipping over hard pebbles and chilly splashes of water, Sellers incorporates a funny little sidewards jump. It's tiny but there. Just a reminder of the wackiness that beats hard within the heart of the actor.

Peter's truth as an actor gives his character of Harold complete believability, complete integrity. His message of love and kindness and understanding is never mocked, by himself at least. The powerful line to the hardened cop, explaining that Sellers himself once had a gun . . . in my heart, is the most perfect summing up of the peace movement you could ever hope for. It's rather beautiful. Everything's better with love . . . and a little brownie recipe from the cookbook of Alice B. Tolkas, whether you like it or not. It may not last, it may not be practical, but, by heavens, it makes for a happier life.[1]

That Sellers was at the spearhead of this revolution was important to him as both a comic actor and as a barometer of social understanding. If Cary Grant hadn't retired a year or two earlier, it's a role that he could have worn like a slightly ill-fitting velvet jacket, or, with a few more movies under his belt, it could have been played by Woody Allen. It's the exact morphing that Sellers wanted. The cool youth and comic consciousness of his hip co-star from *Pussycat*; and the urbane, fish out of water handsomeness and ageless elegance of a screen idol from his own youth. In Harold Fine, Sellers becomes the zeitgeist for the American Jew.

Still, despite happily taking the American dollars – and lots of them – Sellers pocketed the, by now, expected Blake Edwards-sized profit-share King's ransom for *The Party* and another, not-so-small, fortune for *Toklas*, the old, old cry of once a Goon, always a Goon remained a relevant one.[2]

Yes, even at the very moment when the comedian emerged from the chrysalis and became the dashing leading man, Peter eagerly got

---

1 Yes, *The Alice B. Toklas Cook Book* was published in 1954 and does indeed include the recipe for "Hashish Fudge". The ingredients are fruit, nuts, spices and cannabis, and described as "the food of paradise". Little wonder it sold so many copies.

2 Another hip and happening project, *Pardon Me, Sir, But Is My Eye Hurting Your Elbow?* was set to be filmed in late 1967, with Peter playing nine – count 'em – nine characters! An anthology of satirical sketches lampooning modern American man, the project was to be directed by Arthur Hiller but remained unmade. The skits, written by the likes of Allen Ginsberg, Philip Roth, and Sellers favourite Terry Southern, were published in book form in 1968.

behind Milligan's quest to make as many old radio episodes of *The Goon Show* as possible commercially available. The best-selling long player *Goon . . . but not forgotten* had been issued by Parlophone Records in the November of 1967.[1] And within Spike's sleeve note he proclaimed that a new generation should have a chance to hear *The Goon Show*, not that repeats of both the radio series and *The Telegoons* were infrequent in the slightest. Not to mention their charity reunion in the spring of 1967, which had seen them as caring, and crucially, relevant comedy titans.

Besides, Sellers, Spike, and Secombe were not only archive Goons but active Goons, once again, in the summer of 1968, when Thames Television presented a full half-hour of *The Goon Show*. It had been discussed when the Goons reunited, round at Peter's house in Elstead, Surrey, in a jolly gathering which also included Peter's wife Britt and the future King of England, Prince Charles. It was a very Peter Sellers happening. Something wonderful had to come out of it.

Indeed, in a reflection of *The Frost Report*'s place as *the* comedy byword of the mid-sixties, John Cleese, a pre-Python, basking in the after-glow of the first batch of *At Last the 1948 Show*, was recruited to be the on-screen, and on-mic announcer. It's a lovely continuation of the Goon tradition of recruiting the freshest and most cutting edge of contemporary comedy talent. Half a decade earlier Peter and Spike had worked alongside Jonathan Miller and Peter Cook up the River Wye. Now Cleese joined in the fun. The show, a re-working of the vintage Goon classic, 'Tales of Men's Shirts', was produced by the same pair of hands Goon producer Peter Eton. The gloriously fraught director was Joe McGrath, not that battle-scarred since the long, long days of *Casino Royale* to return to the hot Goonish coalface, although McGrath remembered: "it was utter madness. Anybody who attempted to put *The Goon Show* on television, must have been insane. Well . . . I admit it. But I loved it. At one point Peter and Spike were deep in crazy conversation . . . what am I talking about . . . they were deep in anxious

---

1 Serial number: PMC.7037, the two episodes, sans musical interludes, selected for this disc were 'Six Charlies in Search of an Author', and 'Insurance – the White Man's Burden'.

consuming of brandy. They were both heavily into the brandies at that time, and had a few bottles hidden behind the studio set-up. I was desperately trying to hatch a plan to get us through the next – of many – hurdles. At that point dear old Harry Secombe tip-toed over to me, gently tapped me on the head and muttered: 'It must be hell in there!' It was. A glorious hell though. And we did do it!"[1]

Do it they did, indeed . . .

And Goonantics were treated to another Parlophone Records release, in the October of 1968, when *Goon Again* immortalised – once more, with just the Goon segments included – another couple of vintage episodes, 'China Story' and 'The MacReekie Rising of '74'.[2]

It was gleefully unwrapped by many that Christmas morning of 1968. For Peter Sellers and Britt Ekland, December 1968 brought nothing but divorce papers. The marriage officially ended on Tuesday, 17th December.

Exactly four weeks later, on Tuesday, 14th January 1969, Peter Sellers was hanging out with the Beatles, during their fateful *Get Back* recording sessions, at Twickenham Studios. Sellers – with a bland and humourless persona which he would channel into *Hoffman* later that year – was joined by producer Denis O'Dell, and, again, director Joe McGrath, who were conducting casting sessions for Peter's upcoming film project, *The Magic Christian*. McGrath had directed the promotional films for the Beatles' singles releases 'Day Tripper' and 'We Can Work It Out', and although original casting to play Peter's adopted son, John Lennon, had proved reluctant, alternative Beatles choice Ringo Starr had proved very willing. Having been dubbed a new Charlie Chaplin – "He's an old one!" quipped Lennon[3] following his 'This Boy', hungover solo clowning for *A Hard Day's Night* – Ringo had pursued his acting career as a result of the curtailing of the Beatles touring schedule from August 1966.

Lennon's reticence over *The Magic Christian* simply reflected his preoccupation with making love and art with Yoko, for a Sellers

1 Interview with the author, July 2003.
2 Serial number: PMC.7062
3 *The Beatles at the BBC*, Apple/EMI Records, 1994.

admirer he had long quoted *The Goon Show* as an influence. The performance of Chuck Berry's 'I Got to Find My Baby', for the radio show *Pop Go the Beatles*, recorded on 1st June 1963, for a transmission on 11th June 1963, includes the enthused Lennon ad-lib introduction: "Don't know where she's been, pardon, hello? Love these Goon Shows!"[1] *The Goon Show* had, for one week only, been current currency once again, for following the extensive 1960 repeat season, 'The Dreaded Batter-Pudding Hurler (of Bexhill-on-Sea)' had been heard on the Home Service, on 13th October 1962.[2] In the end, *The Magic Christian* would add to its Beatles connection by featuring John and Yoko lookalikes on board the huge ship of the title. The reaction of the Lennons to this went unrecorded, although Paul McCartney happily wrote the oh, so catchy 'Come and Get It', for Badfinger, for the film's title sequence. McCartney also co-produced the Badfinger album, *Magic Christian Music*, which was issued on the Beatles record label, Apple Records, on 9th January 1970. This was beautifully slotted between the film's British release, through Grand Films Limited for Commonwealth United Entertainment, on 12th December 1969, and its American release on 11th February 1970.

Domestically troubled, and professionally intimidated in that January of 1969, Peter certainly seems out of sorts and certainly out of his depth during the encounter with the Beatles, professing to being "incredibly bad" at ad-libs and celebrity introductory jobs and the like. The Beatles joke that they want Sellers to announce them for a – never to happen – appearance back on *The Ed Sullivan Show*. Having now reviewed his decision Lennon may well be cruelly bristling at the fact that he's not about to make *The Magic Christian*, while Ringo is clearly excited and gleeful at the fact that he is about to make *The Magic Christian*.

When consciously in work mode though, Sellers could happily turn on the hip guest star charisma. On 9th February 1969 he appeared on

1 *The Beatles at the BBC*, Apple/EMI Records, 1994.
2 Ray Ellington, that unsung pioneer of rock 'n' roll in British Light Entertainment, had delivered his unique take on twenties show tune 'Ol' Man River' in that show. Max Geldray was in something of an Ellington mood, offering up 'They Were Doing the Mambo'.

the ATV variety series *This Is Tom Jones*, affectionately joining the Welsh superstar in a mockery of all things Welsh. At least the sit-down chat was stuffed to the gills with 'Boyo!' this and 'Appreciate' that. As Sellers says, he has: "come inside for a quick appreciate . . ." and Tom Jones is clearly delighted to have him. He gushes about the fact that every series they had tried to secure Sellers but he was: "always too busy making pictures." That wasn't going to change in a hurry, but Peter had his Hollywood party movies – *The Party* and *Toklas* – to promote, and *The Magic Christian* to sell. The film is all about money, after all, and it was going to take a hefty chunk to get it made.

It had been a pet project for many years – all the way back to when Sellers had actively fallen in love with Terry Southern's novel during the making of *Dr. Strangelove*. Southern had been around the place too, writing additional material for the film, and Sellers had been so taken with the idea to star in a film version of *The Magic Christian* that he had gifted a copy of the novel to friends and followers and even *Strangelove* director Stanley Kubrick. You can see why Sellers was so taken. It's a sketch-format satire on the perils and powers of wealth. Many episodes from the novel make the cut of the film, although the book has no part for an adopted son; while the wallowing in filth for financial gain is rather thrown away as a retrospective memory early on in the prose.

With Joe McGrath attached to *The Magic Christian*, Republic Pictures took a chance on this ambitious and controversial and cynical all-star celebration of human nature and greed. In its ethos *The Magic Christian* is very much a big-budget realisation of Spike Milligan's vision of *The Goon Show*. Anybody will do anything for money, folks. Indeed, Milligan enjoys one of his best film cameos, as a frantic, authoritative and humourless traffic warden who agrees to eat the parking ticket he has just issued Peter's character, Sir Guy Grand, on his Rolls Royce. His reward: a tasty wodge of £500. Everything about the film is all for money, of course. Money, money, money! As Joe McGrath remembered, Sellers and Spike were as one when at work: "If they liked a script and respected a script they would give me everything. Complete commitment. I remember we had two days set aside for their scene, filming on Putney Bridge with Joe Public looking on. Well, Peter and Spike were so in tune, having such fun with the scene, that we started at eight in the morning and were wrapped by lunchtime! That included Peter ad-libbing about Spike not needing to eat the plastic and all that. It was joyous. We could have made a whole film about Sir Guy and the traffic warden. The two of them together was comedy alchemy. It's as simple as that. The funniest thing of all was that our producer, Denis O'Dell came up to me over lunch in a panic: 'We are two days ahead!' he said. 'What are we going to do?' He was the only producer I ever worked with who was worried about being *ahead* of schedule!"[1] The speed and skill of Peter and Spike was born of mutual respect and longevity, of course.

The ongoing Goon connection and cult could be clearly made during the film's production, for BBC Radio 4 mounted a summer 1969 repeat season of five editions of *The Goon Show*.

The connection went deeper, and more prevalent than that. Joe McGrath, having directed or, at best, referred *The Goon Show*'s 'Tales of Men's Shirts' had, of course, already worked with John Cleese on that project. Cleese, with Cambridge Footlights chum and comic co-writer Graham Chapman, had been recruited to contribute additional material to Southern's own adaptation of *The Magic Christian*. Sellers joins them on the credit, although Peter's contribution was more arbitrary, more advisory, more interpretative. Moreover Cleese and Chapman were cast in the film: as art dealer – a lovely, true to the greed cameo – and an Oxford boat race oarsman – a nothing cough and a spit – respectively. *Monty Python's Flying Circus* took flight in October 1969, and it can be argued that rather than them being the comedy equivalent of the Beatles, the Beatles were the rock 'n' roll equivalent of the Goons. Or both. The connections are deep and satisfying. And Sellers was there, active and invigorating, at the beginning of one and the ending of the other.

Peter and Ringo were certainly cultivating a show business

---

1 Interview with the author, July 2003.

friendship at the time. Sellers had just sold Ringo his beloved Brooksfield House. Indeed, the newly changed-hands property was the location for the 1969 summit meeting that saw George Harrison temporarily leave the Beatles. Ringo subsequently sold the property to Stephen Stills, of Crosby, Stills, and Nash, less than a year later.

On 10th April 1969 Peter and Ringo were together to attend the film premiere of Richard Attenborough's *Oh! What a Lovely War*, at the Paramount, in London. It wouldn't have been possible if Peter had got his way with regards locations. Originally, it was planned for *The Magic Christian* to be filmed in New York City, with the climax – of the mass of humanity swimming through excrement for a few banknotes – scheduled to be shot at the foot of the Statue of Liberty. The authorities were not enamoured with that idea. Not one little bit. London was less fussed. This was Sellers, after all, and with Terry Southern in tow, he finally settled on the spruced-up South Bank, complete with his spiritual home, the National Film Theatre. Firmly establishing the link as a rather credible and financially-viable film-maker. Sort of. And, indeed, the film opens with a portrait of the Queen – as seen on a ten-pound note – and, as Sellers in Sir Guy guise explains in the opening narration, we'll be getting through an awful lot of the stuff over the next two hours: "Enough for all of us!"

The London skyline: the clock tower of Big Ben loud and proud outside Sir Guy's luxurious townhouse, his English wake-up ritual of a nice cup of tea, the plethora of – largely – British-based guest stars and, most importantly, the indulging of Peter's seemingly endless supply of funny character voices, all screams that *The Magic Christian* just had to be a British-based film. Certainly, the American market – even in 1969 – would have baulked at allowing Sellers so much leeway. It certainly baulked in 1972 when Roy Boulting pulled together *Soft Beds, Hard Battles*.

Peter is all over *The Magic Christian*: in the guise of William Mate he is the jobsworth park keeper who moves vagrant Ringo Starr on, thus setting up the plot himself. Sellers too is the humble bobby on the beat who moves Ringo on from outside of Buckingham Palace. The third homeless encounter – with a loud-mouthed old hag – was too much, even for Sellers. Luckily Rita Webb was on call. Cor, blimey! Peter is the American announcer on the ship, heralding the main feature film, and he is the Yankee doctor *in* the film. He's both Scots and American seconds during the boxing match, and the Scots voice over the train station tannoy system. Sellers dubs a snatch of David Lodge's announcement as the ship's officer too. There's even a role for dear old Bloodnok, as the new Captain, complete with Fred the Oyster stomach gurgles. It's totally fitting that Sellers should resurrect the Colonel in this back-handed salute to the glories of greed.

Peter's genius with a unique comic voice is beautifully sent-up when he, rather touchingly, reads Ringo *The Wind in the Willows* as a bedtime story and uses his mannered, monosyllabic voice throughout, pinpointed by his straight reading of another character "in quite a different voice". The voice, of course, is exactly the same. A subtle highlighting of the fact that, while it may have been easy for Sellers to dip in and out of complete characters, it *wasn't* easy!

In terms of Peter's performance it is grand and bland. He effortlessly possesses the frightfully posh, refined, and suave manner of a man who has only ever known wealth. That he puts on the silly-ass mannerisms for effect is a masterstroke – such as when he is ordering a Hot Doggie from Victor Maddern's vendor. Talking of which, as a spotter's guide to folk from Peter's British cinema heyday, *The Magic Christian* is a joy indeed. Graham Stark is present and correct, naturally, joining forces with Harold Berens and head waiter Ferdy Mayne, as Sellers displays his surreal gourmet ways.[1] John Le Mesurier pops up during the boat race, as

---

1 This is very much taken from *Magical Mystery Tour*; even to the point of Ringo's auntie from that television mind expansion, Jessie Robins, being gainfully employed as an extra, barging through the pop-up shop on the hunt for bargains. A pop-up shop which, in itself, is very much like the Apple Boutique. The essence of gluttony would, in turn, inspire *Monty Python's The Meaning of Life*. Sellers originally wanted Stark for *The Magic Christian* art gallery owner, as played by John Cleese. Eric Idle, having achieved an ambition to work with his comedy hero in Jonathan Miller's *Alice in Wonderland*, was drafted in for just one scene, during one of Peter's absences during *The Fiendish Plot of Dr. Fu Manchu*. It was a scene Sellers insisted on being cut from the final film. One must assume it was nothing personal. Peter was proud to be one of the midwives of *Monty Python*.

Sir John, wonderfully regaining composure when needed to pose for a photograph; Johns ex-wife Hattie Jacques – having given one of her favourite, and thinnest, performances in *The Bobo*, is there, with Sellers, on the train; Dennis Price, as Wagstaff, is a Yes Man advertising consultant – alongside monocled mirth-maker Fred Emney, silly ass Jeremy Lloyd, and belligerent *Dad's Army* actor Robert Raglan. There's a pompous Roland Culver, a Scots Frank Thornton, and Harry Locke gamely blowing up game birds . . . What a film!

It's also perfectly bonkers, as befits a Peter Sellers film of this crazed era. At one point, and to add to his roster of characters, he dons the outfit of a nun – in wimple and very heavy make-up – in a surreal, mad disco cum gentlemen's club melee . . . If memory serves. Oh, yes. It *is* bonkers, but brilliant, and very much the epitome of the comedy of excess that Sellers had embraced . . . and would continue to embrace until the end of his days. As Sir Guy mutters as the Magic Christian orgy reaches its zenith: these old Hollywood moguls can still show us a thing or two . . . Boom! He remembers all the names of the female members of staff too.

Indeed there's a lovely call-back to the one that really started all this Sellers excess: the hugely successful, hugely excessive, *Casino Royale*. In the on-board ship casino scene there is a distinct refrain of Tijuana Brass Band music. The soundtrack is incredible. Not least the three Badfinger tracks, but also Thunderclap Newman, heavy rock anthems when Ringo's co-starring credit is revealed, and wonderfully weird refrains at every avenue.

The pivotal plotline that people will do absolutely anything for money informs a relentlessly odd, often uproariously funny, loosely-linked string of comic vignettes: including valued cine-chum Richard Attenborough as the cigar-puffing, easily-bribed Oxford Blue. There's Laurence Harvey – as himself – performing a full monty striptease to Hamlet's soliloquy. The sense of truth and reality is forced home with the casting of proper and respected broadcasters: Michael Barratt reports on the carnage at the dog show – when a disguised panther devours the competition; Michael Aspel interviews clearly insane new Captain of the Magic Christian, another old Sellers chum, from *Two-Way Stretch*, Wilfred Hyde-White; while Raymond Glendenning keeps calm and cool as he commentates on the Boat Race. Perhaps the most beautiful meta appearance of all is Christopher Lee, as a dour steward aboard the dream ship, who puts down his tray of drinks and proceeds to sprout his all-too familiar Count Dracula fangs – and only then be revealed as the Ship's Vampire, in flowing cloak, and on the prowl for Captain Wilfred Hyde-White. Although he would soon be back at Hammer Films, giving his vampire once more in *Scars of Dracula*, and putting the fake fangs back in for two subsequent romps at Hammer, Lee was already being very vocal in his disparaging remarks about the films. That he would give his Count for a half-day comic cameo – purely for the money – is the very essence of *The Magic Christian*.

Sellers himself had agreed to a silly cameo in another money-centric romp 'Who'll Bid Two Million Dollars?', an episode of the Universal Television series *It Takes a Thief*, starring Robert Wagner, his old chum from *The Pink Panther*. Peter's role was as a Man in the Harbour Records office. Not too taxing, but it filled the time between American-based promotions for his pet project, *The Magic Christian*.[1] And the joke was decidedly not lost on Sellers. He may not have the bottomless, disposal riches of Sir Guy, not quite, at least, but he certainly liked money. And he liked to work. If he could continue to make people laugh and get paid handsomely for it, where was the moral dilemma in that?

---

1 Peter's *It Takes a Thief* episode was broadcast on 2nd October 1969. It was during this same press junket that Peter recorded his appearances on *Rowan & Martin's Laugh-In*, featuring on the pioneering NBC sketch comedy show on 15th September and 17th November 1969, as well as the 16th March 1970 edition. They sure got their money's worth for a little publicity for *The Magic Christian*. Look that up in your Funk & Wagnalls!

Chapter 12

"I have a burning sort of fire inside me to do certain things which I know I'm going to do. I'm going to defeat all these berks that are around me, and I'm going to do it."

Peter Sellers, 1971

The Magic Christian was an intriguing and integrity-filled film for Sellers to take on. It was very him, of course, and its problems and pressures made it even more precious. His concerns and causes are to the fore: the casual viewing of violence is of *A Clockwork Orange* – the novel being published in 1962 – while Peter's anti-smoking campaign prohibits the dreaded weed being sold in his manic pop-up shop because it causes "cancer of the lung".[1] Sellers chats to 'Major' Terence Alexander about the lack of people of colour on the *The Magic Christian* ship. The racial commentary is a set-up for Alexander's pompous idiot to be embarrassed by a white and a black Mr. Universe: both well-greased and homoerotic. The boxing match too ends in a homoerotic coupling. The satire of *The Magic Christian* may be crass, and it's supposed to be: that final sight of bowler-hatted businessmen literally wading through a vat of shit – and piss, and animal blood – in order to grab a few fivers – is flagged up as an obtuse and obvious metaphor by Sellers and Starr while the scene is playing out. The ending sees Sir Guy join his adopted son sleeping rough in the park – with a lovely cameo by *Dad's Army*

---

1 Since Dr. Isaac Adler's findings in 1912 the link had been discussed, with the evidence growing in momentum throughout the forties and fifties. Still, joyfully in the spirit of *The Magic Christian*, Peter's integrity was bought when, during the filming of *Ghost in the Noonday Sun*, he filled a half-day off by filming a very lucrative advert for Benson and Hedges.

verger Edward Sinclair as another park-keeper – and glories in the fact that their moneyed ways have not been abandoned. Things haven't changed that much either now, which is a fact that would amuse and anger Sellers, probably in equal measure.[1]

Sellers spent the last few months of the sixties wrapped up with Alvin Rakoff's film version of the Ernest Gebler novel *Shall I Eat You Now?* Well, quite. The film, distributed by Anglo-EMI, and released on 16th July 1970, was simply named after the lead character, as played by Sellers: *Hoffman*. The basic premise is of this middle-aged lead protagonist blackmailing a young girl (played by Sinead Cusack, whose father, Cyril, had locked horns and umbrellas with Sellers in *Waltz of the Toreadors*) into spending a week with him. The poster promised it was a new kind of Sellers. Well, every Sellers seemed to be a new kind of Sellers at the time. What the poster meant, of course, was that it wasn't a funny Sellers. Sellers had done serious roles before, of course, but this was rather unusual casting for an actor who longed to be a romantic lead. But it was all on Peter's terms. As the screenplay had it, Mr. Hoffman is one of those many, many, plain, sad-faced men who lust and dream and desire the female form. Its basic in its language. The language of Gebler's sex-obsessed novel. Sellers, as the personification of the bland, moneyed businessman, mutters about breasts and bottoms and thighs. The monosyllabic and, yes, frankly rather creepy utterances and staccato movement around his own palatial apartment, are more than disconcerting for the central female figure of desire, not to mention disturbing for the audience. Still, Sellers being Sellers, and this being a Sellers vehicle, flashes of humour were inevitably and deliciously unavoidable. Though Cusack

---

1 The plot of *The Magic Christian* infiltrates *The Simpsons*: 'Homer vs. Dignity', with its counter-culture buttons set to kill. Peter's contribution to Marty Feldman's analysis of comedy, *One Pair of Eyes*: 'Marty Feldman: No, But Seriously . . .', was filmed during the making of *The Magic Christian*, in the spring of 1969, for broadcast on 7th June 1969. Marty was a fellow guest with Sellers on the 9th November 1969 edition of *London Aktuell*, a film-centric variety chat show which also featured Alfred Hitchcock, Roger Moore, and Pan's People. What a bill! Sellers once more promoted *The Magic Christian* during the Tony Palmer interview for *Will the Real Mr. Sellers . . .?* transmitted 18th December 1969. The film had been on general release in Britain for less than a week. Even a reading of a religious tale for *Stars on Sunday* would be accepted in order to keep his profile buoyant.

reflects that he seems very different from the way he behaved in the office, Sellers is very different again once the odd couple are seated in a posh French restaurant. Hoffman has all the chat; he knows the right wine; he orders for himself and the young lady and, yes, indeed, there is a moment of Goonish levity, as he relates the tale of when his father introduced him to snails – how do you do, goes the old joke – and it is enlivened and invigorated by Peter's metamorphism into the French back chat of the snail he consumed as a youth. The flash of that winning smile, the sparkle behind the eyes – of both lust and superiority – is an echo of the polished comedian behind the desperate, rather pathetic Hoffman. The revelation of a discarded invitation he has made to this Miss Smith to join him at the theatre – a year or so before this proposal of sexual conquest – is haunting, as is the memory of the ridicule shown to him by the other girls in the office.

It's a beautiful, painful performance. Peter's eyes darken and die when his youthful muse packs her bag and walks away from him. With the drinking in solitude, the lacklustre movement, and the recurring bleak fantasies of strangling girls, it's all rather bizarre. However, even this deep into the plot, there are still joyous moments of comic relief: the drunken swerve past his hallway table; the startled leap as the bread rockets out of the toaster; the gleeful greeting to Fred the plumber, downstairs in his new flat, and played, with grizzled reliability by Sellers acolyte and chum David Lodge.

The melting of Cusack is glorious too: the Wimbledon Common walk; the piano duet of 'Chopsticks'; the playful phone call to her intended (Jeremy Bullock) – with Sellers getting even more posh to pretend to be the switchboard operator, and mock-mime a tennis match when the boy's mother informs the girl he is at the club.

Bullock, though: "rather working with Sellers at all" in *Hoffman*, did indicate a crucial facet of the actor in the studio: "He certainly didn't make any attempts to chat with me. He was distant, rather aloof. Not unpleasant, just not really there. Very much like the character of Hoffman really. He became that character during filming. At least toward me. To be honest with you, anybody who has seen the film – and that's not many of you – probably know Peter Sellers as well as I got to know him. Which is a brilliant compliment for his performance. He was the complete actor."[1]

The new decade saw Sellers achieve complete reinvention as a new man: fitter, wittier, and very much a comedic cornerstone of the establishment. He had long held court in Royal circles, and his wealth and celebrity had made him a friend to the young comedy generation while still young enough himself to be the hippest of the old-timers.

On screen and in high society, Sellers basked in the confident air of a romantic leading man. So yes, at last he was a Cary Grant. Albeit a Cary Grant with that sheen of surreal subversion very much within easy grasp, should it be required. That Cary Grant on his own terms he had longed to be since 1965.

By the very end of the sixties Sellers still had a deep-rooted desire to prove he could do a proper Cary Grant-styled role. And, indeed, *There's a Girl in My Soup* proved it without doubt. There is an essence of the cold and calculated Grant of Alfred Hitchcock's *Suspicion* in Peter's performance. A glacier-like confidence in his own sureness. There is also that deftness of touch that Grant brought to tail-end romantic comedies like *That Touch of Mink*, and *The Grass Is Greener*: an older, debonair, occasionally self-parodying edge.

Sellers has all that and more in *There's a Girl in My Soup* but once he had been able to show his hand, he swiftly got tired of this frothy, post-swinging-sixties confectionery.

This was Sellers as an unstoppable force of comedy and sex appeal. A Sellers strengthened not weakened by heart attack and divorce. It was a fire fanned by his wowing of twenty-two-year-old champagne socialite and high-class fashion model Miranda Quarry. She suited this flamboyant, man about town persona. The couple were married, at Caxton Hall, on 24th August 1970. Sellers himself was a fortnight away from forty-five, and the lavish celebration saw

---

1 Interview with the author, September 2015. The location for Hoffman's flat, should you wish to visit and get to know him better, is Ruvigny Mansions, in Putney, South London.

the uncorking of enough bubbles to sink the Royal Yacht Britannia.

Little wonder then that Sellers was more than happy to have signed up to reunite with old friend and frequent fifties director Roy Boulting, in order to play the lead role of Robert Danvers in the screen adaptation of Terence Frisby's *There's a Girl in My Soup*.

A supremely confident, charismatic television chef, the character of Robert Danvers is a fiercely proud bachelor who happily and causally beds several women before facing the effervescent charm of a girl half his age. This was art imitating life in the broadest of terms. In reality it was the frightfully upper crust Miranda Quarry. On screen it was the ditzy blonde Goldie Hawn, fresh from small screen stardom in *Rowan and Martin's Laugh-In*.[1]

The blurring of reality and fiction would have appealed greatly to Sellers. This was the role to fully transcend from anarchic character comedian to suave leading man. It was himself. Heightened to the nth degree.

The fact that the play was a notorious, sexy and sparkling West End hit and, thus, a well-known commodity made it an even greater fit. Even if people didn't pay their one and nines to see the film, they would have heard what the role of Robert Danvers entailed. And here was Peter Sellers playing it on screen.

Donald Sinden had created the role in 1966, playing it for over a year on the pre-West End tour before opening at the Globe Theatre (now the Gielgud). By the Summer of 1969 Gerald Flood, the most prolific Robert Danvers, had taken over.[2] By the time the film rights had been secured and Sellers was filming at Shepperton Studios, the stage production had transferred to the Comedy Theatre (now the Harold Pinter) with Peter Byrne and, from June 1970, Charles Tingwell, in the lead role.

Terence Frisby adapted his own play for the screen. It was hardly surprising that Columbia Pictures was head-over-heels in lust to

---

1 Peter had worked opposite her during his time on *Rowan & Martin's Laugh-In*. In one sketch he had revisited his Second World War angst once again as another crazed Nazi alongside Arte Johnson. Very Interesting!

2 With the West End run coming to an end Flood returned to the role for the UK tour in 1973, eventually playing Robert Danvers for over 650 performances.

present it in cinemas, snapping up the screen rights as early as 1967. Goldie Hawn was signed up to star as the girl in the first weeks of 1969 but it wasn't until the Boulting brothers were assigned to make it that Sellers was cock-a-hoop about accepting the leading role. It was his ultimate Cary Grant performance. A romantic lead of the old school, with lashings of permissive sex appeal, and just the right amount of seventies cynicism. It was in particular the hip and happening Sellers as Robert Danvers that gave the film version of the hit play its knockout clout. Sellers had long been the world's most adult comedy film star. Even as far back as *Only Two Can Play* he was pushing the boundaries of what could be debated within a film comedy framework. Through the excess of *What's New Pussycat?*, and the uneasiness of *Hoffman*, he was an actor who could judge high laughter with shades of complex romance. *There's a Girl in My Soup* was the pinnacle. It was also a plateau.

Sellers was still hot box office, although he had been much more selective in recent months. Far more importantly, in terms of publicity for the film, was Sellers the celebrity. His recent marriage; his cool public appearances at press nights and premieres; his languid, hilarious domination of chat shows; all of it made him a valuable product. His slightest move could sell newspapers. Who better to play this big-headed, pretentious, and prestigiously sexual central character.

Through the film he beds at least one gorgeous young creature (picked up at the wedding that opens the action, and played by a terribly young, terribly good Gabrielle Drake). Romping topless – because of rather than in spite of his terrible reputation – true to form he has her and promptly forgets her name. It is a brief snapshot of the way of life of this man.

The free-spirited Marion (here, in the film, that wide-eyed, frank-talking Yank, in the shape of Goldie Hawn) is a challenge at first, then an enigma, and finally his comeuppance. He actually falls in love with her. The character, on paper, is deeply unpleasant. Still, in the hands of Sellers there are strong traces of humanity, particularly in that pivotal denouncement. When she explains that she's going back to her sluggish, wastrel boyfriend (Nicky Henson) Sellers is at first incandescent with rage and disbelief. Then it is despair. And then deep sadness. It's in the written words, of course, but much more than that, it's in the eyes of Sellers. Not dead, perhaps, but destroyed. A new, more caring man emerges. Naturally, this being an influential British sex comedy, this moment of epiphany doesn't last long.

The catalyst is the gorgeous young French au pair girl – played by the gorgeous young Francoise Pascal. Even off camera Francoise was a distraction, quite naturally. "Roy Boulting called me the 'Trouble-maker!'" she chuckled. Within the narrative, Francoise initially catches the eye of Peter's character, and he asks her out for a meal, a date, food with sex, basically. With typical chauvinistic disregard he promptly forgets all about her when distracted by Marion. Still, as soon as he has licked his wounds and regained his old composure, post-Marion, he is swiftly back on the tail and on the phone to the French beauty, picking up plans for a candlelit rendezvous. It would work too, no doubt. Robert Danvers is that kind of man. And so was Peter Sellers. Real-life was pretty much a carbon copy of the script, as Francoise Pascal remembered: "Peter was a charming man. We first met during the filming of *There's a Girl in My Soup*, and we got on very well. He would phone at the most ridiculous of hours, usually from his lavish suite in the Dorchester Hotel. He would purr: 'Darling. Get over here, your ice-cream is getting cold!' Such silliness just couldn't be resisted."[1]

Sellers too would often use the eternal chat-up line deployed by Danvers: "My God, but you're lovely!" "Oh he would say that all the time", laughed Francoise Pascal, "he sent himself up when he said it, but he said it very well!" That very last insert of Sellers in the film, intoning the immortal phrase into a mirror. To himself. That's as near as we can now get to understanding the Peter Sellers of the early seventies. You can just about see a crack of light between screen personality and reality.

---

1 Interview with the author, October 2022.

There's a Girl in My Soup marked the end of this particular box-office purple patch. In the early seventies Sellers was rather more famous for being famous than being lauded for his film performances. When the realisation bit, he didn't seem to care much. Not at first in any case. He was newly married, and he was keen to accept projects – many of them, with the best will in the world, misguided – simply because they appealed to him. That's fair enough. There's a personal sense of integrity at play there.

As well as being a convex mirror of himself, *There's a Girl in My Soup* was certainly the last commercially savvy choice he would make for nearly five years.[1] The film premiered at the Astor Theatre, New York City, on 14th December 1970, ahead of a hugely successful exposure across America and the United Kingdom for the Christmas season. Its free-wheeling attitude to sex and simply having a great time caught the mood of the era. It wallowed in the sullen waters of ephemera celebrity and easy lays, and it won Terence Frisby the Writers' Guild of Great Britain award for Best Screenplay of 1970.

Still, that pounding hangover from the swinging sixties was really kicking in by now.

Sellers, with his glamorous third wife on arm, was both a famous film star and officially part of the British aristocracy. He was exactly where he wanted to be. He was looking fit. He was feeling funny. His glasses, now subtly tinted and of top-class design, reflected his self-satisfied poise. Quite literally. The wedding celebration had been held in a favourite London nightspot of Peter's, Tramps. The owner, Johnny Gold, recalled Sellers was at his happiest at this time,

---

1 It also helped that Peter was pleased with it, and agreed to several promotional interviews, which usually drifted away from the topic in hand very swiftly. Sellers charmed the ever-charming Gay Byrne on *The Late, Late Show*, on 20th November 1971; and chatted about *There's a Girl in My Soup* in the documentary 'This is my Wife' or Life with Goldie. Peter was interviewed for *Cinema*, transmitted 14th January 1971 – hosted by Clive James, and Sellers enjoyed it so much he was back on 19th October 1972. On Thursday, 4th March 1971 he attended the British Screen Awards, at the Royal Albert Hall, in the presence of Her Royal Highness The Princess Anne, who presented the Society of Film and Television Arts trophies. *There's a Girl in My Soup* didn't win a thing! On 9th March an interview for German television, on *V.I.P. – Schaukel*, was broadcast. A relaxed Peter, in purple jacket and tinted glasses, is, at turns, affable and gloriously bemused.

writing: "My eyes would light up whenever Peter came into the club: he always had a stream of stories, which he would more re-enact rather than merely tell . . . Peter could make me laugh more than anybody I ever met before or since. We got the giggles in an Indian restaurant one night and we had to leave – we couldn't eat our food. We had to ask them to make it a takeaway!"[1]

Now beholden to no one save himself, Peter gleefully turned down script after script on a whim. The financial incentive was irrelevant to him. Now he was free and content to do exactly what he wanted to do, and to divide his time between swanky parties and making films, often as favours for valued chums.

Enfant-terrible film-maker Roman Polanski was one such valued chum. Having readily agreed to a free and for gratis cough and spit in *The Magic Christian* – Polanski is seduced by a dragged-up Yul Brynner, serenading him with Noel Coward's 'Mad About the Boy', aboard the luxury dream ship – the director called on Sellers to repay the debt. Sellers agreed, and with chum Graham Stark in-tow, he dutifully jetted off to Denmark to give a scene-stealing cameo in Polanski's *A Day at the Beach*. The entire shoot was three weeks, it's unlikely that Sellers was needed for more than three hours. Credited as A. Queen, Sellers, with Stark matching him mince for mince, plays an outrageously effeminate boutique owner besides the beach of the title. The film was never commercially released.[2]

If nothing else it galvanised Graham Stark to try his hand at directing a film: "For years everybody had said that I understood comedy so well and that I was so helpful in my advice that I would make a brilliant film director. Peter was as encouraging as ever. He had tried it, after all, so why shouldn't I? That was his argument not mine! Then he promised to do me a favour and be in it. So it was a fait

---

1 *Tramp's Gold*, by Johnny Gold (Robson Books, 2001).
2 Discussed in hushed tones as a lost masterpiece, it remained out of circulation for decades. Having spent twenty years gathering dust in the Paramount vaults, it emerged on the Odeon Entertainment DVD label, in October 2007, as part of their Best of British Collection. The film still occasionally pops up at self-indulgent film festivals.

accompli."[1] Typically starting small, the film was a twenty-minute short subject called *Simon, Simon* and, as well as Sellers, Stark called in influential chums Bob Monkhouse and Eric Morecambe and Ernie Wise, as well as old mates from *Alfie* Julie Foster and (another Dennis Selinger client) Michael Caine, to give it a shedload of star appeal. A wordless comedy of errors, Sellers is typically a man of such substance that he is the owner of two cars. A touch of passive road rage with a car thief (Kenneth Earle) results in the tiniest scratch on the vehicle Peter is driving. Mild angst sees Sellers get out of the vehicle. He ushers forward a lackey to drive it away. Another lackey pulls up in another car. Sellers gets in it and drives away. And that's it. It's a playful heightening of the kind of car-obsessed escapade Sellers *could* have done for real. All directed in a knowing, surrealistic, jolly style akin to *The Running Jumping & Standing Still Film*. *Simon, Simon* was enough of a success to convince Horror specialist Tony Tenser at Tigon to invest in Stark's all-star comedy feature film *The Magnificent Seven Deadly Sins*. Sellers wasn't in that one, but everybody else was, including Harry Secombe, in the Envy segment, and Spike Milligan, who also scripted the absurdist Sloth segment.

As the financial tax year of 1970 was coming to an end Peter was contemplating quite a quiet 1971. On the evening of 25th March 1971 he threw a lavish party at a favourite Knightsbridge Italian restaurant, San Lorenzo. The starry guest list included Royalty (Princess Margaret), an ex-Beatle (Ringo Starr), and even an ex-wife (Britt Ekland), as well as the obligatory Spike Milligan. In between cracking music-hall jokes and singing Italian songs Sellers announced that he and Miranda were moving to Maynooth, in Ireland, for tax reasons: "I am going to open a restaurant, an Italian restaurant . . . in Dublin!" he stated. Despite the venue being festooned with balloons bearing the legend: 'Ciao Ciao Peter', he didn't go.

Instead, Peter chose to indulge something of a borderline

---

1 Interview with the author, October 1999.

obsession: a passion for poking fun at the Hun.

Silly Nazis and a manic Adolf Hitler in particular had long been part of his repertoire, even if the BBC were more inclined to broadcast his Winston Churchill in the few years immediately after the conclusion of World War II. Still, Sellers being Sellers he could never resist injecting a little frantic fascism into his work. Witness Doctor Strangelove as the stand-out showstopper of all.

By 1972, with his film career and his third marriage failing pretty much in tandem, Sellers began accepting strange television assignments. Very strange television assignments. Some of them he really wanted to do. Others proved a useful avenue to earn a little extra cash. Perhaps the most bizarre of all of these was *The End of the Pier Show* which finally emerged in 1974. A satirical offering from John Bird, John Fortune and John Wells, it was ostensibly an affectionate pastiche of a Victorian variety bill, complete with ramshackle audience and knowing playbill matter. In the end, it was something of a mess, and not a particularly funny mess, despite the – albeit – brief participation of Madeline Smith, Neil Innes, and Sellers. Completely going against the Victorian music-hall grain, Sellers insisted and was indulged in giving his off-kilter Hitler. Madeline Smith recalled it came about through: "a ribbon of events. Peter could make things happen, of course. He was a huge star. John Wells was the chief satirist and drive for the series of *The End of the Pier Show*, and he was in total love with Peter Sellers." The feeling was mutual. Sellers had had a ball balling the jack with Wells, in Rome, during the filming of *The Bobo* in early 1967. Wells, though dubbed for the international release, had embodied the flamboyant camp of Louis XIV. Sellers had particularly loved all the business with the drinkie-poos and the brief but telling character arc from impassioned showman to dejected wage-slave. So much so that he had insisted Wells be in *Casino Royale*. Sellers enjoyed the most fun of the entire shoot during the scene in which M-like John Wells and Q-like Geoffrey Bayldon kit him out with his James Bond gadgets. You can see on Peter's face that he's having a high old time. Thus, any favour John Wells wanted was a shoo-in.

Madeline Smith explained that: "*The End of the Pier Show* was gloriously spontaneous. We rehearsed and recorded on the Sunday that it was broadcast. John paid Peter Sellers in a crate of fine wine, at least three bottles of which he had happily drunk before we did our sketch and song. Him as Adolf Hitler, me as Eva Braun. That was the only scene Peter had in the whole show . . . in the whole series. He loved playing Hitler it would seem. Particularly for such a great deal!"[1]

For Sellers 1972 had proved to be a monumental year. For gloriously self-indulgent reasons he had taken his eye off the ball in terms of his film career. The one thing he was determined to do was both international and truthful. No silly costumes or elaborate pratfalls. He wanted to be a good-looking leading man, who got the girl. Or girls.

Typically though there was a conflicting beating heart from his past that he too could easily afford to indulge. The ethos of the Goons had never left him. It never would. It just couldn't. It was part of him. In his very soul. In 1972 the British Broadcasting Corporation was celebrating its fiftieth anniversary, and they wanted to get the band back together again. Again.

This kind of obsessive behaviour was certainly nothing new. Although very happy to take part in the Goon reunion, and one-on-one interview with Michael Parkinson, Sellers was adamant that he would only make the customary walk-on to set if he could wear a leather trench coat and German Army helmet. The BBC and Parky acquiesced. So indulged, Sellers was red hot comically, paraphrased great chunks of the Nazi dialogue Kenneth Mars glories in in Mel Brooks' *The Producers*, and then settled down to reminisce.[2]

"I can really say that it was the happiest professional period of my life. I never had such fun, enjoyment or fulfilment either before or

---

1 Interview with the author, May 2023.

2 So enthused and impressed was he that Sellers paid to take out a full-page advert promoting *The Producers* in *Variety* although, in the occasional interview codicil, he would claim to have been offered the role of the German Bloom, accepted the role, and never heard from Mel Brooks again! No sour grapes at all then.

since . . ." said Peter Sellers on making *The Goon Show*.[1] He would say it a lot. So would Secombe. Indeed, Neddie was very keen to record another series, if all three were available. Spike, doubtlessly having Vietnam-like Goon flashbacks to actually having to write the thing, proved reluctant. Although admitting the revival script came easily, Spike would only consider perhaps one show a year . . .

Even before his two Parkinson appearances Sellers had been attached to an intriguing project that, alas, never would get greenlit. Based on a popular American comic strip cartoon, *The Phantom vs. the 4th Reich* was to have starred Peter Sellers. Three times. He was to have played the heroic Phantom, a masked avenger on the side of good and righteousness. All bulging, skintight purple jumpsuit and skull-emblazoned outer-underpants. This guy was 'The Ghost That Walks', who had first appeared in February 1936, and, thus, was the legendary first costumed superhero of them all. Sellers rather fancied the over-the-top derring-do of all that. He also very much wanted to play the main baddie too, of course. Sellers was to have been an eighty-year-old Adolf Hitler, who had survived the bunker and happily continued his evil ways into dotage and in exile in South America. Not only that, but Sellers was set to play the energetic young son of Hitler: something of a milksop who lounges about the place, sporting long white socks and a very short pair of white shorts. As Sellers explained at the time: "He [Hitler] never had a son, but Henrich would have been his name if he had." So Henrich was to have been the son's name.

A shooting script, written by Philippe Mora, was ready and waiting, and had been approved and financed by King Features Syndicate, the brand owners of the Phantom comics. Leslie Linder was to produce, and they had even assigned a director to the project: Ted Kotcheff.

Of course, it had been Sellers that had fast-tracked the project. By glorious serendipity, the scriptwriter Philippe Mora was able to have an audience with Sellers, whose US agent at William Morris,

---

1 *Radio Times*, interviewed by Ray Connolly, 28th September 1972.

Sandy Lieberson, had once visited one of Mora's art exhibitions and bought a painting off of him. It was this connection that promoted Mora to show Lieberson the script who instantly knew that Sellers would want to do it. Not only that but it was Sellers who insisted on playing all three characters. It was in the bag. The budget was found, and with a shooting schedule set for the July of 1972 all looked set fair, but, at exactly that time the Head of King Features Syndicate, died on holiday, atop a ski-lodge, in Switzerland. More than cold feet resulted.

The project was blocked. And it has yet to happen.

Still, Peter was desperate to play Hitler. All the time. Even turning up to press conferences dressed like the Fuhrer. Both Funny Ha Ha and Funny Peculiar.

He finally gave his Adolf Hitler for the cinema by arranging a joyful reunion with the Boulting brothers – his first film with Roy directing and John producing since *There's a Girl in My Soup* three years earlier, and a decade since their regular collaboration. All the elements were right, so Sellers signed up for the wartime farce, *Soft Beds, Hard Battles*, for production at Pinewood Studios in the spring of 1972. Hitler was the plum of plum parts. Although merely a cameo in the pantheon of military antics, Roy Boulting indulged Sellers and the character with the showiest of entrances. The camera is trained on Hitler's back, as he storms into the Parisian brothel with his stormtroopers. Wagnerian sweeps of orchestral music pound out his crusading gait. It's majestic and cinematic and – as with the whole performance – played for power, not laughs. There isn't an ounce of send-up in Peter's Hitler. He is dogged, determined, and damnable. The only moment of humour is not even at his expense, but a loving, and light playfulness around Peter's multiple performances within *Soft Beds, Hard Battles*. Perhaps the most endearing and certainly most sustained and substantial is frightfully British officer Major Robbie Robinson. While, casing the whore house for Nazis to bump off, he spots the prize of all prizes. Hitler, of course. As Sellers is playing both parts the Britisher mutters: "I know that face!" Of course he knows that face. It's Hitler. The ultimate enemy. Of course, he also knows that face because it's the one he sees in the mirror every morning when he shaves. It's Peter Sellers! The role of Hitler also allows Sellers the most dramatic and potent moment in the film. A moment of pure film. He is exercising his pointer across the map of the world. A world he wants to invade and conquer. As he hovers over Moscow his gaggle of Hun acolytes shift nervously in their seats. Again, the camera is on the back of Hitler, before he senses the unease in the room, swiftly turns, and glowers. No dialogue is needed. Just Sellers, at his most intense, his most assured, his most terrifying. This truly is a dictator one can believe in . . . at least in truthfulness of performance.

In a sense Peter's Hitler is so thoroughly unrepentant and clearly clinically insane, that we simply step back in awe. His vile outburst at the black prostitute Mademoiselle Tom-Tom, played with frantic abandon by Hylette Adolphe, is a shocking moment too. Moreover, it sets up the hypocrisy of the Nazis: all violent bed-hopping and champagne-quaffing.

Unfortunately and rather shockingly, the powers that be at the distribution house of Charter Film Productions, lacked the courage of their own conviction, and certainly the courage of Peter's conviction in making Hitler such a rounded catalyst for the war and for the film. It was lucratively picked up for a release across America, under the rather lacklustre, almost clever, title of *Undercover Heroes*. When the film was premiered in London, on 24th January 1974, it ran ten minutes longer than its final version and, most intriguingly of all, included a narration recorded by Sellers himself. This was in the character of a French observer of the proceedings: a contemporary look back to thirty odd years in the past. The role was an additional or, at the very least, an extension of an uncredited, vocal cameo by Sellers as a French radio newsreader. In the end the film, set in the Paris of 1940, and already giving great swathes over to American embassy employees (a young buck played by Rex Stallings and his superior Don Fellows) had the narration re-recorded with a gruff old GI looking back to the war years. The misquoted Voltaire quote: "history is but a fable that has been agreed upon", was originally and rather lovingly complemented with a cheeky dedication to all those servicemen who have written their memoirs. This little touch was also jettisoned from the final release print.

The mere whiff of an audio-only Sellers did, however, indulge the actor in his successful attempt to out-do his acting hero and out-Alec Guiness Alec Guinness. *Kind Hearts and Coronets* had laid down the gimmick casting challenge twenty-five years earlier and Sellers was up for it. Admittedly the majority of Peter's roles in *Soft Beds, Hard Battles* are glorious vignettes. A mere scene or two – as with Hitler – but beautifully observed and, despite the repertory theatre bald-pate and aged make-up of his grizzled French General Latour, perfect showcases for Peter's quick change, gear-shift acting. The Japanese warrior, Prince Kyoto, is another case in point. The make-up is B-Picture Poverty Row but the subtle performance, measured mannerisms, and little boy sexuality builds to an impressive, contained performance of frustration, conceit, and childlike point-scoring. Typically of Sellers, even in this military sandpit of play and parody, the cultural appropriation is too good to be offensive. The performance merely shocks in every atrocious and parsimonious way in which it is meant to shock. Within the framework of a fantastical farce, the Jap is flawless, funny, and faithful to the cause. It's Sellers rising above the budget and even above the precise and powerful script. It's an oriental gem, touched with comic clout.

Shocking too in *Soft Beds, Hard Battles* is the casual death. This is a war film comedy with an alert and unerring sense of the fact that it *is* a war story. The burst of Vera Lynn – impersonated by Joan Baxter – and the stoic reassurance of the BBC is as powerful as the determined bravery of the French in *Casablanca*. Here, the Nazi hordes are stopped in their tracks; stunned; fearful even. This is satire, this is the reality of war. Sellers, giving his best of the seven roles here, as the British officer is clumsy and gung-ho and rather slapdash in that way that only horrendously brave and calculated and really rather hardened fighters can be. He is nonplussed over shooting Nazis – really more annoyed at himself for forgetting to put the silencer on his revolver. He even kills – or at least brings about the death – of his seasoned old screen pal and fellow Boultings favourite Thorley Walters, who happily gave a day or two of his time to bring seedy life to an overweight and over-come German high-up. This casual dismissal of death as simply a byproduct of the situation, is counterbalanced and bookended by the shuffling, inscrutable Gestapo Herr Schroeder (Sellers again, of course). Pebble-glassed, thin-lidded, his eyes dart on the look-out for the next victim, and the next act of duplicitous skullduggery. Whining of voice, and with a creepy limp,[1] a monster in a tacky trench coat, this is Peter's other major role in the film, invested with all his bitterness and bewilderment at the doctrine of the Third Reich. There is a stillness; a nervousness, in his awkward, reprimanded scene with his superior officer, Curt Jergens, endearingly and gloriously, that rare character in a British war film – a likeable, reasonable Nazi. He is a charmer; he is certainly a valued, old client of Madame Grenier (Lila Kedrova) herself; and in that there is a dignity and fairness in him. Indeed, the audience roots for him, and is chuffed that he gets out of the line of fire alive.

No, it is the Gestapo worm that Sellers embodies. The British fop is fun – beautifully measured, but fun. Schroeder is a gift for the sublime character comedian. If anything this is what Doctor Strangelove would have been during the war – twenty or so years before he was wheelchair-bound and embroiled in deep Cold War politics. The sinister vocal tics are the same, the staccato movement, the cold and calculated dedication to the war effort. Sellers and the Boultings imbue him with a couple of farcical moments – his playful behaviour pretending to be a whore as he bounces on the bed results not in death but embarrassment: he is caught in the deadly mechanism

---

1 Channelled by, first Richard Gibson, as Herr Flick in the David Croft and Jeremy Lloyd situation comedy *'Allo, 'Allo*. Gloriously enough Richard Mercer, who would play Colonel Kurt von Strohm throughout *'Allo, 'Allo*, pops up in *Soft Beds, Hard Battles* as a philosophical Nazi. Philip Madoc had, of course, found immortality within the David Croft and Jimmy Perry canon in *Dad's Army*: 'The Deadly Attachment'. "Your name will also go on the list . . ." *Soft Beds, Hard Battles*, while far from a smash hit, generated a non-hit single release too. 'The House on the Rue Sichel' unleashed multi-Sellers characters from the film on the Sovereign label: SOV126.

like a fly in a spider's web. His ultimate death – as the Fuhrer screams down the phone at him – is cartoon-like in its explosive violence. So much so, and reinforced by his previous escape, that I'm very happy to think that Schroeder did indeed survive to get steadily more insane, changed his name to Strangelove, infiltrated the American government, and the rest is military mock-history, mein Herr.

While Sellers the actor was more than satisfied with his multi-character assignment, Sellers the man was very well catered for in terms of a bevy of beautiful female co-stars. The very plot populates the action with sexy sirens, all scantily-clad. Indeed, such is the dedication to this war comedy as very much a war film that it is not only death that is treated so casually, but nudity too. In the whorehouse scenes, the girls wander around quite unfettered and unashamed, naturally. Moreover, Sellers was so happy because, even before the opening credits, he has – in two very different character guises – found himself in bed with a scantily clad Jenny Hanley; and a completely topless and unbothered Rula Lenska. Sexy and funny, these femme fatales include Peter's beloved favourite Francoise Pascal, as much, much more than glorious decoration. Their bravery and service to the war effort is the very core of the story. The very backbone of the action. Francoise recalled: "that film was such fun. We all had the best time – and I met my best, long-term girlfriend, Jenny Hanley, while making it. Peter seemed in the very best of places too. He thoroughly enjoyed himself on that set. What red-blooded male would not? But he was lovely and respectful and charming . . . and terribly, terribly funny. He had a trigger in his head when it came to the war, and if he could both pay tribute to those brave Englishmen and allies who won it, and savage the nations that lost it, and make it both funny and true, then he was in his element. For me, I don't think I remember Peter being more relaxed in his own skin – or should that be several skins? – as on that film. I have heaps of the happiest of memories from making it. For a little while Peter even adopted his silly British officer's line of 'Keep in touch!' It was very funny."[1]

---

1 Interview with the author, September 2022.

As is Sellers. Throughout – even when it reaches the bottom with an outbreak of killer flatulence. Yes, funny throughout. Except of course when he doesn't want to be. Whether as The Englishman. The Japanese. The Frenchmen . . . Indeed, the final role reveals all. The last Frenchman role is one that Peter relishes. This officious official has the delightful duty of bestowing the medals on the ample chests of the brave ladies at the heart and soul of the film. With pretty and petite Daphne Lawson who has played the baby doll Claudine, with great savvy, throughout, even keeping her payment within a cuddly bear, Sellers eyes her briefest of brief outfits and acts a little inward breath as a suggestion to her. In order for him to pin on the medal without discomfiture, you see. It's a delicious moment. Saucy and sweet. This bureaucrat is tempted by all of them, naturally, but finally gets into lust when faced with youthful Beatrice Romand, as Marie-Claude, who has blossomed throughout the film. She is the one who has stroked the ego and the nether regions of the Jap.

Still it is undoubtedly Peter's Hitler that is the performance that resonates the most. It is far from a comical interpretation. His Hitler here is fooled, yes, but never foolish. The role allows the film to have very serious things to say, very much in the comical mould of a war-time romp. These were rife at the time, be it the Second World War (Danny La Rue in *Our Miss Fred*) or the Great War (Frankie Howerd in *Up the Front*), but Sellers is a brutal, cold killer. Every inch the dictator. Not to be messed with. Certainly, even thirty years on, Sellers viewed the war years with a mixture of wistful memories and paranoia.

This paranoia had certainly informed an earlier film. One of the less loved and less screened of Peter's entire film career. The true story of seven men . . . only two of whom will survive. And that's a paraphrasing of the legend that starts the film. There's not a lot of laughs here, in this D-Day escape of June 1944. It's grim and gritty, but *The Blockhouse* was a major production, through Cannon Films, for a release with MGM. It was made entirely on location, in a discarded military hospital, built by the Germans, in St. Peter Port, on Guernsey, and it was very, very dark. Both in terms of subject matter, and cinematography. Many of the scenes are lit purely by the natural candle light and struck matches. The relentless shooting schedule reflected French hours, with cast and crew meeting at 10.30 a.m. for the day's filming, and descending into complete darkness from midday for an eight-hour session, without a break. The sound is muted; tense; whispered. The plot was simple, and bleak: during a heavy bombing raid a mixture of Allied forces prisoners of war make their escape in the mayhem and find solace in an abandoned German bunker. They have resources to last them years. In the event, they are trapped forever. Under the strict guidance of Sellers himself, director Clive Rees and cinematographer Keith Goddard, filmed the scenes within the actual blockhouse, which is the majority of the film. And it was Sellers that insisted on the use of natural light, from a box of candles. This is stark realism. At one point, a drunk and going slightly mad Peter Vaughan is in complete blackness and screams out: "I can't see! I can't see!" Well quite. Like the characters in the film, the cast had to amuse themselves while waiting for a scene to be set up. Vaughan remembered that: "my friend Jeremy Kemp and I would organise a bit of impromptu cricket. We made a ball with gaffer tape, our bats were pieces of wood, and stumps were chalked on a wall. But it was good fun and keenly fought. Peter Sellers, who normally did not mix or join in socially with cast and crew, asked to have a bat. He was very funny when preparing to bat, taking an elaborate stance and looking to see where exactly the fielders were placed."[1]

Sellers plays Rouquet, a calm and collected, bespectacled French schoolteacher. Brilliantly. There is not a hint of caricature

---

1 *Once a Villain: A Memoir*, by Peter Vaughan (Fantom Publishing, 2016). Incidentally, fifty years later, Vaughan would play Peter's father in *The Life and Death of Peter Sellers*, the only actor in that biopic who had worked with the genuine article! In the book, Vaughan continues his memory of Peter Sellers as a great cricketer. Having expressed an interest to play professionally in that *Radio Fun* piece in 1951, he told the ensembled film personnel that he was a relation of the celebrated Yorkshire cricketer Bill Sellers. Vaughan believed cricketer Bill spelt his surname Sellars and, thus, pretended to be impressed during the production of *The Blockhouse*. During his research for the role of Peter's father, Vaughan read a biography and: "found to my amazement that when Peter was a boy on a variety tour with his family, they arrived in a town to find their name wrongly spelt on the posters: they were billed as Sellers. They preferred it to their real name Sellars and kept it that way thereafter. So was he really related to the great Brian Sellars? Who knows." Well . . . actually that proves that Peter Sellers was stringing them along, living out a fantasy, or trying to impress. Howzat!

here. Not a wisp of farcical over-playing that had, and would again, have them rolling in the aisles as Clouseau. He is the custodian of hope throughout. And, yes, Sellers does provide moments of joy. He teaches his fellow inmates how to play dominos; and oversees the impromptu bicycle race, but these are not hints of laughter but smiles. A glimmer of humanity amidst the despair. Here, with dirty face make-up and a logical mind, Sellers keeps a grip on the number of days the seven have been incarcerated by the time it takes for a candle to burn down – five hours – and, in a poignant, subtle, and bewitching speech, his own heartbeat. As long as that holds out . . . Just relish his final scene. Quietly jaw-dropping.

The Blockhouse and *Soft Beds* are, very different, bookends of Second World War angst. Peter's personal Second World War angst. There could have been a third wartime film. The centre of the Ven diagram. At the time Jerry Lewis was starring in, and directing, his infamous and unfinished *The Day the Clown Cried*. The tragi-comic tale of vaudeville comedian Helmut Doork forced into leading Jewish children into the Holocaust. Sellers had been a hot tip to play the role at one point. It was an idea that, on the surface, had Oscar-winner written all over it. Still, Peter had enough battle-scarred offerings and declined. *The Blockhouse* looked deep within his anxiety for the drama of a slight, intimate incident, while *Soft Beds, Hard Battles* took lavish strikes at the entire conflict, in a farcical romp of human weaknesses and bed-hopping slapstick. Breathless tension and broad strokes. As an actor both stretched Sellers in different ways, and different directions, but it was a need to reflect on the conflict that gives both such clout and importance. Neither were box office hits. Indeed, *The Blockhouse* was such an atypical Sellers film – so out there, so different – that it vanished without trace for many years. It premiered on 6th June 1973, while *Soft Beds* emerged in the following January.

Despite two important films, these were films that failed. Sellers was disappointed. They were important to him. Still, he was not complacent. He faced the reality that this was a rather lean time in terms of success. He was also contented that the times were rich indeed in terms of enjoyment. And the most enjoyable and thrilling had been *that* reunion with the closest of comedy chums. Peter had needed absolutely no persuasion at all to sign up for a last, last *Goon Show* of all.

Chapter 13

"I made a little jokules. Pause for audience applause. Not a sausage. Does I Don't Care pose."

Bluebottle

1972 was quite the year. If not the blockbusting, almost flatlining, maelstrom of 1964, then the free-wheeling, familiar plateau of fun assignments and old comrades. It was a continuation of a comedy friendship that stretched right back to those wartime experiences that Sellers was still reliving. Yes, *The Last Goon Show of All* would rekindle and reinforce Peter's obsession with Hitler and the Second World War, and Winston Churchill and the fear of want and the desire of money and all that had very much been at play as the very fabric of the flag-waving resurrection of *The Goon Show*.

Still, while the euphoric glee of all that was in his mind, Sellers was committed to a very cynical slice of cinematic satire tailormade for the American television generation. On the big screen. *Where Does It Hurt?*, for director Rod Amateau, cast Sellers as the silky smooth and oh so sinister "horse's arse" of a hospital administrator Albert T. Hopfnagel: a man who you would seriously think twice about buying a used car from, never mind allowing him to tot up your accounts honestly. Just before recording *The Last Goon Show of All*, Sellers was asked the question most actors dread: What has been his favourite part to play? Despite a whiff of contractual obligation around a role he had just completed and was awaiting a release date, there is much sincerity in his answer: Albert T. Hopfnagel. One can understand why, for the character has absolutely no redeeming features whatsoever. His cold, dead, shark eyes dart around behind those dark-tinted glasses, looking for the next subterfuge, the next excuse, the next untruth, the next patsy on whom to pile the blame. Photographed beautifully in a blue suit, and sporting an attractive Los Angeles tan, Sellers looks a million dollars. The actual satire at the heart of the film, was based heavily on the novel *The Operator*, written by the director Rod Amateau and Budd Robinson. In retrospect, the joke is obvious, and one-note. Indeed, the cheeky prologue flags up the fact that no-one in America trusts their doctor, asking the three genuine, compassionate medics in the country – and presumably in the audience – to stand up. Clod-hopping but powerful, the corruption and greed at the heart of American healthcare is the driving force of the comedy, although Peter's performance isn't intrinsically funny at all. Shocking, yes. Hilarious, no. Very much an ensemble piece, with Peter's sly and smiling anti-hero at the very core of the intrigue, it is Harold Gould's hopeless surgeon Dr. Zerny who gets most of the pratfalling moments. While the hapless patient, Lester Hammond, played by Rick Lenz, gets most of the action . . . and the girl, bronzed and beautiful Jo Ann Pflug, who stitches up Sellers, thanks to his flirting with buxom nurse, Eve Bruce.

Indeed, Peter's one sign-posted moment of physical comedy is rather thrown away: he nips into the linen cupboard for a little bit of 'Doctors and Nurses', the Fire Department is called in, and the tryst is interrupted . . . but there is no comedic exposure, no frantic, farcical explanations; nothing. Just sweet revenge on the part of his two-timed girlfriend. Peter's role doesn't require the funnies. It's a softly-spoken, almost whispered, gleeful figure of corrupt authority and money-grabbing one-upmanship. While the film itself laudably embraces the commonplace ethnicity in a working hospital, Hopfnagel himself is racist as well as self-centred: he has a go at the black orderly; the Italian doctor; the oriental laboratory assistant (Pat Morita as the gleefully duplicitous Harry Nishimoto). Peter's is a single-minded superiority over everybody. An untouchability that he never, willingly, relinquishes. Even in the face of employment termination. Like a low-rent James Bond villain, this figure of mystery and Machiavellian shenanigans operates from behind a soft drinks dispenser: crafty, as well as a neat bit of product-placement for Pepsi. There's a neat bit of product placement for a previous Sellers incarnation too, when hatchet-faced comic doyen Mrs. Mazzini (Kathleen Freeman) – in the hospital for a hysterectomy on savers stamps – calls him Hoffman by mistake. Sellers, those eyes narrowing in uneasy distrust, momentarily pauses before correcting the woman. His juggling of half-truths, playing people off of each other, spinning plates of financial gain, and attempting to bribe anybody and everybody with dud cheques, is channelled through a relentless and unfaltering charm seemingly learned from television commercials. Indeed, the film looks like it was shot for television, with *Columbo*-styled closing credits, and a multi-camera, low-grade film stock quality. Even Peter's habit of culminating every statement with "10-4" is lifted straight from television cop shows – it was the familiar sign-off of Broderick Crawford in *Highway Patrol*, an oft-repeated time-filler since its demise in 1959. It's a telly link that anchors Peter's character in American culture, big business commercialism, and unapologetic deceit.

This was the elevation of Sellers to a slick and cynical romantic lead, of sorts, with a full submergence in the satire and sensibilities of life and love in an affluent American setting. Alien though it may be, it was proof positive of where Sellers wanted his film career to be. Steeped in Stateside savvy and, thus, international. Sadly, when the Cinerama Releasing Corporation unleashed the film, on 29th September 1972, with the film's poster screaming that *Where Does It Hurt?* is "a prescription for laughter!", the great viewing public failed to see it that way. Before long the film was coupled with a surefire box office winner, *There's a Girl in My Soup*, for a saucy Sellers double bill. It helped *Where Does it Hurt?* limp into profit. Just.

And it made the prospect of Sellers turning his professional clock back twenty years all the more sweet, in that return to the medium and, indeed, the programme, that had made him famous. And which he loved. In serious, reflective mood, he spoke at the April 1972 *Goon Show* recording session: "Coming back to it is like a strange dream, as though we had never parted."[1]

The Goon Show had never gone out of the public consciousness, of course. The three would continually leap into each other's projects, and Parlophone had long realised the commercial sense in releasing the shows on long-playing record. In October 1971 *First Men on the Goon* appeared. Hardly timely – it had been two years since the moon had been conquered – and not science-fiction in the choice of episodes,[2] the record still sold in the bucketload. The BBC, slowly, sat up and took notice. A 1970 Indian Summer of Radio 4 repeats, under the previously utilised title of *Vintage Goons*, had delighted audiences. There was clearly a market for this stuff. So, for the 50th . . . the idea was simple and inspired. In order to celebrate the fifty golden years of the British Broadcasting Corporation, far-reaching plans were put in place to resurrect some of the Beeb's flagship offerings. *The Goon Show* was a natural. And, so it was, that on Sunday 30th April 1972 at the Camden Palace, London, that Messrs. Milligan, Secombe, and Sellers, and beloved Goon acolytes Ray Ellington, Max Geldray, and announcer Andrew Timothy, were rounded up by producer John Browell: the producer of the previous last radio *Goon Show* of all, twelve years earlier.

It was so important, so crucial, that *The Last Goon Show of All* received a rare simulcast on both BBC Radio 4 and BBC2 television, from 8 p.m. on Thursday, 5th October 1972. The BBC had dug deep into its pocket – which was most unusual: Max Geldray had been flown in from America. That Colour Sergeant now a Chelsea pensioner Ray Ellington was a little nearer to the microphone – geographically, while John Browell proudly presented: "all the original ladies and gentlemen . . . what more can I say but please welcome the Goons . . ."

---

1 'Goons let loose on air again', by Peter Waymark, *The Times*, Monday 1ˢᵗ May 1972. Sellers and Spike had, several years earlier, also riffed on the Goons and everything else under the sun in an interview for *Film Night*, broadcast on 8ᵗʰ November 1970.

2 'Foiled by President Fred' and the jolly Christmas episode 'Robin Hood and His Merry Men' were the selected episodes, on PMC 7132.

Indeed, announcer Andrew Timothy was back for the first time since halfway through series four, in 1953, having left because he was "fearing for his sanity".[1]

This last *Goon Show*, show number 161, was so regal that Harry Secombe was cast as the Queen. Not that any acting was required for many regal people in attendance at the recording. An emotional reunion, it may have been, but it was also by Royal Appointment.

The Duke of Edinburgh and his daughter Princess Anne were there, as well as her auntie, Princess Margaret, and her squeeze, Lord Snowdon. Prince Charles, serving overseas with a "shipful of SeaGoons" sent his written apologies. One can imagine that the "trainee King" was devastated. Indeed his kneecaps turned green with envy and dropped off! Sellers was very in with the Royal family, of course. Indeed, at the time he was living in an apartment in Roebuck House. As Johnny Gold, owner of beloved nightclub Tramp's, wrote: "He had a huge telescope with which he used to scan the gardens of Buckingham Palace . . . He said it was better than television. Prince Charles, who was mad about the Goons, would come and visit him. You could see he was absolutely in awe of Peter."[2]

Of the other 500 in the audience, such notables as Keeper of the Goons Jimmy Grafton and scriptwriter Eric Merriman, were joined by

---

1 In 2001, Dirk Maggs produced a new episode, another last Goon Show if you will, *Goon Again*, and Andrew Timothy's actor son, Christopher Timothy, was the announcer. In the autobiography of the *All Creatures Great and Small* star, beautifully and punningly entitled *Vet Behind the Ears* (Pan, 1979), Christopher Timothy wrote of his father as "a shadowy figure throughout my childhood, who occasionally materialised to take both my brother and myself out for the odd Sunday . . . after being a military chaplain [he] had become a broadcaster. He became famous as the straight-man in *The Goon Show*, a fact of which I was inordinately proud." For *Goon Again* it was Jeffrey Holland who took on the myriad and various roles of Peter Sellers: "I had renewed my interest in *The Goon Show* when, in the wake of the death of Peter Sellers, the BBC repeated a load of programmes. Brilliant. I loved them. I still do. In fact I estimate car journeys in the number of episodes I can listen to in the time it takes me to get from A to B. The Goon voices that Peter created actually came quite easily to me. They were in my DNA. I found I could do all of them. All except Grytpype-Thynne. I just couldn't get him quite right. So, Peter, you remain the greatest. No contest." Interview with the author, February 2024.
2 *Tramp's Gold*, by Johnny Gold, (Robson Books, 2001).

young pretenders and broadcasting movers and shakers.[1] At the time of recording Secombe wrote: "I wonder how many people realise how near we have become in real life to the characters we played. Scratch Peter and you find Bluebottle. Discard the trappings of the jet set and there he is – querulous in his Mum's old drawers, thinking lecherous thoughts about Gladys Twit and wearing boxing gloves to bed."[2]

Indeed, the whole show is a return to Milligan's usual celebration of idiots: Sellers is Grytpype-Thynne, a bumbling policeman, Henry Crun, Bloodnok, and, of course, Bluebottle – whose arrival gets the expected huge applause. Nothing had changed. Nothing changes.

The show itself – subsequently broadcast, and commercially released in an extended version – was nothing more than a lengthy list of misty-eyed introductions and a script, solely pulled together by Milligan, of relentless one-liners. Regardless, it is heart-warming, and very, very funny. All the old characters get at least one vignette in which to shine: the last fully-fledged vestiges of full-blown Goonish comedy. Although, unsurprisingly, it is much more in the style of Milligan's most recent sketch-driven television work in 1969's *Q5*, and guest spots on *The Marty Feldman Comedy Machine. The Last Goon Show of All* is also, understandably, very nostalgic, with jolly references back to their own variety theatre schtick[3] . . . with Harry's shaving routine resurrected, and Spike considering singing some of Irving Berlin's songs (and then thinking better of it, because "he never sings any of mine!") . . . although whether Sellers had

---

1 The influence of the Goons on current comedy teams was clear. Sellers often mentioned the Monty Python boys as their natural heirs. *The Goodies* too were working on their third series of BBC episodes at the time. In 'Robin Hood' Sellers and Spike comment on the single release of 'You Gotta Go Owl!'. In the mid-seventies the Goodies would often reference the chart position for their latest single. Even as late as 2014, with Monty Python at the O2, as here with the Goons, the team would acknowledge and send-up the members' current activities, memorably those "boring travel programmes" of Michael Palin!, miles away from the anarchic comedy that first made them known. It was a direct throwback to Peter Sellers on Harry Secombe in *The Goon Show*: 'The Greenslade Story', broadcast 18th December 1955, when he summed him up simply as: "All that singing and shaving . . .". *The Last Goon Show of All* has the star clowns emerge from three coffins. Python would wallow in this deliciously black humour, billing their Graham Chapman-lite O2 reunion as 'One Down, Five to Go'.

2 Backword by Harry Secombe, *The Goon Show Scripts*, Woburn Press, 1972.

3 Spike's latest BBC sketch special, *Milligan in Autumn*, would air on Sunday, 1st October 1972, with the other three seasons following in order, folks, until August 1973.

ever whistled the soliloquy from *Hamlet* before then is debatable. It's also Milligan's scripted commentary on Sellers himself that is key to where the Goons as a unit were in 1972. While Milligan has orchestrated and, yet again, taken on the scriptwriting structure of the revival, he gleefully takes a poke at his old colleague's wealth and position as the world's leading comedy actor. Not to mention his well-documented obsessions that would be splashed across the newspapers. When Andrew Timothy introduces Sellers to the audience it is noted that: "Mr. Sellers will now sell a gross of his cars . . ." Later on, a burst of comic gibberish is explained away as: "That was Mr. Sellers practising his comeback."

Such thinly-veiled pokes were received with tickled snickering. Always. Sellers preferred this childlike name-calling from old friends to the reverential yes-men of Hollywood. As such, the recording of *The Last Goon Show of All* is a pivotal moment in the last decade of Peter's life and work. It was a rather pivotal moment in the history of a nation too. As Vincent Mulchrone noted the day after the show's recording: "With a bit of foresight, we could have imprisoned them in a luxurious studio for life so that their unique idiocy could sustain us in a world going crazy in quite a different way."[1]

For the BBC it immediately warranted a repeat of 'The Jet-Propelled Guided NAAFI', in November 1972. Now it was Radio 2, and dusted off as part of *The Great Shows 1938–1963* season. Peter's old wireless champion and mentor Ted Ray introduced the repeat. There's something very reassuring about that.[2]

If nothing else *The Last Goon Show of All* galvanised the need Sellers had to wallow in nostalgia. He relishes the team huddle, affectionate banter, and free-wheeling spirit of *The Goon Show*. This need for fun would determine Peter's choice of work for the rest of

---

1 'The Goons come back by Royal Appointment', by Vincent Mulchrone, *Daily Mail*, Monday, 1st May 1972.

2 The reunion had also led to the Woburn Press publishing *The Goon Show Scripts*, with drawings by Sellers, Secombe, and Spike, in October 1972: a venture so popular that there were two more print-runs within a month of its publication. It was noted that this was to be the first in a planned series, although in the event only a second volume – in this format – followed. *More Goon Show Scripts*, was published by the Woburn Press, in 1973.

his life. Certainly, the next five years would invariably spin round halcyon memories of past glories and past associations.

Without doubt *The Last Goon Show of All* inspired in Sellers a near-mania for working alongside Spike Milligan again. If the madness and camaraderie of the war years had never left Sellers, that same madness and camaraderie had been the bedrock for the whole life of Spike. He craved the uniform and uniformity of army life: "roll on World War III" he would say.[1] For Sellers to drag Spike into his own floundering projects, and for Peter to eagerly swim in the ken of Spike's work was at fever pitch throughout the early 1970s. It was a decision that undoubtedly contributed to Peter's own mental waywardness. It was a soothing balm of shared lunacy, with Sellers and Spike often merging their nutty neuroses together on projects with little or no commercial mileage at all. So, deep breath: alongside a dusting down of old recording and cinema collaborations, there would be two hugely unprofitable co-starring film ventures, one not even released during Peter's lifetime; two long-playing albums; a book; a couple of small screen reunions, one Goonish excess, one painfully introspective; and even an aborted television situation comedy. Most wasteful of all would be a multi-star re-telling of the wild and wacky world of Lewis Carroll which, stupidly or wisely, kept the two Goons separate on-screen.

In an unpicking of each and every one of these Sellers and Spike projects, there is just one constant. Regardless of how disastrous it may have ended up, the initial objection was clear and simple. Sellers did it simply to have fun. There was little regard for any logistics of furthering his career, nor any bother about promoting the end result. Sellers wasn't even that bothered about finishing the job. For him, the work was his route to that rarest of commodities for Sellers in the seventies: happiness.

---

1 Interviewed by David Dimbleby: *Face Your Image: Spike Milligan*. This programme also had Sellers quoted as saying about Spike that: "he used to like people. Disillusioned in that area. Frightened of people. Romantic." A mis-reading of his friend, or even a transference of his own thoughts about himself. Certainly Peter's accusation of hating women leaves Milligan – watching the filmed interview in isolation – clearly baffled. Spike fervently denies it: "I don't hate women. [Although I] love children and animals.'

Alice's Adventures in Wonderland, as directed and adapted by Australian William Sterling, making his one and only cinematic release, not only gathered together a staggeringly impressive cross-section of theatre luminaries and comedy pioneers but also got to the wildly imaginative heart of Lewis Carroll's source publications. An experienced producer for British television, Sterling was perhaps more inspired than foolhardy in keeping Sellers and Spike in separate environs of Wonderland. He got the film finished, on schedule, and released, successfully.[1]

It was the film venture the two embarked upon after the recording but before the broadcast of *The Last Goon Show of All* and while Milligan is gangling and gleeful in song as the Gryphon, Sellers is pitched in with a gloriously eccentric gaggle of well-known personalities. Roly-Poly satirist Roy Kinnear is the Cheshire Cat; classical actor and ballet-dancer extraordinaire Sir Robert Helpmann is the Mad Hatter, while Dudley Moore is the dozy Dormouse, and embraces the comedy cross-fertilisation of *Goon* and *Beyond the Fringe* once again.

Sellers, wide-eyed and bushy-tailed, is the frenetic March Hare, a performance of concentrated otherness and energy. 'The Pun Song', by John Barry and Don Black, is Peter perfection.[2]

After the fragile charm of Anne-Marie Malilk in 1966, Peter now enjoyed dewy-eyed Fiona Fullerton as a gorgeous Alice. The film was the Fox-Rank Distributors hope for the Christmas market, being released across America, on 20th November, and in England, on 4th December 1972.

And if that rather muted distribution of *Where Does It Hurt?*, in September 1972, had dented Peter's confidence he didn't show it, for the following month was a veritable fanfare of a return to his roots.

The Last Goon Show of All went out to terrific press coverage and

---

1 Still, it would have been hugely satisfying to have Sellers and Milligan play together. Messy and expensive, but satisfying. So, as it is, there is a shade of the disappointment that also taints Irwin Allen's *The Story of Mankind* which reunited Groucho, Harpo and Chico Marx only to segregate them in three different historical settings.

2 Peter, both in character and out of character, contributed to the *Alice in Wonderland* special edition *Film Night*, BBC2, 24th November 1972.

universal praise, on 4th October. Sellers had also, at the same time and on that same trip home, eagerly agreed to do another old Goon chum, Eric Sykes, a favour. 'Sykes and a Stranger' – Peter was the stranger – was so meta, and so cool, that it was even referenced in Peter's biography within *The Goon Show* scripts book. The Sykes episode went out on 19th October 1972, a scant fortnight since the last of the Goons.

'Sykes and a Stranger' was the sixth episode of a brand-new series of Eric's domestic situation comedy, which co-starred Hattie Jacques as his identical twin sister. Now in full colour, it had been seven years since the original run and Eric needed all the help he could get. Or so he thought. The show was a massive success, running until 1979.[1]

Despite being performed before a BBC Television Centre studio audience Jacques and Sykes at least try to keep the situation comedic rather than farcical. There are acknowledgements of the viewer in the auditorium, but the plot drives the laughter. That is until Sellers arrives. The pressure cooker is shaking during the build-up of his reputation. This little Tommy Grando who used to play with the twins as children but went bad and went inside. What Sellers brings to the half-hour comedy is a gusto and off-the-scale bravado that not only takes over completely but completely leaves his accomplished co-stars fighting for breath between bouts of uncontrollable corpsing.

There is too a sense of a rich old playmate coming back into the community. Sykes and Jacques had stayed put, happily paddling in the waters of the British Broadcasting Corporation and British film. Sellers had tasted Hollywood excess and fortune. He's happy to return to the old country and the old ways, safe in the knowledge that he can go back to his international fame whenever he wants to. Not so much in the quality of the work which, at the time, was wavering purely on whether he wanted to do it or not, but because he could well afford to stop entirely if he wanted and still live in the manner to which he had swiftly and irreversibly become accustomed. Once

---

1 *Sykes* had run on BBC Television from 1960 through to 1965, with this colour resurrection, often harking back to familiar sketches of slapstick, fuelled by an unexpectedly large financial demand Sykes received from the Inland Revenue!

tasted, the high-life was impossible to curb.[1]

Sporting a repertory company five o'clock shadow and a spiky fright wig, Sellers is a caricature, but played with such verve, such disrespect for Eric's carefully-chiselled script, that it is arguably the most powerful comedy showstopper in all of British television. The genius of the performance lies in its very incongruousness. Sellers is a Goon character unleashed in suburbia. Peter's vocal choice is something akin to the unruly grandson of William Mate: a hard-boiled cockney youth with as much disregard for the law as Sellers has for the script. Wildly going off-piste when he sees Hattie Jacques begin to laugh, Sellers twists the knife with a completely off-the-cuff bellow of "Flabberknackerjawers" – itself resurrected from the nonsensical ramblings of William Mate on the 'Any Old Iron' recording from 1957. It's an inspired moment of madness that pulls the entire cast over the edge of breaking down with laughter. Certainly in the five years since making *The Bobo* together, in Spain, when both Sellers and Jacques had never looked leaner, life had thrown curveballs that would resonate for the rest of their days.[2]

All this feelgood insanity was a direct result of the Goon reunion of '72 and, suitably enough, the interest in the last show was further fuelled by a landmark get-together for the *Parkinson* chat show, on 28th October 1972. A lifelong fan of the trio, Michael Parkinson would be disappointed by his producer's furtive attempts to get all the Goons in the Shepherds Bush studio at one time. Spike Milligan, who had flown off to Australia to promote poetry and his cough and a spit in *The Adventures of Barry Mackenzie*, was struck down by the dreaded lurgy and had to beam his thoughts and opinions from his hotel sick-bed. Still, Sellers and Secombe, live and in-person, were on-hand and on-form, to happily run slipshod over Parkinson's preconceived line of questioning. It was a reflective and celebratory

---

1 Certainly Peter's always constant fascination with television, coupled with his love of a quick, easy, and well-paid job, saw him gleefully accept a glut of small-screen bits at this time. There was *The New Bill Cosby Show* on 18th September 1972 and 5th February 1973 for CBS; an appearance on the New Year's Eve 1972 episode of *Festival of Entertainment* for the BBC; and *The Dean Martin Show* on 5th April 1973 for NBC.

2 Hattie's own heart would give out, just ten weeks after Peter's, in October 1980.

75 minutes . . . and the Ray Ellington Quartet were on hand to add authenticity.

Milligan's momentary loss of good health was instrumental in him agreeing to assist Sellers with his pirate romp, *Ghost in the Noonday Sun*. The Cyprus location would certainly have appealed to a convalescing Spike. Unfortunately, during his time on the film, Turkey were actively threatening to invade the country, while enemy Russian and American ships patrolled the surrounding waters, forever on the verge of attack. Such world-shattering negative vibes were as nothing, however, to the beleaguered production's chief disruption: a totally apathetic Peter Sellers. Both Sellers and Spike had suffered a pivotal upheaval in health: massive heart attack for Sellers; debilitating mental breakdown for Spike. However, while Spike struggled to mask his madness with stoic reasoning in the face of authoritative conflict, Sellers capitalised on his well-documented health issues to get his own way. At one point during the location filming of *Ghost in the Noonday Sun* he even fabricated a massive heart attack in order to get time off the shoot. And promptly jetted off to London in order to take luncheon with Princess Margaret.[1]

Ostensibly brought on board to cheer up and gee on his fellow Goon, Milligan was powerless and implicit in Peter's desire to enjoy the experience, spend hours water-skiing and, basically, do everything save cooperate with their director Peter Medak. After all, they were getting their payment out of the $2 million budget and Milligan had done all he could to add some funnies to the script.[2]

The nautical narrative of the film had Sellers as the charmingly named Dick Scratcher – an echo of the deliberately cheeky and controversial ethos of the Goons if ever there was one. He is a pirate

---

1 The Queen's sister had been very much part of Peter's swinging sixties scene, visiting Sellers on the Shepperton Studios sets of both *Casino Royale*, and *The Magic Christian*. As early as 1964, Margaret, her then husband Antony Armstrong-Jones, and Peter's then wife Britt Ekland, larked about for the home movie *I Say I Say I Say*. The delightfully Goonish film, featuring Sellers as variety turn 'The Great Berko' and shot at the home of Jocelyn Stevens, *Queen* magazine editor and financer of the recently launched Radio Caroline, was, along with many other Sellers treasures, commercially released on DVD by the BBC as part of the Collectors Edition of *The Peter Sellers Story . . . As He Filmed It*, in 2005.

2 *The Ghost of Peter Sellers*, Medak's 2018 documentary, lays all the facts bare. Clinically so.

who has killed his rascally Captain and now faces a problem. He can't locate the old seadog's buried treasure. Befriending the young cabin boy (Richard Willis) who maintains he can see dead people, the scurvy Scratcher hopes to perhaps, just perhaps, commune with the not-so-dearly departed and ascertain the whereabouts of the doubloons and diamonds.

As director Peter Madak later admitted: "as an artist he was a genius, as a person, he was insane", and this fragile state was further heightened by Sellers being in a love-life maelstrom. The relationship he had been enjoying with Liza Minnelli had lost its fizz. Sellers was still married at this point, but the union was clearly as shaky as Dick Scratcher's shivering timbers.

If galivanting around on location in Kyrenia and Cyprus, or even on the sainted sound stages of Bray Studios, in Berkshire, was an exercise in licking his wounds, then Sellers was seriously convinced that Spike Milligan's input could lick the film into shape. A re-write here; a scene re-work there did little but make Sellers and Spike laugh, however. They also laughed all the way to the bank when, with James Villiers, playing Parsely-Frack in the film, in-tow, they shot that silent slapstick gold bullion vault heist commercial for Benson & Hedges. The sun was shining and the water was lovely and Sellers was initiator in both the deal and the on-screen heist: all finger-pointing instruction and silent movie mugging. Frankly, it was a nice excuse to take an enforced break in Kyrenia harbour, and was the only use of that Cyprus-location filming that contemporary cinema audiences saw. A jolly romp for money, *Ghost in the Noonday Sun* director Peter Medak helmed the advert, even though it was on his Sunday off. His hope was that it might cheer his star up. It didn't work. Sellers refused to hold the packet of cigarettes because he was the Chairman of the Anti-Smoking League! Spike couldn't do it either. He was the Deputy Chairman of the Anti-Smoking League. Villiers was happy to help! Mortified once the commercial was in the can Spike pleaded with Benson & Hedges to give his twenty-five-grand fee to public health charity ASH: Action on Smoking and Health. They refused, and Spike donated it to charity. Sellers pocketed his fifty grand and drove off in his new Mercedes.

Wolf Mankowitz had written the first draft of the *Ghost in the Noonday Sun* screenplay, pretty much imagining it as a straight pirate yarn. And, don't forget dear reader, he had written *The Millionairess*. The film that had kickstarted Peter's star film career in the first place. A safe haven on rocky seas, for sure. However . . . the final print was deemed un-releasable by Columbia Pictures.

Undeterred, Sellers was convinced that, together with Spike, he could still salvage something from the wreckage. Sellers mounted a campaign to buy the rights from Columbia, bring Milligan back again, and home-record a Goonish, two-hander narration for the film in order to signpost the plot and fill in confusing elements that did not or could not be filmed.

Ever the business brains, the bosses at Columbia, had their price. It was over double what Sellers had expected and anticipated. Sellers too, being no fool, abandoned the idea. *Ghost in the Noonday Sun* languished, unloved and pretty much unfinished, in the vaults until long after Peter's death.[1]

However, if Miranda was tolerating her husband's affair with Liza Minnelli, then Peter's own distress at the breakdown of the relationship was swiftly swamped by a punishing work schedule. Again, this was work that Sellers wanted to do for the sheer fun of it, rather than any notion of increased profit margin.

And for Sellers, in the early seventies, fun could only be had with Spike Milligan at his side.

---

1 His subsequent re-found fame with the relaunch of the Pink Panther franchise, and the continuation of the series in the wake of his relatively early passing, made Sellers a comedy cult figure and, thus, any scrap of previously unseen material commercially viable. It finally emerged onto the home video market, via Virgin Vision, in 1989.

Chapter 14

"I'm not what you'd call a full-time professional funny man.
I don't do funny voices in restaurants. I just eat!"

Peter Sellers, 1975

Still, the glowing aftermath of the Goon reunion didn't get past Decca Records either, who, on 4th August 1973, re-issued the 'Ying Tong Song', coupled with 'I'm Walking Backwards for Christmas'.[1] It was a successful cash-in, with the single peaking at number nine in the charts.

Sellers and Spike were happy to count the royalties. Besides, they were basking in a fresh and funny joint project, the recording sessions for which were taking place at Decca's studios in Hampstead: the home of the fifties Goon songs that were still selling, nearly two decades on.

The inspiration for this fresh lunacy was once more ripped from the world's screaming headlines: *He's Innocent of Watergate . . . or Dick's Last Stand*. Yes, Sellers was playing another Dick here: disgraced American President Richard Nixon, who just eighteen months after being elected, had resigned from office in the August of 1974.

Peter's recent squeeze Liza Minnelli is indeed name-checked, during a final fantasy casting of the film of Nixon's life as a biopic of Hitler: Sellers living his happiest comedy life again, in Nazi rant. Minnelli, in a sketch scripted by Spike, is, unflatteringly, suggested as the ideal person to play Rudolf Hess. One can imagine the mirth that Milligan and Sellers shared. Like a couple of tickled kids in the

---

1 Serial number: Decca F.13414.

playground. Mind you, Liza is very much not alone in the satirical patter which seems as equally obsessed with corruption in the White House as it is of gleaning the maximum laughter out of flatulence. Suitably enough, as a lively Sellers and Spike collaboration, this even includes archive Bloodnok bowel-movements from the Goon vaults.

Sellers had long been a lover of the gadget and a follower of innovation. As a fledgling performer he had cited one of his hobbies as: "collecting unusual gramophone records",[1] and believe me there are few gramophone records as unusual as *He's Innocent of Watergate*. It certainly displays a love of mucking about with tape-recording from the outset with speeded-up, slowed-down and tape jams riffing round cache celebrities and political scandal. Frank Sinatra, Sammy Davis Jr. and Jack Ruby are just some of the name-drops insinuated within the first few minutes.

The lion's share of the album was written by Spike Milligan and he happily pops up in various guises – from a gibbering lackey, to jazz legend Duke Ellington. Really! Sellers is dour, desolate and desperate as Richard Nixon with many of these: "fragments of fifteen tapes recently found secreted in the false bottom of a flowerbed in the White House Gardens", indulging Milligan as song-writer and Sellers as piano-pounding singer. Somewhat relentlessly on 'He's Innocent of Watergate'. The song, a recurring ear-haunting throughout the album will stick with you. You have been warned. He's innocent, you know!

Sellers even sings it at prayer, with frantic asides from Pat, his good lady wife, the first lady, played, in the briefest of almost off-mic cameos, by June Whitfield. *He's Innocent of Watergate* is an invaluable newspaper of comedy: a read-all-about-it satire which would have resonated with every thinker in the Western world at the time. Over the decades the barbs may have dimmed slightly, but only slightly, and there's no doubting Peter's complete emergence within the deluded and delightfully vague President.

---

1 *Radio Fun*, January 1951.

The initial recording sessions for the record had taken place at the time *The Last Goon Show of All* had been broadcast and, suitably enough, the record's producer was Peter Eton, the most prolific *Goon Show* producer of them all.

The atmosphere should have been convivial and fun . . . but it wasn't. Sellers swiftly got bored and jetted off to South Africa to take photographs of Doctor Christian Barnard's pioneering heart transplant operation. It was a procedure very close to his, well, heart. Sellers did return to the Nixon spoof, in the spring of 1973, by which time Eton himself had grown tired of the production. Eventually Eton relinquished any credit at all, opting for an old W.C. Fields nom de plume, Pismo Clam. Well, quite.

The intro and the outro seem to suggest an invited live audience were in attendance, but in actual fact it was simply the result of Sellers and Spike meddling with the final cut. The crowd were added to give an air of *Goon Show* spontaneity; a spontaneity that was lost by the time the record was finally released on 11th February 1974. Despite Nixon's resignation just two months before dragging it back into the news again. However, in February 1974 Sellers considered the joke spent, and refused to take part in any promotions for the release.[1] Regardless, the sheer joy of Sellers and Spike riffing off of each other again, is palpable indeed.

And, during the recording of *He's Innocent of Watergate*, an even more financially-appealing notion was conjured up: a thought that it was time for Sellers and Spike to return to the BBC, for a new television series.

This was to have been a major coup indeed. In September 1974 BBC Records released the first *Goon Show Classics*: the sleeve screaming it was the first time on record. If hardly that for the show as a whole, it was certainly the first time on record for these particular two episodes ('The Dreaded Batter-Pudding Hurler', and 'The Histories of Pliny the Elder') and, more importantly, the first

---

1 Nixon remains a touchstone for corrupt politics, of course, and his likeness has been used for everything from a Hallowe'en mask to many a corrupt gag appearance in *The Simpsons*. The David Frost interviews added wood to the fire too, and the last Mrs. Sellers married Frost, for less than a year, six months after Peter's death.

time on record that *The Goon Show* retained the musical interludes for a commercial release. Thus, this disc fully captured the essence of the original broadcasts: that of a colonial and military-obsessed asylum of loveable idiots, with a hot jazz and rock 'n' roll musical accompaniment.[1] As a post-Christmas, spend-your-gift-money-here-folks push, a ten-week repeat season of *The Goon Show* ran under the heading of *Encore the Goons*, on BBC Radio 4, from 17th January to 21st March 1975. Goonery was, once again, reverberating round the corridors of Broadcasting House.

Thus Sellers and Spike once more walking the hallowed halls was a big deal.

The news broke, or more to the point, broke down, in the April of 1975 when Jack Bentley's TV Spectacular column in the *Sunday Mirror* revealed that: "it was to have been the BBC TV's comedy coup of the year. Peter Sellers and his Goon buddy, Spike Milligan, were to be in a pilot show for a series called *The Melting Pot*. With a brilliantly observed script by Spike, about two Pakistani illegal immigrants, the BBC cameras were all set to roll. Then came a call from Sellers in America saying that he was sorry, but unforeseen film commitments made it impossible for him to appear."

It was indeed a last-minute disaster for BBC producer Roger Race who was faced with the unenviable prospect of recasting Peter's part at the eleventh hour.[2] Luckily for him he spotted renowned satirist John Bird in the BBC bar, a performer: "almost as famous as Sellers for his many voices and impersonations." That was as may be, and rather generous despite Bird's great skill, but Bird was certainly part of the flotsam and jetsam of the surreal universe of Sellers and Spike. It was Bird who had written the sketch for the *He's Innocent of Watergate* album which featured Sellers, as Richard Nixon, meeting Sellers, as a savvy Indian mystic. Moreover, as Jack Bentley

---

1 Two months later, in December 1974, EMI Records issued *The Very Best of the Goons – 1* EMC 3062. There was no volume two. As if to prove they had faith in the brand, BBC Records issued 'The Jet-Propelled Guided NAAFI' and 'The Evils of Bushey Spon' on *Goon Show Classics Vol. 2*: REB 213 in October 1975, and every year after until 1985 when double-cassette and then CD repackages and continuations followed.

2 It had been Roger Race who had directed, or refereed, Peter's performance in *Sykes*.

maintained in his *Sunday Mirror* column, Bird's recent comedy album *The Collected Broadcasts of Idi Amin* "comes very close" to out-classing *The Best of Sellers*. Sellers too had had a bash at Amin on the *He's Innocent of Watergate* recording, injecting cruel quietness to the racial misunderstandings.

John Bird remembered that: "later I got a call from Spike who asked me to step in for Sellers, who I heard had got tied up with a US TV commercial. I agreed to take his place, although I had only four days to go before the start. The idea of these two Pakistanis who have been conned into thinking they have landed in Britain legally in a rowing boat would seem a certain hit whoever played the Sellers role." Bird was keen but philosophical, admitting that: "I kept on thinking the viewers would be saying: 'Pity, that should have been Sellers'."

Spike had recent form for this kind of comedy, of course, having played the Pakistani Irishman Kevin O'Grady in Johnny Speight's *Curry & Chips*, for London Weekend Television in 1969 – later resurrected for *Till Death Us Do Part* – and adopting the blackface of Victorian music-hall turn E.W. Mackney in *'Wilton's' – The Handsomest Hall in Town*. This, even then, controversial comedy of his colleague, also promoted Sellers to have a moment of quiet reflection. The previous October, on 18th October 1974 to be precise, Peter had been the very special guest of black comedian Flip Wilson in his Clerow Productions special *Flip Wilson . . . Of Course*. Although Flip's hugely popular series *The Flip Wilson Show* had been axed eight months earlier, this sketch and stand-up show was a big deal . . . and Sellers relished working with some of the greatest black artists in America, including Richard Pryor, Don Bexley, and Martha Reeves. The thought of racist stereotyping for an easy laugh was certainly the antithesis of Flip Wilson. Even as late as 1979 Sellers was pointing out the comic heritage of the Goons and cultural appropriation, and whether a funny thing also being an offensive thing is an acceptable thing. In his final EMI album, *Sellers Market*, the Indian George Formby impersonator in 'The All-England George

Formby Finals' – voiced by Peter, of course – is dismissed from the competition because he sounds too much like Peter Sellers and Spike Milligan. There's Meta Get-Out-of-Jail comedy commentary right there!

The Melting Pot was just out of sync. Filmed in the May of 1975 for an 11th June broadcast. A subsequent series of six remains one of comedy's great mysteries. Filed away and untransmitted, rumours have abounded that the BBC deemed it inappropriate. However it was Spike who warned that the show was guaranteed to offend everyone and, most telling of all, explained that: "the BBC reckon I've got a winner. Maybe. But it doesn't make me laugh."[1]

Television reviewer Ken Burgess seemed to agree with Spike, dismissing the pilot of *The Melting Pot* as a "Ragbag of Racial Jokes"[2] and perhaps unwittingly raking up memories of the original casting by commenting that: "it is not enough just to imitate Peter Sellers imitating Indians."

And what of Sellers and that lucrative TV commercial? Well, yes, he was picking up a hefty fee at the time, donning various outlandish outfits – from Highland Scots to suave Italian – for TWA: Trans World Airlines, out of New York City.

However, the debacle and mistiming of *The Melting Pot* didn't dent the friendship and on–off comedy partnership of Sellers and Spike. In a Goonish bookending of *The Melting Pot* escapade, the two reunited to celebrate an abstract hero of longstanding: Scottish poet of the absurd, William McGonagall. Sellers had brought him vividly to life, and most vicariously with a wintery twist, in *The Goon Show*: 'The Hastings Flyer', on 3rd January 1956, and over the course of the programme's history both Sellers and Spike would relish the groan-indulging doggerel.[3]

The raw heat radiating from *The Last Goon Show of All* had long-

---

1 *Sunday Mirror*, 11th July 1976. The suggested August 1976 premiere date for the series came and went, and Spike published the scripts, with Robson Books, in 1983, adding a cover sticker dubbing it: 'The TV show they wouldn't release!'

2 *Coventry Evening Telegraph*, 11th June 1975.

3 A reading of 'The Railway Bridge of the Silvery Tay' was Spike's only contribution to *Curiouser and Curiouser*, recorded in June 1956 for transmission that August.

lasting shockwaves. In the hinterland between Christmas 1974 and New Year's Day 1975, Sellers and Spike eagerly guest-starred on the BBC1 Television spectacular *Sing a Song of Secombe*.

The contribution of the two guest Goons was a filmed insert, busking, with Secombe, in Oxford Street, with Spike on trumpet; and a videotaped sequence, as The Brothers McGoonagal, performing a reading of 'The Famous Tay Whale' by William McGonagall.[1]

The glee was all the more apparent because Sellers and Spike had already filmed *The Great McGonagall*: a feature-length love-letter to the master of bad poetry, which was released or, at the very least, made a fairly successful attempt at escape, on 22nd January 1975.

Directed by long-time friend and collaborator and *Casino Royale* survivor Joe McGrath, *The Great McGonagall* was filmed in just three weeks, at the gloriously ramshackle but historically pivotal 'Wilton's' Music Hall. Financed by eminent British pornographer David Grant, under the respectable auspices of Tony Tenser of Tigon British Film Productions,[2] Spike was the cheaper option to claim the leading role of McGonagall, weaving a sketchy, surrealist and just plain silly biography of the poet against the backdrop of variety conventions and remnants of half-remembered acts. At one point Spike even wears the stage suit of the Cheeky Chappie himself, Max Miller, while John Bluthal sports the distinctive, white-eyed diamond on black-face stage make-up of comedian G.H. Chirgwin.

Sellers was on the film for just a week. We first see him like all the cast, as himself, or at least a version of himself, playing the contemporary make-up artist to Spike Milligan. Joe McGrath recalled that: "Spike and I liked the idea of seeing all the actors, or mountebanks as McGonagall would have called them, preparing to tell this story of this terrible Scottish poet. Those opening scenes were all improvised and Sellers came in wanting to play it like a very camp make-up artist he had worked with in Hollywood. You'll notice

---

1 The show was directed by Stanley Appel, produced by Stewart Morris, and written, reassuringly, by Jimmy Grafton, with Peter Vincent, for broadcast on 29th December 1974.

2 Who had funded Graham Stark's magus opus *The Magnificent Seven Deadly Sins*.

that Sellers only makes up Spike. The rest of the cast are seen being made up by the genuine make-up artist Alan Boyle, who later went on to work with Stanley Kubrick. Talking of Kubrick, Peter paid me a very lovely compliment while we were making the film. He said: 'You know, I will never work with a director twice if they are not good enough and I don't respect them. Kubrick, the Boultings, Edwards, and you, Joe. I respect you all!' I thought, 'My God! I'm in some company there.'" Joe had that quality which Sellers quantified during his interview with Michael Parkinson in 1974. The directors he could not tolerate were those who "can't communicate!"[1]

Spike not only relished the opportunity to sleep in the rat-infested portals of 'Wilton's' but, according to Joe McGrath, was one of the few people that Sellers would really take notice of: "You know, if I wanted to give a note to an actor or advise them to tone it down or, quite frankly, stop over-acting, I would quietly take them off set and tell them one-to-one, but with Spike on *The Great McGonagall* he would stop Sellers on a rehearsal, with everybody there, and actually correct him, and Peter, bless him, would say: 'Yes, okay Spike!' Spike could get away with that and I asked him about it once. He said: 'Look, I'm the writer and he's a friend!' And that was that. Whatever you may hear about Spike and Sellers, the truth is they loved each other."[2]

That mutual respect notwithstanding, it is true that Spike's dialogue is often muffled and hard to follow, in comparison to Sellers. Joe McGrath admits: "that's my fault. I should have re-recorded a lot of Spike's dialogue. I had first done a McGonagall sketch, on television, with Peter playing the part, and as with that occasion, in the film, as Queen Victoria, his lines are absolutely crystal clear. Spike is lost on occasions because he gets emotional, whereas Sellers was simply a better technician as a screen actor. His dictation is perfect. He's not only a proper film actor but he knew about cameras and about sound and about everything within the film business. He was brilliant. Even when playing a ridiculous old Queen on a skateboard!"

1 *Parkinson*, BBC Television, 1974.
2 Interview with the author, July 2003.

Still the brief scenes when Spike and Sellers are together the sheer enjoyment is palpable. Both were brilliantly bad piano players too, although in the scene where Queen Victoria tickles the ivories it was that renowned jazzman Erroll Garner, who happily came in to play as a favour: "that was incredible", remembered Joe McGrath, "and I over-dubbed the silly singing of the Queen. When Peter saw it he said: 'I'd forgotten I sang along with it!' and Spike said: 'You didn't, you fool. It's Joe!'"

Sellers was certainly very happy not only to over-play character comedy parts but also drop any pretence of handsome leading man and don outrageous make-up once more. Indeed, a perfect companion for a double-bill with *The Great McGonagall* is *The Optimists*, a film that Sellers had just wrapped for director Anthony Simmons. Simmons had adapted his own novel for the screen, and it was the Sellers assignment ahead of linking comic arms with Spike on *Ghost in the Noonday Sun*. *The Optimists of Nine Elms* – shortened to just *The Optimists* for its American release – had cast Sellers as Sam, a veteran of the music-halls and now a wandering vagabond: part street entertainer, part wizard. When the novel had been published, and first mooted as a feature film, in 1964, Simmons had wanted 'Buster' Keaton for the role. A decade on, Sellers was the perfect replacement, bringing a real sense of both slapstick and of magic to the film. As the poster set him up: "Meet Sam, the wonder man. He's got madness in his closet, everybody in trouble, the police in circles – and the world in his pocket." That's Sellers. The key people "in trouble" were a couple of children, who the traveller befriends. Sister and brother Liz and Mark, played by Donna Mullane and John Chaffey. It was the first really shabby, craggy or just plain eccentric character film role Sellers had played since *Waltz of the Toreadors*. The nose here is ski-slope sharp and smooth, the temples greying, the face enlivened by a near-permanent gormless grin while giving his cheeky banter and street entertainment songs. Charm is the word. The story is simple. A grumpy old music-hall star, down on his luck, and protective of his humble, private dwellings, has his heart warmed by two kids. Never work with animals or children said professional grouch W.C.

Fields, but for Sellers it encouraged one of his most delightful of all film performances. And it was a real return to his London roots. It is the London that nobody knows or nobody wanted to know. The London that, nearly twenty years on from *The Ladykillers*, had been built over and neglected even more. Indeed, there's a lovely echo back to the Ealing classic that boosted Peter's film career, when he spits out an insult to the young girl, calling her Mrs. Lopsided. The wistful look on Peter's face plants visions of Katie Johnson in the head of the soppy cinephile. Still, it's the long-shot slapstick – very much in the style of Peter's own directorial effort *Mr. Topaze* – and the effortless lapses into nonsense variety – be it Scottish, Russian, or pure gobbledegook – that beats at the heart of the film. The faded variety posters; the sepia snapshots; the lonely comedian. It is Sellers in reflective heaven. *The Last Goon Show of All* had been recorded at the Camden Theatre, the hallowed hall in which Marie Lloyd, Little Titch and the essence of music-hall lived on in stone-wall tape splendour.[1] *The Optimists* wallowed in this essence too. Perfect for Sellers. So much so that he genuinely told journalists that during the making of the film he felt he had been inhabited by the spirit of music-hall comedian Dan Leno.[2] Leno clearly inspired Peter's broad eyebrows and the streets in which it was filmed – Cinema Verite style with actual members of the public strolling past, unaware, that the great Sellers was walking amongst them. This was Leno's manor. So too, Peter's Northern twang and strummed songs of Sam Hall evoke the spirit of George Formby Junior and Robb Wilton. Sam Hall was the music-hall creation of W.G. Ross – one William Gribbon Ross, born in Glasgow in the summer of 1819. The fictionalised figure of Sam Hall, as played by Sellers in *The Optimists*, even lapses into a snatch of the aggressive ballad of this violent jail-bird who hates everybody. Indeed, the anti-social place we find Hall in at the film's start, coupled with the flamboyant variety theatre business and miraculous acting opposite Bella the dog, showcases one of Peter's most multi-faceted,

1 Now known as Koko, the venue boasts a Comic Heritage blue plaque to *The Last Goon Show of All*, unveiled by Sir Harry Secombe, fittingly on a Sunday, on 17th September 2000.

2 The pioneer of the modern pantomime, and the long-in-residence Mother Goose of the Theatre Royal, Drury Lane, Leno had spent time in an institution for the insane before his death, in 1904, at the age of 43.

heart-warming and personal performances. Indeed, there is much of Chauncey Gardiner in his straw slouch hat, Chaplinesque waddling, and joyous, cockeyed philosophy of life. The songs, by Lionel Bart, and the plaintive musical score by trusted old Abbey Road cohort George Martin, bed Peter's performance in the essence of 'Wilton's' too. That bridge between *The Optimists* and *The Great McGonagall* had been provided by Peter's eager agreement to appear in *'Wilton's' – The Handsomest Hall in Town*, screened on BBC2, on Boxing Day 1970, produced by Michael Mills, and written by variety fountain of knowledge Jimmy Perry. Among the starry cast was Peter's old *Orders Are Orders* army comedy mucker Bill Fraser but, as befitting his international status, Sellers was the top of the bill, playing the actual G.W. Ross performing the song 'Sam Hall'. It is a seriously electrifying performance. Straight, chilling, precise and with a barely suppressed air of pending violence. Indeed Peter's frantic, leaping to his feet movements on the killer rant to the audience: "Damn your eyes!" is so swift and unexpected as to beat the cameraman and bob out of frame. With a permanent scowl on his face, two-finger salutes and deadly thumb-biting actions to the baying crowd, this is the dark underbelly of Victorian England in microcosm. Yes, *'Wilton's' – The Handsomest Hall in Town* is the shortcut between Peter's layered portrayal of Sam Hall in *The Optimists* and the tangible venue for the filming of *The Great McGonagall*. It is a pulsating soul and a rooting of Peter's excitement and love for the ancient palaces and traditions of variety.

The Optimists was distributed by Scotia-Barber, in the UK, and by Paramount Pictures in the US, premiering on 18th October 1973. The joyous caricature of Sellers on the poster, is Willy Wonka-like, just two springs since Gene Wilder's wizard-like chocolate-maker had only dented the box office too, and a hint at how Peter may have played Dahl's beloved madman. Still lukewarm reviews didn't stop *The Optimists* from being of just minor interest to cinemagoers. That fact though didn't dent any sense of magic and merriment during the music-hall-infused filming of *The Great McGonagall*.[1] Indeed, if you think laterally it's almost as if Peter's Sam Hall has just played about in the dressing-up box and is giving his Queen Victoria for a select audience at 'Wilton's'. The joy and sheer fun in larking about is tangible. The ups and downs and shared music-hall passion that Sellers and Spike lived, breathed and loved is tangible too. Indeed, through the debacle of *Ghost in the Noonday Sun* and *The Melting Pot* and through the giddy delight of *The Great McGonagall* any petty jealousy on Spike's part was gone forever: "It had been there", remembered Joe McGrath, "Spike would moan about how much money Sellers was making in films, and he would moan about Harry Secombe getting paid thousands just to sing! I did try to explain to him that there was more to it than that but he wouldn't listen! Anyway, by the time we did the McGonagall film Spike's Adolf Hitler book and his other war memoirs had made him an absolute fortune, so he was more relaxed about his place in the pecking order, if that makes sense."

Peter was relaxed and engaged throughout, with a healthy obsession with Victoriana and the traditions of music-hall: "Oh, yes. Peter loved 'Wilton's'", said Joe McGrath. "He thought that place was wonderful, even though he didn't sleep in it like Spike! There's a scene, right near the start of the film, that Peter has with John Bluthal. The music-hall turns are entertaining the Queen and Prince Albert – who has a distinct look of Adolf Hitler. Spike's idea. Anyway Sellers was in hysterics during this scene. He managed to keep it together for a take or two, but you can see him twitching, on the verge of a laugh, in the film. It's rather lovely."

Sellers had also moved on since the near decade-old debacle of *Casino Royale*: "Peter was charm personified on *McGonagall*", said Joe McGrath. "I mean he was still late, as usual, so I had to improvise some extra scenes with the extras being made-up, like the leading actors had been made-up. That was purely down to Sellers, because he wasn't there for his scene. So you can blame him, or thank him,

---

1 Although rather tragically Peter's spell-bindingly beautiful performance in *The Optimists* remains one of his rarely unearthed screen treasures. It got a very limited VHS release in 1989 from Parkfield Publishing in its Pick A Pic range. The sleeve was branded Missing In Action. Well, quite!

depending on whose side you are on! Victor Spinetti told me that for him it reminded him of his days with Joan Littlewood at the Stratford East Theatre. So that was rather nice. Anyway, Peter came up to me and suggested repeating a gag from *Casino Royale*. In that film he's larking about as Toulouse-Lautrec with Ursula Andress. Doing the short man, on his knees, on shoes, with his trouser legs rolled up. He said: 'Let's do it again! Unless it brings back bad memories for you . . .' He paused, smiled, and I hugged him. And we got the take. First time. Peter was in a very happy place making that film."

Peter enjoyed two performances, both of historical standing, for as well as the regal anarchy of Queen Victoria he is also, once more on film, the voice of Winston Churchill. It's that sort of wacky, wonderfully ramshackle, *Oh! What a Lovely War* kind of project.

As for the Queen, it's an unashamed and unabashed drag performance. All strangulated vowels and outrageous flirtation, it is, in essence, Crystal Jollibottom on the throne, but at its heart it is pure, undiluted fun. Just two mates in the dressing-up box, enjoying each other's company and the perfect pleasure of behaving stupidly together. This free-wheeling carnivalesque happiness with Spike was the only thing that seemed to make life worth living for Sellers. There's certainly a reflection of his personal life in the, then, crumbling and desolate portals of the disused and decaying 'Wilton's' Music Hall. Certainly his marriage to Miranda had been unstable, and had finally come to its inevitable end, in divorce, a couple of weeks after his 49th birthday.

So, if the question is begged as to why the greatest comedy actor in the world would, on the surface, scupper his own career and agree to a frantic cameo as a dead old Queen, the answer is simple. Because he could, and he wanted to: "Peter was all out to enjoy himself", confirmed Joe McGrath. "My God, why shouldn't he? He had earned the right to make whichever film he damned well wanted, and he wanted to make ours! A week larking around with his best mate, Spike, and me, and a cast of like-minded professional idiots. Wonderful. And he loved McGonagall. I had directed him in an episode of *Tempo*, that time he had played McGonagall himself, but this was Spike's show and Peter just wanted to play."[1] That Joe McGrath directed occasion with visual interpretation of McGonagall in *Tempo*, transmitted on 15th October 1961, is rather grand, dapper in fact. Clad in a tartan cloak and waistcoat, Sellers recites with piqued reverence, as befits this worthy Arts programme from Associated British – other guests were all four members of *Beyond the Fringe*, Joan Greenwood, and Franco Zeffirelli – regardless of whether it is intrinsically a funny piece or not. In contrast, Spike's McGonagall is a mess. A funny mess, but a mess nonetheless. So, if for Sellers the shared insanity with Spike was a cooling balm and a licking of his wounds in the weeks and months leading up, and scurrying away from, the failure of his third marriage, then who could question the appeal of a little bit of pleasure. It was a rather rare commodity for Sellers at the time.

In the immediate wake of *The Melting Pot* controversy and parallel with *The Great McGonagall* film, Spike himself found additional solace back with the bizarre rhyming couplets of the gloriously rubbish scribe. Alongside his frequent book-writing collaborator Jack Hobbs, he wrote *William McGonagall: The Truth at Last* – a fantasia riff on the life story of the notoriously terrible Scots poet, published by Michael Joseph in January 1976. As if to signal that Sellers and Spike were still alright, the black and white illustrations are credited to "anybody & Peter Sellers". The jolly, juvenile fist of Sellers proudly identified by his signing of 'P. Sellers' on the drawings that were all his own work, you know.

Joe McGrath lamented that: "although *The Great McGonagall* did get a release – it was screened at the Curzon Cinema, in Bloomsbury, for a month – the producers, one of which was Malcolm Fancey, the son of E.J. Fancey who had produced those Goon films of the fifties, were using it as a tax scam and promptly disappeared to foreign parts! There was no budget in any case, but I certainly didn't see any

---

1 Interview with the author, July 2003.

profit from it!"[1] Even so, none of those principals involved ever fell out of love with William McGonagall: "Oh we loved him!" said Joe McGrath. "He was so bad. And so funny. Once a year, even after that film, we would all three of us meet at the Piano Bar in the Dorchester Hotel – myself, Peter and Spike. And Alan Clare, the jazz pianist and friend to the Goons, would join us, and Eric Sykes came along a couple of times, and we would recite McGonagall poems to each other. Within minutes word would go round the hotel that Sellers was performing and we'd have a hundred people packed in there, listening. We loved that!"[2]

Whether it was turning fifty, in September 1975, or simply the vast amount of money on offer, *The Melting Pot* was swiftly put in file thirteen – i.e. the waste paper bin – and those Trans World Airlines commercials were gladly accepted. Not that they would have been a challenge for any competent comedy actor, let alone someone of the magnitude and experience of Sellers. The trio of jokes were obvious to say the least: Sellers as a frightfully upper-crust, frilly-shirt-wearing, champagne-supping Englishman by the name of the Right Honourable Jeremy Peak-Tyme: praising the food glorious food (allowing a lapse into cockney when waxing lyrical about the fish 'n' chips) and the quality of the on-board entertainment. In another commercial, Sellers was a swarthy Italian, all open-necked shirt and dark glasses, wining, dining, and chatting up the ladies (including *Young Frankenstein* beauty Teri Garr trying to enjoy a foreign-language film). Finally, and most obviously of all there was Thrifty McTravel, a broad Scots, long-kilted, bulbous-nosed laddie who praised the airline for its economical services. It's McGonagall again, and Sellers clearly enjoys this penny-pinching Scot the most, even calling long-distance to Glasgow and chatting to his Goonish

---

1 Almost thirty years after the making of the film, I was asked to produce some bonus material for the Fabulous Films DVD release, and this included an audio commentary with Joe McGrath. At the time he chuckled: "I'm only seeing money now!"
2 Interview with the author, July 2003.

chum Fred.[1] What the commercials lack in comic originality they certainly make up for in the star's gusto of performance. Sellers also shot a promotional film advertising his adverts, nailing his commercial colours to TWA, and indulging in some hilarious out-takes, including a delicious pratfall from a luggage trolley. Playing someone as near to himself as he would allow on screen, this is Sellers, International Jet-Set Film Star, relishing his place as the company's spokesman or spakesman!

Although reunions and reminiscences with his Goon brothers would buoy Sellers until the very end, it was fitting that this maelstrom of chaotic collaboration with Spike would culminate with a press photograph session accepting the Silver Disc for sales of 200,000 copies of *The Last Goon Show of All*. That same year, of 1976, the fifty-year-old Sellers was still very much an active Goon. He may have been momentarily shocked by the huge sales of the disc, but he recovered swiftly enough to tell any BBC ear within his hearing, that the next vinyl collection of two classic episodes simply must include one of his personal favourites, 'The International Christmas Pudding'. Among its many delights is Sellers, tremulously channelling McGonagall, his enthused introduction of Ray Ellington's 'Crocodile Crawl', or as Bloodnok sees it Crocodile Cringe, and Bluebottle entering to his expected round of applause, on cardboard horse. Both Bottle (extra applause) and Grytpype-Thynne (champagne cork-popping) indicate the sound effects on gramophone too: an indulgence for the techno-obsessed Sellers.

And when Sellers spoke, the BBC listened, for the Christmas 1976 release *Goon Show Classics – Vol. 3* did indeed include this beloved seasonal episode, from precisely twenty-one years earlier. In cheeky reference to the Silver Disc, John Browell's sleeve note commented that: "the venerable Goons desire they may ultimately receive a Gold

---

1 Peter gave his full-bloodied Scots broth for the country & western variety show *Glen Campbell: The Campbells Are Coming*, which starred the singer-songwriter from Arkansas taken to discover his roots in the Highlands. The show, which also featured *Dad's Army* star John Laurie – "We're doomed!" – aired on ATV on 12th June 1974.

Disc – the melt-down value being higher."[1] It was a joyful package of a comic ensemble that Michael Bentine wistfully concluded were: "all smashed out of our heads with the sheer joy of living."[2] Money and fun. Combined. What a Christmas present indeed.

That year of 1976, the legacy of the team had been immortalised in an essential guide penned by cultural historian Roger Wilmut and Goon maestro Jimmy Grafton. *The Goon Show Companion* professed to be both a History and a Goonography, and by heavens it was. All four Crazy People contributed an introduction, with Spike fearing it could be: "my obituary", while Sellers introduced himself thus: "My name is Peter Sellers. I am a human being." He concluded that: "I was paid certain monies for my appearances. They were very small.[3]

"When I first visited Major Grafton's public house in Victoria I was five years old. I am now ninety-two, and still enjoy a good laugh."

The next generation of comedy adventurers had already long ago picked up the baton and, in one of the most remarkable acknowledgements in popular culture history, film-making innovators Terry Jones and Terry Gilliam harkened back to the fifties for the release of their first feature film, proper.[4] As a support picture for the release of *Monty Python and the Holy Grail*, Jones and Gilliam hand-picked none other than gloriously crusty, twenty-year-old short subject *The Case of the Mukkinese Battle-Horn*, enjoying its third and undoubtedly, most exposed international cinema release.

Not only a tangible fragment in the relay race between the Goons

---

1 The Transcription Services remake was selected, while the other featured episode was 'Lurgi Strikes Britain', from November 1954, on BBC Records: REB 246. "Yakka-Boo!". Browell is identified as: "latter-day Goon Producer and possessor of an untarnished Silver Disc".

2 *The Goon Show Companion* (Robson Books Ltd, 1976).

3 This affectionate mockery of low pay from the corporation still has comic relevance, witness Steve Pemberton in 'Plodding On', the wonderfully meta final episode of *Inside No. 9*, in June 2024. Following another near-death experience, this tongue-in-cheek dismissal of the low pay was gone completely in the poignant and famous Sellers telegram, dated 28th May 1980 to Mr. Spike Milligan, pleading that he was "desperate to have some real fun again . . ." and reunion the Goons. "I don't want any money", Peter wrote, "I will work just for the sheer joy of being with you both again as we were."

4 The Pythons, as a six-man voice, actively discounted *And Now for Something Completely Different*, 1971. The film, directed by their television director Ian McNaughton, was dismissed by the group as nothing more than a reworked collection of old television sketches. Which is exactly what it is. Fun though.

and Monty Python, but a very nice little earner for the fifties comedy crime potboiler. Little wonder then that producer Michael Deeley called *The Case of the Mukkinese Battle-Horn*: "the most profitable film I have ever made – relative to cost – having recouped its original budget ten times over."[1]

For a 1975 audience to see Sellers, in black and white, in fledgling form from variety turn to skilled comedy actor, was a revelation. For Sellers himself this hive of Goon-inspired activity, both in the moment and from out of the archives, had been like hitching a tank of oxygen on to his back. It gave him a nostalgia kick but more than that it reinforced the absolute joy he got from making people laugh and, even more key, laughing himself.[2]

As a result *The Case of the Mukkinese Battle-Horn* was an unaware pilot fish for an even more successful, personal resurrection: *The Return of the Pink Panther*.

If so much fun could be gleaned from bringing beloved elements from his past right bang up to date in his troubled now, then why not accept that call from Blake Edwards that would unleash upon the mid-seventies the bumbling slapstick artistry of Clouseau?

The Melting Pot debacle; the *Ghost in the Noonday Sun* dilemma; the speedy decline and failure of his third marriage; nothing could stop, or more importantly, dampen the inevitability of *The Return of the Pink Panther*.

With that divorce from Miranda, on 27th September 1974, to be precise, came a clearing of the Sellers consciousness. *The Return of the Pink Panther*, the project that would, single-handedly, elevate his career, was finally released, in cinemas, on 21st May 1975.[3] In between these two Sellers-shattering events he gave an in-depth and candid interview to Michael Parkinson, broadcast on 9th November 1974.

---

1 *Blade Runners, Deer Hunters & Blowing the Bloody Doors Off: My Life in Cult Movies*, by Michael Deeley (Faber & Faber, 2008).

2 Audiences had also seen a contemporary black and white Marty Feldman blowing his instrument – very much like a Mukkinese Battle-Horn – in the Mel Brooks horror pastiche *Young Frankenstein*. With Gene Wilder having snaffled Willy Wonka, and Stanley in *Rhinoceros*, one can only smile and imagine Sellers as Fred Frankenstein!

3 On 4th June 1975, Peter guest-starred on CBS Television's *Dinah!*, the popular musical comedy variety show hosted by evergreen entertainer Dinah Shore.

Although Peter's reluctance at giving interviews as himself dictated that he, in this Churchill centenary year, insisted on coming out to the studio audience clad in that World War II Nazi uniform – again – and spend the first few minutes in Cod Germanic rant. With this request duly granted, Sellers quickly relaxed. In a combination of Parky's stoic Yorkshire bluff and Peter's inability not to play to the gallery, it was a whistlestop gallop through his early life and work, complete with all the old impressions – from Peter Lorre to George Formby – and gleeful lapses into the voices of the Goons. Peter is also very free in his praise of Blake Edwards. The two had reconnected for the first time in seven years. Edwards had co-written and directed *Julie: My Favourite Things*, a musical variety spectacular for his wife, Julie Andrews, for broadcast on Associated Television, on 18th April 1975. Sellers, now back in the fold, was pretty much contractually obliged to give his pebble-glassed Mad Doctor turn in a comedy sketch. Peter also notched up the frightfully posh Binky Barclay and the heavyweight Reggie. Peter also channelled the long-haired weirdness of Dr. Fritz Fassbender from *What's New Pussycat?*, while Julie, once more, donned the garb of Mary Poppins. It's that kind of free-wheeling, tongue-in-cheek, self-mocking romp. A colourful, gleeful, mutual love-in of creative chums back on friendly terms.[1] It certainly brought the three superstars into alignment ahead of the imminent release of the major motion picture event of the year.

The Return of the Pink Panther was the first time Sellers had played Clouseau in a decade. And, despite his last massive box office success having been *There's a Girl in My Soup* nearly five years earlier, Sellers was still a film star: a twinkling personality with clout and marquee value. Laudably, Sellers professed to be philosophical and realistic whilst measuring his success. He would recall: "going through a very bad patch [in Hollywood, when] several well-known

---

1 Julie Andrews was also on the bill of ATV's *Salute to Sir Lew – The Master Showman*, on the same day, an all-star celebration of Lew Grade which, although best-known now as showcasing the last public performance of John Lennon, gathered together the great and the good of show business, including Lauren Bacall, Kirk Douglas, Tom Jones, Gene Kelly, Peter's leading ladies Goldie Hawn and Shirley MacLaine, and Peter himself, in tux and tinted spectacles, speaking at the New York Hilton Hotel.

people would cross from one side of the road to the other in order not to bump into me!" We are talking of the days of *Where Does it Hurt?* here. A time and a town in which if: "two films don't do any good. Out. Elbowed." This is exactly why Peter relished a return to London. Home. Where he could make *The Optimists* and *The Great McGonagall* and *Soft Beds, Hard Battles*, and enjoy himself whilst doing it: "As long as you don't think of yourself seriously. If you think it's going good. Money is coming in; parts are coming in. Thank you!"[1] In other words, never believe your own press and always be grateful you are working. So, while it is not to overstate the fact that *The Return of the Pink Panther* single-handedly boosted his comedy credentials, Peter's name attached had never lost the ability to secure a budget and decent distribution. That huge name in lights during the opening credits; his Richard Williams caricature self interacting with the Panther in the guise of Chaplin, Frankenstein's Monster, John Wayne, Fred Astaire . . . all of it sets up Clouseau's revival as a major cinematic event. It was an international affair, and whipped up a frenzy of interest during its production. Indeed, while on location filming in the south of France, Sellers was interviewed by Annett Wolf Senior for *The World of Peter Sellers*, broadcast, on Denmark Television, on 19th May 1975. *The Return of the Pink Panther* certainly was the best fiftieth birthday present Peter could have ever wished for. It heralded Peter's perfect final act. The Indian Summer that came and went too soon, like a precious bloom. The last flowering of comedy greatness within the shards of a broken life.

So, divorced from Miranda and with the spirit of his Goonish past buzzing in his psyche, Sellers turned back the clock once more. Any reluctance had now gone. He was determined to revive Clouseau and, as a result, make the world laugh again. And again. And again. And again.

Sellers is slightly less-controlled than the sixties Clouseau but certainly more stable than he would become by 1978. The mad disguises begin to take hold, but fundamentally this is *The Party* with a joyously

---

1 *Whicker's World*, 'California: Nothing Is Utopia, This Comes Pretty Close', 7th May 1980.

exaggerated French accent. The comedy of Sellers, in the main, comes from his one-man disaster area struggling to cope with the world at large: it is man against machine. He encounters a doorbell which refuses to ring; a radio that refuses to turn off; a shower that refuses to stop gushing water; and a super-suction vacuum cleaner that refuses to stop sucking! Sellers is a laughter-stock that never, not ever, admits that he is wrong or has made a mistake. The inspired pratfall and slapstick peaks early, with the investigative museum scene as Clouseau doggedly searches for clues, waxes lyrical on different waxes, spills fingerprint power over the crime scene, loses his hat, regains his hat, and destroys valuable exhibits with the merest hint of a shrug of the shoulders. It is all in the game of solving crimes, you know.

Typically, Peter is happy to be surrounded by reassuring and familiar faces: David Lodge is the street-wise muscle in the employ of the Littons; while recent *Great McGonagall* cohorts John Bluthal (as the 'blind' look-out man with the "minkey!") and Victor Spinetti (as the petulant Swiss hotel manager) effortlessly engage and feed Peter's determined, disillusioned master sleuth. This fourth Clouseau film – and the third with Sellers – brings back three central figures from *A Shot in the Dark*, ten years earlier: Herbert Lom and Burt Kwouk and Graham Stark each chalking up their second in the franchise. A franchise that would secure them irregular employment as part of the Pink Panther family for the next twenty years. Lom and Kwouk would be a constant thorn in the side, playing the same characters, the increasingly barking mad Dreyfus and the assault missile manservant Cato, while Stark was called upon to play various, ever more outrageous characters. Indeed, in *The Return of the Pink Panther*, Stark is Pepi, part of the subplot with the Phantom (re-cast, without comment, with Christopher Plummer) and doesn't encounter Peter's Clouseau at all. Stark, a crawling minion, gives his salute to Peter Lorre, while Eric Pohlmann is the Fat Man. The espionage and intrigue screams *The Maltese Falcon* and *Casablanca*, with film buffs given the opportunity to smile in satisfaction as the refrains of 'When Time Goes By' strike up.[1]

Mike Grady, who admitted to having been as green as grass as a film actor, was chuffed to land the role of the Bell Boy and eagerly jetted off to Gstaad in Switzerland for location filming. "It was this glorious ski resort – out of season in the summer, but full of movie stars improving their tennis! I was certainly no threat to Peter Sellers, but the person I met was sweet, focused, upbeat. He hadn't had a hit movie in quite a while, not that that seemed to bother him overly much. I wasn't interested in all the celebrity stuff in the papers but even I was aware that one marriage was in the press, then it was a divorce, then it was another marriage. The comedy and the films – popular or not – didn't seem to be covered, but throughout all that, Peter's passion for his work and for the comedy seemed to remain all-powerful. It was certainly to the fore in the man that I met and got to know. Peter just seemed determined to knuckle down and deliver as many funnies as he could. And he did. As far as I know when Peter was either in love or using drink or drugs he could be impossible. He was the complete opposite on that film, so he obviously wasn't using. Or else other people's recollections and experiences are clouded. Regardless, Sellers was great. I arrived with absolutely no fanfare. Of course. I was billeted in a tiny room in this hotel, and that was quite alright by me. I was a nobody. Victor Spinetti and Peter Arne were very welcoming, but the crew completely ignored me. That all changed when I met Peter Sellers. I'm certain he wasn't aware of his powers. He was being genuinely nice to me but on that first day I was there, I wasn't in the scene but they took us down – in the limousine – to watch the filming. This was all so far from home, I have to tell you. I was so out of my depth! Vic Spinetti was with me so that was great because he told me how to behave on a massive film like this and Vic knew absolutely everybody. I had met Blake Edwards before so he acknowledged me but that was about my lot. He was a very nice man was Blake Edwards but always very still, behind dark glasses. Like a chameleon. He moved

---

1 Pohlmann had played an identikit Sydney Greenstreet-styled Fat Man in *Carry On Spying*, over at Pinewood Studios a decade earlier, while Sellers was shooting the first Clouseau outings. His Peter Lorre-like henchman in the Carry On was none other than John Bluthal.

very slowly, very quietly, almost imperceptibly. Then somebody else said: 'Have you met Mr. Sellers?' and suddenly there was Clouseau. The full getup. The lot! We shook hands and he said: 'Ah, yes. I've seen you on television. In Britain. A commercial.' I was indeed in a very successful commercial at the time. Peter very graciously and very loudly said: 'As far as I'm concerned, the commercials are the funniest things on television.' That did it. Suddenly there was a chair for Mr. Grady; a cup of tea for Mr. Grady; a drink in the hotel bar later for Mr. Grady? That was purely down to Peter's kindness. He didn't have to do that and I honestly don't think he was aware of what he had done. He was just being nice. That having been said, he could be impossibly difficult and I'm sure long-term friends of his didn't know what Peter Sellers they were going to meet from one day to the next. His driver was Bert Mortimer, and Bert's wife was Peter's personal dresser. The couple had been loyally with him for fifteen years or so. One day during the shoot Peter dismissed them, by letter, and this poor bloke was lost. He had no idea what he had done. That was Peter. He had a personal priest too. Seriously. This bloke was six foot seven or something and looked like he had walked out of a John Wayne film. Every morning before we filmed Peter and this priest would pray. For what I don't know. Good weather maybe! It worked whatever they were doing!"[1]

So much so that Sellers and Edwards had already made the decision to make another Panther. During that filming schedule in Gstaad, Sellers confidentially talked of "the next one" to Barry Norman, for *Film '75*.

Mike Grady also remembered hanging out with another Hollywood superstar, Mrs. Blake Edwards herself, Julie Andrews: "Julie Andrews was phenomenal. She was there with Blake, of course, and she and Peter went back a long way. Back to the days of variety on the BBC Light Programme, so they would chat about the wireless days, and be hilarious together. I had no idea at the time but one day there was this whole new set-up in the hotel. I was told to stand in a certain place and

---

1 Interview with the author, April 2024.

just walk from point A to point B while this old cleaner, on her hands and knees, was wiping the floor around Clouseau. This old character actress, as I thought, was all boils on her face and shaggy hair and blackened teeth. Well that was Julie Andrews. Just doing it as a favour, you know. A little in-joke. The scene wasn't in the finished film but for fifty years I have told anybody who cares to listen in our business that I once made a film with Julie Andrews. Well I did. Sort of. The whole atmosphere of the *Pink Panther* film was like that though. It was one long joyous time. Hardly anything I did with Peter got into the film, but we laughed all day long."

That prevailing atmosphere of laughter for the simple sake of laughter, echoed time and time again from within memories of *The Goon Show*. Even Clouseau's cry of: "You swine!" was steeped in fond, funny, halcyon recollections of the BBC: that's Bluebottle and Bloodnok and Crun, folks. And a tangible talisman for those happiest of days was, of course, Graham Stark.

Mike Grady recalled that: "Peter Sellers was still tickled by silliness. They sent-up Graham Stark something rotten. Peter would be giggling uncontrollably in the corner. There was no superstardom about him. I was in my twenties, and very happy in my own skin. I would dance on my own at the hotel disco, and I would occasionally catch Peter watching me, head to one side, bemused by this kid who seemed blissfully happy. He was quiet. Not shy. I only overstepped the mark once, in my mind. A family staying at the hotel asked me if I could ask Mr. Sellers to sign a few autographs. I approached the great man, and he was more than happy to oblige. Delighted, in fact. A lovely, considerate man."[1]

Carol Cleveland, Monty Python's ageless sex symbol, also saw most of her work for *The Return of the Pink Panther* cut from the film: "It's a great shame, but I did have a marvellous time on location in Gstaad. In between takes Peter remained in character as Clouseau. He was so focused. After filming he tended to keep himself to himself and go back to his hotel suite. One evening about a dozen of us were

---

1 Interview with the author, April 2024. Despite the dismissal, Sellers instructed David Lodge to base his performance on Bert Mortimer.

off to a fancy restaurant. To be honest we hadn't even mentioned it to Peter. We didn't think he would want to come because he tended to go to bed early, but then he appeared, asked us where we were going and, to our amazement, accepted our invitation to join us. He was in high spirits and spent the evening regaling us with hilarious jokes and funny stories. I've never laughed so much in my life. And at the end of the meal, when the bill arrived, Peter insisted on taking care of it". What's more, the eagle-eyed will not fail to see that Carol Cleveland does appear in the film. It is her unmistakable figure at the swimming pool that attracts Clouseau. He watches her dive so intently that he falls in the water after her![1]

All the ingredients came together in *The Return of the Pink Panther*. Although its emergence from ITC Entertainment and, hence all the ATV and Lord Grade love from Sellers and Mr. and Mrs. Edwards, and the fact it was made by a different production company dictates it has been orphaned from the other Sellers Panthers in subsequent box set releases. However, as the Channel 5 video label release of 1986 yelled: "The title says it all. You know who's making it, who's starring in it, who's writing the music, and that it will be a very funny movie." Even with a few cast shifts. In the absence of an initially approached but unavailable David Niven, who was filming Ken Annakin's *Paper Tiger*, in Malaysia, and with Rex Harrison (heading for Broadway in *In Praise of Love*) and Douglas Fairbanks Jr. (tied-up with a stage run in *The Secretary Bird*) both out of the running, Christopher Plummer stepped in to play the notorious diamond thief Sir Charles Litton. He's married to a new Lady here so perhaps it's a different Litton. A younger Litton. The Son of the Phantom, perhaps. Still, this was always going to be Peter's film. Perhaps Niven was still smarting from *The Pink Panther* a decade earlier. That wouldn't last, with his original Lady, Capucine, back on his arm, and Sellers dead, Niven would return. Not that Niven *was* bothered. He was still with Peter's agent, Dennis Selinger, as was Roger Moore, now riding high as the new James Bond. With that cinematic clout, Roger picked up a film

---

1 Interview with the author, July 2024.

project Sellers had discarded: *That Lucky Touch*. Producer Dimitri de Grunwald had originally seen it as a reunion vehicle for Peter Sellers and Sophia Loren. When Sellers dropped out, so did Sophia. The plot, involving NATO, international arms deals, and a *Washington Post* journalist (ultimately played by Susannah York), suited the James Bond actor down to the ground. It was released for the Summer of 1975.[1] Although there was certainly no hard feelings, with Sellers and Niven working together brilliantly in the up-coming *Murder By Death*. Despite all the casting bingo, during the lavish production of *The Return of the Pink Panther* it was clear something very special indeed was going on. Groucho Marx, having been invited to the Screen Actors Guild preview, was seen leaving, darkly muttering to himself: "And they think that's funny!" The Top Marx was alone in his opinion, for the whole world laughed. And it made an utter fortune. Mike Grady remembered that: "the premiere was unbelievable. Vic Spinetti, who was very upset at lots of his scenes being cut, tried to upstage the party by inviting his friends Richard Burton and Elizabeth Taylor. The next day, the press was full of the Burtons and not the Panther, but it didn't stop the film being a success. It added even more glamour!. You have to remember that I was an actor at the Royal Court at the time. I was a billion miles away from what Peter Sellers was used to. They flew us all back to Gstaad in Switzerland – and I mean all of us – the entire cast, even the Henry Mancini Orchestra who played during the flight! Oh, and the actual plane we were on. Oh, boy. The plane was pink! With little panthers dotted all over it! That was an experience that I had never had before . . . and have never had again." The stops had well and truly been pulled out. The anticipation of a massive hit was palpable. Clouseau was back!

---

1 Roger and Peter remained close friends, Roger even giving a slapstick tribute cameo, as Inspector Clouseau, in *Curse of the Pink Panther* (1983). Both James Bonds too! And good pals of fellow Dennis Selinger client Michael Caine. It had been the 1961 television drama *The Compartment*, written by Johnny Speight, that had first brought Caine to Selinger's attention. It was a role written for Sellers, who proved unavailable. Marty Feldman played it in the 1969 remake. Sellers and Sophia Loren had remained friends too, Peter having taken the official photographs of mother and second son Edoardo Ponti, in January 1973.

Chapter 15

"Start the show - we're dying, you know!"
Henry Crun

In the spring 1975 slipstream of publicity for the *The Return of the Pink Panther*, Sellers once more threw himself into an orgy of nostalgia. As if to compound the trend he guested, twice, on *Looks Familiar*, the clip and chat show of bygone songs and silliness. The second of these appearances, transmitted on 5th January 1976, even reunited him with Goon chum Ray Ellington. On 3rd November 1976 Sellers cropped up as a surprise guest on the *This Is Your Life* of *Two-Way Stretch* co-star Wilfred Hyde-White. A real blast from the past for Chalky, also making headways in America in the decade or so since, charming Marilyn Monroe in *Let's Make Love*, and playing Colonel Pickering in *My Fair Lady*. He would even be a suspect in two episodes of *Columbo*: muttering anachronistic Americanisms in 'Last Salute to the Commodore'.

Sellers had spent the spring of 1976 being a suspect himself. And a detective. A great detective: in Neil Simon's deliciously dark crime fiction pastiche *Murder By Death*. Shot at the Warner Brothers Burbank Studios in California, it cast Sellers as Oriental super sleuth Sidney Wang, a delightful slit-eyed sideways shade of the Earl Derr Biggers creation, Honolulu police detective Charlie Chan. The sleuth had been culturally out of favour in Hollywood since 1949 but Sellers clearly harks back to the 1930s masterpieces starring Warner Oland as the great man. Neil Simon's affectionate script gives Sellers plenty of fanciful fortune-cookie philosophy to deliver and while injecting the dialogue with typical pidgin-English and lapsed pronouns Peter's performance never for a moment lapses into racial over-play or insult. There is integrity and grace at the heart of the performance; a real humanity and humility; and total conviction in the cool, calm and calculated, razor-sharp mind of a great thinker. There is real kindness and parental devotion to his son too, continually bubbling under the surface of elder acid and weary shake of the head. Played by Richard Narita, the son is all wide-eyed wonder and gauche naivete, in a splendid approximation of Keye Luke's gutsy portrayal as Chan's number one son in the classic series.

That Sellers is protective and ridiculing of his son, in pretty equal measure, is an emotive and effective portrayal of a loving father. Indeed, Sellers as an actor seems to envelope and elevate Narita who, in his first major movie role after a handful of uncredited bits in the television series *Kung Fu*, is a good measure of Sellers as mentor.

That Sellers also effortlessly steals the picture in a cast that drips with weighty friends, old and new, is something of a miracle. Director Robert Moore who, despite a long association with Neil Simon stretching back to the 1969 Broadway production of *Last of the Red Hot Lovers*, was helming his first feature film after several seasons with Valerie Harper on the television series *Rhoda*. Not only does Moore master the iconography of vintage film thrillers but he acts as cheerful ringmaster for a lip-smacking cast of seasoned scene-stealers: David Niven and Maggie Smith as Dick and Dora Charleston, cocktail-swigging New York socialites in the mould of William Powell and Myrna Loy's Nick and Nora Charles in *The Thin Man* films; and Elsa Lancaster as Jessica Marbles the face-pulling, forthright spoof of Margaret Rutherford's Miss Marple. Another Agatha Christie mixed concoction is James Coco, who had starred in that original Robert Moore production of Neil Simon's *Last of the Red Hot Lovers*, at the Eugene O'Neill Theatre. Here Coco plays Milo Perrier, the waspish, pernickety image of Albert Finney's Hercule Poirot from the 1974 bloody blockbuster *Murder on the Orient Express*. And there's Peter Falk as Sam Diamond, Humphrey

Bogart's Sam Spade from *The Maltese Falcon*, with just a dash of Falk's own Columbo for television's generation X.[1] That Sellers can hold his own and more against such a cast is heightened by his interplay with two outstanding showy cameos: the non-actor Truman Capote, who instruments the whole thing and allows Sellers moments of true concern and consternation; and Peter's hero and inspiration Alec Guinness. The two hadn't worked together for over twenty years, since the Sellers breakthrough in Ealing romp *The Ladykillers*. At that time Guinness had predicted Sellers would become a huge film star and advised him not to tell the press anything about his private life. The prophecy had come true – and then some – although Sellers had not heeded the warning about keeping his domestic life to himself. Still, the panache and the respect fair fizzes off of the screen in the *Murder By Death* scenes between Guinness and Sellers. Guinness, as the blind butler Bensonmum, is a masterclass in underplayed slapstick. Sellers can only stop, stare and observe the feats of sheer audacity that Guinness performs. There is no overt eye-roll from Sellers, slanted or otherwise, simply peaceful disbelief at such skill. He even turns the heat down on his own comedy, in respect and awe.

By all accounts the shooting of *Murder By Death* was a happy one. A gelling ensemble of actors who all knew their worth individually, with none of them ever up-staging or upsetting the flow. More than that, it was a hoot. It still is. A relaxed Sellers relished such a rich, resonant script and such a distinguished and diverting cast of actors. And it shows.

Sellers wasn't to be diverted for long. Miranda had already swiftly remarried, in 1975, to Nicholas Nuttall, the 3rd Baronet and heir to the Edmund Nuttall construction business.[2]

---

1 Neil Simon built an entire film round Peter Falk's Bogart pastiche, *The Cheap Detective*, released in June 1978, and again directed by Robert Moore, with *Murder By Death* alumni Eileen Brennan, James Coco and James Cromwell featured in different roles. Moore would direct just one more feature, Neil Simon's *Chapter Two*, before his sudden death, in 1984, at the age of just fifty-six.

2 Miranda, having been Peter's third wife, was Edmund's third wife, and the union lasted until 1983. Nuttall said at the time of the separation that: "Miranda is too exotic for me. I am the pig who loved the leopard."

Soon after wrapping on *Murder By Death*, Peter's agent Dennis Selinger threw a dinner party. Naturally his top comedy client was on the guest list. As was a young actress Selinger wanted Sellers to meet: twenty-two-year-old Lynne Frederick.

Lynne could well have met Sellers four years earlier, as she had auditioned for the lead role in *Alice's Adventures in Wonderland*, losing out to her friendly rival Fiona Fullerton. That same year Lynne earned the role of Catherine Howard in the film *Henry VIII and His Six Wives*, opposite Keith Michell. It was a performance that helped win her the Evening Standard British Film Award for Best New Actress the following year. Now represented by Selinger, Lynne had just wrapped in Stuart Rosenberg's star-studded wartime drama *Voyage of the Damned*, and Pete Walker's psychological horror *Schizo*.

Then the dinner party was held. True to form and now free to do so, Sellers proposed less than forty-eight hours later.

Peter was happy professionally. *Murder By Death*, although only a muted success upon its summer previews, was screened to great acclaim at the Venice International Film Festival, on 5th September 1976.

Two months later, Sellers was back in cinemas, resurrecting his best-loved detective, Clouseau, for *The Pink Panther Strikes Again*.

It was the great pink hope – not that anybody connected with the film had any doubt at all that it would pull in the crowds. From the very outset the lavish Richard Williams animated opening credits scream confidence. It is an affectionate salute to Hollywood's past – all through the prism of the pink panther – as the character reacts and interacts with pitch perfect pastiches of *The Sound of Music*, *Singin' in the Rain*, even *King Kong*. That Sellers could duet with Welsh matador Tom Jones . . . or, at the very least, take over for the final few lines of 'Come to Me' . . . was testament enough of his international clout. This was a James Bond singer, after all. The voice. Sellers was the clown. Back at the pinnacle. It was a kind of international success bookend with *What's New Pussycat?* Jones the

Voice was a talisman for Peter's street cred.[1] As was Julie Andrews who, apart from the call-back to her own, Oscar-nominated role in *The Sound of Music* in the opening credits, was back, by proxy, dubbing the drag cabaret artiste Ainsley Jarvis as played by Michael Robbins – this is why Robbins sings so well! Still, despite all this jollification, the atmosphere was not as convivial as it had been, as Mike Grady revealed: "I wasn't on that film, sadly, but my very good mate Dudley Sutton was. I asked him how it was going and he told me that Peter and Blake just weren't talking anymore. They had both made so much money from the one that I was in that they were just giving people gifts of Ferraris rather than actually communicating!"[2] The world was still laughing though.

Now with a budget and the panache of a James Bond epic itself, the Panther franchise had become appointment cinema, with a shooting schedule that lasted from December 1975 through to September 1976.[3] An event. Fittingly enough this is the one when Herbert Lom's twitching Former Chief Inspector Dreyfus goes completely crazy and takes on the mantle of a fiendish Bond villain in his ever-thwarted attempts to assassinate his bete noire, Clouseau. Having strangled his psychiatrist (Sellers favourite Peter Jones in a Clouseau-less scene) Dreyfus tricks his new shrink, played by Geoffrey Bayldon, into thinking him sane and releasing him. It's a direct sequel to the very last scene of *The Return of the Pink Panther*, a fact that makes that film's non-appearance in several 'complete' collections beyond frustrating. However, by 1976 the Pink Panther franchise was that

---

1 United Artists Music Limited released the track as a single, composed by Henry Mancini with lyrics by Don Black, and an uncredited Tom Jones supplemented by Sellers: UAS30012. The James Bond connection was completed when *The Pink Panther Strikes Again* was coupled with the Roger Moore thriller *The Spy Who Loved Me*. As the poster had it: "Nobody Does it Better Than 'Bond' and the 'Panther' Together!".

2 Interview with the author, April 2024.

3 This was an intense shoot for Sellers who was also on constant call for hungry journalists, joining Blake Edwards to contribute to the eight-minute promotional short *Clouseau, the Greatest Fumbler in the World*, for Professional Films. An on-set interview and behind-the-scenes footage with Sellers was also featured on the 26th November 1976 edition of *Clapperboard*, hosted by Chris Kelly and directed by Dave Warwick. The intellectual film show for cine kids drew loveable parallels between the Panthers and vintage comedies of Laurel and Hardy, Harold Lloyd, and 'Buster' Keaton. A double episode *Clapperboard* tribute to Peter Sellers, directed by Richard Guinea, would be transmitted across 22nd and 29th September 1980.

rare commodity in the film industry – a guaranteed box office winner.

"It was business as usual", remembered Cato himself, Burt Kwouk, "and great business at that. Peter was very happy to be doing Clouseau again. The one thing that has annoyed me over the years – I did get over it," he chuckled, "was that people would say, 'Oh, it's all stuntmen that do the fights for you!' Well, of course it was. Those guys are professional and very well-paid for a job that only they could do. We would have been mad to do them! And audiences are mad if they think we should have done them! We were actors. Peter was a brilliant one, but believe me, Peter knew exactly the choreography of those fight scenes. His facial reactions and feedlines in our epic battles were always perfect. It's Clouseau and Cato, regardless of whether it is Peter and myself. And every crash landing and smashing of furniture and breaking through walls is a laugh that Peter got. The brilliant stuntmen would be the first to tell you that."[1]

For that Christmas of 1976, Sellers was firmly back at the top of the comedy box-office pile. Still, with the international box-office turnstiles spinning and movie executives courting him for more, Peter was in poor health. He would tell inquisitive journalists that he was: "trying to give up heart attacks. I'm down to two a day!". But this was no joke. As a result, more and more of the elaborate pratfalling stunt work that the Panther punters had come to expect was giving over to Peter's double and dependable stand-in Joe Dunne.

Peter was keener on expending his energies in the persuading of Lynne Frederick to become the 4th Mrs. Sellers. It took him a little longer than usual but Peter's persistence paid off, and the couple were married less than a year after the whirlwind proposal, on a Valentine's elopement to Paris, on 18th February 1977. It was a happy and compatible match but that first month of married bliss clearly took its toll on Peter's already weakened heart. Akin to the Britt Ekland bedroom acrobatics of thirteen years earlier, in March 1977 Sellers suffered a massive heart attack.

---

1 Interview with the author, May 2012.

However, that spring 1977 heart attack didn't deter Peter from fulfilling his commitment to start filming with Blake Edwards again, this time on the even bigger budgeted follow-up comedy *The Revenge of the Pink Panther*.

Sellers had even found time to schedule a ghost-written autobiography, *Sellers Market*, which he was working on alongside film journalist Joe Hyams. Joe's biographies included one that Sellers particularly loved, *Bogie: The Biography of Humphrey Bogart*. Besides, Hyams was married to a favourite leading lady of Peter's, Elke Sommer, who had cavorted in *A Shot in the Dark*, and was soon to smoulder in *The Prisoner of Zenda*. *Sellers Market* was never completed and the notes remain unpublished but, at the time of Peter's death, Hyams remembered him as: "a very courageous man who refused to allow his heart problems to interfere with his professional life. He had a heart attack while we were doing the book, but when I visited him in the hospital, he wanted to get to work on the manuscript the very next day. When I told him he was too ill to work, Peter said 'Not at all. You have to live before you die, or you will die before you live.'"

The period of working on his autobiography also coincided with the death of a champion and mentor from his earliest success in show business. Ted Ray died in November 1977, just a few weeks shy of his 72nd birthday. Upon hearing the news, Sellers was magnanimous and modest in his praise: "Whatever I know about timing I learned from Ted Ray." David Lodge recalled that: "Peter was very cut up about that, actually. You know, in this game, you lost mates along the way. It happens. But Ted Ray was very important to Peter. He never forgot the encouragement and kindness. Ted was a big star. It meant a great deal to Peter. I remember him saying that these journalists and writers would bleat on and on about the Goons cutting down the old guard like wheat before the sickle. Peter would always say, first of all, it's rubbish. *Ray's a Laugh* was not only running concurrently with *The Goon Show*, it was still going after *The Goon Show* finished. And secondly, Spike and Peter and all of us loved those old variety turns. They were the business. Ted was still making us laugh on panel shows like *Jokers Wild* and *Does the Team Think?* right up to the end of his days. Peter would also say, we are all in the market to make people laugh. We are all pitching our wares to get Joe Public to crack a smile. Old or young. Ted Ray was one of the greatest. That's coming from Peter Sellers. And it's coming from me!"[1]

How the old clock does go round, indeed.

By the time Sellers was filming *Revenge of the Pink Panther*, his fifth Clouseau with Blake Edwards, for United Artists, he had had a heart pacemaker fitted, and the device had already failed and been removed. His worsening health was no more apparent on screen than in previous Panther romps, however. It just meant even more days on call for the ever loyal and jovial Joe Dunne who did an awful lot of the heavy comedy lifting. Still, Peter was no less energetic in his character acting skills and Goonish delight in the most outrageous of disguises: from bloated, Marlon Brando-like Godfather,[2] in a lift with a hood with whining flatulence, to a salty sea dog with blow-up parrot on a foggy dockside; to a slant-eyed Chinaman; to the diminutive Toulouse-Lautrec . . . again . . . with Sellers on his knees and stumbling through another hilarious, crazy disguise created by Auguste Balls.

Premiered at the Odeon Leicester Square, in London, on Thursday, 13th July 1978, *Revenge of the Pink Panther* was one of the most eagerly awaited releases of the summer. At a budget of just over 12 million dollars, the film's initial release grossed just shy of 50 million. Lucky for its star then that United Artists was so flushed with the success of the previous film that they had agreed a Sellers-Edwards Productions deal. Sellers coined in a huge profit.

The cracks in the relationship between actor and film-maker

---

1 Interview with the author, August 2003. *The Goon Show Compendium Volume 5* includes studio chatter during the recording of 'The Nasty Affair at the Burami Oasis', from Sunday, 30th September 1956. Sellers mentions an amusing sketch from the previous evening's Ted Ray show *Hip Hip Who Ray*, on ATV. Sellers always laudably appreciative of the writer, acknowledges the sketch as one by Sid Colin. Secombe agrees on the quality of the gag.

2 When after much courting James Cagney turned down the role of Hyman Roth in *The Godfather Part II*, Francis Ford Coppola seized upon the idea of casting Sellers. In the end Lee Strasberg played the role.

were widening now though. Edwards had taken ten months on the schedule for *The Pink Panther Strikes Again* and over-filmed to such an extent that great swathes of hilarious, unused material was ripe for plundering. Edwards had suggested using some of this footage in the new film. Sellers was appalled at the idea, and not just because he wanted his old pit prop Graham Stark on hand to play eccentric provider of disguise Professor Auguste Balls. The character had been played by Harvey Korman in *The Pink Panther Strikes Again*, although all these scenes were removed from the film. Scenes that Edwards wanted to include in the new one. In the end Edwards did get his way. But only after Peter's death. Korman's deleted scenes as Balls are included in *Trail of the Pink Panther* (1982). Reassuringly, and, undoubtedly, much to Peter's post-mortem delight, Stark was back as Balls in *Son of the Pink Panther* (1993).[1]

In 1978 though, the debate still raged. While Sellers insisted on filming all-new material for the new release, Edwards was adamant he was going to make an epic, of new and old bits and bobs. As a result there was an edit of over three hours at one point, muted for release at an increased cinema ticket price. While not having the artistic integrity of Sellers, United Artists baulked at the notion of an epic-length Panther comedy. They favoured lots of people paying a standard price, rather than a select few opting for the increase. In the end, sanity prevailed and the film was edited down to the usual hundred-minute-or-so mark.

The Goonish humour was at a peak in this, Peter's last Panther proper. The one with the China Town subplot; and, once again, the, by now, obligatory and relentless torrent of outrageous disguises. It's also the one where Cato, in the ever-faithful form of Burt Kwouk,

---

1 The final active film credit for both Blake Edwards and Henry Mancini, the *Son* was Robert Benigni, the brilliant Italian comedy actor and film-maker. Ironically, Benigni achieved what Sellers longed to do, winning a Best Actor Academy Award, for *Life Is Beautiful* (1997). And, so to sum up, the mad genius disguise creator Auguste Balls had featured in *The Pink Panther Strikes Again*, in among all those hours of excised scenes that Blake Edwards was keen to include in his epic cut. Harvey Korman had played the role here, in 1976. By 1978 it was Peter's dependable pal Graham Stark, who would return to the role in 1993. In order to utilise that 1976 footage, Professor Balls was played – in archive and new interview footage – by Harvey Korman in *Trail of the Pink Panther* and *Curse of the Pink Panther*. Confused? It's all balls, you know!

gets a position of authority and some wonderfully funny, scripted interaction with Sellers: "For my part, *Revenge of the Pink Panther* was my favourite, by far. I had some nice dialogue scenes with Peter and, one day on set, he said the nicest possible compliment and told me that he felt Cato and Clouseau were working like a Laurel and Hardy double act of slapstick . . . with kindness, now. That was Peter's intention, in any case, and if you watch the film there is a moment or two when Peter does that Oliver Hardy thing of looking into camera after I've done something particularly funny and foolish. That was Peter telling you, the audience, that that was what we were doing. We were both in the tradition of Mr. Laurel and Mr. Hardy in that film. What a thrill for me. Peter was always very generous with sharing the laughter. There was plenty to go round."[1]

According to Valerie Leon, cast as exotic dominatrix Tanya the Lotus Eater, this comic clout is all the more amazing when you consider: "Peter was really very, very unwell at the time we made that *Pink Panther* film. My scheduled dates were extended, simply in order to allow for a few good days for Peter to feel fit enough to work. When he *was* fit enough though: Wow, he was brilliant. So funny. And so focused on what he was doing. I had been doing the very successful Hai Karate after shave commercials, playing a similar sort of character. It was all very empowering. With Peter I just had to keep a very straight face when he did all that: 'You two should be ashamed of yourselves!' business. My bossiness and my bosom being vital parts of a very funny scene. And popular. I kept the whip for years afterward. In-fact, I only sold it, at auction, a year or two ago. So a lovely fan of mine and, one must assume, a lovely fan of Peter's too, now owns it. But, as a comedy actor, Peter really was remarkable. You tell me he completed three more feature films, as well as lots of other jobs, after the Panther film. Incredible. I can only believe he was surviving on sheer will power . . . and the sheer joy of making people laugh."[2]

Revenge of the Pink Panther is loud, silly, and gloriously

---

1 Interview with the author, May 2012.
2 Interview with the author, July 2024.

entertaining. All this ridiculousness inevitably seeped into the massive promotional push too. Sellers and Edwards held court during a three-day press junket in Hawaii and, although contractually sensible so to do, Peter maintained that this was the greatest Panther they had ever made. It certainly pushed Clouseau into more of a romantic lead, with the whistle-worthy Dyan Cannon making for a playful leading lady in the comic love story at the film's core. And, as warbled in the film in character as Toulouse-Lautrec, Peter's recording of 'Thank Heavens for Little Girls' was commercially released as a tie-in.[1] Despite its undoubted joyfulness, this purely audio manifestation of Peter's *Pink Panther* slapstick genius does somewhat expose just how easy Sellers was making his life at the time. There is really none of the deep skill of Peter's acting finery here. Pretty much anyone can put on a strangled French accent and garble their way through a cod tip of the titfer to Maurice Chevalier. Few would have the charm of Sellers, it's true, but it certainly doesn't take the great nuanced acting talent at his disposal to do it. What it does take is nerve, and aplomb, and comic heritage. Three factors that Sellers had in spades. It was all that was required. That and the playful childlike innocence which is at the beating heart of Clouseau's clowning. An indulgence of the inner infant. It is a beautiful trait that Sellers was exercising rather a lot at the time.

Peter had joined beloved fellow Goon Harry Secombe on Keith Michell and Jeremy Lloyd's all-star anamorphic fantasy *Captain Beaky and His Band (Not Forgetting Hissing Sid!!!)*, which took the charts by storm for the Christmas of 1977.[2] The album encompassed various notable turns as various infamous creatures, with Peter's dexterity for accents utilised on two cuts. Billed alphabetically but with cover design skilfully edging the Sellers name to the highest position, he brings, from out of the vocal banks, a perfectly-pitched,

---

1 United Artists: UAS30012, while Peter also recorded a Clouseau version of 'We'll Meet Again' which remained unreleased until the EMI box set *A Celebration of Sellers*, in 1990. Peter had contributed a cheeky comment to The Pink Panther EP (RCA Victor: RCX-7136), in 1964.

2 Keith Michell had appeared just before Sellers on the bill of *'Wilton's – The Handsomest Hall in Town*, on BBC Television for Boxing Day 1970 – portraying that sophisticated turn George Leybourne, with a rendition of his most famous song 'Champagne Charlie'.

burly Scots brogue for the Christmas hunting yarn of 'The Haggis Season'. Peter also played, rather poignantly, 'Jacques, a Penniless French Mouse'. Despite Sellers sprinkling a pinch of his usual strangled garlic warble on the track, there's real character in this short, and sweet tale of a gnawer and his passion for Roquefort. Quite beautiful.

It was in celebration of the 50th anniversary of the world's most famous, and financially secure rodent, Mickey Mouse, that Sellers was, rather incongruously, interviewed for *The Wonderful World of Disney*: 'Mickey's 50', broadcast 19th November 1978.

Sellers too had guest-starred on *The Muppet Show*. He was fabuously at ease in a world of cloth and ping pong balls that talk. His episode was broadcast on New Year's Day, 1978, debuting on New York screens that 27th February. It's from the days when I, personally, was more interested in the muppets than the megastars who interacted with them. When that interest flips, or more to the point, merges, then you are in business. As a comedy historian studying the comedy legacy of Sellers, *The Muppet Show* is a colourful, free-wheeling encapsulation of the characters that made him great in the first place. There is a madcap, unofficial resurrection of his Germanic madman Doctor Strangelove. Peter's Third Reich masseur is called Merkwurdigliebe, quite literally Strangelove in German. Here he terrorises dashing porcine leading man Link Hogthrob with a very thorough session. Throughout the show there is a running joke concerning Peter's desperation to perform the soliloquy from *Richard III*. Straight. No Beatles lyrics. No scouse. This mini gallop through Peter's life and work even informs the big finale song, 'Cigarettes and Whiskey', in which Sellers is a temperance preacher, and returns to his wartime showbiz days by beating a drum! The show opens with Peter as Inspector Clouseau, having knives hurled at him by grotesque specialty act Gonzo. Filmed in a break during the shooting schedule for *Revenge of the Pink Panther*, which stretched from the Autumn of 1977 until the April of 1978, this is a lovely hook on Clouseau for the tiny tots.

Moreover, *The Muppet Show* ends with Peter, as 'himself', joining the gathered muppet cast. At the very close Sellers is in his favourite, twisted, comedy state of mind: grinning widely from underneath a German tin helmet. So, as a twenty-five-minute introductory Peter Sellers package, *The Muppet Show* is perfect. It's his comedic *This Is Your Life*; a playful autobiography through a View-Master. It's also very, very funny. A total joy.

Peter was in equally frivolous and relaxed mood when he eagerly lent his voice as multi-character narrator of *The Great Pram Race*, a cinema short written and directed by James Hill. Within just over twenty-three minutes there's seven Sellers performances, ranging from his upper-crust commentator Dick Dingleberry to Irish (Dermot O'Reilly) and Scots (Angus McConk) commentators. Filmed with the good and, frankly, bonkers people of Hertford Heath, Hertford, Hertfordshire, it's a celebration of the gloriously-fictitious, British tradition of on-road pram racing. That it has the air of Michael Bentine's 'Drats' is absolutely right. This suitably Goonish nonsense, fuelled by alcohol and mild insanity, was an extremely happy assignment for Sellers. He practically knocked it off in real-time. The session also reignited Peter's interest in recording, and would inspire the long-form comedy monologues of his final album, *Sellers Market*.

Sellers also voiced the slightly larcenous Mayor in the animated feature film *Kingdom of Gifts*, co-written and directed by Ted Kneeland. The supporting cast were no slouches either, with Gemma Craven heading a cast including swashbuckling legend and Sir Charles Litton contender Douglas Fairbanks Jr. and Peter's beloved old British film playmate Terry-Thomas.

Voices from out of Peter's past were given contemporary clout too, for in the autumn of 1978 it was a case of Needle Nardle McNoo as 'The Treasure of Loch Lomond' headlined the latest *Goon Show Classics* release. That episode ends with Spike warbling 'I'm Walking Backwards for Christmas', and it was, once again, back in the charts! A blast from February 1956, backwards was right.[1] By now a dusting-off of Goons was a known Christmas cert, and the episode is particularly infectious, as Sellers cracks up at Secombe's Scots accent, and Milligan translates. The sheer unfettered joy of it all is palpable, and one can imagine Sellers, sitting at home in Switzerland, listening through the latest hi-tech headphones to his complimentary copy from the Beeb Beeb Ceeb, chuckling at memories past. These dear old comrades-in-comedy, when life sort of made sense. In 1978, when Peter's life really didn't make a lot of sense, he turned to the balm of old: it was time for the Goons.

The one fixed point in an ever-changing Sellers world. Moreover, to add weight to the fact that once a Goon always a Goon, Sellers was back in a Decca recording session with Spike Milligan and Harry Secombe and the chaps' fifties singles producer Marcel Stellman – to put their own slant on the hoary old Leslie Sarony number 'Rhymes'. The A-side release, 'The Raspberry Song', allowed Secombe full-wind for his legendary sound effect, while the reunion resurrected all the old inspired infantile joy of old: Sellers threw in bursts of Grytpype-Thynne and Bluebottle and Bloodnok. There's also a parade of semi-familiar vocal traits from his subsequent career in there: the obligatory Nazi, which sort of combines his Hitler with his Strangelove; the fussy Indian; the fidgety Jew; even an echo of Fred Kite on the reading of the line: "jolly little song, mother".

The recording session was clearly a jolly one. Spike can barely get his first lines of 'The Raspberry Song' out without collapsing into laughter. Sellers too seems on the brink of bursting when he pleads for the prison warden to hold his ball. As he intones, in a different guise, "Oh, they are rude those Goons, you know!"

Rude . . . and imperishable.

The new single was certainly timely for an extra, fresh inclusion

---

1 *Goon Show Classics Vol. 5*, BBC Records REB 339 also included 'The Greenslade Story', from December 1955. Both selected episodes were hand-picked by Spike Milligan. That episode, a glorious deconstruction of the BBC, features Ray Ellington in a seasonal mood too, belting out a jazzed-up 'Jingle Bells' and pre-empting The Goodies' barking dogs by twenty years. *More Fun at One*, a BBC compilation of comic cuts, also released in late 1978, featured Peter's 'Party Political Broadcast', from 1958, as well as a brief burst of *The Goon Show*'s 'The Flea', lifted from *Goon Show Classics Vol. 4*, from 1977.

on the Decca Records compilation release of *The World of the Goons*, also for the Christmas sacks of 1978. How spoiled we were!

The World of . . . range had cornered the market in budget vinyl, consisting of re-recorded numbers, a simple reissue of an existing record or, in the Goons' case, a hastily cobbled-together collection, safely gathering in 'The Raspberry Song' and 'Rhymes' alongside glorious creaky old favourites from the first flush of fifties success. As per usual it was Spike, the senior Goon and, now at the ripe old age of sixty, who was called upon and agreed to write the sleeve notes. In them he proclaimed that the recordings were the result of: "a psycho power brought about by the intake of whisky impregnated porridge . . .". And, basking in the ongoing legal wrangling within the Beatles empire, Spike stated that "unless this record was issued on the date it was issued on, Peter Sellers had threatened to get married again . . .". It was just a year after Lynne and Sellers had tied the knot. Sellers didn't get married for a fifth time. He didn't have the time. Not quite, at least.

He did, however, have time to shoot three roles, in tandem with his young bride, for The Mirisch Corporation and Universal Pictures. All in the one film, naturally: *The Prisoner of Zenda*. The oft-told and re-told yarn of Anthony Hope, first published in 1894, was reinterpreted by British comedy scribes extraordinaire Dick Clement and Ian La Frenais, as a breakneck and, at most times, very funny romp.[1]

Sellers stars as the foppish regal figure of Rudolf V, who has trouble with his Rs; as well as the lithe and lively English tourist Syd Frewin, who happens to look exactly like the Prince. Funny that! Sellers being Sellers, he slipped in a third performance too: as the aged and doddery Rudolf IV who, celebrating his 80th birthday by touring his domain by hot air balloon, swiftly meets his end at the start, and sets up the gloriously convoluted plot. So, typically, *The Prisoner of Zenda* is not so much starring Peter Sellers and Peter

---

1 Although the Carry Ons had already done a send-up, on television, with the *Carry On Laughing* episode 'The Prisoner of Spenda', transmitted in January 1975. Here it was the late Sid James who acted opposite himself. The brilliant Clement and La Frenais, now writing for Sellers, had, as we will see, also fully plundered *Two-Way Stretch* for their *Porridge* movie.

The World of Henry Orient:

The sparkle, the 'tache, and the duplicitous self-possession were all still in place for Peter's first Hollywood film: when he took on the eponymous role of the pretentious concert pianist in *The World of Henry Orient*. "An often-funny and always fetching production", according to *Variety*.

Photo 12 / Alamy Stock Photo

Dr. Strangelove:

Stanley Kubrick called Peter "the hardest worker I know. I'd come into the studio at seven o'clock in the morning and there he would be. Waiting, ready. Full of ideas." The director certainly got his $333 thousand money's worth for the titular, twisted tactician in *Dr. Strangelove*. *Landmark Media / Alamy Stock Photo*

The Wrong Box:

Friend and film-maker Bryan Forbes only needed to wind Peter up and let him go for the largely improvised guest star cameo of Doctor Pratt in *The Wrong Box*. A room full of cats are his unforgettably funny soft props. *Everett Collection Inc / Alamy Stock Photo*

There's a Girl in My Soup:

The transient and conceited essence of celebrity was at the centre of Terence Frisby's West End play. Peter's real-life playboy personality added extra tabloid inches clout to the Boulting brothers' feature film presentation of *There's a Girl in My Soup*.

Everett Collection Inc / Alamy Stock Photo

Soft Beds, Hard Battles:

Peter's war informed his entire comedy life. He would hastily morph into a comic Nazi at the drop of a tin helmet. However, his depiction of the Fuhrer himself in *Soft Beds, Hard Battles* is no cardboard cut-out dictator. This Hitler is an extended cameo of mad malevolence.

Album / Alamy Stock Photo

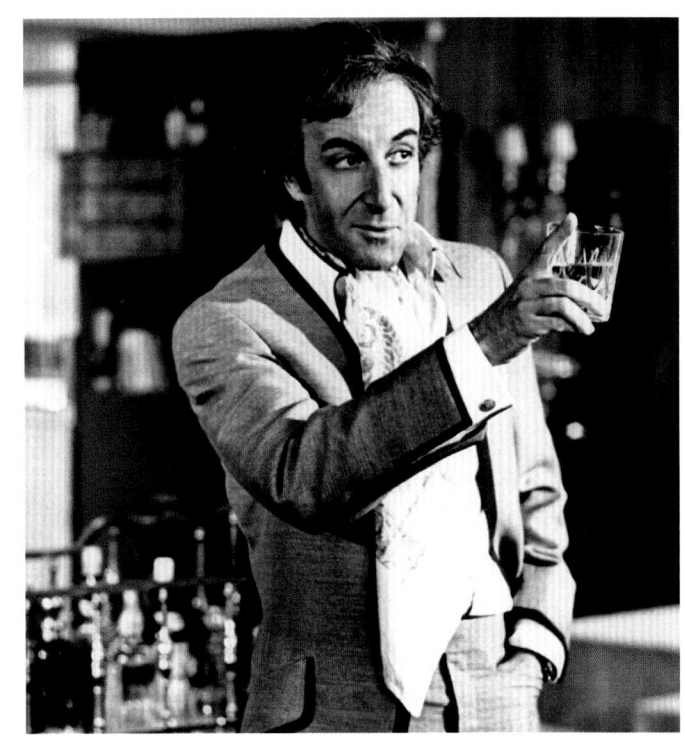

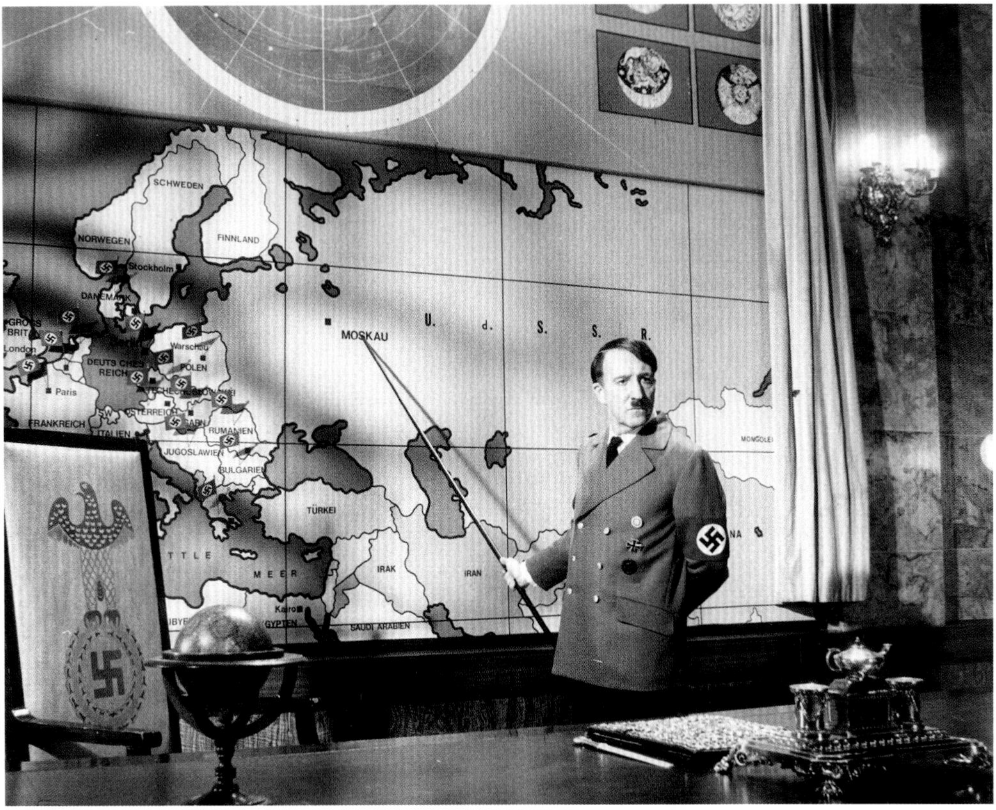

"I Love You, Alice B. Toklas!":

An hallucinogenic daydream of retrieved lost youth and embraced West Coast counterculture. In other words, Sellers at the summit of his swinging sixties satire, as the groovy Harold Fine in *"I Love You, Alice B. Toklas!" Album / Alamy Stock Photo*

The Pink Panther Strikes Again:

The Pinkest and the Funniest! Peter always threw himself into promotion for the series that cemented his reputation as a slapstick comic genius, and still makes the whole world laugh. Here joined by a friendly furry fellow to launch *The Pink Panther Strikes Again*. *Roger Tillberg / Alamy Stock Photo*

Murder By Death:

Even without the use of Prepositions and Articles, Sidney Wang is determined to find out what meaning of this in *Murder By Death*, Neil Simon's loving pastiche of vintage detective fiction. Not only a battle of sleuths but a friendly fight between a clutch of screen greats to be number one! *Everett Collection Inc / Alamy Stock Photo*

The Fiendish Plot of Dr. Fu Manchu:

Umm . . . wrong oriental! The brilliantly befuddled Nayland Smith, in Peter's last completed film *The Fiendish Plot of Dr. Fu Manchu*. A performance of subtle stillness in a manic *Goon Show* plot. As Roger Ebert's posthumous review noted: "just the kind Sellers loved to work on."

Being There:

As the *Daily Mirror* said of Jerzy Kosinski's novel: "Take a note of it, write it in big letters, scrawl it on walls. But remember it . . ." And remember Peter's performance in *Being There* too. In the "blank page" of Chance he achieved his goal to do something better. Much better. Just in the nick of time. *United Archives GmbH / Alamy Stock Photo*

Sellers, as starring Peter Sellers and Peter Sellers with Peter Sellers. The aged cameo is the most outlandish, and most Goonish. It's pure Bloodnok, really, with the silly old duffer engaging in the befuddled business of trying to drink out of his telescope and putting a champagne bottle to his eye; while the rightful King is all dewy-eyed debauchery, arrogance and spineless cowardice. He's got an eye for the ladies though and in that department *The Prisoner of Zenda* is a veritable Sellers harem, with Elke Sommer, from *A Shot in the Dark*, Catherine Schell from *The Return of the Pink Panther*, and Lynne Frederick from the marital bed. All three are excellent, in particular Lynne who displays a likeable mix of wide-eyed innocence and haughty pomposity as befits a Princess. She is refined, poised, gentle, and sweet. The scenes with Sellers – in the guise of Syd Frewin – are enchanting and, with hindsight, rather moving. The waltz is danced divinely, with no whiff of send-up, and the enforced pairing, with Sellers muttering: "I'll dream about you for the rest of my life" is loaded with meaning, and poignancy. Henry Mancini, on sweeping romantic musical score and rollicking action adventure duties, fully shines in these moments of quiet reflection. Having provided the soundtrack to many of Peter's biggest successes, there's something reassuring in the Mancini strings here.

Although, as Rudolf, Sellers looks meek and pale, as befits the milksop he is playing, as the cockney cabbie commoner, Syd Frewin, he looks in rugged good health. Full of face and fit of limp, the stuntmen on full-term duty notwithstanding, there is a heroic sense of derring-do about this performance. Indeed, the Dick Clement and Ian La Frenais adaptation is a fairly faithful retelling of the old, old story. There is a comic preoccupation with arse jokes, although the slight moments of slapstick and pratfalls are not for Sellers but others, most memorably that cherubic, white-bearded character actor Tony Sympson, who, having been a Panther suspect in 1976, hilariously topples backwards at the train station. And, although much of the Looney Tunes cartoon slapstick is played out by Gregory Sierra, as the cuckolded husband Gilles, Sellers vented his anger on the studios for trying to turn his romantic romp into a *Panther*.

However, the film is packed with reassuring faces for Sellers to interact with. Lionel Jeffries, in the furiously loyal role immortalised – twice – in Hollywood by Lewis Stone, is his exemplary self; while fresh-faced newcomer to the Sellers universe Simon Williams equips himself well. Mike Grady is in the mix, greeting the old King; Jeremy Kemp, an ill-fated chum from *The Blockhouse*, has a glorious time as the evil half-brother; Norman Rossington is on scene-stealing form as a jolly torturer; Michael Balfour is a ruddy-faced explosives expert; while Arthur Howard and, in particular, John Laurie as a bonkers Bishop, excel in the Coronation scenes. And of course Graham Stark is on hand as a St. Bernard's dog-handling flunky at court.

Sellers need do little but look on with a weary shake of the head. In large part this is a serious action hero performance, played like Michael Caine, with an air of Bethnal Green charm; the skill of a horse-whisper (which prompts a hearty ad-lib or two), and a sense of truth and decency that never sends up the source material. Director Richard Quine juggles the two Peters beautifully, most memorably in that first meeting when London Sellers is all speechless distrust and amazement and Ruritanian Sellers is all clenched gleefulness and awkward squeaking. There is a beautifully mad moment when the two sing a duet on the George Beauchamp music-hall number 'She Was One of the Early Birds'. It's a half-brother link, of course, but there's something so gloriously dotty in the drunken camaraderie with Sellers and Sellers. It sums up the uncluttered and life-affirming fun of the entire film.

Frantically busy character actor Robert Gillespie, who had popped up as a Swiss banker in the Sellers-less *Inspector Clouseau*, pops up here as a wine waiter. For Gillespie, it was: "very interesting to watch Sellers operate. Fascinating. Our director Richard Quine didn't have to do very much. Peter was in complete control of that ridiculous, languid character of the King. When the cameras weren't turning over he was quiet, slightly giggly, floaty. He seemed to drift around the place. Both as an actor and as a person. It worked, of course.

Sheer brilliance. An utter privilege to observe him, from within my minute involvement in his comedy."[1]

As for that reunion with Mike Grady, from *The Return of the Pink Panther*, that had been complete serendipity, as Mike was holidaying in Austria and clocked there was a film crew in town: "Suddenly there was Peter Sellers with his director Richard Quine, and Peter saw me and said: 'Mike! I didn't know you were on this!' First off I was dumbstruck that he remembered me at all and before I could say, with a laugh, 'Actually, Peter, I'm not!', I was! That was just lovely. Peter seemed as relaxed and loveable as he was four years earlier. A lovely man."[2] Unfortunately for the box-office reputation of Sellers, this wasn't a *Pink Panther* movie.

The Prisoner of Zenda made $8million at the box office. The problem was it cost $10million! Result: misery. It certainly wasn't the *Pink Panther*-sized box office smash that Universal had hoped for, when it was released across America, and then internationally, on 25th May 1979. No, this was not a *Pink Panther*. The Evening Standard British Film ceremony of 1976 had named the year's Best Comedy as *The Return of the Pink Panther*, with Sellers winning Best Actor. In 1977 the Evening Standard named the year's Best Comedy as *The Pink Panther Strikes Again*; while in 1978 it was, you guessed it, *Revenge of the Pink Panther*. In 1979 it *was* a win for screenwriters Dick Clement and Ian La Frenais, but not for the Sellers film but the feature film spin-off from the Ronnie Barker BBC sitcom *Porridge*. Having borrowed many elements from the Peter Sellers comedy *Two-Way Stretch*, this full-length presentation of the Dick Clement and Ian La Frenais sitcom went the full hog and lifted the entire, intricate heist plot of the twenty-years-old Sellers classic![3]

Unsurprisingly United Artists were pushing for yet another *Panther*. And, Sellers was more than willing. He was sitting in the catbird seat,

---

1 Interview with the author, November 2023.
2 Interview with the author, April 2024.
3 The 1980 ceremony followed hot on the heels of Peter's death and saw the inaugural Peter Sellers Award for Comedy presented to Leonard Rossiter for another sitcom film, *Rising Damp*. Rossiter, as Quinlan, had memorably locked comic horns with Sellers in *The Pink Panther Strikes Again*.

after all. They wouldn't and couldn't make one without him. Not now. Could they? And certainly his production credit and star bankability gave him a lot of clout. He green-lit the idea and a screenplay was written. *Romance of the Pink Panther* was to have teamed Sellers with blonde comedienne and gleeful gush of nature Pamela Stephenson, who was currently wowing the nation on the BBC sketch show *Not the Nine O'Clock News*. There's something cyclical and right about the pairing of Sellers and Stephenson. And the script is very, very funny. Sellers, though, had a couple of conditions. One was revolutionary. Although Blake Edwards was co-writing and producing the film, he was to be forced to relinquish the director's chair. Out went Blake Edwards and in his place was to be . . . yes, Peter Sellers.[1]

That United Artists agreed to this is testament to their desperation for more *Panther*. And, although, as pre-production continued on *Romance of the Pink Panther*, Sellers relinquished the directorial chair to Oscar-winning actor Sidney Poitier, who had just enjoyed a box-office hit directing Peter's comedy scavenger Gene Wilder, and Richard Pryor in the prison comedy *Stir Crazy*, the Panther was all set to pounce on box office records once again. But Sellers wasn't done yet. He also wanted to show the public that he could do more than silly slapstick and funny foreigners. One offer on the table was a sure signifier of his standing as a truly great actor on the world screen. It wasn't for a funny foreigner but it was to have given Sellers a chance to broaden and strengthen his already comedically heralded Indian. This was no *The Millionairess* or *The Party* though. This was an invitation from respected Indian film-maker Satyajit Ray, who had cast Sellers as a Marwari businessman in his film treatment for *The Alien*. Ray was not only an admirer of Sellers, but also an admirer of his Indian portrayals. Within their comic veneer, Ray had seen truth and understanding. Ray was not gimmick-casting, he was courting a highly valued character actor. Moreover, the attachment

---

1 Despite their full-blown creative arguments, Sellers remained loyal and respectful to Blake Edwards. He even filmed a gag appearance, as a dance band drummer, for Blake's *10*, which launched the Hollywood career of British satirist Dudley Moore. Peter had, of course, been first choice for the role of George Webber in *10* – and it was to be a huge hit. Moreover, Peter's little scene was cut from the final print, although ironically it was Cuddly Dudley who stepped into Peter's shoes to star in the remake of the jet-black Preston Sturges comedy *Unfaithfully Yours*, which was released in 1984.

of Sellers to the project would secure the budget. Immediately. A situation compounded by the fact that Marlon Brando had already agreed to co-star, as long as Sellers signed up too. In the end *The Alien* was never made.

Never idle, not even when holed-up in his Switzerland hideaway, Sellers used the time between making pictures to record the comedy album *Sellers Market*, largely at the Mountain Studios, in Montreux. The project, re-cycling the title of his aborted autobiography, had been kick-started thanks to that Goon reunion in the spring of 1978, with Sellers also fitting in a solo recording of 'Singin' in the Rain', in cod Clouseau mood, at the same session. It was the seed for a new album of comic cuts which beautifully basks in Goonish humour throughout. It begins with a monotone, nerdy introduction to Cole Porter's 'Night and Day' played in Morse code by none other than Sid Prunes of East Finchley. International clout there. Not! Glorious. This is Sellers playing with the very codes and conventions of recording once again, and having a playful time setting up this most outrageous and audacious track. *Sellers Market* also indulges him with 'Peter Sellers Sings Rudolph Friml' which, rather than repeating the old George Gershwin gag, has Sellers, revisiting the vocal of that aged thespian Warrington Minge to actually warble his way through Friml's composition for *The Vagabond King* 'Only a Rose'. It certainly fits the vibe of Peter's latest comedy film, *The Prisoner of Zenda*. 'The Eaton Square Blues' has Sellers as a drunken toff, without his girl, 'Bobo', and in his sozzled state sings his way through corrupted Cole Porter. *Sellers Market* also, rather wonderfully and rather poignantly, reunited Sellers with Irene Handl, late of being Mrs. Kite and of the *Songs for Swingin' Sellers* album. 'The Whispering Giant' is a twenty-years-on sequel to her own 'Shadows on the Grass', and her dithering 'Squidgy'.[1] The album also took in hilarious sessions at the Pathe-Marconi Studios in Paris, and

---

1 Prince Charles, always a devoted Sellers-phile, would get embroiled in Squidgygate in 1992 when taped phone conversations between his estranged wife, Diana, Princess of Wales, and confidant James Gilbey revealed that Gilbey called her Squidgy. Sellers was long gone, of course, as was Irene Handl, who had died in November 1987, just after filming a contribution to *Wogan's Radio Fun*, a show that also reunited Goons Spike Milligan and Harry Secombe.

allowed Sellers to go back home to work at the old Pye Studios, in London. This was his summer of 1979, fleshing out the collection of new tracks, all in time to celebrate his final birthday in the September. Split into two sides, y'know, both The Musical Scene and The Cultural Scene, the *Sellers Market* cut everybody seems to remember, even though they may not know where it's from, is 'The All-England George Formby Finals': the elephantine salute to the comedy legend. Although Formby had been dead eighteen years, his films were still staple BBC2 television fodder. Over the previous ten years good old Decca Records had issued several, popular George Formby Greatest Hits collections in The World of . . . range. Besides George Harrison was a Formby fan and disciple, and Peter had rounded off his very well-received 1974 interview with Michael Parkinson with a burst of George Formby. In 1975 Peter had even been invited to play ukulele on the Steeleye Span track 'New York Girls'. Of course, he couldn't resist some Goonish babble either. It was released on the album *Commoners Crown*.[1] Thus, it was in the Sellers tank of talent and of the zeitgeist, of sorts. The track is Peter's full-scale, affectionate salute to his variety days, and the story that even he believed now, that his father had taught Formby how to play. Within the sketch Sellers utilised a myriad of characterisations – from upper-crust toff to authentic and – as it turns out – dishonest Lancastrian. William Fruit – Sellers, of course – gets my vote as the best, despite being disqualified for not starting his rendition of 'Chinese Laundry Blues' with George's "Turned Out Nice Again" catchphrase. Peter's Major Ralph Relph character – recreated from 'So Little Time' from *Songs for Swingin' Sellers* – is on hand to cash in on the winner: a new Formby-style song composed by Grant Rees and performed by Sellers as a variation on his cockney cabbie from the just released *The Prisoner of Zenda* . . . and then it's all the Formbys in a multi-tracked Sellers. Fabulous. The *Sellers Market* track 'Gefrunk' is a duologue between an American nut job and a German psychiatrist. It's Gefrunk with Funk. The flip side of *Sellers Market* includes 'The Compleat (sic) Guide to Accents of the British

---

1 Chrysalis: CHR1071. The track was laudably licensed for inclusion on the EMI box set *A Celebration of Sellers*, in 1990. One for the completist indeed.

Isles' which again echoes old Sellers recordings, in its academic and analytical examination of the British, through the eccentric prism of a foreign microscope. This is from the American stance, with Peter's character, Don Schumann, escaping the States and drifting through Europe. Fitfully funny, its main value is an encapsulation of Peter's gear-shifting prowess and relentless ear for detail, not least of which is the muted resurrection of William Mate; a groovy evocation of hip and happening John Lennon; an essence of Noel Coward; a final comic punch in the stomach of Nazi Germany; and a cockney knees-up version of Tim Rice and Andrew Lloyd-Webber's 'Don't Cry for Me Argentina', *Evita* having opened in the West End from 1978 and, at the time of the record's release, just wowed Broadway. The track was co-writtenly impoverished by Sellers with Ken Barnes, who also produced the whole joyful bundle of the album.[1]

A fanciful man may say that the contents of *Sellers Market* are more than enough to be a satisfying conclusion of a body of work from a performer's twilight years. And I am a fanciful man. Listening to the album you get a sense of Sellers looking back through a clutch of faded photos from his own glittering past. Indeed, the interior gatefold album leaves this in no doubt. Laid out like a tabloid newspaper, it is peppered with sepia snaps of past Sellers glories: from Clouseau to Ladykiller Harry, to *The Battle of the Sexes* to the wedding pose of the Kites. *Sellers Market* is an artefact of career closure.[2]

If the winter of 1979 was to see Sellers back in the charts, that last Christmas would also see him in the cinemas with the realisation of a long-standing project – straight from his weakening but determined heart.

---

1 In 1977 Ken Barnes had overseen Bing Crosby's final recordings. In turn, *Sellers Market* was the studio swansong for Peter Sellers. Unbeknown to Sellers, forty-year-old John Lennon would be shot down in December 1980, while Steve McQueen, referenced in 'Gefrunk', had died in November at the age of fifty. Peter had been around in January 1980 to hear of Jimmy Durante's death. The source for his 'Never Never Land' impression was 86.

2 Peter's Goon past was still profitable too. In 1979 EMI Records repackaged three previously released Goon Shows as *Goon Show Greats*: PMC 7179. 'Tales of Old Dartmoor', 'Six Charlies in Search of an Author' and, split between sides, 'Dishonoured'.

Chapter 16

"I happen to be one of those sorts of people who was born in England and I will die in England."

Peter Sellers, 1980

So, while he was recording silly voices and scratching up remnants of his own recorded past, Sellers was knee-deep in the dream film he had been obsessing over for nearly a decade. *Being There*. Sellers had long hailed Jerzy Kosinski's 1971 novel. As was his wont, he had been lending it to influential friends in the hope that he could get interest from a studio. In collaboration with Robert C. Jones, National Book Award-winning Kosinski had adapted his own work into a screenplay. Sellers saw Chance as his ultimate screen legacy. This bland, misunderstood prophet would be informed of ghosts from his past. He was a little bit Stan Laurel; a little bit his own father; a little bit John, the herbal-pipe-smoking gardener of Brooksfield House, which Sellers still had fond memories of, over a decade since moving out. All three were will-o'-the-wisps for Sellers to tap in to. The novel even likened his naturalness to the retired Cary Grant. That man again! Still, the character was the very essence of the blank, vacuous canvas that had long been the very essence of the real Peter Sellers, as Sellers saw himself. Or, at least, the very essence the real Peter Sellers had sold to the press. In *Being There* he somehow made this nonentity flesh: a vibrant, truthful philosopher, whose only secret was simplicity.

United Artists only put up the money . . . as long as Sellers pinky-promised that he'd do another *Panther*. He would. He had promised. Besides, the Sellers name was more than enough to guarantee the studio an audience and get the star what he wanted. *Being There* was put into production, with a filming schedule in and around the Biltmore Estate, in North Carolina.

The heart of the plot is the heart of the character. *Being There* is about love and innocence and kindness. It is Peter's total dedication to these principles that makes the performance and the film so lasting, so important, so good. This pure, gentle man. Honesty as a way of life. What a revelation. In this 'sue you', 'sue me' world, a reasonable man is a stand-out thinker. Even his champion, Eve Rand (Shirley MacLaine) has initial leanings towards kindness merely to avoid a legal claim: after her chauffeur-driven car damages his leg in an accident. That it is MacLaine, a spectre from Peter's sixties jet-set life, adds an extra layer of clout and relevance. But in *Being There* the moments of the peak standard blue print Peter Sellers comedy of awkward embarrassment are never milked: when he struggles with a cigar or when he double-takes at the dinner table, it is subtle; real. This man's life's knowledge is gleaned from television. It's a tunnel-vision of cartoons and commercials and men in drag and puppets and silly-voiced foreigners. A microcosm of Peter's own comedy world. Chance's accompanying soundtrack – from waking up alone to emerging into cold, hard reality – is classical. Old-fashioned but reliable. Dependable. When it and he meets the new, he and the music are forced to adapt. Just a little. That funky, disco riff on Wagner's 'Thus Spake Zarathustra' as he quietly and sedately wanders through homelessness and poverty, and politely raises his hat to the hobos, is a masterly piece of composed Sellers acting. This is the world beyond his world. It is the pivotal transition moment, of course, but in that methodical walk on the wild side, Peter touches true cinematic greatness. That he gleefully infiltrates and influences the White House is as nothing to this cheerfully bewildered embracing of modernity. On his own terms.

Peter being Peter he couldn't resist just one, tiny Goonish moment. When faced with eviction from his home, the home of his recently deceased boss and benefactor, Chance momentarily ponders on his photographic memory of the visiting handyman from nearly thirty years before. Joe, the guy who came in to fix the wall of the garden, showed him a book, with pictures of men and women. The naughtiness of this voyeuristic memory makes him chuckle like a schoolboy. For a second, Chance is pure Bluebottle. It's a delight. As is the entire film. Peter's dedication is palpable throughout.

The pre-production of *Being There* and, for an ailing Sellers, the shooting schedule was long and arduous but totally rewarding. It was, indeed, the pinnacle of Peter's creative life. It is that "full potential" that Michael Parkinson had pushed him on, during the most candid and reflective moment of his 1974 interview, when Blake Edwards and the Pink Panther were just back in his life. While praising Edwards and Kubrick, Sellers revealed that: "I always think I can go one better before I die. I don't want to be remembered by that lot!" *Being There* is the one better before he died: a worthy epitaph to a great career in comedy.[1]

When United Artists released *Being There* as their feelgood Christmas film, on 19th December 1979, critics agreed that a happy Sellers had clearly delivered a brilliant Sellers performance. Indeed, *Variety* commented that *Being There* was: "an unusually fine film . . ." and that, personally, it: "represents Peter Sellers' most smashing work since the mid-60s." Sellers was vindicated. Chance was his perfect performance. A conjuring up of nothingness, of innocence, of kind charm. He had also worked himself to a standstill in accepting every press interview he could to promote his prized *Being There*, including *Today*, on 12th March 1980; and *Good Morning America*, on 19th March. Sellers felt even more vindicated when the awards season came around. He won a Golden Globe. He was nominated for a BAFTA, and he was given the nod for a National Society of Film Critics Award, and a New York Film Critics Circle Award. Sellers was also nominated for the biggest prize of all: the Academy Award for Best Actor. When the winner was announced as . . . Dustin Hoffman for *Kramer vs. Kramer*, it broke what was left of Peter's heart.

---

1 *Parkinson*, BBC Television, 1974.

Hosted by Johnny Carson, the date of the lavish 52nd Academy Award ceremony was Monday, 14th April 1980 – on 17th April, a recorded interview with Peter for *The Don Lane Show*, resulted in less than a plug for *Being There* and more an opportunity for the wild-haired host to discuss the Sellers classics of the sixties and push his buttons as a silly voice and accent juke box. Although chuffed that the film and a co-star got acknowledgement, Melvyn Douglas winning Best Supporting Actor was probably the last, gruelling straw, but Sellers reserved his spite for *Being There*'s director Hal Ashby. Sellers made it perfectly clear that he considered the decision to run fluffs and out-takes and breaking of the fourth wall during the film's closing credits had not only undermined his performance but also revealed the mechanics behind the role. For Sellers it was that closing gag reel that had lost him the Oscar. One can see his point of view. Sort of. Although, in 1979 it was the kind of thing that British television viewers got joy from at the end of *The Dick Emery Show*, Peter's old Goon chum. Moreover Sellers had not only agreed for the hilarious breaking wind in the lift out-takes to be screened on *It'll Be Alright on the Night 2*, hosted by another old cohort Denis Norden, with his ever-present clipboard, on 28th October 1979, but he was a Special Guest to introduce the brilliant bloopers; and those, along with other moments of Sellers collapsing into giggles during the *Panther* shoots had been a highlight of the 1978 promotional documentary *That's Panthertainment*.

Still, all that was fine for a bit of Light Entertainment nonsense. Not for his masterpiece of subtle acting in *Being There*.

The fall-out between the star and the director was apocalyptic . . . although, typically, not long-lasting. By that early spring of 1980 when the Oscar had just slipped through his fingers, Sellers was happily back in talks with Ashby. This fledgling fresh film collaboration never came to fruition.

However, for a dying man on borrowed time, Sellers was extremely busy. He was vetting and polishing the new *Panther* script and he had reunited with another high-octane collaborator, Joe McGrath, on a series of Barclays Bank commercials. These were nicely lucrative and an unchallenging comedy coast for Sellers: clicking his internal dial to a financially untrustworthy Jewish agent by the name of Monty Casino: his very last comedy role. Sellers filmed three in the series of commercials, advising a young classical cellist, played by Brian Pettifer, to go punk – much to the shock of the ecclesiastical Arthur Howard; he also persuaded Cambridge University student, Robert Longdon, to punt to his rental abode – a dilapidated mobile home; and he ruined landed gentry toff, John Fortune, planting the seed of inviting a circus to his estate. Peter even had the opportunity to mug his way through Shakespeare's Winter of Discontent speech again. Sort of. McGrath remembers that: "Peter was taken very ill during the shoot and had to drop out. He had a commitment to attend the Cannes Film Festival which he was determined to honour, because it was for *Being There*, and then he was back to the Dorchester. And that was that. Very sad."[1]

Still, while the narrowly lost Oscar was a massive blow, Sellers was hardly on a course to capitalise on any renewed critical credibility. And he knew it. Gleefully so! The film he had wrapped just before shooting the commercials was one with no award-winning potential whatsoever. It was a silly romp, and proud of it.

Peter had been thrilled to sign up for *The Fiendish Plot of Dr. Fu Manchu*. Not least because, as co-star David Tomlinson remembered: "Peter was to collect a million dollars plus a percentage of the gross. He needed that kind of money, as he had just spent five thousand dollars on a pair of eighteen-carat gold spectacle frames."[2]

The Fiendish Plot of Dr. Fu Manchu was a pastiche of the Oriental fiend, created by Sax Rohmer in 1912. This comic resurrection was the first time the Yellow Peril came back to the silver screen since

1 Interview with the author, July 2003. This Barclays Bank campaign was still ongoing at the time of Peter's death, with other instalments written and prepared, so McGrath completed the contract, with Peter Cook stepping into the breach. The full Cannes experience, meanwhile, was recorded in *Diary of the Cannes Film Festival*, an Ian Johnstone documentary film, for producer Billy Baxter, which was broadcast 16th July 1980, a little over a week before Peter's death.

2 It's a lovely, affectionate snapshot of the extravagant Peter Sellers, still vital and vibrant to the last. *Luckier Than Most: An Autobiography*, by David Tomlinson, (Hodder & Stoughton, 1990).

Christopher Lee had bowed out, after his fifth outing in the role, eleven years earlier.

The project appealed to Sellers on several levels, not least the gloriously Goonish take on a subject that had previously been treated thrillingly rather than comically. Delights include the wind-up clockwork tarantula, the music-hall auditions for a female policeman to be a decoy Queen Mary, and, best of all, the fact that, while working the laundry at Eton, everybody called the evil emperor Fred. It's like Spike Milligan was whispering in the ear of his old pal. The *Fu Manchu* script also revived shades of Peter's aborted film *The Phantom vs. the Fourth Reich*, with its central conceit of pitting Sellers as dignified protagonist vs. Sellers as aged villain. As well as a more youthful incarnation of the big bad as a bonus feature to boot. Spoiler alert here: the end of the film sees Fu Manchu, having celebrated his 168th birthday (and had "Happy Birthday to Fu" rather endearingly sung to him by his cronies) survive for the duration of the film on electric shocks, only to regenerate into a '70s style Las Vegas jumpsuit era Elvis Presley. Played by Sellers, of course. It's certain that Sellers would have welcomed such a time-reversing elixir in the studio canteen.

Problems with the director Piers Haggard notwithstanding, Sellers brings a tail-end, trail-blazing energy to the film. Fu Manchu himself is a lip-smacking, multi-layered, and suitably inscrutable characterisation. There is an air of Vincent Price's Dr. Phibes as he emerges, to the strains of Bach's Fugue in G minor, straddling an organ, while the performance has a throbbing energy, even in his decrepit state. A thirst for world domination is quaintly contrasted with an edge of surreal joy in piano-pumping and harmonising with a slightly drunken Helen Mirren on 'Daddy Wouldn't Buy Me a Bow Wow'. There's a crisp determination in this Oriental Peril: eagerly throwing himself into the bolts of life-reviving electricity in the electricity chamber. Even when he's being dragged from pillar to post by his minions, there's a playful gusto at work. This mastermind of crime is played straight and strict, with no mugging on the funny, overly silly high demands of the pompous dictator. Even his nonsensical ramblings – half Confucius half Chinese restaurant menu – during the on-trend Kung Fu Disco opening credits is played deadpan and with total conviction. It is never an obviously funny performance, nor an offensive stereotype. It is merely a ghoul from the pages of history dropped into a visual, feature-length edition of *The Goon Show*. No less of a send-up is Peter's pitch perfect performance, the plum in the pudding, the world-weary, ashen, and dilapidated hero of the action, Nyland Smith. Sellers is weakened as a man but not weakened as an actor, particularly when playing such, superficially, humourless and nondescript characters as this. There is an elegance and charm in the performance. He is a proper *Boy's Own* hero, a British bulldog doggedly keeping his cool and keeping his head while on duty. First spotted mowing the lawn through a rainstorm – manufactured by a sprinkler system – Peter's Smith is otherworldly throughout. His eyes are mad. They twitch and double-take for no apparent reason. At times they glaze over completely. He is not there, or so it seems. At other times he is sharp, focused, quietly relaxed in the knowledge that his brain is up to speed once more. He is a total eccentric, of course, blocking his right eye in order to read small print, drifting into a rendition of 'San Francisco', and name-checking Jeanette MacDonald, who warbled the song throughout the 1936 film of the same name. Smith's house is as eccentric as himself, living, as he does, in a 400-year-old Wiltshire cottage which can transform into a hot-air balloon. There are shades of *The Naked Truth* here, while his old family retainer, Perkins, is played with wonderful detachment by a favourite face from many aspects of Peter's past, John Le Mesurier. Pipe-smoking and softly-spoken, almost to the point of a stage whisper at crucial plot points, Peter Sellers as Nyland Smith is, at times, my favourite of his film roles. Honestly! It has the control and calm of *Being There*, mixed with the all-out battiness of Bloodnok. Without planning it, Sellers somehow meshes bookends from the very start and very end of his legacy and, in Nyland Smith, personifies his whole crazy career in comedy in this one performance. Gaunt but stoic. A bit like a transference of Sellers himself.

The Fiendish Plot of Dr. Fu Manchu had completed filming and was in post-production when, with much annotated script of *Romance of the Pink Panther* under his arm, Sellers checked into his favoured London abode, the Dorchester Hotel, in July 1980. *Daily Mail* show business reporter David Lewin considered Sellers: "a workaholic . . .", claiming that "he can't slow down. It isn't that he needs the money. He's just happiest when he's working . . . He sets himself a fearsome pace. It's as though he's driven to accomplish as much as he can." His sixth Clouseau misadventure notwithstanding, it wasn't work and it certainly wasn't money that Sellers was most focused on that July day. No, rather it was an exciting reunion with his closest show business pals, Spike Milligan and Harry Secombe. Goon projects were always bubbling under the surface. This was simply to have a good time and, yes, let's dream a little, planning for some new episodes of *The Goon Show*. It's not beyond reason to assume that the last editions of *The Goon Show* Sellers had heard were those collected for *Goon Show Classics Vol. 6*, which had been the annual audio treat for the previous Christmas.[1] The consecutive January 1957 episodes 'Wings over Dagenham' and 'The Rent Collectors' were the programmes personally selected by Spike this time around, and showcased all the old Sellers favourites, including a very able display that he could even do Kenneth Connor's *Ray's a Laugh* character, the whiningly nasal Sidney Mincing. 'The Rent Collectors' also allows Sellers to effortlessly merge from Grytpype-Thynne to Crun, and unsubtly flag-post the shift. The joy fair busts, and Sellers was near desperate to recapture it. Even complaints of chest pains on Tuesday, 22nd July 1980 wouldn't deter his plans for the Friday evening of fine food and world wines . . . and lots and lots of laughter.

In the first few hours of Thursday, 24th July 1980, from the Middlesex Hospital, Fitzrovia, it was announced that Peter Sellers

---

1 BBC Records REB 366, 1979.

had died of a massive heart attack: "entirely due to natural causes", as a spokesman for the hospital reported. "His heart just faded away. His condition deteriorated very rapidly." Lynne, the current Mrs. Sellers, at least one ex-Mrs. Sellers, Britt Ekland, and Peter and Britt's daughter, Victoria, were at the hospital when the world's press started to spread the news. Peter Sellers was just 54 years old. Once a Goon, always a Goon. Forever.

With an exclusive insight from Front Line Ambulance Man Ted Taggart it can be revealed that: "when I arrived at the Dorchester Hotel, on the evening of Wednesday 23rd July, Peter Sellers was dying. I understand he called the Grim Reaper the Fellow in the Bright Nightgown. Well, whatever he called Death, it was in that hotel room that evening. I can honestly say I was the last person to see him alive. In the room was a member of the hotel staff, presumably the one who raised the alarm and called for medical assistance. Mr. Sellers was totally unresponsive to all the First Aid I gave him. Once in the ambulance, on blue lights and siren, I drove him to the Middlesex Hospital, in Fitzrovia, while my colleague tried to revive him. He was dead. I believe he had died at the hotel, in my presence. When we arrived at the Middlesex, a crash team had assembled in the casualty department. That team too got no signs of life, but regardless Mr. Sellers was taken to the intensive care unit. I was very young at the time. A Peter Sellers fan – as I still am. Naively I thought all this urgent, special treatment was because of his celebrity, but an older colleague told me it would have been standard practice for someone of his young age, despite the long history of heart problems that Mr. Sellers had suffered. By the time I left, a man had arrived to represent him, and was on the phone to America. This was to tell his wife, Lynne Frederick, the news. She would have caught the next arrival flight for London, but would not have been present at the death of Mr. Sellers. He was dead, on that evening of Wednesday, 23rd July 1980."[1]

---

1 Interview with the author, July 2024. Once Lynne had arrived, the announcement of the death of Peter Sellers could be released to Reuters News Agency. This was early on Thursday, 24th July 1980, the official date of the death of Peter Sellers.

The BBC hastily made space for a repeat of *The Goon Show*. The selected episode was 'The Jet-Propelled Guided NAAFI', last heard in 1972, with an introduction by Ted Ray. For this transmission, as part of a *Smash of the Day* repeat season, an audibly shaken Harry Secombe came into studio to record a brief tribute, explaining that "the entertainment profession lost a truly great international comedy actor, and I lost a very dear and close mate . . ."

Two weeks later on Friday 8th August 1980, with terrible comedy timing, the Warner Brothers release schedule saw *The Fiendish Plot of Dr. Fu Manchu* unleashed on an unsuspecting and, in terms of Sellers, a deeply saddened world. The health issues of Sellers had been tabloid fodder for many years, but the death of such a popular and current superstar was a shock. It certainly would have made that first viewing of his last completed film a very tough watch indeed.

With forty-plus years' hindsight, the viewer can and should detach the tragic loss of its star from the film itself. If one can do that then *The Fiendish Plot of Dr. Fu Manchu* gives a lot of joy, not least in that pleasing story arc of a decrepit super mastermind of crime doing a Benjamin Button and ending the film as a youthful, energised version of himself: attempting a tongue-in-cheek wiping-out of humanity through the power of rock 'n' roll. In 1933. Maybe. That the mirthful chaos of the film ends with such a wacky kind of logic leaves a contented smile on the face. Bonkers, brilliant and never, ever boring. It's nonsense, of course, but there are joys along the way: memorably, Helen Mirren playing the saxophone while tap-dancing. Indeed, it is thanks to Helen Mirren that the eyes of Sellers are bright and boyish at least twice in the film – once, while playing Smith, as he praises her acting prowess as the Queen (a nice echo of things to come for Dame Helen's Oscar-winner turn as Elizabeth II) and once as Fu, as he giggles and claps at her ambition to embrace the music-hall. Indeed, while Lynne Frederick was happily behind the scenes as Executive Producer on this one, Helen Mirren as Peter's final leading lady is one of quality, conviction, and nuance in this mad comic strip come to life. She even takes on the mantle of Lady Warrington Minge when her duty is replaced with love for the arch criminal. There is also the added delight of the befuddled pillar of British authority from David Tomlinson as Sir Roger Avery. Tomlinson had been there at the dawn of Peter's cinema stardom in *Up the Creek*. The actor revelled in Peter's love of gadgets. A personal tape recorder had been a favourite Sellers toy back in the late '50s and, as always: "he was delighted to have someone and something to play with." The dreaded boredom, having set in during the filming of *Fu Manchu*, was alleviated by Tomlinson. Certainly when director-less and rudder-less, Peter turned to his old and trusted friend: "when Sellers was in a scene himself, he put me behind the camera. We had a great time and I took it as a great compliment that he trusted me to check his performance: 'How was that, old cock?' he would ask. 'I'd do it again if I were you,' I would say occasionally. And so he would, without question, but mostly he was perfect."[1] Yes he was. That Simon Williams is back, here playing silly ass assistant and nephew Robert Townsend, certainly aided that too, and is more than enough to couple this film with the previous all-round roller-coaster spoof of *The Prisoner of Zenda*. It's an interesting, fun double-bill. Sellers was delighted by Simon Williams, as both a confederate and a colleague. He had gone to see, and went back after, to the 1977 production of Oscar Wilde's *An Ideal Husband*, in which Simon played Lord Goring, the dashing, dandy son of Lord Caversham. The old duffer was played by Peter's chum Wilfred Hyde-White. It was all very civilised, and very much up Peter's street. The camaraderie of good actors in a good company on a piece peppered with Goonish humour was how Peter saw *Fu Manchu* working. And, above everything else combined in *The Fiendish Plot of Dr. Fu Manchu*, of course, are these final, completed film performances from a stricken Sellers. Not just the lead rivals, Sellers also dubs

---

1 *Luckier Than Most: An Autobiography*, by David Tomlinson (Hodder & Stoughton, 1990). Tomlinson makes the point that: "in retrospect it is perhaps easy to see that it could have been marvellous on radio, just as *The Goon Show* was. The surreal images were best left to the imagination". And, indeed, Spike had written 'The Terrible Revenge of Fred Fu-Manchu', for series 6, in December 1955. Sellers was reverting back to that happy place "as we were" once more.

Rene Arana as the real King George; indulges his love of disguise as Manchu transforms himself into antique dealer Charles Rotten, and even answers his own commands, voicing a Chinese servant in the deep den of Fu Manchu. Yes, somehow, against all the odds, he delivered a couple of cheeky, cheery cherries on the cake as Fu and Smith. Quite extraordinary under the circumstances. And there's undeniably something heart-warming at the rejuvenated Fu wanting to give his old adversary Nyland the elixir so they can exchange in a battle of wits forever more. This is comic genius for an eternity.

Christopher Lee's Fu Manchu was very fond of declaring that: "The world shall hear of me again . . .". On screen, so far, it hasn't heard of him again since Sellers.[1]

Burt Kwouk, enjoying a cheeky and cheery cameo himself in *The Fiendish Plot of Dr. Fu Manchu* is the catalyst for the whole plot. It's his clumsiness with the life-giving elixir that necessitates the concoction of a fresh batch and the re-gathering of the ingredients, including the ultra-rare canary diamond 'The Star of Leningrad'. The museum tour; the hi-tech, overly complicated lifting of the jewel; the tense, thrills-masking Goonish comedy. All of it is pseudo-*Pink Panther*. Burt's casting was pure Clouseau too, of course, with the wary Manchu muttering: "Your face is familiar . . ." "Peter was delighted I was on set for that day", recalled Kwouk. "All that nonsense about him hating the *Panther* films. Come on! He had the freedom to do what he wanted before that series, but once it was resurrected, he had the freedom and then some. He could get his pet projects made, he could have his pick of any comedy script doing the rounds in Hollywood. The Panthers were good for all of us and Peter was very grateful. That little gag moment in the *Fu Manchu* film was fun. He was relaxed and funny and kind. As always. And we were already signed up for another *Panther*. That was so sad . . . we couldn't make that. The script was hilarious."[2]

---

1 At the time of his death Sellers was committed to resurrect another long lost fictional character, Chandu the Magician, who had been an American radio sensation in 1932. He hadn't been seen on screen since Bela Lugosi had played him in the 12-part 1934 serial *The Return of Chandu*. Lugosi had previously played the villain, Roxor, in the feature film, opposite Edmund Lowe. Sellers, no doubt, would have played both parts.

2 Interview with the author, May 2012.

As Sellers had chuckled in the face of a cuddly Panther in 1978: "he's getting pinker every day!"[1] The return of Clouseau was, of course, unlike *Fu Manchu*, a guaranteed hit, and Blake Edwards was happily in pre-production for *Romance of the Pink Panther*, with the shooting schedule to begin in the autumn of 1980. With Sellers gone, and United Artists hungry for more *Panther*, Edwards returned to his old idea of doing something with those hours of Sellers out-takes. Regardless that Sellers had fervently vetoed this idea, Edwards had little course of action and, in a roundabout sort of way, it was the film-maker's celebration and tribute to his fallen comic genius: it is affectionately dedicated 'To Peter . . . the one and only Clouseau', although, in all honesty, he wasn't that, even at the time. All this laudable sentimentality notwithstanding, the bottom-line was that United Artists thought the film would make them a lot of money. In the end, it didn't. One critic would call *Trail of the Pink Panther*: "the worst case of grave-robbing he ever saw!"

Viewed disparagingly, the salvaged Sellers material *is* hilarious and undeniably treasurable as scraps of finely-woven cloth from a master-craftsman of comedy. The bulk of the footage is retrieved from the filming of *The Pink Panther Strikes Again* but, in a laudable and believable attempt to flesh-out the full story of Clouseau, Edwards included scenes from early sixties *Panther* too. Critics laughed – and not in a good way – at the inconsistencies, but as a mockumentary *This Is Your Life Clouseau*, it all works well. Right from that oh so modern Pac-Man inspired Clouseau vs. Panther animation. Still, critics too, unfairly, sneered at David Niven, returning to the franchise for the first time since the original, *The Pink Panther*, in 1963. Tragically depleted by the motor neurone disease that would kill him, Edwards was forced to have Niven's scenes dubbed by master impersonator Rich Little. It's ironic to think that, in a parallel universe, it's the kind of cut-and-paste cinematic gig that Sellers himself would have gladly knocked off in his lunch-break.

---

1 *That's Panthertainment*, Premacy Productions, broadcast 7th November 1978 in promotion of *Revenge of the Pink Panther*. Ken Kramer and Carolyn F. Russell were the directors of the documentary.

Other survivors of the series, including ever-faithful Burt Kwouk and Herbert Lom and Graham Stark, genuinely saw it as a patchwork quilt salute to Sellers. A clever and affectionate way to preserve some of his hitherto and potentially dispensable work. It's worth the price of admission for Peter's 'Singin' in the Rain' routine alone. A desperate attempt to cover embarrassment, opposite a bemused April Walker. Beautiful.

The chink in the armour was Lynne Frederick who was the custodian of Peter's flame, legally and quite rightly. Despite the shadow of divorce hovering once more.

In the wake of Peter's death the BBC, in particular, were very keen to salute his recorded legacy with the corporation.

Since Christmas 1974 the *Goon Show Classics* long-player albums from BBC Records had become almost as traditional and eagerly-awaited as the *Giles Annual* and *The Morecambe & Wise Show*. Volume 7 was well in the works when the news of Peter's death filtered through. Fittingly, one of the selected episodes was 'The Man Who Never Was', the perfect Sellers epitaph for Sellers. When the album went to press, in September 1980, there had just been time to include on the back cover an early, fresh-faced portrait of Sellers with a BBC microphone, and the loving dedication: "with grateful thanks for all the pleasure and laughter which he gave to so many people."

In November 1980 a cleverly cobbled-together compilation of solo classics by the trio was issued on the One-Up label, as *Dark Side of the Goon*. The sleeve joke might not have been cutting edge – Pink Floyd's *The Dark Side of the Moon* had been released seven years prior – but it was no less potent. The multi-coloured spectrum converged through a wedge of cheese, while the opening tracks came from Sellers: the 1957 single 'Boiled Bananas and Carrots', and 'Any Old Iron'.[1]

---

1 Serial number: OU 2232. Other Sellers tracks included were 'Fuller's Earth', 'My Old Dutch', 'A Drop of the Hard Stuff', and 'I'm So Ashamed'. The album culminates with not one but two belted-out belters from Harry Secombe. In early 1983 Australian record label Hammard secured the triple record release of six previously available *Goon Show* recordings, producing an impressive gatefold collection *The Best of the Goons*: (HAM 084). The episodes included were 'The Dreaded Batter-Pudding Hurler of Bexhill-on-Sea', 'The Histories of Pliny the Elder', 'Lurgi Strikes Britain', 'The International Christmas Pudding', 'The Treasure of Loch Lomond', and 'The Greenslade Story'.

BBC Records continued with their Sellers tribute with a release of *Parkinson: The Peter Sellers Interview*,[1] which cemented the platter in the present with a resplendent Switzerland-based Sellers on the front cover. Parkinson had recorded a new introduction, the week of Peter's death, while the small print whispered the fact that: "at the request of Mrs. Lynne Sellers, the royalties due to the Estate of Peter Sellers shall be paid over to The British Heart Foundation in perpetuity." By the time the BBC pulled together an edited television compilation *Parkinson* episode in tribute for transmission on 11th February 1981, the ex-Mrs. Sellers had become the new Mrs. Frost, having married broadcaster and satirist David Frost, in the Suffolk village of Theberton, on 25th January 1981. It was six months since Peter's death, and almost exactly four years since her marriage to Sellers.

While the Frosts were still on honeymoon, Blake Edwards had seen the public appetite for delirious detectives whetted once more with the 13th February 1981 release of *Charlie Chan and the Curse of the Dragon Lady*. The Chinese sleuth was played by Peter Ustinov, who Sellers had poached Clouseau off of back in 1962. The poster for Ustinov's film screamed that he was the "funniest detective". Not unreasonably, Edwards wanted to give the audience the real deal.

David Frost and Lynne Frederick were divorced in June 1982, after just seventeen months of marriage. Meanwhile, the legal battle over what Sellers had left behind was really hotting up. Lynne, once more, saw herself as the protector of her first husband's image and legacy, and demanded a legal settlement of $3 million from Edwards and United Artists. Not only that, she insisted that *Trail of the Pink Panther* be shelved and never released, in any format. She was not going to sit back and see a profit made from work she knew Sellers didn't want his public to see. In the end, the courts awarded Lynne a cool million, to go with the just over seven million Sellers had bequeathed her in his will.

However, for the "gratification of Mr. Sellers' many fans across the

---

1 Serial number: REH 402.

world", the courts also agreed that *Trail of the Pink Panther* could be released. Typically it was slated for the lucrative Christmas market. The film went on international distribution on Friday, 17th December 1982. To that universal condemnation and critical savaging.

It certainly may not have been "the funniest Panther" as the optimistic poster claimed; it may not even have been "the pinkest" as it also staked itself; and it certainly wasn't the last, but *Trail of the Pink Panther* was, by proxy, Peter's cinematic swansong. The last Sellers film proper, whether you like it or not.[1] Despite the simplest of plotlines – Clouseau has gone missing and investigative journalist Joanna Lumley tries to track him down by interviewing personalities from his past and, thus, neatly setting up flashbacks to moments we haven't been privy to – it is an ingenious way to mop up those discarded remnants of Sellers at full-pelt, turbo-charged slapstick. It certainly wasn't the way Sellers would have wanted it, and it may have been out of his hands but it was in the hands of a director he owed his twilight years renaissance to and in the hands of a bunch of chums, not least of which were close allies Graham Stark and Burt Kwouk, who took on the funny flame with a respect and affection that is palpable and rather moving. In the end, Sellers had left us laughing, and, somehow, from beyond the veil, he was still making us laugh.

I like to think that Sellers would roll his eyes and accept the inevitable. Very much like he would have done when he heard Spike and Secombe and son Michael had insisted that his funeral service include a recording of Glenn Miller's 'In the Mood', a tune that Sellers, in life, had detested. It was Peter's final joke.

Was fame and fortune and everything that goes with it what it was cracked up to be? Did Sellers ever find true happiness in anything that life tossed at him? Apart from in the sheer joy in making others and himself laugh. Probably not; but we can at least agree, I trust, that Peter Sellers should be back on his comedy pedestal. The very best of the best. Pre-Jet Set; Pre-Clouseau; even Pre-*The Goon Show*,

1 There are several Sellers sounds in the 1983 follow-up *Curse of the Pink Panther* too, but that is stretching it a bit. Even for me!

he admitted that: "I have a strange whim to own an old antique shop in a quiet English town – say in a place like Marlborough. The bright lights of London, the gaiety and the excitement are not really what I want. For me, the steady job – maybe as proprietor of that antique shop – a wife and a family spell happiness far more than fame ever will."[1]

So, for all the wealth and wives and weirdness, there was always just a simple man who wanted to make us laugh. And he did. Close friend and frequent director Joe McGrath revealed that: "Peter did write me a letter of apology after all the pain of making *Casino Royale*. He never apologised to anybody, and just before his death he phoned me and asked for the letter back! He must have known the end was near because he whispered: 'I want it back because you'll publish it when I'm dead!' I paused and he hurriedly said, 'Well, keep it then, but will you promise me that you will never publish it?' That I did, but I did tell Spike that I had this letter of apology from Sellers. Milligan yelled: 'Tell everybody, Joe. Tell everybody. You see, he is human!'"[2]

Thank heavens Peter Sellers lived his life for comedy. He is a tonic distilled from the silliness and the madness. Laughter eternal.

Cut to the final, funny chase. Fade Out. Laughter. Applause. Standing Ovation. The End . . . or is it?

---

1 *Radio Fun*, January 1951.
2 Interview with the author, July 2003.

A Fun Little Bit of Afterwords

by David Barry

I have known Robert Ross for many, many years. Robert is quite rightly described as Britain's Comedy Historian, but even after all those hours together, laughing and drinking in West End public houses, I had no idea he had such a passion for, and vast knowledge of, Peter Sellers. One of my absolute comedy heroes.

Having read this brilliant celebration of Sellers I also had no idea just how extremely busy Peter Sellers was, throughout his life in comedy. I certainly didn't realise Sellers was quite so willing to take on fun little telly jobs, even after he had become a massive, international star. I realise now that it would not have been beyond the budget of London Weekend Television to attract Sellers to a guest star role in *Please Sir!* or *The Fenn Street Gang*. Oh, just imagine Sellers tackling my comedy kid character of Frankie Abbott. What sparks could have flown! I also didn't know that the Tyrone Power and Mai Zetterling film *Seven Waves Away* – in which I played the young lad – was an important part of the road to Peter making *The Mouse That Roared*. What a small world.

However I did, in actual fact, and thrillingly, work with Sellers. The occasion was with another young actor, Hugh Halliday. Hugh and I became involved in one day's uncredited non-speaking roles in *Lolita*. We were both at Corona Academy and agent Hazel Malone got us the job.

It was a scene where Lolita appears in her high school play, and Sellers is ogling her from the wings. We were decked out in these ridiculous medieval costumes, and given long trumpets on which to blow a fanfare signalling the opening of the performance.

Presumably, as it was all set up and lit, Kubrick wanted it in one take. He came over to us and said on the word 'Action' raise the trumpets to your lips and blow a fanfare: "What, actually blow it?" I said. "Yes, of course", Kubrick replied, as if we were stupid. That was it. "Turn over, speed, action!" We blew what we thought was a fanfare and what came out were two strangled farts. Sellers was doubled up in hysterics.

Kubrick came over and said, "When I said 'blow' I meant mime it!" After he returned to his camera position, I turned to Hugh and said, "Well, why didn't he say that?" The second take was ruined, because when we mimed the fanfare, Sellers was doubled up again, because now he could imagine the fart sounds! Every take was the same. Kubrick eventually took him aside and I saw him walking, an arm over the shoulder of Sellers, trying to calm him down. But I have seen the film and we are not in it, thanks to the strangled fart sounds and the glorious inability of Peter Sellers to stop laughing!

David Barry
Royal Tunbridge Wells
August 2024

Acknowledgements

This passion publication came about in the immediate wake of our first Write On Comedy Book Festival, in 2022. It was also the first time I had met David Burrill of Great Northern Books. I immediately knew I could work with him – blissfully. Particularly when we got to talking about comedians who could, and should, have dozens of books written about them. "Peter Sellers is one, for sure", said David. "Would you fancy writing one on him?" Would I! So, a huge Thank You to David for the time and encouragement. It's been a humorous revelation. And much admiration to Ross Jamieson who skilfully picked his way through the manuscript and reminded me that many of my references could confuse a stupid person. And everybody else . . . but me. Cheers. Many thanks to Tim Stark for his invaluable assistance in sourcing the stunning cover photograph, as taken by his father and Peter's dear friend, Graham Stark. Also respect to Ned Pierce, builder extraordinaire, who was working on Comedy Cottage during initial Sellers film viewing right through to final corrections. A jolly companion as I scribbled within the rubble!

I have conducted new interviews with old friends, and delved back into my own collected archives for telling insights into Peter's work ethos from those who knew him best. My admiration and respect to all his cohorts and colleagues who are quoted within these pages.

A thousand thanks – as always – to the vaults of the British Film Institute, and the BBC Written Archives Centre, for holding all the answers and clarifying my misted memory. Thanks to Tyler Butterworth for care and kindness above and beyond. If you have walked a mile in Peter's shoes, Mental Health UK is there.

Finally, all my love and laughter to Gemma – the power behind the Comedy Historian throne. You keep me focused when I need it; and distracted when I need that. And you make me chuckle. At least once a day. That's reality.

Proud as punch:
as Welsh Lothario John Lewis
in *Only Two Can Play*.
(The Comedy Cottage Collection)